Slovenia 1945

# Slovenia 1945

## Memories of Death and Survival
## after World War II

**John Corsellis**
**and**
**Marcus Ferrar**

I.B. TAURIS

LONDON · NEW YORK

Published in 2005 by I.B. Tauris & Co Ltd
6 Salem Road, London W2 4BU
175 Fifth Avenue, New York NY 10010
www.ibtauris.com

In the United States and Canada distributed by Palgrave Macmillan,
a division of St. Martin's Press, 175 Fifth Avenue, New York NY 10010

ISBN 1 85043 840 4
EAN 978 1 85043 840 3

A full CIP record for this book is available from the British Library
A full CIP record for this book is available from the Library of Congress
Library of Congress catalog card: available


Typeset in Century Schoolbook by Dexter Haven Associates Ltd, London
Printed and bound in Great Britain by MPG Books Ltd, Bodmin

# Contents

# Maps

# Main Characters

**Aloysius Ambrožič**
Cardinal Archbishop of Toronto. Son of a Catholic Slovene farming family which narrowly escaped wartime Italian reprisals after a Partisan attack. Fled with 18,000 other anti-Communist Slovenes on foot over the mountains to Austria at the end of World War II. Lived in a refugee camp for three years, attending its grammar school. Emigrated with his family to Canada.

**Andrej Bajuk**
Fled to Austria at the end of the war with his family, who pushed him over the mountains in a pram at 19 months. After three and a half years in a refugee camp, he emigrated with his family to Mendoza, Argentina. After a career with the Inter-American Development Bank, he returned to Slovenia and served as Prime Minister in 2000 and Finance Minister from 2004.

**Director Marko Bajuk**
Andrej's grandfather. A former headmaster and inspector of Slovene schools. Set up a thriving refugee camp grammar school for Slovene children who had to flee with their families. The cultural leader of the Catholic Slovenes in the camps. Also a musical composer and conductor. Emigrated with his family to Argentina.

**Major Paul Barre**
Canadian commandant of the camp in Viktring, southern Austria, where the Slovene Catholics first settled after their flight in 1945. Allowed them maximum autonomy, and played a key role in preventing the British military from repatriating 6,000 civilians after *domobranci* (Home Guard) soldiers had been sent back to their deaths in Slovenia.

**Jože Jančar**
Slovene Catholic student leader who fled to Austria in 1945. Acted as John Corsellis' aide and interpreter in the camps. Helped arrange admission for Slovene refugee students to Graz University. Later became a distinguished psychiatrist in Bristol, England.

**Dr Valentin Meršol**
Leader of the Slovene community in the refugee camps. Together
with Major Barre, was instrumental in saving the 6,000 civilians from
being repatriated to Slovenia. In Ljubljana, headed the infectious
diseases department of the hospital. Personal physician to Yugoslav
King Alexander between the wars. Emigrated to Cleveland, US.

**France Pernišek**
Catholic social insurance official in wartime Slovenia. Kept a diary of
his flight in 1945 and the hard years in the refugee camps. Portrayed
the Slovenes' fervent Catholic faith, their bitterness at the British deceit,
the despair over hunger, harassment and poverty in the camps, and the
joy at making new lives overseas.

**Dr Franc Rode**
Youngest son of a farming family which fled to Austria in 1945. Schoolboy
in the refugee camps, before emigrating with his family to Argentina.
Returned to Europe six years later and came back to Slovenia as a
priest in 1965. Metropolitan Archbishop of Ljubljana 1997–2004. As
Prefect of the Congregation for Religious in the Vatican, he is responsible
for monks and nuns around the world.

# Preface

*... While with the eye made quiet by the power*
*Of harmony, and the deep power of joy,*
*We see into the life of things.*

– *William Wordsworth*, Tintern Abbey, *1798*

For 30 years, the head of a language school in Britain had been suppressing the memory of terrible deeds he witnessed as a relief worker at the end of World War II. Then, in the middle of the 1970s, a student walked into his office and changed his life forever. It was an innocent query about a work permit. John Corsellis looked at the passport and his flesh tingled. Standing before him was a Slovene who lived in Argentina. John knew why he lived there. He knew only too well.

Back in 1945, John witnessed a deceit which led to the deaths of 12,000 people, and played his part in the rescue of 6,000 others sheltered in a refugee camp. The Slovenes were Catholics who fled their country in May 1945 after losing a civil war against the Communist Partisans. The British sent those in uniforms back to be killed by the Partisans, using a trick to deceive them. The student was one of the civilian survivors.

As they talked, he asked if John had any documents or souvenirs of those days. John went home, rummaged in his attic and found a cardboard box with letters he had sent his mother at the time. He read them through and it all came flooding back. In his late 40s, he was deeply moved at the confrontation with himself at half that age, witnessing a horror he had buried deep in his mind. He tapped out the hand-written letters on a typewriter and kept a carbon copy for himself. Some months later, his testimony was published in an almanac by Slovenes who had emigrated to Argentina.

A year on, John was sitting on the hill overlooking Tintern Abbey in Wales with one of Britain's most distinguished psychiatrists. He was not a Briton by birth: he too was one of those Slovene survivors. When John was caring for the Slovenes as an aid worker in the Austrian camps, Jože Jančar had been one of his closest co-workers. Jože gently took John through the strong emotions he had felt since transcribing the letters.

'You must write about this,' said Jože. 'Let me show the letters to my daughter's godmother.' That godmother was Iris Murdoch, the distinguished writer. She too knew all about the Slovenes. She too had looked after them in the Austrian camps, and helped Jože and others get university educations.

'Fascinating...most interesting and touching...splendid text,' wrote back Dame Iris.[1] She urged him to write the book but said he needed more material. The question was: how? By this time, John knew the book was to be his life's mission. Grants from Quaker trusts enabled him to reduce his paid work to half-time and travel to interview Slovenes in North America. But many threads of the story remained out of reach. Then one of his hosts mentioned an emigrant had just published his diaries in Buenos Aires. That was his breakthrough.

The diarist was France Pernišek, who wrote about the Slovenes' flight, bereavement and long years in the camps. Pernišek arranged for a friend flying to England to take John a copy to enrich this book. John tried in vain to apply his knowledge of Serbo-Croat to the Slovene text before him. He could not make it out. Who could translate it?

Jože warned him about the suggested candidate, Sister Agnes Žužek, a retired Slovene medical missionary living in a convent in the London suburb of Ealing. She had a reputation as a difficult character. But John found her to be 'sweet and massively generous'. She translated the lengthy document into English in long-hand, sending it in instalments as she gradually worked her way through. She asked for no money. So John had a text in English, but the style remained resolutely Slovene. He sat down, now equipped with a computer, to rework it into idiomatic English.

The diary was a jewel. This was the first-hand evidence he was looking for. He was touched to see himself mentioned as 'the good Mr Corsellis'. Many of the other references to Britons were bitter and resentful. John realised that his trauma was resurfacing, trauma rooted in guilt for what the British did. As a British witness of the events, he considered it his duty to ensure that the truth about what had happened should be publicly recognised.

Over the next decade, John tracked down and interviewed scores of survivors, of a diaspora spread worldwide from Canada to Argentina. Three years ago, he asked me to work with him as a co-writer. I leaped at the task. I had just left Reuters after a career which included Cold War assignments in Eastern Europe. I was about to marry a Slovene. It seemed an ideal fit. Our mutual friend, Keith Miles, warned me the book had been long in gestation and I risked a long-term entanglement. I took little notice. I was used to investigating a story, writing it, checking it and dispatching it all in the course of an afternoon.

Within months, I too was hooked. Instead of just helping pull his material together, I was off to North America, Argentina and Slovenia to find out more myself. We both wrote large parts of the book, but decided that John should appear in the third person, since he was a prominent actor in the drama.

As one year passed and then the next, the story settled into my psyche too. It recalled elements of my own life. My mother, who left Germany in 1939 because she fell foul of the Nazis; and my father, who served in the British Army in World War II, with all the accompanying fears, hopes, frustrations and comradeship. I was fascinated by the immense complexities facing human beings in this part of Europe. As I peeled layer after layer away, it became ever more complicated to understand. This was the supreme challenge: to understand.

The refugees were equally moved by telling their stories. Many began their impassioned accounts as soon as one of the authors walked through the door. Their experiences remained etched in their minds. Often the best morsels came after the interview, over drinks and a meal.

Likewise with John. He told me the full story above, after two and a half years' intense collaboration, just a few weeks before going to press.

Marcus Ferrar
March 2005

# Prologue

As World War II slumped to a conclusion, the road leading from Yugoslavia to Austria over the Ljubelj Pass, high in the Karavanke mountains, was black with a mass of Slovenes fleeing their homes. Europe's map had been redrawn and vast numbers of men, women and children were taking to their feet all over Europe in the largest migration the continent had ever seen. Although they did not know it, most of the Slovenes trudging up the dirt road to the Ljubelj were to meet their end in mass executions in remote forest pits a few weeks later. Others won a reprieve, literally at the last moment. This is the tale of those survivors – their dilemmas, betrayal, bereavement and neglect – and their determination and solidarity in building new lives thousands of miles away. The background is a civil war between Partisans and anti-Communist Catholics during enemy occupation of Slovenia in World War II. The conflict which led them to flee tore families asunder, and remains alive today in modern Slovenia, which has been independent from Yugoslavia since 1991.

This is therefore more than just a refugee story. It also re-assesses a part of ex-Yugoslavia's wartime history, which has hitherto been largely written from the viewpoint of the Communists. That history simplistically condemns the refugees as traitors, causing resentment not only among those who fled, but also among many Catholics in Slovenia today. Some of the refugees, who eventually had to resettle overseas, are now at the peak of successful careers, at ease in the rough and tumble of a competitive world. Others have arrived at an age at which they can stand back and philosophically accept their lot. Many, however, remain angry and misunderstood. They long for an opportunity to set right what they see as an injustice.

On the other side, the Partisans, who fought under Communist leadership, object that the emigrants belittle their struggle as a selfish grab for revolutionary power. For them, it was a patriotic fight against the German and Italian occupiers.

With the passage of time and the advent of democracy, it should be no problem for new generations to view the events more objectively. But there has been no reconciliation. The post-war emigration and the civil war that preceded it remain an issue around which political and religious disputes swirl anew. As this story unfolds, it delves into a dark side of Slovenia's history. The people we have quoted have a particular point of view to put across. The authors' aim throughout, however, has been to tell the truth objectively rather than take sides. Where a viewpoint or a fact is contested, the opposing version is also given.[1]

Slovenia has existed as an independent state for little more than a decade and is still unfamiliar to many. It is a beautiful land of Alpine peaks, meadows, forests and a short Adriatic coast. It nestles to the north-east of Italy, is smaller than Wales and has less than one third the population of Switzerland. For the last 650 years, Slovenes have undergone the decisions of others rather than ruling over their own destinies. They avoided much of the prolonged fighting that occurred elsewhere in the former Yugoslavia, seceding from the disintegrating federation after a ten-day war in 1991. Slovenes have a disciplined, down-to-earth reputation. They have converted to democracy and built a market economy which, while still poorer than most parts of Western Europe, is the most prosperous of the ex-Communist countries. As they entered the European Union in 2004, foreign commentators remarked how smoothly the process of integration had gone. Yet this tranquil image can be deceptive. Twentieth-century history still casts a long shadow over the Slovenes. Some of the worst slaughters in both World Wars took place on their soil.

Europeans today principally remember the civil wars of the 1990s that tore Yugoslavia apart on their doorstep. But the history of violence in Yugoslavia has long roots. When the decline of the Ottoman Empire left a power vacuum in the Balkans in the 19th century, Austria-Hungary, Russia, Germany, France and Britain jockeyed to fill the void, exploiting ethnic tensions and rival local political ambitions that were only too ready to be inflamed. People were treated as pawns to be manipulated, tossed aside and expended at will. This phenomenon hit Slovenia with full force in World War I, when a series of battles was fought between the Italian and Austrian armies in Slovenia's Julian Alps. Casualties were huge, and the emerald green waters of the Soča* (Isonzo) river ran red with the blood of stricken soldiers. Around 300,000 died on Slovene territory. Most were not Slovenes, but a number were. Slovenes fought as conscripts in the Austrian army, and by the time the conflict ended, the nation had lost 3% of its population.

Worse was to come in World War II, when Yugoslavia as a whole lost approximately one million people. While the rest of Europe ended hostilities on 9 May 1945, the war continued in Slovenia for another week. When it ceased, nowhere in Europe was the population so divided as in Slovenia, according to the country's long-standing President, Milan Kučan, the only former head of a European Communist party to continue in power into the 21st century. Scarcely anywhere was the post-war settling of accounts more ferocious.

---

\* In Slovene pronunciation, č = ch, š = sh, ž = zh, c = ts, j = y.

In May 1945 the British 8th Army was sucked into this turmoil, having just arrived in southern Austria as the occupying force after a victorious campaign up Italy. It was confronted by a challenge it was ill equipped to deal with – the arrival of fleeing troops and civilians, bringing horribly intricate politics in their baggage. The presence of the British Army should have been good for the fleeing Slovenes, but it was not. Most of those making their way over the Ljubelj Pass were sent back by the British into the hands of the Communists, who had embarked on a frenzy of killing aimed at eliminating their remaining opponents and enforcing a proletarian dictatorship. The British military may not have known exactly the fate to which they condemned the Slovenes coming under their protection. The Partisans had been Britain's chosen allies in the war against Nazism. However, a brutal reaction was predictable, in the light of the extreme force used by Communists elsewhere, and the Partisans had scores to settle after a two-year civil war with their anti-Communist opponents. Certainly, the British knew enough to suspect that death was the most likely outcome.

It is easy to jump to moral conclusions. The slaughtered victims belonged to a military force called *domobranci*, set up by anti-Communist Catholics to defend themselves against the Partisans. The Italians and the Germans persecuted many of them as nationalists and Slavs in the early part of the war. But these Catholics also collaborated, first with the Italians and then with the Germans. When they arrived in Austria, they were wearing uniforms supplied by the German occupiers and were armed with German and Italian weapons. It would be all too easy to condemn them as puppets of the occupying powers. However, the objective truth is more complex. This is a story of people caught up in the maelstrom of war. Practically every Slovene of that generation lost a father, mother, son or uncle at the time. People were confronted with difficult moral choices. That some of them erred is not surprising. Amazingly, many ordinary people *did* find the way out of the labyrinth and took humane decisions in almost impossible situations. This is a tale that enjoins humility on those who rush to pass judgment on fellow human beings.

Nevertheless, there *are* lessons to be drawn. Slovenia may be a small corner of Europe, but the story has implications for anybody who wants to evaluate the war in a more objective light. This re-assessment is taking place in one European country after another. The settled images of black and white are giving way to the shaded tones of reality. In Slovenia, the questions of wartime guilt, innocence and heroism are particularly complex. We now know that the Third Reich and its satellites were to collapse. In 1943 or 1944 this was not so clear to those involved. Was it thus better to fight the tyranny of Communism, even at the expense of sidling up close to the enemy occupier? Was collaboration with an enemy occupier always evil? Was resistance always the right course? Were heroic raids by resistance fighters noble if they resulted in lethal reprisals among defenceless civilians? Was it better to keep your head down, or at least have a go against an enemy occupier? How were the victorious nations to distinguish between friends and foes once the conflict had ended? What were helpless civilians supposed to do in the midst of all this?

And with Europe today confronted with a growing number of refugees and asylum seekers, this story poses questions relevant for those who have to decide what to do with them. The Slovene refugees overcame incredible difficulties, were accepted as immigrants and eventually integrated successfully into their new societies. But during the long course of what in the end was a success story, the key questions of refugee policy were constantly being posed. Are those responsible for refugees primarily there to ease their plight and help them establish new lives? Or is their task to persuade refugees to return home, with whatever hard-line measures work best? The Slovenes underwent both approaches, and represent a case study drawn from human experience.

The Slovenes fleeing in May 1945 were not alone as they struggled up the ever steeper slopes, heaving at their lurching wagons. They had embarked on what they thought would be a two-week absence, but they found the road choked with fellow-travellers – German troops retreating from southern Yugoslavia and Greece; Serb Chetniks, who had been fighting against the occupiers, the Muslims in Bosnia and the Partisans; Croatian Ustashe, who sided with the Nazis in order to suppress minorities and resist Serbia; and anti-Communist Russians and Ukrainians who preferred service in the German military to oppression in the Soviet Union. Slovenia's mountain passes to Austria were the last funnels through which this throng squeezed to reach the Western Allies and escape the advancing Communists.

When the Slovenes made it to Austria, the British Army shepherded them into a field outside the village of Viktring. Exhausted after a week on the road, they lay down among the furrows to pray to the Virgin Mary, ponder what fate held in store for them, and slip into a dazed slumber under the stars.

There they met John Corsellis, one of the authors of this book. A pacifist, he was working for the Friends Ambulance Unit, which was run by Quakers. At the age of 22, he had been caring for refugees in camps in Egypt and up through Italy in the wake of the Allied advance. Slovene refugee accounts recall a tall, gangling young man striding around in shorts, helping them in the desperate months ahead. They remember him as one who cared.

Slovenes at home view this cruel story of civil war, emigration and massacres with mixed emotions. Belief in Partisan heroism still runs deep. Today they find it hard to acknowledge that some of their best people had to flee into exile, while thousands of others were slaughtered by their own countrymen in cold blood. It has not been easy for them to find out the whole truth. The subject for many years remained taboo.

Some are reluctant to confront the dark side of their history because they feel modern Slovenia should turn its face to reconstruction and integration into Europe. They want to avoid the pains that over-vindictive exposures of Communists brought in the Czech Republic. Ex-Communists and anti-clerical Liberals resist historical revisions since they do not want to rehabilitate their Catholic opponents. Some are concerned that returning emigrants might demand trials or return of property. But others feel it is time for the whole tale to be told after years of Communist suppression. They are curious: it is their own history – history that until a few years ago was that of a small federal republic but is now that of an independent nation.

Meanwhile, the Grim Reaper wields his scythe into the ageing ranks of survivors. Classical scholar Justin Stanovnik was in 1945 a *domobranec* teenager whose main concern as he trekked up the mountain was to steal a superior Mauser gun from a German soldier, which he did. Now, 60 years later, he sits in a tenement block in Ljubljana in the chill fog of winter, marvels that he is still alive when he could have died at the age of 17, and muses over the boatman of the Classical legend who rows the dead over the River Styx: 'The boatman is waiting for us all now, and we want the truth to be told before we set out on our final voyage.'

# *1* OVER THE MOUNTAIN

*A wild beast is most dangerous when about to die.*

*Friday 4th May 1945.* The German army is retreating: it has relaxed its combat readiness, but the Gestapo continues with its persecution of our people. The prisons are full of them. A wild beast is most dangerous when about to die. Because of yesterday's proclamation by the [non-Communist] National Committee for Slovenia, the Gestapo surrounded the People's Printing Press, and for two days people have not been allowed to leave. Liberation Front sympathisers in our building are proud of approaching victory and happy. The whole house is full of the smell of freshly made pastries. Their women have been baking all night to be ready for the arrival of the Partisan army.

In our clean, white Ljubljana there is a strange atmosphere. The usually empty streets today are full of people. They gather in small groups and talk in subdued voices. Our people are very worried at news that the international Communist brigade, which goes under the name of the Yugoslav Army, has landed in Rijeka and is advancing towards Trieste and Ljubljana. The Partisans are coming down from the mountains and the first refugees have arrived in Ljubljana.

France Perniŝek, a Slovene Catholic community leader, picked up an unused address book and penned these lines in a precise copperplate hand-writing. He was to keep this diary[1] until he arrived in his country of emigration, Argentina, four years later. It is a passionate account of a refugee adrift in post-war Europe.

For three years, a central core of Slovene Catholics had been fighting a civil war against the Communist-dominated Partisans during the occupation by the enemy Italians and Germans. Confronted by a wave of assassinations by the Partisans, they set up their own Home Guard – the *domobranci* – and accepted arms and organisation from the occupiers to mount military campaigns. Now things were coming to a head, and the Catholics were losing. The Soviet Red Army had captured Belgrade, the German Army was in headlong retreat, and on 3 May the Catholics and other non-Communists convened a Parliament to preside over Slovenia as a reconstituted nation. Franc Kremžar, a deputy in the Yugoslav Parliament of the 1920s, was chosen as its President. The Communist leaders of the Partisans were having none of it. They were on the verge of victory in their revolutionary war, and had no intention of letting others take power. With the Germans pulling out, and the Allies supporting Tito, the *domobranci* had no hope of holding on. The Parliament got a letter off to the Allies but lasted just one day.

Pernišek, a trim, austere figure, was one of the few who sensed that he was abandoning his old life forever. He lived to his nineties, but never returned to his homeland. His daughter Cirila remembers him telling the family: 'We leave for one week, for two weeks or forever.' On 5 May he wrote in his diary:

> The hardest moment in my life faces me: to tell my wife and children that, if we want to stay alive, we must leave home and all our possessions and go abroad to an unknown but terrible future. In resignation I pray for God's help…Our hearts were torn with sadness and fear. I left it to her to decide whether to stay at home with the children, but she said: 'Wherever you go, we all go. Whatever happens to us, we'll be together. If you go on your own, we'll probably never see each other again. And if we die, we'll die together.'

Most of the others thought they would return in a few weeks. They believed the British would occupy Slovenia. This was no fantasy, since Winston Churchill did have such a plan, though unbeknown to the refugees it had been abandoned some time ago. Churchill, concerned at the slow pace of the Allied armies up Italy, wanted a landing on the coast of Istria south of Trieste. The invading army would move through the Ljubljana gap on to Vienna. He had tried to sell it to Roosevelt, who vetoed it so as not to offend Stalin. The Slovene Catholics identified with British democracy, fair play and the rule of law, seeing them as bulwarks against social revolution. 'We totally adored the British. They walked on water. They had been fighting the Germans and we did not like the Germans,' says Frank Jeglič.*

The Slovenes were in for a shock. Pernišek was not the only one who never saw his homeland again. The British arrived in Trieste and the Austrian province of Carinthia in time to forestall Tito's plan to grab

---

* Where not otherwise indicated, quotations are from interviews with one of the authors. See Acknowledgements and Verbal Sources.

both as part of Slovenia, which he intended to keep within Yugoslavia. But the British never came to Slovenia itself.

Word was spreading that it was time to leave. That meant not just political activists. As Slovenia was predominantly a Catholic country, many of those in positions of authority were religious. Catholics were the Communists' main rivals for power and the hearts and minds of the population. Prominent Catholics also had their hands on the levers of the economy. Quite a few of those who left were farming people, but it was also an exodus of the educated, the successful and the qualified. For the Communists, capitalist came to mean collaborator. In the strict sense of the word, of course many had been collaborating – as had practically anybody else in German-occupied Europe who wielded authority or ran a business. Defeat of the enemy, besides raising hopes for social change, was also an opportunity for the ill-willed to exploit personal grudges and seize property. Jealousy, greed and a feeling of inferiority were all pretexts for denunciations.

The Germans had been protecting a nearby paper mill for strategic reasons, so its financial director had to flee. The head of a brush factory had to go too because he once sold a batch to the Italians. He had spurned the love of his secretary, so she denounced him. Another left because he kept his bedding firm solvent by selling mattresses to an Italian military brothel, delivering them clandestinely on a tricycle after curfew. A headmaster had to leave because he once apologised to an Italian Fascist chaplain, in order to save his pupils from expulsion for refusing to say the Lord's Prayer in Italian. A flourmill owner in Logatec southwest of the capital fled after a neighbour threatened to ensure that he and all his family would be executed.[2]

Former Communists today claim many of those who left could have carried on without problems under the new regime. Possibly rumours and fear panicked some people to flee unnecessarily. Nobody seems to have given any order to go. The decision spread like a virus. However, there is little reason to doubt that large numbers were marked men and women. Several had Partisan relatives who tipped them off that they were on lists for liquidation known as 'Black Books'.[3] The trials and executions which followed bear this out. Others saw Partisans and sympathisers waiting outside the homes they were vacating so that they could remove the contents or move straight in – a practice by which Communist regimes across Europe rewarded their supporters. Pernišek put a rucksack on his back, grasped two suitcases, took his children to pray before a small statue of the Sacred Heart of Jesus, and crossed the threshold of his home weeping. Neighbours watched but showed no surprise.

Others hesitated. Milči (née Lekan), future wife of Uroš Roessmann, recalls that her father, the former Director of Utilities in Maribor, refused to leave at first because he was in the middle of planting his peas. The guns on the ramparts of Ljubljana Castle were thundering over his head, but he kept digging because the garden was his family's means of survival. They were living uneasily on the outskirts of Ljubljana in a block of flats with plenty of Communist sympathisers. Window curtains twitched and doors opened when they went out. Milči said:

When I ran to inform Dad that some friends were already leaving, I saw a convoy at the military barracks preparing to do the same. It was clear he had no option but to go – along with me and my twin sister – since we were all members of the Catholic Action lay organisation. My Mom and younger sister opted to stay, so we would have a home to come back to. Dad burned a lot of papers which could implicate other people, and Mom used the heat to bake some bread – a rarity since we mostly ate corn mush. The following morning, we left on foot and for good. It was ten years before we saw Mom and the younger sister again.

Paula Hribovšek's family had two hours to decide. Her mother, who had lost a son in the war, said she would go if the neighbours went. But they did not, so she stayed behind with Paula's sister. Within two hours the Partisans occupied their home and sent them to prison for two weeks. By that time, Paula had gone, on her own.

Uroš Roessmann's brother Matej was in the *domobranci* and took a couple of civilian suits with him, just in case. They saved his life. Tine Velikonja, aged 16, who had just joined the *domobranci*, was advised by his father to put on the uniform to be safer. It nearly killed him. Others took with them rolled-up paintings of ancestors or the lake resort of Bled. They now adorn homes thousands of miles away.

Frank Jeglič, whose father was the Director of Slovene primary education, set off with his parents equipped with an identity card around his neck and iron rations taken from their bomb shelter. As an 11-year-old, he was looking forward to the adventure. His American grandchildren now read the diary he kept on the way. The first entry went:

*Sunday 6th May 1945*: I went to Mass early in the morning. I was in the sacristy when a young lady came to tell me to go home quickly. I learned we were going to Villach in Carinthia. I put my most important things in my knapsack and went to the railway station. We waited in a train until 1.30 p.m. and it did not move. After that we walked until 7 p.m. Then on to Brdo, where we arrived at 9.30 p.m. We are in a little room and there are 11 of us. The Kožuh boys want to have a lot of room. I am going to sleep on the floor, but I am sure I am going to sleep, because I am so tired.

Frank's Sunday excursion ended in America, with a job at NASA on the space programme many years later.

Dr Valentin Meršol, who was to help save the lives of thousands of the fleeing Slovenes, was called into the Gestapo and advised to leave. He had treated German officers for rashes they picked up in Africa. When he got

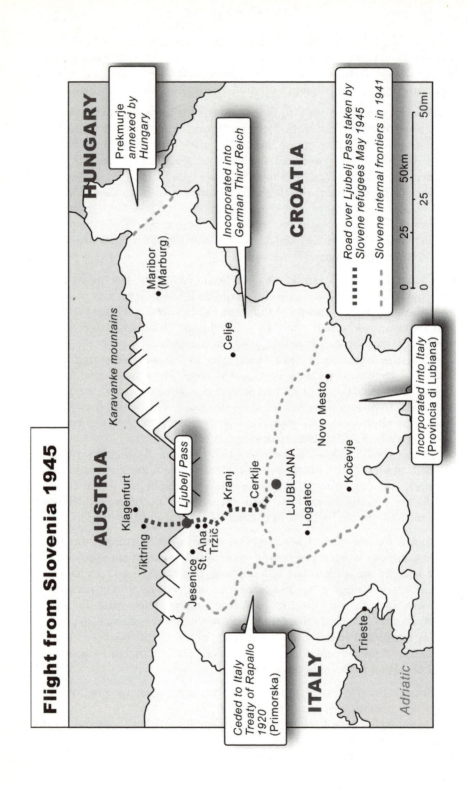

# Flight from Slovenia 1945

**HUNGARY**

Prekmurje annexed by Hungary

Incorporated into German Third Reich

**CROATIA**

Road over Ljubelj Pass taken by Slovene refugees May 1945

Slovene internal frontiers in 1941

| 0 | 25 | 50km |
| 0 | 25 | 50mi |

Maribor (Marburg)

Celje

Karavanke mountains

Novo Mesto

Incorporated into Italy (Provincia di Lubiana)

**AUSTRIA**

Klagenfurt

*Ljubelj Pass*

Viktring

Jesenice
St. Ana
Tržič

Kranj

Cerklje

LJUBLJANA

Logatec

Kočevje

Ceded to Italy Treaty of Rapallo 1920 (Primorska)

Trieste

**ITALY**

Adriatic

up to go, the officer added: 'It was very clever of you to hide those Allied pilots in the hospital.' The *domobranci* had rescued shot-down Allied airmen, and Meršol had concealed them in his infectious diseases department, reckoning no Germans would risk contamination by searching it.

Sixteen-year-old Gloria Bratina's headmaster interrupted her class and told the pupils to go home. Home was an hour's walk away and she ran the whole way, skipping through the doors of a train stranded on a level crossing. Her father rented a horse and cart and they departed immediately, leaving everything behind. On the way out, people gave them soup and food. Two Partisan uncles helped with bread and cheese.

Judge Edvard Vračko, an outspoken anti-Communist, knew he had to leave, but his wife decided to stay as she was sick after an operation. His 16-year-old daughter Majda plucked up courage and said she was going too. She told her mother they would be sleeping outside, so she did not need pyjamas in the rucksack, just food. By the time they set out, ten friends and acquaintances had joined them, one of them blind.

Out in the countryside, Magdalena Šimenc, then eight years old, remembers her uncle coming up from the valley on a sunny morning and telling her family they had to go. Everybody looked at the ground as if there had been a death in the family. The 60-year-old grandfather dragged the big hay-wagon out of the front of the house, and fixed nets to both ends with hay for the oxen. In between, the women loaded bedding, clothes and provisions – flour, a big sack of dried fruit and a barrel of fat. Little Magdalena stood and watched silently, and then went for a few of her own things. The grown-ups were astonished that she knew exactly what to take. Nothing frivolous, just the essentials for a little girl going into exile. They were ready:

> A yoke of well-fed, well-trained oxen was led from the stable, watered and attached to the heavily laden cart. Grandpa knelt, crossed himself with the words 'let us go in God's name' and cracked his whip. The oxen strained as if set to plough. Grandma and the aunts followed in tears, and I with them. Where the track curved we paused to look back – for Grandma the last sight of the farm she'd worked for 35 years. Grandpa went to say goodbye to a family in the next village. By the time they'd 'comforted' him his footsteps had grown decidedly unsure and he had to ride on the cart, while the others walked to spare the animals.

Aloysius Ambrožič, now Cardinal Archbishop of Toronto, escaped with his parents at 7.30 p.m. on 8 May. By 8.45 p.m., the Partisans had arrived in his village and his neighbours could not follow. 'My mother didn't want to leave, but she knew my father had to go. Father said, "It's all or nobody," and that was a blessing as we stayed together and eventually went as a family to Canada.' Joseph Plevnik, now a Jesuit in Toronto, retreated with his *domobranci* unit northwards through Ljubljana when the sound of guns approached. He wanted to stop at his home to say good-bye, but did not dare.

Jože Lekan, brother of Milči, had just captured military plans and archives of party members from the Partisan 7th Corps in the hills around Kočevje in the south and was taking them back to Ljubljana on a mule.[4] By the time he reached the capital, his fellow *domobranci* were preparing a general retreat. He was among the last to leave, exchanging fire with snipers as he walked down the street. He commandeered a bicycle at a post office and the next thing he knew he crashed into a wagon because he went to sleep pedalling. His hips ached and bled with the weight of a bag containing a Schmeiser machine-gun he had taken from a German, as well as hand grenades and clips of ammunition. 'I was determined to survive even if I had to kill everything around me,' he said.

Jože Jančar rushed to his fiancée Marija Hribar. It was her birthday, but he had not come to celebrate. He was an activist in a Catholic student movement and was in danger. While earlier in an Italian concentration camp at Gonars, Partisan fellow-prisoners told him they had been ordered to murder him in a maize field back at home, but had been forestalled by an Italian patrol. 'Jože had a bicycle, and said to me: "We are going to Austria for a while, until the Americans and British arrive. Do you want to come with us?" I packed a few things, and we left straightaway. We could hear the sound of guns behind us. My birthday was forgotten,' said Marija.

It was soon clear the journey was going to be no picnic. Confusion and panic spread. The sound of gunfire grew closer. Rumours spread that the Partisans were only half an hour away. German soldiers, cars and trucks were all over the place. Trains were no longer running. Many setting out on the 60 kilometres to the frontier were families with children and elderly relatives. A few had wagons, particularly those from the farms. Stane Snoj loaded provisions from his family's village shop on a trolley. Others had bicycles, or just rucksacks and a pair of feet. As night fell, many were tired and hungry and had nowhere to sleep. For some, it would take more than a week to reach their destination. Pernišek, a social security official, wrote:

> Crowds of refugees wait at the station. We wait until a column is formed. Everyone keeps silence, our hearts full of sorrow. There are flashes and the roar of guns from Ljubljana; every salvo increases our fears. We want to move as quickly as possible…It's like a funeral, but this massive cortege has no hearse. The procession is sunk in sorrow and prayer and even the beasts of burden are silent. Ljubljana is left behind and the guns grow fainter.

Twenty-five kilometres north of Ljubljana, the arrival of the dispirited column at the village of Cerklje on a fresh Sunday morning caused a stir. The whole village had turned out to celebrate the end of the war with pealing church bells and a brass band. Festivities came abruptly to a halt, the bells and music fell silent and people stood around in consternation. The priest appealed to villagers to be hospitable, and the congregation began weeping. It was the same in other villages, where friends and relatives were shocked and incredulous at the headlong flight – though ready with food and a bed of straw for the night. Nobody could take in the scale of the disintegration before their eyes. Enemy occupation was coming to an end, but the old familiar society was crumbling before social revolution.

Slovene Catholics in flight across the mountains to Austria. They thought they were just going for a few weeks, but for many it was the last time they saw their home country.

Some families had to split up on the way. Dr Franc Puc left a four-year-old daughter behind because she was ill. When the rest of the family reached the town of Škofja Loka half way to the border, two children aged seven and nine could walk no further, so they left them with their grandparents. The two parents and their remaining daughter and son set off again, and it was nine years before the family was reunited in Canada.

While adults worried and despaired, many of the children found it exciting. To Milči Lekan, a teenager at the time, it seemed an unreal adventure as she joined a column ten kilometres long. Eight-year-old Magdalena Šimenc, sleeping under the stars in the hay on the wagon, declared: 'So far I'd enjoyed the outing. It was something really new. Normally we never left the farm apart from the Sunday walk to church, an occasional wake and the annual visit to the sewing woman.' Pernišek's children begged to linger in the beautiful countryside they were passing through, and were allowed to play for a few hours by a stream. Majda Vračko debated with university students about Thomas Aquinas before bedding down for the night in a barn. Tear-away young Val Meršol crammed his pockets with ammunition discarded by German soldiers, 'but not for long, as subsequently my mother disarmed me'.

Thirteen-year-old Rudy Kolarič and his family were attacked on the road by Partisans and dropped everything and fled. Together with his mother, uncle, two aunts and three cousins, he took shelter in a roadside tavern, but a bomb injured his mother and a cousin. A passing ambulance picked them up and in the confusion he found himself alone.

'I was petrified, and put a bucket over my head as I walked up the mountain road. There was shooting going on all the time. Once I lifted the bucket a bit and looked around. I saw Partisans to the left and the right, and when I looked back I saw a horse drop dead from a rifle shot. I jammed the bucket back on my head and walked on. I am sure I was protected by Divine Providence,' says Rudy. He eventually found his mother again in Austria.

Fellow-refugees ripped the rucksacks off the daughter and wife of Dr Meršol. Mrs Meršol, a doctor of philosophy and daughter of a famous literary critic, already weak from cancer of the womb, for the rest of her life could never forgive the affront. Rumours spread that Partisans were killing stragglers. Corpses of humans, horses and cows littered the roadside. Everywhere, the refugees mingled with an endless train of German soldiers, cars, tanks and carts – the defeated army, in a hurry, pushing civilians into the ditch, driving over fallen horses, whipping and stealing to get out first.

When Jože Lekan reached the little town of Tržič at the foot of the mountains, he spotted a young man about to be shot by *domobranci* for hiding weapons. Jože recognised him as a boy he used to play with on holiday, and saved him by training his machine-gun on his comrades.

As Lekan left the town with the *domobranci*, they came under shellfire that ripped through roofs and cratered the ground around them. A man fell screaming nearby, cut in half by a shell. A German tank ahead opened fire on them. Confusion was total, and they lay pinned down in a meadow until they could scramble off again at nightfall. Lekan said:

> It was a river of humanity and animals, streaming up into the mountain, where fires were burning in a camp where Germans had housed slave labourers. The whole camp was ablaze and that gave us some illumination, with black silhouettes standing out against the red background. Once I saved myself from falling down a cliff into a river 70 metres below by grabbing the tail of a horse and hanging on. Horses pushed me left and right; there was nothing I could do; I was just a little pebble in an avalanche.[5]

As they moved on up the mountain, underlying mistrust between the Germans and the *domobranci* came to the fore. Until now, both sides had used each other, and the Germans kept the *domobranci* on a short rein. Now the balance of power was shifting. As they reached the village of St Ana, they saw the German tank that had been firing on them blocking the road, with German SS and Gestapo soldiers standing beside it.

'The Germans were laughing at us and thought we were just a defenceless mass of civilians. All of a sudden a Chetnik fighter threw

Refugees on the way to the Ljubelj Pass. Civilians, soldiers, horses, carts, tanks and cars mingled chaotically as they fled from the advancing Partisans.

himself down with a machine-gun and threatened to mow down the entire German staff. We jumped to the left and right of him and aimed our rifles at the Germans. We made clear that we would kill everybody in sight if they did not move the tank off the road. They moved it and the civilian refugees and wagons could resume their climb.'

Lekan and his unit spread around the sides of the congested road and walked into a minefield that blew off the leg of one of his friends. Lekan, near the end of his strength, crawled the last few hundred metres out of the minefield on all fours.

As Uroš Roessmann's *domobranci* unit headed up the hill, Partisan artillery rained shells on them, wounding soldiers, blocking the road and causing panic at the end of the column. 'The company disintegrated, and we never saw our commander again. I got into a strange group of Serbs, Croats and Slovenes, and we mounted a rear-guard with a heavy machine-gun. Exhausted after three nights without sleep, we were just approaching the pass, when the man in front of me stepped on a mine and was killed.'

Marian Loboda, 14 at the time, described the chaos: 'Now we could only move at night. The nearer the frontier, the greater the crowds. Pauses for rest were impossible. Then the whole mass got stuck with our wagon in the middle, and we were terrified when we heard shots from behind and from the hills. People seized anything they could carry and rushed up the hill, and I was told to hold on tight to a member of the family. The fully loaded wagons were stranded and later taken over by pursuing Partisans or the locals. The valley grew narrower, the path steeper. A munitions truck caught fire and exploded with a deafening report.'

France Pernišek recorded the apocalyptic scene as he and his family headed up from the last village of St Ana:

> The horses whinny, the carts groan, all the men push the carts to help the beasts climb the hill. St Ana now lies far below and the whole valley is lit by a huge conflagration: the camp at Ljubelj is on fire. We are horrified by the dark red flames reflecting like blood on the rocks. The higher we go, the darker and more frightening the sight of the burning valley. We hear repeated explosions. How we'd have suffered if we had still been at St Ana.

Gradually, they struggled up to the two-kilometre-long tunnel that would take them under the Ljubelj Pass to safety in Austria on the other side.

The tunnel was blocked. SS soldiers guarding its opening were only letting German troops through. It had been built by slave labour – French, Polish, Russian, Belgian, Italian and Yugoslav civilians drafted in from Mauthausen concentration camp.[6] Intended to give German armies speedier access to the Adriatic, in the end it only served to facilitate their flight in defeat. Nearby lay the burned-out remains of the camp which housed the labourers. In an old baronial hunting lodge requisitioned by the SS camp guards, the refugees found bread, biscuits and unwashed dishes abandoned in a hurry.

At the tunnel entrance a huge mass of refugees milled around haplessly under a beating sun. It was a gigantic encampment of awnings and shacks, carts, horses and meagre stew-pots. People crammed into a tiny chapel to pray, while priests said Mass and tolled the bell.

Among the throng was 60-year-old Director Marko Bajuk, headmaster of the principal classical secondary school of Ljubljana, former inspector of secondary schools, composer and conductor. He too was to play a key role in the fleeing Slovenes' destinies. With him were his wife, son and daughter-in-law and their four children. Andrej, the youngest at only 19 months old, was to return many years later to govern his home country as Prime Minister. They had left Ljubljana with two prams, a bicycle and a small suitcase, and made their way to the pass on foot, taking over an abandoned horse and cart as they neared the top. The son, Božidar, a teacher of Latin and Greek, recalled the scene:

Lord, what crowds and chaos, what traffic! Tanks, carts, cars, lorries, people on horseback, columns of soldiers, people on foot, civilian refugees, all pushing their way towards the tunnel – the soldiers, specially the Germans, screaming while the refugees were silent, thoughtful, worried. We spent all next day on the ground in front of the entrance. There was pandemonium, people growing more and more neurotic, the crowd thicker and thicker. Planes circled overhead and people grew panicky. On top of mental trauma we suffered

The Slovene refugees enter the uncompleted Ljubelj tunnel, built by slave labourers for Nazi troops occupying Yugoslavia and Greece.

acute physical discomfort. Starving and out in the intense heat, our bodily strength was totally exhausted. Columns of tanks, artillery, lorries and men on foot passed us. Father baked a few potatoes. We were terrified at the thought of another night in the open and stood wearily in columns, hungry, sleepless, cold.[7]

Some headed up the old track to the top of the Ljubelj Pass at 1,538 metres. A few slept on top among patches of snow under the gleam of a full moon. Zdenka Virant, now living in Argentinian Patagonia, woke up to find an unexploded bomb lying a metre away.

The crowd by the tunnel stared threateningly at the SS soldiers and began to move closer. A German officer was seized, taken down the hill and did not come back. A group of *domobranci* arrived, took their guns from their shoulders and prepared to fire. The SS capitulated, the tunnel was opened, and the huge convoy of refugees stretching far down the mountain road began to heave into motion.

They poured into the tunnel, into another hell. Pitch-dark and incomplete, it was strewn with rocks and in places was knee-deep in water. Rail tracks laid by the construction workers ran through the middle. A few of the refugees had torches or candles protected by paper cones. Most felt their way through in the dark, holding on to family or friends as they negotiated the curves. Every ten or twenty paces, they were forced to a halt by the crush and had to wait in stinking mud. Foot soldiers thrust past the civilians, and German tanks forced their way through lines of Russian horsemen. The air was rent with cursing. Women and children screamed as horses pushed them against the wall. The blind companion of 16-year-old Majda Vračko held on to her white bicycle. Eight-year-old Magdalena Šimenc clung on to her father's. Tone Suhadolc was so frightened when blocked in the middle that he lit the first and only cigarette of his life. Somebody pulled a gun on Val Meršol's brother when he lurched into him. But little Gloria Bratina, pulling a handcart with her small sister, felt her neck nudged by a horse, encouraging her onwards until they reached the end.

Then they were out in the air again. For the Bajuk family, it had taken three hours to negotiate the two kilometres of tunnel which motorists today pass in a few minutes. Their children were screaming and crying when they emerged. One had disappeared with a student on a bicycle. Any hope they had reached safety was quickly dashed, for the Partisans had got ahead of them, blocking the road at Borovlje (Ferlach) down in the valley. Once more, fear spread through the weary masses. Some, like Gloria Bratina, Milči Lekan and the whole Pernišek family, went straight back through the tunnel to the Slovene side. Milči, teenage sister of Jože Lekan, felt her head spinning. A human foot sticking out of a shallow grave brought her to her senses. She found a wheelbarrow, put their rucksacks in it, and set off on foot over the pass above the tunnel. 'I was young and could walk, and I was thrilled to see the mountains bathed in moonlight at the top. But the euphoria had vanished by the time I reached the valley on the other side – shaky on my feet from hunger, thirst, lack of sleep and walking for 24 hours.'

Eventually, a unit of *domobranci* shock troops led by Major Vuk Rupnik headed down to Borovlje and drove away the Partisans. The *domobranci* mostly wore German-supplied uniforms, but Major Rupnik's battalion went into this last encounter wearing British battle dress and firing British Bren guns. They had taken them from dead Partisans, who received them in the British government's wartime airlifts. The Partisans did not retreat far. For weeks, they roamed Austrian Carinthia, reinforcing Tito's claim to the region and co-existing uneasily with the British Army.

The dirt road leading down from the tunnel dropped away steeply in serpentine bends. The farm-carts had no brakes, and the refugees had their hands full keeping them on the road. 'Our horse kicked, reared and bit ever more furiously, and the cart kept sliding down towards the edge of a precipice or into the ditch, so that I had to lift it by the back spring every 20 paces and straighten it. My arms were giving way and blisters were bursting,' recalled Božidar Bajuk. Pernišek lifted his sleeping younger child on to his shoulder and wrote in his diary: 'Today the children are our sweet though heavy burden.' By now, the refugees were carrying dead and sick with them. A woman gave birth in one of the farm wagons. A German Panzer crew traded food for civilian clothes. As flares lit by the *domobranci* illuminated the surrounding mountains, the road levelled out and people started reciting the rosary.

Then they met the British. A few small dishevelled Tommies greeted them morosely at the roadside. 'It was one of the big disappointments of my life,' says Maria Hribar, who later emigrated to Britain as Mrs Jančar. 'We were so pleased to see them, but they were stealing watches. It was like finding out that Father Christmas doesn't exist any more.' Ten-year-old Franc Rode, later Metropolitan Archbishop of Ljubljana, found the British decidedly unfriendly.

Lekan saw bodies strewn around in Borovlje after the battle between *domobranci* and Partisans. Amid fields covered with trucks, tools and ammunition discarded by the Germans, he saw a British officer smoking a pipe as he calmly surveyed the scene from the turret of a tank.

They plodded over the long bridge across the river Drava, and on the other side 14-year-old Marian Loboda spotted a huge pile of pistols, rifles and automatic weapons. He jumped to help himself – a pistol at that time was worth two pounds of bacon – but a young British soldier shooed him away. The British Army was forcing the *domobranci* and Germans to give up their arms as they crossed the river. Many *domobranci* handed them over without a second thought, glad to be in the hands of the British. Others felt uneasy without their arms. A group of

Partisans stood nearby laughing. Heading down the road, the *domobranci* were aware of other bands never far away. A Partisan on horseback told Maria Suhadolc: 'You are not going to achieve what you want. It's going to get worse. You'll be disappointed.' He seemed to know something they did not. But what? Two Partisans drove by in a jeep with British Army officers. The fraternisation did not bode well. Marching along in their German-supplied uniforms, it began to occur to some of them that the British might not necessarily see them as friends. Lekan was furious at having to give up his huge arsenal just after the *domobranci* had defeated the Partisans at Borovlje:

> I was so hurt to see that the Allies were taking that stuff away from us that I cried and ground my teeth and broke a tooth clean off. I disassembled the Schmeiser machine-gun I got from the German and threw the parts in the faces of those Englishmen standing by the road. I was mad, disgusted and disappointed. I was ready to die. To see those people for whom we risked our lives to save their pilots disarming us and treating us as if we came with a bunch of Germans – I couldn't swallow it, all the more because they were stealing watches and wedding rings.

Some of the refugees had been walking non-stop for 36 hours. Pernišek's daughter Cirila refused to give water to a Partisan, and was scolded by her father, who told her: 'Don't ever refuse water to anybody. Water is for everybody.' Little Gloria Bratina, still perky and combative, did her best to revive the spirits of her flagging parents. Her father had blisters and was carrying the two youngest of his ten children in his arms. Her mother looked desperate. Gloria gave them a lecture on this not being the right time to get depressed. She tried to ask the way in French from a British army patrol they met on the road. The family climbed over a fence to spend the night in a garden, and Gloria decided to keep watch in case Partisans came. The next thing she knew she was waking up in early morning sunshine.

Božidar Bajuk was near the end of his tether as his family stumbled on into the night:

> Mentally and physically exhausted, we noticed lights at the top of the hill. From the fires we could hear shouting, yelling and singing. Army vehicles drove towards us, blinding us. We came upon a monstrous red light on the tarmac road. The two British soldiers standing in front realised we were Slovenes. We turned off into the camp and from all sides came shrill shouts from our own people who'd already settled – we were now in their way. I tried to calm myself. Never had I been so close to a complete breakdown, shaking, dizzy as if drunk. I got out matches and found we were in a corn field.

They had arrived outside the village of Viktring (Vetrinj), just south of Klagenfurt. The British were halting the refugees there to sort out what to do with them. After seven days on the road, Pernišek staggered in with his family around nine in the evening, and confided to his diary:

> Viktring, a new station on our Way of the Cross. Here we are. What next? My wife looks at me hopelessly, the children ask for food, it's a long time since we last ate. Where will we sleep? What shall I tell them? How can I console them? 'We love Jesus and he loves us. Now we're like Lord Jesus who had nowhere to lay his head. Let us trust him.' For supper we had our bitter tears. We flopped down exhausted. After 30 hours walking we slept well on the hard bare ground under the open sky.

# 2 PAWNS

*We've let the golden apple of our freedom*
*Slip into the blood and the mud,*
*And before it shines again in pure glory,*
*We'll all be muddy, all so bloody.*

*– Slovene poet Oton Župančič, October 1943*[1]

When Hitler declared war on Yugoslavia in spring 1941, Slovene student Leo Čop joined the Royal Army as a volunteer, took a train to Zagreb and reported to a barracks to defend his country. Something seemed wrong as soon as he got to the Croatian capital; he wondered why Croats gave him peculiar looks as he made his way to his unit. After a week's rifle training under a Serbian commander, he was about to be dispatched to Bosnia; he glanced out of a barracks window and was shocked to see Croatian girls sailing by on top of German tanks. Yugoslavia had disintegrated, not for the last time. A pro-German Ustasha Croatian government had been proclaimed, and the girls were regaling the Germans as 'liberators' from the Serb yoke. It was no time to be part of the Serb-dominated Royal Army. Now he understood the strange looks.

He slipped out through a back door and headed off over fields, shedding his military insignia and stamps with the head of the King. He jumped on a train back to Ljubljana. As he crossed into Slovenia, the mood of rejoicing changed abruptly. Germans were searching the trains and took some other young men away. When he arrived in Ljubljana, it was swarming with Italian elite Bersaglieri troops.

For Slovenes, it was an awakening to the grim realities of war that had so far passed them by. When Leo got back home, his father snapped to him: 'Don't ever volunteer for anything again.' This was not a surprising reaction, since independent initiative had rarely been an option for

Slovenes. Under the Austro-Hungarian Empire, they had their own homeland, and their cultural influence spread to Trieste (Italy) and Klagenfurt (Austria). But there was no self-determination, no independent Slovene state and no real democracy. Vienna ruled, and Austrians assimilated Slovenes into their own culture or treated them as 'a nation of servants'.

After World War I, the Austro-Hungarian Empire was broken up, and Slovenia became part of the Kingdom of Serbs, Croats and Slovenes – subsequently Yugoslavia. In practice, this brought little emancipation. Now they were subjected to the authoritarian Serb monarchy in Belgrade instead of to Austria. Although only a bit player in World War I, the Slovene death rate proportionate to its population was twice that of Britain, one of the principal belligerents.[2] The western part of their homeland, with a quarter of the population, was ceded to Italy. The Italians had been defeated at the battle of Caporetto (Kobarid) on Slovene soil, but got the territory as part of a secret reward agreed with the British, French and Russians in 1915* to entice them into the conflict.

Leo was already on the wrong side of authority between the wars. At his high school in Kranj, he risked expulsion by agitating in student organisations for an independent Slovene state. When World War II reached Yugoslavia, he was studying chemistry at Ljubljana University, and had joined a Catholic organisation which was both anti-Communist and nationalist. They brawled with Communists on the campus, but also tangled with the occupying Italians and Germans. In one prank, they sprayed ink over the white knee socks of a group of Germans.

None of this did Leo Čop any good. Like millions of others all over Europe, Slovenes counted as no more than pawns once war took a hold. Well-intended personal initiative often led to disaster, as it finally did for Leo. Patriotic, religious and a hearty mountain-climber, Leo Čop had human qualities that in normal times should have served him well. But at that time, in that place, they brought no protection.

While Čop did a few absurd days of military service for the Kingdom of Yugoslavia, two other men who fled over the Ljubelj Pass could recall more intimate connections with inter-war Yugoslav Royalty. Dr Valentin Meršol, the Ljubljana hospital doctor, had been personal physician to Yugoslavia's King Alexander, assassinated by a Macedonian funded by the Ustasha in 1934. Short, bald, with a round face and glasses, Meršol already had a well-travelled career. Taken prisoner by the Russians while serving in the Austrian Army in World War I, he moved via Odessa, Samarkand, Moscow and Ekaterinburg to a post as sanitation inspector in 1919/20 in the Arctic port of Murmansk. He learned English with the British Army fighting with White Russians against the Red Army. Subsequently, he studied on a Rockefeller Scholarship at the prestigious

---

*    Treaty of London, 1915, ratified in the Treaty of Rapallo, 1920.

Johns Hopkins Medical School in Baltimore. Earnest, fluent in languages, cultured and independent of mind, he personified Central European professional values. In the Slovenes' Odyssey, he modestly exercised a natural gift for leadership which proved decisive.

Jože Jančar, then a schoolboy and later a distinguished psychiatrist in Bristol, England, was invited with the 40 best pupils of Yugoslavia to spend a week at the 'White Court' of teenage King Peter, who had succeeded his father Alexander:

> The Court sent a royal railway carriage to Ljubljana and five of us, with a teacher, travelled in this. When we arrived in Belgrade, we were taken to a hall, where each of us was fitted out with a Crombie overcoat. Every night, we went to the Palace to visit the King, where we were received by the Marshal of the Court, and had a meal with him. On the last night, we all had a few drinks. Suddenly our teacher came over to me with a bunch of carnations, and told me to present them to the King with a vote of thanks. I said I wasn't prepared, but he said I had to. The next day I read my speech in the newspaper *Politika* and it seemed quite good, but I don't remember giving it!

By spring 1941 all this seemed a remote fairy-tale. Peter had fled to exile in England after his Regent, Prince Paul, had concluded a pact with Hitler and been overthrown by a coup. Yugoslavia had fallen easy prey to the Nazi military machine. Jančar too would have to join the flight to Austria. Unprecedented death and destruction was to afflict Yugoslavia, and the Slovenes would not be spared. As a Royalist diplomat put it: 'The appalling conditions throughout Yugoslavia following Hitler's blitzkrieg in 1941 froze the blood of all who lived there, and of their friends and foes as well. There was a general feeling that hell had been let loose, and that any return to normal standards was impossible. It was as though the Four Horsemen of the Apocalypse had swept through the land, sowing the seeds of strife, carnage, death, famine and pestilence.'[3]

Slovenia ceased to exist. From being one of Yugoslavia's eight provinces, it was dismembered into three parts. The area nearest the Austrian frontier was incorporated into the German Reich. Hitler swept into the city of Maribor and declared: 'Let's make this land German again.' Schools switched to German, the city became known by its German name of Marburg, and the area was sealed from the rest of Slovenia. Hungary, allied with the Axis powers, was given the small eastern part of Slovenia. The rest went to Fascist Italy. In the Austro-Hungarian Empire and inter-war Yugoslavia, Slovenia had been recognised as a territory and a people. Now even that small measure of nationhood was gone.

The Slovenes were at square one. Their darkest hour had come. Every detail of their lives was controlled with totalitarian thoroughness. It was practically impossible to move between the different zones of occupation. 'During the war my world was 15 kilometres long and two wide,' says Cardinal Ambrožič, then a schoolboy. Joseph Plevnik lived in a corridor one kilometre wide between two sets of barbed wire fences. Another village was split in two by the zonal border running through its centre.

There was a significant difference between the German and Italian occupational regimes. The Nazis adopted the same racist practice as in other Slav lands, removing Slovenes from positions of authority, rooting out the intelligentsia, expelling priests and teachers to Serbia, and burning books from libraries and schools. In their zone, it was forbidden to speak Slovene in a public place. Over 80,000, or 7%, had to go into exile.[4]

Milči and Jože Lekan's father, as Director of Utilities, was the highest administrative official left when the Germans took over Maribor. The mayor had been drafted into the German army. 'My dad was a man of great integrity. Some urged him to leave too, but he believed it his duty to see to the orderly transfer of authority. So one day the German military marched into his office – "Heil Hitler" and all. Dad showed them the books, was thanked and dismissed,' said Milči.

Marian Loboda, then ten years old, saw the first German invaders in his neighbourhood on Palm Sunday, 1941:

> On the way to Mass in my native village 12 kilometres from Ljubljana I saw black planes with white crosses hovering like falcons over their prey and releasing bombs whose roar we could hear a long way off. The war had started for us, and a couple of days later a column of German troops appeared in our village on motorcycles, young lads in dark brown uniforms, very friendly and cheerful, throwing sweets and chocolates at us children. A week later another kind of people appeared, in green [SS] uniforms with shining black boots and caps from which shone silver-plated skulls and crossbones. They were more sullen and didn't smile.

Marian's primary school was closed and the teachers expelled or arrested. After a few weeks it reopened. A blonde teacher who could not speak a word of Slovene took over and began teaching them in German. She started with patriotic German songs, which the children happily picked up within a few weeks. Later Marian went to a ski camp in Austria and was entertained in a tavern by young German soldiers on leave from the Russian front:

> One day I returned home from school singing the German national anthem 'Deutschland, Deutschland über Alles' at the top of my lungs. I can still feel how my uncle welcomed me with a formidable box of my ears. He subjected me to a long sermon on how the Germans were torturing and killing our people, how they forbade us to speak our own language, banned our papers and books and caused us all kinds of evils every day.

The Germans ruled in their zone with such an iron fist right from the start that few of the inhabitants there were accused of collaboration after the war. There was no free choice. If men served with the German forces, it was because they were forcibly conscripted. A total of 35,000 had to serve in the German or Hungarian armed forces, and 7,000 were killed.[5] One Slovene now living in Patagonia remembers being drafted into the Hitler Youth at 16, fighting in France and deserting in 1944. His father was forced to serve in a paramilitary unit in Slovenia. When they went into action, the Partisans shouted, 'Don't shoot!' The men had to 'keep their heads down and make bangs', but they fired high. Neither son nor father faced any charges of collaboration after the war.

In the Italian zone, which was declared an integral part of Italy, the image of kind, romantic Italian soldiers turned out to be a myth. In August 1942 the commanding general, Mario Roatta, outlined to his staff a policy of wholesale deportation of Slovene villagers suspected of harbouring Partisans, which was to include men, women and children: 'Don't worry if those expelled include innocent people. Operations must be brief and effective: if necessary don't shy away from using cruelty. It must be a complete cleansing. We need to intern all the inhabitants and put Italian families in their place, families of dead or wounded soldiers.'

He added that internment was no substitute for 'shooting all those elements guilty or suspected of Communist activity'.[6] Italian units took photographs of their soldiers shooting hostages and standing over dead bodies in villages. One published in a recent Slovene book[7] shows the Italian Alpini regiment carrying the severed head of a Partisan on a pole around Slovene villages in November 1942.

The Italian oppression was often arbitrary. Uroš Roessmann, who later became a neuropathologist in Cleveland, US, remembers: 'There were frequent *razzias* when the train taking us to school in Ljubljana from our village of Polje pulled in to the main station. Italian soldiers picked us all up. Some were released, and others were sent to concentration camps. Nobody knew who decided, or on what grounds.'

One of those detained was Tone Suhadolc, now living in Hamilton, Ontario. The youngest in a family of 14, he was arrested in a round-up of students at Ljubljana University in 1942, and sent for 18 months to Gonars concentration camp over the Italian border. 'Why? The Italians just wanted to make sure that we young men did not go up into the hills and join the Partisans.' Leo Čop had a narrow escape in another raid on the University campus, when the Italians lined up the male students and sent every tenth in the line to a concentration camp.

France Kozina, later to make an amazing escape from the Partisan execution squads, was arrested in 1942 and sent to one of the worst Italian concentration camps on the Adriatic island of Rab. It was filthy, muddy, overcrowded and swarming with insects. Prisoners, who included pregnant women and children, were quartered six to a tent and slowly starved. Another Rab inmate, Metod Milač, described the appalling conditions in his memoirs.[8] Wracked by dysentery, infested by lice and covered with excrement from the primitive latrines, many could hardly crawl out of their tents for roll calls. Food consisted of thin soup, a few grains of rice and small pieces of bread. Guards let the prisoners fight with each other for scarce water from a barrel. Flash floods washed away part of the encampment, and work included lugging coffins laden with two bodies apiece to burial.

Many died, and lines of crude crosses stretch into the distance in the island's cemetery. Kozina was eventually transferred to Padua, weighing 40 kilograms. Released after a year, he was never given a reason for his arrest. Italian sailors ferrying inmates back to the mainland were shocked by their emaciated state and gently helped them ashore. Altogether, 9,000 Slovenes died in Italian concentration camps.[9]

Jože Jančar narrowly escaped with his life after being arrested in an Italian reprisals raid:

> I spent a week as a hostage in the death cell in Ljubljana. They said if any Italian were shot outside, they'd take people from our cell and shoot them. It seems incredible but we became stoically indifferent. They'd call names at 4 a.m. and people would be taken away and we just wrote their names on the wall and went to sleep. Those summoned didn't cry or swear – just defiantly walked out. Then when we were taken to the concentration camp, they chained us together and put us in cattle trucks. At the station we were thirsty, and saw where the railway engines were filled with water. We put our hands out to catch some, but the soldiers beat us back, wouldn't allow it. When we were walking towards the camp, people spat at us and called us 'banditi'. In the camp, they fed us on a thin soup with a few grains of rice in it.

He was released after a Slovene bishop intervened through the Vatican.

The Italians played a more ambiguous game than the Germans. Although cruel at times, they were less direct and single-minded. They allowed civil administrators to continue in their posts, and pressured them to cooperate actively. They planned to introduce Fascism more gradually, rather than impose it instantly as in the German-run areas. By allowing a measure of autonomy, they were setting a trap, and the Catholic politicians fell into it. Carrying on in positions of authority under Italian tutelage meant in one way or another collaboration.

For these Catholics, collaboration was blameless because it was directed against the Communists. Their domestic opponents, who fought and eventually emerged victorious, thought otherwise. For ordinary people caught up in the war, the Italian regime was the more dangerous. If they resisted, the Italians put them in a concentration camp or in front of a firing squad. If they tried to accommodate the Italian authority, they risked attack by the Partisans as collaborators.

Joseph Plevnik saw dangerous weakness in the Italian attitude:

> The Germans decreed they would kill ten Slovenes for every German soldier killed, and we knew where we stood. The Italians did nothing to protect the civilian population. At night, their zone was in the hands of the [Communist] resistance, and during the day they would come storming in to make reprisals. They allowed the Communists to flourish, did deals with them, and were supplied by them with girls and spies.

Stane Snoj, now in Argentina, lived with his family only 100 metres from an Italian guard-post, but Communists still threw a bomb through their window. They were tipped off they were on a Communist death list and felt unprotected by the Italian occupiers.

Marija Hribar, the fiancée of Jože Jančar, agreed: 'The Italians were nice and friendly. But turn your back and they would put their knife into you. The Germans would just tell you straightaway they hated you.'

So what were the Communists doing? For the first two months of the war in Yugoslavia, they sided with the occupiers, taking their cue from the Soviet Union, which in August 1939 signed the Molotov/Ribbentrop Pact with Germany. Following instructions from the Comintern, the organisation set up by the Soviet regime to direct Communist activities worldwide, they initially hailed Nazis as enemies of capitalism, praising the jobs created by the state in Germany for millions of unemployed. They urged soldiers to desert from the Royal Yugoslav Army and sabotaged factories. When Catholic student leader Matej Roessmann organised a demonstration against the Pact, the Communists stayed away.

Marian Loboda remembers Communist sympathisers hanging swastika flags from their houses to welcome German troops and jeering that 'the rich and the vicars are now going to pay for it'. In Jesenice, a Communist knocked on the Markež family's door asking his uncle to join the Hitler Youth. The uncle threw him out, and after the war, when serving a six-year prison sentence imposed by a People's Court, he recognised the same man as his prison guard.

So the Communists, who were subsequently to claim all credit for defeating the Germans, started off on the German side, while the anti-Communist Catholics, later to be branded as collaborators, began the war as a focus of nationalist opposition to the invader. The complex moral mesh was being woven. When Hitler invaded the Soviet Union in June 1941, the Communists did an about-turn. They formed a Liberation Front together with a couple of other smaller political movements.

The Liberation Front started organising a fighting force – the Partisans. Although this force quickly came to be led and dominated by the Communists, it also included patriots who were just interested in protecting their Slovene homes and hearths against a foreign enemy. Since most Slovenes were Catholics at that time, the Partisans had

Catholics in their ranks from the beginning. Even some of those Catholics who later fought against the Communists and had to flee in 1945 had joined the Partisans during this period. The staunchly Catholic father of Franc Rode, later Archbishop of Ljubljana, was with the resistance for a time. 'People began talking of the men of the forest, and there was a certain amount of sympathy with them because they were resisting the occupier,' says Rode. For some the decision to join was voluntary; others were press-ganged.

Among the latter was France Kozina, whom the Partisans 'mobilised' in 1943 when he returned from the Italian concentration camp. He recalls reconnoitring a railway bridge near Ljubljana at night with a Partisan commander, who suggested when they were still a kilometre away: 'What do you say if we all go back now?' They went no further. When his Partisan unit later came near his home, Kozina deserted and joined the *domobranci*.

France Dejak, who like Kozina escaped from Partisan execution pits, had a similar career on both sides. He too had to go with the Partisans in the early part of the war. At night they were all over Slovenia. After two months, lice-ridden, hungry and suffering from dysentery, his column of 800 Partisans arrived close to his home village. He slipped away and went home.

Two months later, the Partisans turned up with a list of 30 people they were looking for, including him. So he was back in their ranks until, once more close to his home village after his unit was broken up by a German attack, he persuaded his commander to let him go and fetch fresh clothes. They went together, but his sister, pretending the Germans were coming, tricked the commander into running away. He was free again. It was hard to distinguish good and evil in this war; it was turning into a jumble of threats, deceit and contradictions. A few days later, Dejak jumped on a truck to Ljubljana and joined the police.

By spring 1942, Catholics and Communists were at each other's throats. The Yugoslav Communist leader Tito had decided to use the world war as an opportunity to launch a social revolution and seize power. Nobody should be surprised he took this course. In 1915, during the course of World War I, Lenin wrote: 'It is simply insane to talk about abolishing capitalism without a frightful civil war or succession of such wars...The duty of Socialists is to transform this war into a war between classes.'[10]

In 1928, the Fourth Congress of the Yugoslav Communist Party, held in Dresden, resolved that 'it must turn any war into a civil war against its own bourgeoisie...to defeat the Yugoslav government and ensure the victory of a Soviet government'.[11]

Tito, who came to head the Yugoslav Party in Moscow in the 1930s, was therefore following a Leninist strategy, ignoring the fact that it had been amended in 1935 when Communists were instructed by Moscow to form 'popular fronts' with bourgeois parties to defeat fascism. Stalin initially feared that Tito's assaults on his bourgeois opponents would jeopardise the new policy and antagonise the Western Allies; preservation of the alliance to defeat Hitler should take priority, and he scolded Tito for excessive aggression. He need not have worried. The British sided with Tito anyway. Later, Stalin certainly resented that Tito took scant notice of his admonitions, and Yugoslavia's growing independence led to Tito's expulsion from the Comintern in 1948. Relations with the Soviet Union were not restored until 1955. In practice, however, Stalin applied a similar principle of forced revolutionary change in the countries which the Soviet Union occupied at the end of the war, using the presence of the Red Army to engineer takeovers by Communist regimes.

Gradually it became clearer that the Germans were losing the war. Among those fighting them all over the world, thoughts began to turn to the political futures of countries under Nazi rule. So too in Slovenia and the rest of Yugoslavia. The Communists consolidated their domination of the Liberation Front, and insisted on leadership of all military action against the occupiers. In 1943, the Communists forced through the 'Dolomite' declaration that they should be the only permitted political party within the Liberation Front. Here too they were acting in the Leninist tradition, seeking dictatorship by the party of the proletariat at the expense of all others. It was a more radical stand than Communists took elsewhere in occupied Europe. In France, the Communists followed Comintern instructions and accepted that other political formations participate in decision-making of the French resistance movement.

In the Slovene Communist Party, which numbered just 800 at the outbreak of the war, the old leadership had been ousted in 1935 by young radicals bent on revolution, as soon as possible, at any cost. Although small in number, they were well organised and used to operating clandestinely. Among them were Boris Kidrič, a leader of the Communist reign of austerity and repression after the war, and Edvard Kardelj, who was Tito's ideologist and later devised a unique but unwieldy system of workers' participation in government.

The Catholic establishment took an equally uncompromising stand. Bishop Gregorij Rožman, the leader of the Catholic Church in Slovenia, reminded his flock in a pastoral letter on 5 December 1941 that Pope Pius XI had forbidden Catholics to cooperate with Communists, describing Communism as 'something essentially evil'. Rožman wrote: 'These Papal principles apply to us and there is no debate about it, so we must adhere to them in awareness and recognition. It is vain to expect cultural progress or national freedom from Communism; it is a fatal mistake which would chain the nation into deepest slavery and destroy it.'[12]

The Slovene Catholics were caught in a pincer movement. On the one hand the occupiers, in particular the Nazis, saw them as enemies both ideologically and in terms of the Slav cultural identity they defended.

On the other hand, they were menaced by a Communist movement that had returned to its traditional revolutionary path.

This split was heavy with consequences. A civil war had become inevitable. It left scars that are still not fully healed among modern-day Slovenes.

From spring 1942, Catholic community leaders found themselves under murderous attack. Mayors, teachers, judges, priests, intellectuals, policemen, organisers of the Catholic Action lay movement, or anybody who challenged Communist-led insurgency were targeted for assassination. It was a text-book Communist exercise, as executed already in the Soviet Union and subsequently in the countries the Soviets were to dominate in liberated Eastern Europe. It threatened anybody who held power or property.

Kardelj, the Communist strategist of the Slovene Partisans, wrote in 1941: 'Without pitiless physical eradication of all kinds of spies and enemy agents, the Partisans won't ensure safety of their movement, and they won't get food, arms, clothing or information.'[13] According to Božo Repe, Professor of Contemporary History at Ljubljana University, the Communist leaders believed in 1942 the war would soon be over and set about liquidating the political opposition so that they could seize power. The Communists later sought to justify their attacks by alleging that the Catholics were by that time collaborating with the occupying forces. This was not quite true.[14] But by then both sides detested each other deeply and were at war.

Dinko Bertoncelj, later to become a well-known ski-guide in the Andes, went with his father one midwinter's day to answer a knock at the door. A Partisan sprayed them both with dum-dum bullets from a machine-gun. His father, a local dignitary, died eight days later. Dinko threw himself to one side and was untouched.

Frank Jeglič, now a business executive in Cleveland, US, remembers how Partisans shot his uncle, a judge, in the back of his head. Matej Roessmann's brother Uroš recalls: 'The first person to die in our village of Polje was an old gendarme. He had been retired by the Italians, but he knew people. One day, the Partisans knocked at his door and shot him. Then other people were shot in the village.'

Marija Hribar saw Partisans come into her family house one night and plunder food and clothes, including a muff with a fur collar she had bought her little sister. On another night in a house nearby, they killed four adults and four children.

Farm-boy Marian Loboda recounts:

One Sunday afternoon, when we children were playing at the edge of the wood, we were surprised by a man with a big beard, a cap with a bright red five-pointed star on it and an enormous rifle on his back. He started talking to us, introducing himself as a Partisan and saying they would soon throw the Germans out of the country. He then told us with threats we must not tell anyone we had seen him...

At 2 a.m. on 29th May 1943 we were woken up by heavy blows on the door. My mother opened it and was met by guns pointed at her. They said they were Partisans. They turned the house upside down, stole what they could, tied my uncle Jože's hands and took him away. He was never seen again, but we learned later that after some days of torture they killed him in the mountains not far from our village. We never found his burial spot.

It was the same uncle who had boxed his ears for singing German songs. A few weeks later, two Partisans appeared again and said he had been sent to Serbia and they needed to take clothes, linen and shoes for him. By that time he was probably already dead, so it was just an excuse to lay hands on his belongings.

Three months later, Germans troops knocked on the door at 7 a.m. and rounded up the family to take them to a transit camp for deportation to Germany, allegedly for sympathising with the Partisans. Marian told a young German soldier: 'I can't go without feeding my rabbits.' The soldier, a simple boy, laid his gun against a tree and with tears in his eyes helped Marian mow grass for the rabbits. The denunciation was false, and after a bit the Germans decided it originated from the Partisans. It looked like a trick to get rid of a Catholic family. The family were released and returned home, but were again threatened by the Partisans, who believed they must have done a deal with the Germans. There was no way civilians could avoid being drawn into the war.

Anica Guden, now living in Wales, remembers how she and her family were seized by the Partisans in the Ribnica area. As Italian troops closed in, two Partisans shot her parents and her three brothers in the temples before her eyes. Her dead father fell across her and a shot pierced her hand. The Partisans realised she was not dead and she heard them discussing whether it was worth using another bullet to finish her off. They were short of ammunition and decided against it.

In this spiralling horror, the anti-Communist Catholics opposed to the Partisans gave back in kind. They operated their own assassination squads, called the Black Hand, against members of the Liberation Front. In cells in Ljubljana, one can see the words 'Avenge us' and a series of female names, which pro-Communist women scratched on the walls with their finger-nails just before they were taken away to be shot. A 90-year-old ex-Partisan woman told one of the authors that collaborating Slovenes tortured her and other Partisans. 'I was never beaten by anyone but Slovenes,' she said.

One of the biggest disputes was how violent the opposition to the occupiers should be. The Communists, as soon as they stopped siding with the Germans in June 1941, launched attacks against the occupiers which triggered reprisals against civilians. Kardelj wrote in 1941: 'The best defence is attack...Abandoning defensive tactics and constantly attacking selected enemy positions, this is the first and most important task of the Partisans...Blow for blow, blood for blood, hostage for hostage.'[15]

The Catholics and their non-Communist allies preached caution and mounted little significant military action. Like authorities in many other parts of occupied Europe, including in the British Channel Islands, they saw little point in provoking an enemy who for the time being could not be defeated. It just led to pointless casualties, in their view. Bishop Rožman wrote in his pastoral letter of December 1941: 'Acts by various liberation movements of irresponsible people bring no good to the nation in present conditions: they can only do harm...Our duty is to save the nation from a greater evil...Let's teach ourselves and others to be patient and wait.'

The Catholics were convinced the Communists deliberately staged attacks near Catholic villages so that the Catholics bore the brunt of the reprisals. One celebrated occasion was a three-day Partisan uprising against the Germans in the village of Dražgoše in 1942, which the Slovene Communists proclaimed as unique in Europe at that time. The locals suffered 41 dead in reprisals once the uprising was put down. The Partisan bands were hunted down and killed by the Germans.

For the anti-Communist Catholics, it was a harmful waste of effort. The Communists felt such attacks helped them win the war for opinion. They calculated that reprisals turned the population against the enemy rather than themselves. Moreover, the upsurge in belligerence caught the attention of appreciative Western Allies.

Aloysius Ambrožič, now Cardinal and Archbishop of Toronto, told what happened to his village after a Partisan attack on an Italian troop column in 1942: 'The Italians came back with tanks, burned houses and shot a dozen hostages. My father was arrested by the Italians because the Partisans denounced him after he refused to join their ranks. The Italians were about to shoot him too when a colonel saw us children weeping, and took him away for four months in prison instead.'

In Loboda's village, the Germans shot ten young local Slovenes because the Partisans murdered a German Army soldier who became engaged to a local girl. He belonged to the Slovene minority living across the border in Austria. 'We were all outraged at the Germans' brutality and at the lack of conscience of the Partisans, who knew the reprisals the Germans would make should their soldiers be attacked.'

Stane Snoj remembers seeing a convoy of women and children passing through his village on their way to deportation in Serbia. The Germans had shot their men-folk and burned their village in reprisal for a Partisan killing of two German gendarmes.

The Partisan combativity prompted Britain to switch support in the middle of the war from the Royalist Chetnik guerrillas to Tito. The British believed that the Chetnik leader Dragoljub Mihailović was using British arms to fight the Partisans and doing little against the Germans or Italians.[16] The Partisans were similarly directing their fight against their domestic opponents. But they fought the enemy occupiers as well. This latter point was crucial for the British, who wanted to weaken and tie down German forces in Yugoslavia. The Communists thereby positioned themselves to come out on the right side at the end.

The episodes described above illustrate the price paid by the civilian populations caught in between. The death toll in Yugoslavia contrasts with the far fewer civilian casualties in most of the rest of occupied Europe. The Partisans deliberately involved the civilian population in the fighting because they did not distinguish between combatants and non-combatants in their ideological war. British military historian John Keegan estimated that three-quarters of Yugoslavia's dead resulted directly or indirectly from Partisan action. He commented: 'It was a terrible price to pay so that Tito should make his political point.'[17]

It is harsh to imply this was the only purpose of the Partisans' warfare. They did indeed exert military pressure on the occupiers. Ljubljana was the only city in occupied Europe which had to be surrounded by trenches and barbed wire to make it secure. According to Partisan leader Milovan Djilas, wartime resistance in Ljubljana was more active than anywhere except Warsaw during the uprising of 1944.[18] The number of Partisans operating in Slovenia had risen from nil to 40,000 by the end of the war, and they started operating the first clandestine radio in occupied Europe at the end of 1941. Britain's liaison officer with Tito, Fitzroy Maclean, wrote eyewitness accounts of how he accompanied Partisan bands attacking serious targets, including the Štampetov viaduct on the Ljubljana–Trieste railway line.[19] Such actions may pale in significance beside the massive conventional warfare which decided the war's outcome. However, the viaduct destruction earned the Partisans a personal message of thanks from Field Marshal Harold Alexander, Supreme Allied Commander Mediterranean.

Historian Barbara Jelavich, who shares the view that guerrilla activity did not determine the outcome of the war, noted the mixture of nobility and brutality among the Partisans: 'Many observers were impressed by the idealism of the young fighters … Despite the idealistic aspects of these movements, they also had their grim side. The emphasis on comradeship, courage, discipline and other noble virtues applied usually only to the relationship with the bands and among friends. Enemies, whether co-nationals or foreign occupiers, were treated with ruthlessness and cruelty.'[20]

In the areas of Italian occupation, country-people organised Village Guards (*vaške straže*) to protect against the Partisan raids. The purpose was self-defence, but it put them on to the slippery slope of collaboration. They were armed, controlled and paid by the Italians. Today's Museum of Contemporary History in Ljubljana displays forms on which Italian authorities recorded details of each Village Guard. A photograph shows an Italian officer inspecting them on parade. Catholic journalist Ivo Žajdela contends this was unavoidable: there was no way they could muster enough force to withstand the Partisan attacks without the Italians knowing about it. Street posters in Ljubljana put up by the occupying authorities boasted of the Guard's successes against the Partisans. They were ruthless. In one episode in the village of Goliše, recounted by a Slovene now living in Australia, the Village Guards accompanied Italian troops to a Partisan farm, tied up the wife and four children and a pregnant neighbour and burned them to death.[21]

The Village Guards were poorly armed, however, and their resistance collapsed once Italy withdrew from the war in 1943. German forces took over the Italian zone of Slovenia, but by that time the Partisans had their hands on much of the heavy weaponry of the disbanding Italian forces.

In desperation, part of the Village Guards tried to make a break to join the Allies in Italy, but were caught by the Partisans. They suffered a major defeat in which hundreds were killed at the castle of Turjak. Italian soldiers were seen helping Partisans fire the artillery they had just handed over. In this and other setbacks, Uroš Roessmann lost a brother and brother-in-law. Thirteen other young men in his village of Polje died too. The Partisans executed several hundred of the Village Guards in cold blood after they surrendered. The civil war had escalated.

Alarmed by the threat to their lives, and also having one eye on the future regime in Slovenia, the Catholics turned to the Germans. With the Germans now occupying all of Slovenia, the remnants of the Village Guards were afraid they would be overrun by the Partisans or dispatched to the Russian front, where chances of survival would be minimal. Major Vuk Rupnik gathered a column of 1,000 men and set out on a march, until they contacted the German army, who asked him who the men were. He replied off the cuff '*domobranci*' – which happened to be the name of an Austro-Hungarian regiment before World War I. And so the new body gained a name, which roughly means Home Guard. On arriving in Ljubljana, Vuk asked for advice from his father, General Leon Rupnik, who had fought in World War I with the Austro-Hungarian army. Rupnik, President of the Ljubljana Regional Administration, in turn asked the local German commander, who said: 'Use them to secure Ljubljana.' The Germans were happy to help with weapons, uniforms and organisation.

So the pieces of the fatal equation fell into place. On the one hand, Communists pursuing revolution with brutal single-mindedness. On the other, Catholics and other anti-Communists, who were ready to accept help from the occupier to defend themselves and regain the initiative. Both sides aimed to take power in Slovenia once the Germans left.

The *domobranci*, however, were not united in their aims. A faction around General Rupnik sincerely believed in the Germans and what they stood for. Another group around Lieutenant-Colonel Ernest Peterlin wanted eventually to link up with the Western Allies. The Germans arranged a parade where 1,000 of them swore an oath of loyalty before a sword. The Ljubljana museum shows a photo of Bishop Rožman shaking hands there with German SS General Erwin Rösener, the *domobranci*'s formal commander-in-chief, as he prepared to celebrate Mass. It was 20 April 1944, Hitler's birthday. The gesture was heavy with symbolic meaning.

In this chaotic violence, families were torn apart. Dr Meršol was a prominent anti-Communist, but another branch of his family was with the Partisans throughout. One of that branch, Mitja Meršol, was a long-time editor-in-chief of the Ljubljana daily newspaper *Delo*. He never knew his father, killed by the Germans when he was an infant. *Domobranec* France Kozina had a brother whose daytime job was a stoker on a railway engine and by night fought with the Partisans. Another Slovene recounted how her father and uncle, who were on different sides, walked down an alley lined on either side by trees, and one brother said to the other: 'If your side wins, I will be hanging from a branch on this side; if my side wins, you will be strung up on the other side.'

Metod Milač, now living in Syracuse, New York, described how extraordinarily varied and dangerous the existence of a wartime Slovene pawn could be. As a student, he was arrested in an Italian *razzia*, freed from a prison train and press-ganged by the Partisans, re-captured by the Italians, sent to Rab concentration camp, released again and arrested by the Gestapo, sent to Auschwitz, liberated by the Soviet advance, returned to Slovenia and finally joined the refugees fleeing into exile over the Ljubelj – all in one war.[22]

The record for family trauma must surely be held by Bishop Rožman's deputy, Monsignor Jože Jagodic, one of nine children of a tailor. The Partisans shot the eldest daughter's husband in front of her and their children; the eldest son joined the Partisans and was taken hostage and shot by the Germans; the second and fourth sons joined the *domobranci* and were killed; the fifth spent nine years in Italian, German and Yugoslav prisons during and after the war; while the sixth became a Partisan major and survived the war, only to shoot himself and his wife in a crime of passion.[23]

A Slovene young man, however little he may have felt concerned by the war, had no chance of keeping out of it. In the German and Hungarian zones, they were conscripted. In the Italian zone, they could not stay in their homes. The Partisan raids triggered reprisals, so any young man found at home was shot or sent to a concentration camp. They could join the Partisans in their guerrilla struggle in the hills and forests. If they chose not to do that, the *domobranci* called them up to fight on the other side. One Slovene now living in Buenos Aires switched to the *domobranci* after watching fellow Partisans kill a 70-year-old couple in their bed with an axe. In the Gorenjska region, 28% of *domobranci* had previously fought with the Partisans.[24]

Some of the *domobranci* were German Army conscripts of Slovene origin who deserted while on leave from the Russian front.* Others had originally been Chetniks, supporting the Royalist Yugoslav regime of between the wars, rather than the Catholic goal of an independent Slovenia or the Partisans' vision of a socialist state. Bo Eiletz, now over 80 and living in Argentina, belonged to a Royalist secret society which ordered him to take to the hills and swear a candlelight oath to fight for exiled King Peter. They had little clandestine expertise however, and were militarily ineffective. After narrowly escaping death five or six times, Eiletz quit his disintegrating unit, came across his 17-year-old brother hiding in a ditch and the two walked back to Ljubljana. There Bo joined an administration and intelligence section of the *domobranci*. Later, when he had to identify himself to the British, he produced a document vouching for him 'in the name of King Peter', which caused the British official to exclaim 'What the hell is *that*?' but helped save his life. King Peter by that time was living under British protection in London.

Justin Stanovnik joined the *domobranci* as a 16-year-old student seven months before the end of the war: 'There was a big movement of national revival in Ljubljana. We thought we were establishing our country and preparing a future Slovene state.'

Joseph Plevnik, also 16, joined in September 1944 against his father's wishes after lying about his age: 'My enthusiasm quickly vanished. The food was bad. We were sent to the countryside to protect a railway line. We didn't have many bullets, but by that time the battle was really over.'

The women were not conscripted, but they had to dig trenches. Maria, who was later to become Leo Čop's wife, was set to work on Italian fortifications surrounding Ljubljana. Today they are preserved as a memorial path, decked with slogans celebrating Partisan heroism. Where Partisans used to lurk in woods at night in front of nervous Italian soldiers in gun emplacements, now joggers run past and cars roar by on Ljubljana's ring-motorway.

'We slacked off digging whenever the guards were not looking. Because they were the occupiers, I refused to give the Fascist Saluto Romano at school. I never learned the Italian they forced us to use for lessons, though now I regret I never picked it up,' says Maria.

Uroš Roessmann enrolled to study medicine at Ljubljana University in 1943, but two weeks later it was shut down:

---

*   Ernst Dichtl, an Austrian Gestapo commander of the *domobranci* in Gorenjska, helped Slovenes to desert and sign up for the *domobranci*. He had an interest in having them serve with his own unit rather than return to the Russian front. He learned Slovene, even though this was forbidden under Nazi rule, and had a reputation for liking Slovenes.

'I joined the *domobranci* because they agreed to assign me as a medic. In 1944, Allied air forces started to bomb railroads and stations. An American pilot was shot down and parachuted to the ground. I was called because he was suffering from burns. I got my bag, and made the first medical error of my career. I put vaseline on the burns and bandaged them. They got infected because the vaseline did no good, and we had to smuggle him into the hospital.'

Tone Suhadolc, now in Hamilton, Ontario, was one of the *domobranci* who picked up the pilot and helped get him to hospital. His family looked after the airman in their home for three weeks. After the war, Captain Maurice A. Brash of the US Air Force described in an affidavit how he was shot down in his P47 on reconnaissance over Ljubljana. 'Dr Anton Suhadolc did all in his power, at great risk to his life, and the lives of his family and friends, to aid me during my distress. He gave me...security from the Germans, excellent medical care, plentiful amounts of food, and shelter from the cold. His Christian kindness and courageous acts of bravery gave me and my 14 comrades great hope and inspiration to carry on in our struggle to return to our forces.' They did not speak each other's languages, so they communicated in French. The vaseline was clearly forgiven.

Shot-down Allied airmen were thus helped by both sides, since the Partisans also ferried a number of them out through the makeshift airstrips. But even these rescues were not all quite what they seemed. The Catholics maintain the Partisans sometimes murdered the airmen in order to steal their warm flying clothes. The Communists say the *domobranci* also hunted the pilots down and handed them over to the Germans. Slovene historian Matija Žganjar recounts two episodes in February 1944 when *domobranci* accompanied by German troops captured and imprisoned the crews of shot-down American B-24 bombers.[25]

Fortified by German arms, transport and strategic direction, the *domobranci* gained the upper hand against the Partisans, regaining control over large parts of Slovenia. The Village Guards had been static units. But the Germans lent the *domobranci* an armoured train, and they were able to surprise their enemy. As the *domobranci* recovered territory, they discovered at Jelendol a mass grave containing 110 bodies of their comrades shot by Partisans after capture from Turjak castle the previous year.

Apart from the small group around General Rupnik, there was not much empathy between the *domobranci* and the Germans. The *domobranci* pursued their own interests and resented that the occupiers suppressed Slovene national aspirations. By 1944, the group of officers around Lieutenant-Colonel Peterlin was making clandestine plans in case of an invasion by the Western Allies, and was in touch with them by radio.[26] Marko Kremžar, now living in Argentina, says his communications unit was designated to secure Ljubljana railway station and hand it over to the Allies. The Germans were aware of this underlying disloyalty and did their best to keep the *domobranci* under control. They declined to supply them with their most modern weapons. In late 1944, the Gestapo arrested the pro-Western *domobranci* officers and sent them to Dachau concentration camp, possibly after betrayal by a Partisan infiltrator. They were executed by the Slovene Communists when they came back from Dachau after the war.

In 1944, after arm-twisting by the British, the Yugoslav government in exile in London agreed to support Tito. Karl Lavrenčič of the BBC remembered broadcasting warnings that there was going to be no British occupation of Slovenia. A British liaison officer, Major William Jones, flew into Slovenia to appeal to the *domobranci* to join the Partisans, but in vain. A Slovene politician in exile in London, Alojzij Kuhar, and Boris Furlan, later Dean of the Ljubljana Law Faculty, made similar appeals over the BBC. Furlan became known in Slovenia as 'The Screamer from London'.* The *domobranci* leadership dismissed these as unrealistic fantasies by outsiders, or continued to believe they would soon be fighting with British troops at their backs. It seems naïve to believe that the British would prolong the war by picking a fight with their ally Tito on behalf of soldiers in German uniforms. Possibly the *domobranci* miscalculated at a time when reliable information was hard to come by, or were victims of their own wishful thinking. One way or another, they could not have been more wrong about British intentions.

In the last wintry months before the end of the war, military activity dwindled, lulling the *domobranci* into a false sense of security. January 1945 was a particularly good recruiting month for them.[27] The Partisans could afford to wait. It was clear the Germans were going to lose, and by autumn 1944 Belgrade was in the hands of the Red Army.

Meanwhile civilian professionals such as Dr Meršol were making do as best they could. The Italian military refused to give him a curfew pass, and threatened: 'We will kill you if we do not recognise you.' He went out all the same. Later the German military offered him an official car, but he declined. For two days, a German car followed him to work as he wobbled over the cobbles on his bicycle. Then they gave up.

His small son Val found the war much more of a lark. In the early months of 1945, school ended at 10.30 a.m., when the morning mist cloaking Ljubljana lifted and Allied warplanes came in to strafe. They roamed up and down the railway lines, waiting for trains to make a dash from tunnels.

'It's not true that Allied pilots never shot at civilians. They shot at anything that moved,' says Val, now a back specialist living in Chagrin Falls near Cleveland. 'We kids used to play tag with the fighters as they came down the long Celovška road firing their cannons. We would jump

---

* This earned Furlan no points with the Communists: in 1947, in imitation of anti-Western show trials in the Soviet Union, he was convicted by a Ljubljana court on a charge of being a British spy.

behind a building just in time. I can still remember the clinkety-clinkety-clinkety of the cannon shells bouncing off the cobbles.'

One day a peasant woman serving as his family's maid cried out to him as planes swooped down low: 'We are being attacked by devils! They have black faces.' Records show the Tuskegee Airmen, the US Air Force's first all-black unit, were operating over Yugoslavia from Italian airfields at this time.[28]

Val made brass rings out of the shell casings, and when Allied bombers flew overhead on their way to Vienna he started a trade in the aluminium foil they dropped to deceive radar. He took it in his stride when a British Hurricane fighter damaged the family house, likewise when Germans nearby shot a woman who had an illegal pig. He even wangled a ride in a German tank after the driver inadvertently frightened his spaniel with a revving engine.

'One evening at the Opera, my mother could no longer find me. She spotted me sitting on the lap of the Italian commandant of Ljubljana in the main box. I was attracted by the extravagant uniforms of his bodyguard. She only got me back at the end of the performance.'

In the last days of the war, Marija Hribar also had her thoughts elsewhere. British fighters had been shooting up her farming village of Ponova vas south of the capital. It was 6 May, and she was at home preparing to welcome her fiancée Jože Jančar to her 23rd birthday tea.

The tea party never took place. 'Death was stalking us,' she says, now aged over 80.

# 3 BETRAYED

*Go down to Viktring, there's a mob of people there, we don't know who they are. Find out and let us know.*

## 13 to 26 May
## 1945

While death was stalking in Slovenia, the British 8th Army over in Austria was feeling overstretched. Its 5th Corps stationed in Carinthia was a combat group with a fine record in battle, but it had little experience with refugees. Besides the Slovenes pouring into Viktring, they were confronted with Serbs, Croats, Cossacks, Germans, Bulgarians and Hungarians – some 70,000 in all. It was hard to decide which were enemies, ex-enemies, prisoners-of-war, camp followers or just civilians. The order to go down to Viktring was given to Major Paul Barre, a 38-year-old Canadian from Montreal. He too had had little to do with refugees, but 6,000 were soon to owe their lives to him.

He found 17,000 Slovenes crammed into an open field, partly sown with corn, partly ploughed with furrows. Horses, carts, *domobranci* and civilians mingled chaotically. There were no shelters, no latrines, little food and just a small stream for drinking water. Soon it started to rain, and the refugees fashioned makeshift shelters with old pieces of sacking and bark they tore off trees in the nearby woods. Others slept under carts, but everybody was splashing around in puddles. The situation could hardly have been more dire. The intelligence officer of the Brigade of Guards, Captain Nigel Nicolson, later an author, publisher and Member of Parliament, compared Viktring with scenes from the Gold Rush in America.[1] British Red Cross nurse Jane Balding described it in her diary as 'like a fantastic film'.[2]

The British were not sure what to make of the *domobranci*. However, they were also beginning to wonder how much they had in common with their wartime allies, the Partisans. The latter plastered Klagenfurt with posters declaring 'liberated' Carinthia to be under Yugoslav authority. The southern part of Carinthia had a sizeable Slovene minority, but had been assigned to Austria in a plebiscite in 1920. The

The Slovenes camped first on a field in Viktring in Austria and built rudimentary ovens and bark shelters. Carers described it as an amazing shantytown.

Partisans claimed it, and reckoned armed occupation would do the trick. The British military, however, were committed under an Allied agreement to restoring Austria, annexed by Germany since 1938, as an independent country. British soldiers tore down the Partisan proclamations and put up their own. Locals in the villages likewise pulled down the Partisan posters but left the British ones, because the Partisans were pillaging and raping, according to Nicolson. Jane Balding's scribbled diary of those days reports: 'Tito's boys running wild causing trouble...Partisans very noisy in the evening, sounds of shooting up, incident in square this a.m., a bit sticky...Tito's boys parading all over town in afternoon, all very warlike.' Meanwhile, the 5th Corps was keeping a watchful eye to the east on a Soviet Army advancing into Styria. British soldiers mounted guard around the Viktring camp perimeters to keep prowling Partisans at bay. Inside, a British soldier had to intervene to prevent the lynching of a suspected Partisan spy.[3]

The Viktring camp was a potential disaster in the making. But Barre, assisted by a team including John Corsellis of the Friends Ambulance Unit (FAU), set British soldiers to work digging latrines, separated the Slovene soldiers from civilians, brought in rations and provided drinking water by draining a fish pond into rubber tanks and purifying it with tablets. A dozen women gave birth in the first two weeks, and despite the primitive conditions and shortage of doctors, all but one of the infants survived. Corsellis 'suggested rather strongly' to the owners of 400 horses that they should be moved to the outskirts of the camp and tied up in lines under trees. Eventually they were sent off to the abattoir at Klagenfurt and came back as horsemeat. The owners had mixed feelings, but the food was sorely needed.

Barre organised a rudimentary news service. 'We found stationery, an old typewriter and an old radio on which they'd listen to the news at night from the BBC, translate it into their language, type it out and post it wherever they could, so that next morning the people could read the events of the night before and keep up,' said Barre. 'I was able to get one piece of soap per person per month for all purposes, and it was very difficult. But these people are very religious, and on Sundays they all turned out in their best attire: the women had frocks and the men dark suits, a white shirt and tie. Where they kept these, pressed and clean, I don't know. It's a bloody miracle.'[4]

Barre arranged for communities from the same areas in Slovenia to group together, and he encouraged self-administration. He saw himself largely in the role of a liaison officer. 'I didn't administer with a stick in my hand. I wanted to give them the feeling they were running their own camp: and I felt that would be perhaps a means of giving encouragement and self-reliance in view of all the misery they'd gone through.'

In a letter to his mother, John Corsellis fretted at the resulting lack of coordination and grumbled that 'it is extraordinarily difficult to work as part of a machine that has no steering wheel or driver'. But as he also remarked, Major Barre was a charming and self-effacing man who was very patient, did his best for his charges and let his staff get on with the job. The refugees were lucky that at a moment when their lives were in the balance, they came under the sway of an officer who had straightforward values, genuinely wanted to help and was ready to allow them a measure of autonomy. Nurse Balding remembers going around with the major raiding Nazi offices for school paper, begging linen from a nearby camp and visiting refugee children with measles in hospital. The earlier disagreeable episode of British watch-looting began to be countered by an onset of humanity.

The Slovenes organised themselves with remarkable speed, making the most of the fact that their community leaders were empowered to act. Dr Janez Janež began operating on patients in the open air, down on his knees in the field. Gloria Bratina, 19 at the time, says:

> We built ourselves a little tent very fast with some blankets we picked up, because we were sporty people – high school students; we cut some branches for the structure; my dad was very good at it. There was a place where you had to pick up your bread and so on, and meat when they were killing the mules or horses: we cooked soup and sometimes went downtown to get onions and lettuce. We were very cold at night, and there were two weeks of heavy rain and mud. It was quite difficult.

After a week, some of the women and children were moved into an abandoned factory nearby. The Roessmann family, nursing a sick daughter, camped under a stairway leading to a British Army officers' mess in a Baroque monastery at the end of the field. The British cooks took pity on them, and a large tin of marmalade, tea, powdered milk and other food turned up. A sergeant ordered the family to be thrown out, but the cooks took no notice and told the Roessmanns: 'He's a master sergeant, he's a monkey, he sleeps in a tree and we don't obey him.'

Some of the refugees had been members of the short-lived Slovene National Council, and soon the camp had a 'National Committee for Slovenia', which issued decrees. Young Val Meršol, whose father, Dr Meršol, headed the camp committee, was enjoying himself roaming around, when he found himself firmly seated down in a school in the open air. 'I felt much put upon, I was not happy,' he recalls. He had fallen victim to Decree no.1.

Within days, Director Bajuk, barely recovered from his gruelling march over the mountains at the age of 60, decided that as a former inspector of Slovene schools and an ex-headmaster, his most immediate duty was to restore proper processes of education. The rapid resumption of schooling not only prevented the children falling behind in their learning. It also symbolised a determination to fight against misfortune and restore normal life. Bajuk described it thus:

I worried about what would happen to our pupils and planned a temporary secondary school, having found that teachers for almost all subjects were available. I invited teachers and pupils to meet and enough turned up to start lessons at once, which led to Decree no. 1 [resuming schooling]. But we had enormous difficulties – no classrooms, books, writing paper or pencils. We cleaned out an abandoned building for classrooms and used what we could lay our hands on for chairs and a few planks of wood for desks, while the English commandant Major Barre got us a blackboard...

There were no books, I borrowed a few Latin and Greek texts from the Jesuit monastery and Božidar copied them on his knees, and we found single books among the pupils, at second-hand dealers and from individuals in Klagenfurt. Teachers had to prepare scripts for all subjects, write down lessons and texts, compose mathematical problems etc.[5]

Thirteen-year-old Rudy Kolarič, who crossed the mountains with a bucket on his head, felt it was more agreeable to go swimming in the stream, but a teacher chased after him, and he was soon back on the school bench in the field.

Dr Meršol, the de facto leader of the Slovene civilians, viewed John Corsellis sceptically at first. For 6,000 people, Meršol had been hoping for at least a major as a helper rather than a youthful conscientious objector. Corsellis, a fast walker, was allocated Jože Jančar as an interpreter, since they both spoke Italian. It was the beginning of a long and fruitful relationship. They were on the move around the camp until late into the evening. Meršol was impressed and relented, not least because Corsellis produced 10,000 sulphonamide tablets to treat a wide range of maladies.

Nigel Nicolson described how he warmed to the Slovenes as they began organising concerts, horse races and religious processions. 'They were very well behaved. They were happy to have escaped into Austria under British protection...We grew to like them very much, and they were all so jolly and gay and grateful, and helpful to us; and we had no trouble with them...I was constantly in the camp.'[6]

Two officials of the FAU visiting from London described Viktring as a fantastic shantytown presenting a frightening picture of dirt and disease from the outside. Inside, however, they noticed it was remarkably well kept by the refugees, most of whom were engaged in building, cooking, laundry or similar occupations.

The *domobranci* believed the British would redeploy them to fight the Communists. Jože Lekan heard they were being sent to Italy to join an army commanded by Polish General Anders to fight the Soviet Union. Their spirits were high as the British served them rations of beef, duck and tinned fish confiscated from German stores.

A Slovene prelate, Dean Matija Škrbec, went to the *domobranci* camp to urge them to keep together to prepare for the impending resumption of hostilities against the Communists. Each morning, the 11,000 uniformed men paraded in their field and a priest said Mass.[7] Božidar Fink, a lawyer responsible for disciplinary matters with the *domobranci* high command, said: 'Our chief concern was to maintain discipline and fighting spirit in the camp and detect people spreading confusion or lowering military morale.'

Pernišek wrote in his diary on 22 May:

> The camp presents a unique sight in the evening. Mighty Mount Košuta sparkles like a giant emerald in the setting sun, while smaller mountains and hills are wrapped in a mysterious bluish hue set off by the magnificent green of the pine trees. Fairy-like white wisps of mist float above the lakes. Daylight dims fast, the day ebbs away and the camp becomes a single huge bonfire. One blaze after another lights up the surroundings fabulously and smoke rises skywards like a thin transparent veil. A cheerful chatter of voices comes from the fires, together with the joyful sound of *domobranci* patriotic songs accompanied by accordions. Now and again horses' neighs pierce the air, and the camp falls silent with God's sublime peace above it. The tents assume a silver colour in the moonlight and the stars twinkle happily...

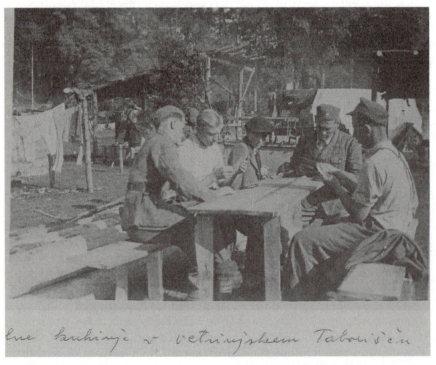

*Domobranci* in the Viktring camp after surrendering to the British Army.

Only the coughing of the elderly and the ominous hooting of the owls disturb this heavenly peace. Ill-omened owls! From early childhood I hate your sinister call. I am trembling and my soul is filled with an inexplicable fear. I cannot shake off the impression that these hoots presage horror and death. I'm suffocated by the feeling and try to escape from it.

## 27 to 31 May
## 1945

Five days later, on 27 May, amid pelting rain which turned the camp into a swamp, the British started sending the *domobranci* back to Yugoslavia, where they would meet their deaths. The return of the Slovene soldiers was part of a larger operation. Almost at the same time, the British Army in Austria was dispatching 45,000 surrendered Cossacks to the Soviet Red Army, as well as another 14,000 Serbs and Croats to Tito. They had to use force against the Cossacks, who knew the lethal reprisals that awaited them on their return. The operation degenerated into violence, killings, suicides and scenes of despair.

In the case of the Serbs, Croats and Slovenes, the British military resorted to a deception to ensure they went calmly to their fate. They spread word that the destination was a better-equipped camp in Palmanova in Italy, west of Trieste. It was a lie.

Why did the British Army decide to send back the Yugoslavs who had surrendered to them?

The Western powers agreed secretly at Yalta in February 1945 that they would return Soviet citizens found with German forces at the end of war to the Soviet Union. Yalta implicitly acknowledged Tito's revolutionary regime in Yugoslavia, but made no mention of repatriating Yugoslavs. The *domobranci* had surrendered and handed over their arms, so the Army, if it had kept to Geneva Conventions, should have given them protection as prisoners-of-war or refugees.

Milovan Djilas, the senior Yugoslav Communist, whose later views were perhaps coloured by his break with Tito, claimed in 1979 that the Yugoslavs were taken by surprise by the repatriations. In an interview with *Encounter* magazine, he declared:

We didn't at all understand why the British insisted on returning these people. We believed, in the ideological context prevailing at the time, that the British would have a good deal of sympathy with these refugees, seeing that they had fled Communism. We thought the British would show 'class solidarity' with them, and some of us even feared that they would enlist them for future use against Communist governments, especially our own. Yet to our great surprise, they did none of these things but delivered them into our hands.[8]

At the time decisions on their fate were being taken, a number of British authorities did in fact take the side of the victims and tried to block the repatriations, though not for the ideological reasons Djilas had in mind. On 27 April, the British ambassador in Belgrade, Ralph Stevenson, in a note on anti-Tito Yugoslav forces, recommended on political and humanitarian grounds that they be disarmed and put in camps rather than repatriated.[9] Two days later, Churchill gave instructions to that effect.[10] On 2 May, the Supreme Allied Commander Mediterranean, Britain's Field Marshal Alexander, followed up with an order that surrendered anti-Tito Yugoslavs be held in camps until their fate was decided at governmental level.[11]

But there was no clear-cut consensus what the right thing to do was. British public opinion in the closing months of the war strongly favoured the Soviets and the Yugoslav Partisans.[12] The 5th Corps commanders dealing with the refugees no doubt considered it normal to seek friendly relations with the local Partisans, because they had been wartime allies. As a corollary, it was natural that the British should find the *domobranci* and other anti-Tito Yugoslavs suspect.

Nicolson commented: 'We were very, very confused at the time about these other Yugoslavs – and exactly what their relationship was. And to us they were a lot of Balkan bandits really, compared to the shining example of Tito's Partisans. That was a totally mistaken view, but it was quite widely held at the time.'[13]

Judgments about friend or foe, however, were just then beginning to swing. In the face of the Yugoslav refusal to withdraw from Carinthia (or Trieste), the possibility of an armed conflict between the British Army and the Partisans suddenly loomed. In the US, the new American president, Harry Truman, took a less friendly attitude to the Communist regimes which had been wartime allies than his predecessor, Roosevelt. The Americans took the same protective stance as Churchill towards the anti-Tito refugees.

This vacillation was just one more problem for the 5th Corps. On top of all that, on 13 May, reports reached them that some 300,000 Germans and 200,000 more Croats were approaching the Austrian frontier in Slovenia. This was reported to Allied Headquarters in Caserta, southern Italy, who asked Tito's authorities in Belgrade if they were ready to accept the repatriation of 200,000 *Yugoslavs*. Belgrade replied yes. Quite why the Croats were now referred to as 'Yugoslavs' is unclear. It may have been an unintentional slip: after all, the Croats *were* Yugoslavs. Perhaps the British meant they would stop the approaching 200,000 Croats and turn them back. In the event, on 15 May, the Germans and Croats had to surrender to a Partisan Army on the Austrian border near Bleiburg, because the thin British forces there declined to take the surrender themselves.

But it was an important modification, since on 14 May, General Sir Brian Robertson, Chief Administrative Officer of the Supreme Allied

Command, Mediterranean, followed up with a signal to the 8th Army: 'All surrendered personnel of established Yugoslav nationality who were serving in German forces should be disarmed and handed over to local Yugoslav forces.'[14] This implied also the Slovene *domobranci*, since they too were Yugoslavs.

On 17 May, Brigadier Toby Low, later Lord Aldington and a British government minister, issued another order, in his capacity as Chief-of-Staff of 5th Corps: 'All Yugoslav nationals at present in Corps area will be handed over to Tito forces as soon as possible. These forces will be disarmed immediately but will NOT be told of their destination' [emphasis in original].[15] This again implied all Yugoslavs, not just Croats, and could be taken to mean civilians as well, not just those who had borne arms.

Within hours, however, yet another command arrived from Alexander that 'all Chetniks and dissident Yugoslavs be evacuated to British concentration area Distone [District One] south of the Po river in Italy'.[16] The 8th Army and 5th Corps ignored this, relying instead on the Robertson order of 14 May. On 18 May, 5th Corps started to send Croats and Serbs back to Yugoslavia.

The Allied Forces Headquarters General Staff, when advised of this, accepted it, with the limitations that nobody should be returned to Yugoslavia against their will, and that no force be used. Should the refugees protest, they should be evacuated to the Distone area.[17]

By deceiving the victims into thinking their destination was Italy, 5th Corps found a way of complying with these restrictions. By 27 May, it was the Slovene *domobranci*'s turn for repatriation.

Were the repatriations offered to Tito in return for his withdrawal from Carinthia? This seems unlikely. Since 12 May, Tito had been exchanging diplomatic notes with the British ambassador in Belgrade over the presence of Partisans in Austria. After a final, sharply worded note from the British, Tito backed down on 18 May, advising Western ambassadors on the 19th. None of the notes mentioned any *quid pro quo*. By the time the British started the repatriations, the Yugoslavs had already given in.[18]

Harold Macmillan, the British government's Resident Minister for the Mediterranean and later Prime Minister, flew to the area and held meetings with British commanders just before the operation began. General Robertson's order of the 14th was issued after Macmillan returned to Caserta. When the American political representative to Supreme Mediterranean Headquarters, Alexander C. Kirk, protested to the military command about the repatriations in early August, he was told it was a military decision with which Macmillan had 'concurred'.[19]

Macmillan himself never admitted taking the decision. He denied any wrongdoing until his death, though his official biographer, Alistair Horne, who discussed the incident with him eight times, felt he was far more tormented by it than he ever let on.[20]

The prime instigators may in fact have been the commanders of the 5th Corps and the 8th Army, acting independently of political authority. 5th Corps had all sorts of problems on its hands – the prospect of an armed conflict with the Partisans, tens of thousands of refugees who could get in the way, the possible arrival of several hundred thousand more, and the menacing presence of Soviet troops in the East. The situation was complex, they were thinly stretched far ahead of the Allied supreme command, and the imprecise and conflicting orders gave loopholes to act on their own initiative. Under such circumstances, they may well have considered their best choice of action was to renew friendly relations with the Partisans, liaise on arrangements for the Partisan withdrawal, keep the undertaking made to Belgrade to send back anti-Tito forces, and clear out refugees who would otherwise have had to be fed and cared for.

At the end of a gruelling war which had hardened spirits, the British commanders were not in a mood to take much care of niceties. As Nigel Nicolson put it: 'There were many people who felt "Well, so many millions of young men have died in this war, what does another 30,000 matter?"'[21] It was a rough, practical solution, for which the victims had to pay with their lives, and the British Army in loss of honour.

Absorbed by their own preparations to continue the fight against Communism, the *domobranci* fell into the trap. They assumed the British Army would protect them after they had surrendered and handed over their weapons. Just a few suspected a ruse. A high-ranking Slovene officer tipped off Uroš Roessmann's father: 'Don't let your boys go back.' Uroš himself came to the conclusion that 'all this was going nowhere'. Leaving the *domobranci* encampment, he exchanged his uniform for plain clothes and joined his family in the civilian camp. So too did his brother Matej, making use of the civilian suits he took with him over the pass. Riko Ziernfeld, now making his life in Toronto, Canada, found nobody tried to stop him as he took off his *domobranci* jacket and walked across. One *domobranec* who came over from the military camp, however, was cold-shouldered by Slovene civilians, who told him: 'If everybody else goes where they go, you should go too.'

Some British officers with consciences were dropping discreet warnings and turning blind eyes. An officer about to be sent back asked Nigel Nicolson of the Grenadier Guards if he would swear on his honour they were going to Italy. Nicolson said he would turn his back for half a minute, and if the questioner was still there, he was going to Italy. When he did look back, the officer had taken the hint and disappeared. The *domobranci* chief-of-staff, Colonel Ivan Drčar, recorded in his diary that the British told him they considered the *domobranci* as prisoners-of-war, but if they changed into civilian clothes they would be treated as civilians. It was another hint how they could save their lives. Drčar wanted to undertake intelligence operations to find out more about British intentions, but the *domobranci*'s commanding officer, General Franc Krener,* refused.

The *domobranci* faced a supreme challenge, but they had a commander unequal to the task. Most afternoons, Krener was absent visiting his wife on a nearby lake shore.

According to Marko Kremžar, then in a *domobranci* communications unit, Krener was put in charge because there was no one else left after the Gestapo arrested the group of leaders suspected of preparing a deal with the Allies in 1944. He was an administration officer. One of his close lieutenants described him later as 'one big holy ego, a disaster for the Slovenes'.

Val Meršol junior described Krener as 'completely out of his depth. His position got to his head. He thought he was totally in charge, and didn't want to be told what to do.' Val's father, Dr Meršol, threw a fit when he found out the *domobranci* were trying to recruit among the civilians for whom he was responsible. He felt they were much safer as civilians. 'He and Krener got into a major fight. Dad never yelled at anybody, but this time he let him have it, and I was surprised at the language he knew. Krener was an appalling person; he called everybody a liar.'

Marko Sfiligoj, then aged 19 and serving in *domobranci* headquarters, recalls: 'I was also at Viktring and went through all the events with Krener. We didn't like him. He was a nasty guy.' Marko owed his life to a change in plan. Originally, headquarters staff was due to leave first for 'Palmanova'. They said good-bye and sat in a truck. Then Krener told them to get down, as plans had changed and they were going last rather than first. 'That's how I am alive and here,' Marko said in Canada 50 years later. His elder brother, however, was sent back and killed.

Most of the others had no such luck and they had no reason to disbelieve British assertions they were being evacuated to Italy. The Slovenes knew nothing of what was happening to the Cossacks, and reported calmly at the appointed times to board British Army lorries. They were driven to railway stations at Maria Elend and Rosenbach in the west and Bleiburg further to the east. Pernišek records a joyful departure scene in his diary:

*Tuesday 29th May*. A glorious sunny day. The lads of the 3rd regiment are leaving; they are happy and their songs echo around the camp. The English load the last truck. Slowly the convoy moves out, accordions sound cheerfully, the roar of the motors doesn't drown the happy songs and cheering of the *domobranci*. A sea of white handkerchiefs waves good-bye to the lads. Girls and women are crying; their eyes follow the column until it disappears. Farther off one can still hear the singing and accordions.

---

\* In some sources, also spelt Krenner.

The happy mood changed abruptly when they were forced aboard trains. To Nicolson, who witnessed the transfers there and knew what was going on, it reminded him more of the deportation of prisoners to a German concentration camp:

> Our guardsmen slid together the doors of the cattle-trucks when they were full, and padlocked them. They also locked the carriage doors. When all was secure, they drew back from the train and their places were immediately taken by Tito's Partisans who had been hiding in the bushes and station buildings. The wagons were old and through cracks in the boarding the [*domobranci*] could see exactly what was happening. They began hammering on the inside of the wagon walls, shouting imprecations, not at the Partisans, but at us, who had betrayed them, lied to them and sent at least the men among them to a certain death. This scene was repeated day after day, twice a day. It was the most horrible experience of my life.[22]

Survivors remember British soldiers shouting at them, pointing their rifles and firing the occasional shot. The British brought tanks and searched knapsacks and pockets, taking cameras, knives, fountain pens and other valuables. As the loaded trains headed back into Slovenia, a handful were able to escape on the way. Ivan Kukovica, who had practised jumping off moving trains as a schoolboy prank, pushed his hand through a shrapnel hole, opened the door and leaped to safety. Kukovica's parents and four brothers were not so lucky. They were among several hundred civilians who volunteered to accompany the *domobranci* because they thought they were going to Italy. Kukovica's family was aboard one of the other trains heading back into Slovenia; the Partisans killed them all.

Marija Jančar (then Hribar) says her *domobranec* brother had a premonition something was going to happen to him. He had been spending his time reading and writing and she visited him on the military side of the camp. He came to say good-bye to her before boarding his transport. She never saw him again. 'Losing my brother hurt me more than anything else in my life, worse than losing my parents,' she recalled 57 years later in Bristol, England.

Maria Suhadolc, now living near Toronto, Canada, was also very close to her *domobranec* brother. 'Just before he left, he came to see me again to say good-bye. The vehicles were ready to take them off. I didn't realise it was the last time I would see him. I was devastated by the news they had been sent back. I couldn't believe it. Years later a friend of his in Argentina who escaped told me of their last few moments together in a concentration camp. The Partisans were sorting out the prisoners and called out his name. My brother bade him farewell, and swore he would become a priest if he ever got out alive.' He did not live to keep his vow.

When young Majda Vračko heard of the rumours, she went over to the *domobranci* camp and found her brother's tent empty except for the radios he liked to tinker with. She never heard of him again. A few days later, her judge father, who had been hospitalised with a strong fever, came staggering in through the door, unshaven and ashen-white, asking:

> Where's your brother Marian? When I told him he had left and I couldn't find him, my father collapsed. In the hospital he had heard they were returning them and he left without telling anybody, in his hospital gown, and walked from Klagenfurt all the way to Viktring, sick as he was, to find out... For me the worse thing was that my brother was sent back and I could not keep him there, and my father expected that I would, and I couldn't. If I'd known, I'd have taken him away before then, but I didn't, and thought I was doing best letting him be where he was.

After a time, the British deceit became hardly necessary. Most of the *domobranci* continued to go meekly to their slaughter, even when it became obvious what was going on. Their instinct was to dismiss the evidence as lies aimed at undermining their morale and panicking them into flight. As *domobranec* Božidar Fink said years later: 'At first, when we heard the soldiers were not being sent to Italy, we thought it was enemy propaganda, but unfortunately later it turned out to be true.'

Shock, disbelief and fatalism spread as those still due to be sent back, collectively repressed the horror that was being perpetrated on them. A *domobranci* commander opened a map as the lorries drove through the countryside and shouted they were going the wrong way, but his soldiers told him to stop trying to frighten them. 'Nobody tried to escape. We sat dejected, absorbed in our thoughts, shocked, hypnotised, paralysed,' wrote survivor Pavči Maček.

When Tine Velikonja arrived at the railway station with his unit, he went into a field to relieve himself, and an Austrian farming woman told him: 'You boys are being sent back to Yugoslavia. You can hide in the hay.' He indignantly rejected the offer and accused her of trying to demoralise him. He was shipped to a concentration camp at Teharje in Slovenia and was lucky to get out alive because he was only 16. One *domobranec* was pulled off a moving train by a comrade, but promptly jumped back on again to join the others going to their death.

Milči Lekan watched the departures: 'At first, they were singing as they marched up to the springs to wash before leaving. But after the deceit was known, I still saw several trucks set off with everybody inside knowing they were going to their death. They said, if my friends go, I go too. It was loyalty. They did not want to abandon their fallen comrades.' They took the view that 'if this is happening to the rest of them, why not to us? I am not going to run away.' Another said: 'If God demands this sacrifice of us, we will follow our brothers and comrades even if it means death: we too are ready to die for the truth.'[23]

News of the treachery was pouring in to General Krener from eyewitnesses, but he did not believe them and took no action to save his men. Civilian leaders in the National Committee for Slovenia likewise buried their heads in the sand. While thousands of young men went to their deaths, the leaders remained paralysed.[24]

The warnings came thick and fast – 17 altogether between 24 May (when repatriations of the Serbs and Croats began) and 30 May. Five came from *domobranci* who escaped and returned to the camp. There were six reports from Serb Chetniks, and two from Slovene civilians, who told of seeing the *domobranci* being herded into the trains. Krener heard the same story three times from his chief-of-staff, Colonel Drčar, and once from his chauffeur, Franc Šega. He turned a deaf ear, declaring some to be unreliable witnesses and accusing the Serbs of trying to trick the Slovenes. He had one of the Slovene civilians locked up for 'spreading alarmist reports'.

One of the civilian leaders questioned General Charles Keightley, the Corps Commander, who indignantly denied the handovers and threatened to punish anyone spreading such rumours. Krener eventually went to British headquarters in Klagenfurt, and protested that the trains could not be going to Italy, since bridges were down on the only available route. The British had no explanation, but Krener still did nothing.

The testimony of Dr Janez Janež tipped the balance. He staggered back on the 30th and was believed because of the accumulated evidence and his own respected status as a surgeon attached to the *domobranci*. He had followed the lorries in a car but abandoned it and crawled into a rye field after he saw what was going on at Bleiburg station. Narrowly escaping discovery by a woman Partisan, he lay for the whole day among the crops. Recalling it later, he said:

> At around 11 at night I decided that I had to leave the rye, go across the field to the road along which we were driven, and then to the hill on the other side. Slowly and silently on my knees I parted the rye in front of me and after repeated pauses, around one o'clock in the morning I looked out on the white road. When I saw that there was no one there, I ran across to the hill 100 metres beyond it. I waited for daylight on the hill, and around six in the morning I crossed the hill and began to go towards the plain. I avoided people.[25]

While hiding in the field, he made a vow he would dedicate the rest of his life to missionary service for the sick and needy around the world if he survived. It was the anniversary of his qualification as a doctor, and he felt he should be accompanying the *domobranci* to their deaths. He considered his life to be 'officially over'. He kept his pledge, spending the rest of his life as a missionary doctor in China and Taiwan.[26]

When Janež came with this story, the camp's National Committee for Slovenia bowed to reality and sent a delegation to warn the remaining *domobranci* and civilian refugees. By that time, nearly all the soldiers had been dispatched.

After hearing the last eyewitness report from his chauffeur, Krener emerged in civilian trousers, stepped into his car and left without a word. Captain Nigel Nicolson recorded in the military log book that the General in charge of the Slovenes was 'missing in his green Adler coupé'. Not for Krener the fatal loyalty to his comrades. He was not in the delegation which went to the *domobranci* camp to warn them. Years later he was spotted as a doorman at a Buenos Aires hotel, prompting a fellow Slovene to comment: 'I hate to see that bastard in uniform again.'

That same night, the senior Slovene officer remaining, Colonel Emil Cof, a veteran of the inter-war Yugoslav Army, summoned his officers and gave his final command: 'I told the sad truth and, because their lives were in imminent danger, I ordered them to scatter and disperse. Other ranks were free to do as they wanted.' Joseph Plevnik's commander came back from this meeting and told his men: 'I absolve you from your obligation to serve. I am 99% sure we are going to be sent back. There is no way we are all going to escape. Smaller groups may have a chance. Save yourselves.' Plevnik picked up his belongings, went to his sister on the civilian side, took off his military uniform and hid under a blanket for several days. The British troops did nothing to block off this escape route.

Jože Lekan's brigade was due to leave on one of the last British transports. Just before the order to disperse, he went down with his full gear and was about to mount a half-empty truck when his father intervened, remonstrating with all the paternal authority he could summon. Jože's watching sister, Milči, thought her father would strike his son. Jože relented, took off part of his uniform and stayed.

Pernišek's wife burst into tears when she heard what was going on: she had two brothers in the *domobranci*. She rushed over to the military side of the camp and found the married one still there. 'Come now, you are no soldier, you are a civilian now. Take my husband's second suit and put it on,' she urged the brother. He refused, insisting he would stay with his comrades. She hit him hard, and shouted: 'You have a family and two children!' Little Cirila Pernišek, who observed the scene, had never seen her mother strike anyone before. He gave in and stayed.

Teenager Gloria Bratina acted with similar resolve. Her two *domobranci* brothers wanted to leave with their units. But she found civilian clothes and surrounded them with her younger sisters and brothers, literally hanging on to them to stop them going. She won.

Others continued to depart on the transports unhindered, refusing to recognise the reality. Jože Lekan watched what happened the next day, after the order to disperse had been given:

> Most of them were so disappointed, so shocked that they just didn't move. They tore down their tents, sat down on them and waited for transport. I went to the empty British trucks where they were lining up neatly to be loaded.
>
> They were just marching up there unblinkingly. Nobody was doing anything except getting on to the trucks. The British didn't have to

force anybody. At the last moment I pulled one of my friends out of the formation and said, 'If you stay alive you can do something in life, but if you are dead, you're dead and that's the end of it.' He left the formation but when the last few transports were leaving, he all of a sudden changed his mind and jumped on the last truck and took off.

Lekan later heard the Partisans killed his friend after beating him and breaking his legs.

Božidar Fink, now over 80 and living in Buenos Aires, says: 'I was due to go back with the last group. I really wanted to return to Slovenia. That was my purpose. But I was seriously ill from dysentery and I could not drag myself to the trucks. A friend took me over to the civilian camp. I wondered whether it was right not to go, and I still ask myself that today. For me, fidelity is the foremost value.'

Jan Lovro, another *domobranec* now living in the Andes in Argentina, went to Mass early that day – it was Corpus Christi – and resolved to make up his mind whether to go when he got back from church. He came back to a deserted camp, with his rucksack lying empty. He decided there was no point in sacrificing his life in such circumstances, and changed into civilian dress.

On 31 May, the final day of the transports, about 500 boarded the lorries and 500 remained. Colonel Cof changed into civilian clothes, slipped past the loose British cordon and made his way to Klagenfurt.

Why did the *domobranci* command not prevent thousands of soldiers marching off to their deaths? And why did the men continue to depart when it was clear they had been betrayed? From a purely practical point of view, the command had little other choice than to go along with the British orders. They could hardly have organised resistance, but they could have given the men a chance to make a break on their own. A few *domobranci* did indeed take to the woods, but only right at the end. Krener and the civilian leaders were evidently still thinking in terms of their civil war against the Communists. Their goal was to reverse the defeat they had suffered, and they wrongly assumed that a country such as Britain must be thinking also of combating the Communists, despite the fact that the British had supported Tito since 1943 in the fight against the Germans.

But they dithered so long, it is clear they were no longer thinking rationally. Deep shock appears to have immobilised them. They were so sure the Western Allies would take control of their country, as in fact happened in Greece, that their whole world collapsed when the Communists took over and they were forced to flee. They went into denial. They hated and feared the Partisans, Germans, Italians and Russians. That left only the British and the Americans, who must be trustworthy whatever evidence to the contrary. They also became paranoid, deluding themselves that the Serbs, with whom they got on reasonably well so far, were also plotting to destabilise them.

As for the rank-and-file, they desperately needed to turn to fellow human beings for comfort, and their comrades were the ones they felt closest to. As Catholics, the *domobranci* were brought up to subordinate individual desires to authority. It was natural for them to go with the group. But their determination to follow each other to their deaths also reflected *esprit de corps*: loyalty to comrades and a sense of honour are qualities all armies seek to instil, since they are major motivations for soldiers to risk their lives in battle.[27] The *domobranci* following their comrades on to the trucks were not just sheep going dumbly to the slaughter. They were making a deliberate choice of loyalty to their fellow-soldiers.

British military historian John Keegan observed that Christian churches had favoured the ideal of martyrdom at least as much as war-making.[28] Curate France Kunstelj gave the doomed soldiers absolution as he rode with them, declaring: 'We are finished in this world, we will be repaid in eternity. Hold fast to the end.' In a detention camp on the other side, he continued giving absolution even after his hands were cut off, according to a witness.[29]

As they realised the enormity of what was happening, the civilians in the Slovene camp were thrown into shock and mourning. Fourteen-year-old Marian Loboda, who saw the first *domobranci* climb into the trucks singing and cheering, recalls:

> A few days later I went into the little church, curious about the uncontrollable weeping I heard. Women and men were praying aloud and crying and sobbing – the mothers, sisters, wives, betrothed, fathers, brothers and friends of the *domobranci* who had left in the English trucks a day or two earlier. The first to escape had arrived and told what had happened. The English had treacherously handed over the disarmed and deceived *domobranci* to their mortal enemies. No one was under any illusion as to what would happen. Everything collapsed completely, above all our faith in the men we'd always believed to be gentlemen. The blow was so great that people lost the most basic instincts of struggle for survival. Young men, previously heroes, seemed to be without the slightest will to save themselves. All that remained for us was God's mercy and prayer.

France Rode, later head of the Catholic Church in Slovenia, remembers the crowd filling the church reciting biblical texts, in particular Job's stark acceptance of cruel misfortune: 'The Lord gave, the Lord has taken back. Blessed be the name of the Lord' (Job, 1:21).

British Army officers, questioned on their honour about the rumours, continued blithely to persist with their lie. Major William Johnson, responsible for Displaced Persons camps in the area, retorted to one

Slovene: 'Don't you trust us?' School Director Marko Bajuk got the same reaction from the Canadian Barre, who was himself a victim of the deception. Visibly hurt, he replied: 'Do you think that the British could really do something like that?'

Dr Meršol was chosen by the National Committee for Slovenia to deal with the British because he spoke English well, had worked with them before and had spent a year in America. A *domobranci* unit had picked him up among the refugees thronging the Ljubelj Pass and driven him to Viktring to establish contact with the British. He was elected to head the civilian camp committee and act as its spokesman. Bajuk went hurrying over to tell him of the treachery and saw Meršol's eyes dart like lightning in every direction. He headed for Barre, with whom he had established mutual personal trust. 'I asked Major Barre what was really happening. Everyone would agree he was our best friend and a sincere man who looked more than others after our welfare and benefit ... He asked the Army – I don't know who – and was told that all our *domobranci* were going to Italy.' Meršol went to Krener too, but Krener threw him out of his office.

The Slovenes were appalled by the British deceit, and for many the bitterness has lasted a lifetime, resulting in a rejection of all things British. Jože Lekan, sitting 55 years later in his brother-in-law's Cleveland drawing room full of Slovene landscapes, declared: 'I hate the British guts. I am still so mad I would shoot them if I had a chance.'

John Corsellis found the hitherto appreciative Slovenes became cold, withdrawn and hostile. They found it hard to believe he was not in the know. As his Slovene interpreter in the camp, Jože Jančar, put it years later:

> I asked: 'John, why didn't you tell me?' and you said: 'I didn't know,' and I said: 'John, is that the truth?' and you said: 'It's the truth, I didn't know.' I asked because nobody trusted you and they were suspicious of me, that I was knowing things because they saw us always together. I remember distinctly I asked you and you were very upset. But people didn't believe – before they were very friendly to you. It took a long time, but then they came back.

One or two never quite did. Years afterwards, Director Bajuk wrote: 'John Corsellis was a man of honour and good heart. He was good to us and understood our circumstances. I am grateful to him for many a thing, but I cannot rid myself of this feeling that he is British, a member of that pompous mob that had betrayed us.'

Pernišek confided to his diary:

> The English have disillusioned us in an appalling way. We never could have conceived that such a vile and hypocritical betrayal was possible. The good Mr Corsellis, who's working for us in our daily needs, admits the English who are with us are ashamed of what has been done.

There's nothing left to us but to lock our grief in our hearts and not complain. We are of course only refugees, delivered up to the mercy of the English.

Many of the British were indeed ashamed. Nigel Nicolson wrote 45 years later: 'These were three weeks that should live in infamy. It was one of the most disgraceful operations British soldiers have ever been ordered to undertake... This brutal act was committed knowing its probable consequences. Compassion was over-ridden. For a momentary advantage (but what?) and a desire to placate Stalin and Tito, a major betrayal was deliberately organised.'[30]

Nicolson said this view was widespread in the officers' mess at the time, and was also shared by lower ranks. He said:

The Welsh Guards who had the major task of forcing these people into the trains – they were at one point on the verge of mutiny. They were saying to their officers, 'Is this what we fought the war for?' And when one company of the Welsh Guards was relieved by another, a sergeant in the first company who'd been through this just for one day said, 'well, I'm very glad we haven't got to do it again because I couldn't answer for what the men would do if we were ordered to do this a second time.' So they rotated the companies: it was as bad as that – the feeling was running as high as that.[31]

Captain Tony Crosland of the Royal Welch Fusiliers, later a British Foreign Secretary, wrote at the time to a friend contrasting the repatriations with the protection the British Army had earlier given to surrendered anti-Tito Chetniks in the Italian frontier town of Gorizia, holding off the Partisans until the Chetniks could move further into Italy. Of the Viktring events, he wrote:

The problem of the anti-Tito Croats and Slovenes is almost causing a civil war within the British Army. We have on our hands at the moment some 50,000 of them. When we accepted their surrender, they certainly assumed that they would not be returned by us to Yugoslavia. It was then decided as a matter of higher policy that they were to be handed back to Tito...

The unarmed lot were shepherded into trains and told they were going to Italy; they crowded on in the best of spirits, and were driven off under a British guard to the entrance of a tunnel at the frontier; there the guard left them and the train drove off into the tunnel. Among the officers here, there is great revolt and resentment against the deception and dishonesty involved... The most nauseating and cold-blooded act of war I have ever taken part in.[32]

His widow and biographer added: 'He spoke of the train and cheerful unsuspecting men going into the tunnel... He really didn't want to talk about it.'[33]

## 31 May to 16 June
## 1945

On Thursday 31 May, Pernišek wrote with horror in his diary:

> Today we celebrate the Feast of Corpus Christi. Our hearts are crushed, sorrowful unto death. We suffered a terrible night: at the moment when we are commemorating the greatest mystery of our holy faith, the English are loading the last of the lads on to their trucks. Poor lads, what a terrible fate they are approaching... What happened to the *domobranci* might happen any minute to us all. We've no more friends on this earth. They've all abandoned us in our most difficult hour. Stay with us at least You, Lord.

That same afternoon, Dr Meršol was told that the civilian Slovene refugees were to be sent back too, beginning at 5 a.m. the next day. Pernišek's premonition was true, but he was wrong that they had no friends on earth. Major Barre was prepared to stand by them. Meršol went to him and said: 'So it's really true the English are sending the refugees home to be tortured and killed? Earlier they sent the soldiers back, now it's time for us civilians. We didn't believe the English were capable of lying and deceit, but the facts confirm these dishonourable acts.'

Barre turned pale. The British had been keeping him in the dark, and he had been defending their truthfulness. In this forthright Canadian, the British had chosen the wrong man to trifle with. As a non-Briton, he felt excluded by the British military establishment, and he hit the roof. 'I deeply resented that my own people at Corps never informed me, either verbally or in writing. I was left up in the air. That of course is something which is intolerable and unacceptable, because in the army, communications and putting everyone into the picture is a very important thing, which all treasured very much. I was left in complete ignorance, and I had to learn of this from Dr Meršol.'[34]

Barre asked Meršol to accompany him to the camp military commander, Lieutenant Ames. Ames objected to Meršol's presence, but Barre insisted he stay. Ames picked up a paper and read: 'I've orders to send 2,700 Slovene civilian refugees tomorrow morning the 1st of June – 1,500 to Bleiburg and 1,200 to Maria Elend station. They must be ready at 5 a.m. They'll be transported by trucks to the stations, where trains will await them.'

Barre had had enough. 'That I refused to accept, because I did not consider that a direct order from my superior, and that is a point I want to make: that I did not act on this order. I completely ignored it...I was terribly upset. It was quite a difficult interview.'

Barre asked Ames to wait so that he could talk with his own direct superior, Major Johnson, in Klagenfurt. He commandeered Ames' car because his own had broken down, and headed off with Meršol, who pleaded with Johnson that it was the British Army's duty to save the Slovene refugees since it had taken them under its protection.

'Johnson was not too happy about it and hedged a bit, didn't want to say yes or no and kept Dr Meršol waiting in the hall,' said Barre. 'So I raised a point with him: why wasn't I informed, how true this was? I found Johnson didn't seem to want to admit anything; he didn't want to agree or disagree. So that made it very difficult. It took me two years to get over the fact that I was treated that way by the British people, by the British forces. I can't blame Britain as a country but I certainly can blame those people.'

After half an hour of telephoning by the majors, Meršol was summoned back into the office. Johnson offered him a chair, looked at him in silence and then in Barre's presence said: 'We've decided the civilians won't be sent back to Yugoslavia against their will. Only those who want to go will go.'

They had won, with just 12 hours to spare before the first were due to be sent back. Meršol was astonished that the breakthrough was so rapid. He started thanking Johnson for helping save the lives of thousands of people, declaring that conditions in Yugoslavia were undemocratic and terrible. But Johnson had just had to back down, and he irritably cut Meršol off: 'You may not inform me about conditions in Yugoslavia. I know a lot about them; therefore we decided thus as I told you.'[35] Indeed he did know. He had been a liaison officer with the Partisans at Tito's headquarters.

Barre and Meršol rushed back and informed Lieutenant Ames of the change of heart. He asked for the order in writing, so they drove back to Divisional Headquarters in Klagenfurt. At 10 p.m., Barre finally arrived back at the camp to find the whole Slovene camp committee waiting to thank him in his office. The major acknowledged their gratitude with tears in his eyes.

Of the 6,015 Slovene civilians asked if they wanted to return, 150 said yes, and left two days later in carts back over Ljubelj Pass. The rest declined. Director Bajuk, not averse to sniping at Dr Meršol, later acknowledged: 'He was the one who saved those who remained, and if he hadn't intervened we'd have all shared the fate of the *domobranci*. We all know that, although we like to forget it. Our whole group must be grateful to him till death for all he did.'

It took half an hour to get the British Army to change its mind about the civilians. Why so quick? Perhaps the commanders had doubts whether the varying orders they had received really covered this. But something else had been going on in the background; a revolt by the British relief workers. Refugee care in the wake of the advancing Allied armies was shared between the British Red Cross and the Quaker FAU staffed by pacifists. In some cases, the military found it hard to overcome their distrust of the civilians. However, a number of the relief workers had been with the 8th Army all the way across North Africa and up through Italy. They had forged strong personal bonds with officers, in particular with Military Government (MG) experts trained to take over from ousted enemy authorities.[36]

Besides Major Barre and Dr Meršol, the Slovene civilians owed their lives also to John Selby-Bigge, British Red Cross (BRC) Assistant Commissioner for Civilian Relief in Austria. Visiting FAU representatives noticed that Selby-Bigge had a privileged position with British Military Government authorities.[37] He was ideally equipped for his delicate task. His father, Sir Amherst Selby-Bigge, came from the British establishment and progressed from Oxford don to head of a government department. He himself received a prestigious education at Winchester College and Christ Church Oxford, but then rebelled and became a painter, with Edward Wadsworth, Paul Nash and Ben Nicholson among his friends. Rebel though he was, he had served as a captain in World War I, which earned him respect from the military in World War II.

Selby-Bigge was on excellent personal terms with the head of the 8th Army's Refugee Section, Colonel Dufour, a French-Canadian. In mid-May, he found Dufour in despair at the 8th Army's headquarters in the Italian town of Udine, some 165 kilometres southwest of the area of Carinthia, where the Yugoslav refugees were pouring in. Dufour had opened his office, but as yet had no personnel or equipment for refugee camps. Because they got on well, Dufour let Selby-Bigge's civilian relief workers move into Carinthia without waiting for a Military Government to be set up. They were thus on the spot and saw what was going on. Selby-Bigge wrote in his memoirs:[38]

> In Austria, the 5th Corps Commander was in charge of the occupation forces. But 5th Corps was a fighting force, and its staff knew little, and cared less, about Military Government. Dufour's Refugee Section suffered the most. As he was unable to cope with the whole situation through lack of personnel, 5th Corps opened many refugee camps on their own initiative and without reference to him. When these camps became congested, 5th Corps loaded the refugees, irrespective of nationality or category, into trucks and dumped them over the Italian frontier. This was done without any notice to HQ, either in Italy or Austria, and caused considerable confusion and hardship.

The 50 relief workers in Selby-Bigge's team, committed to alleviating the plight of the refugees, had to witness forced repatriations, British soldiers rounding up terrified men and women with pick handles, suicides among the Cossacks, and escapees coming back with tales of slaughter and rape. 'My workers got increasingly restless; one of my supervisors threatened to resign; the head of the FAU [David Pearson]* said his team would not continue to work under these conditions; wherever I went I was met by the dejected faces of my workers. From our point of view, as Red Cross workers, the position was untenable; and I don't think the Army officers or their soldiers were much happier,' he wrote.

Selby-Bigge prepared a report for his Commissioner in Rome, suggesting 'the British Zone in Austria is not a suitable field of operations for the BRC'. He showed it beforehand to the Chief of Military Government at 8th Army headquarters in Udine, Air Commodore Constantine Benson, who was perturbed at what he read, and trusted Selby-Bigge's judgment. Within no time, Selby-Bigge, accompanied by David Pearson of the FAU, was brought before the Chief-of-Staff, Major-General Sir Henry Floyd, and had an appointment to see the Army Commander, General Sir Richard McCreery. Dufour muttered: 'Holy Pete. What a fellow. You do stick your neck out.' Selby-Bigge asked him whether he would not do the same.

Selby-Bigge recounted:

> I was taken to his [McCreery's] caravan. He shook me by the hand and motioned me to a chair. He plunged straight into the matter, and for forty minutes we argued the points. On one point I had to be silent and accept his reproof. He wanted to know why I had not reported the matter at once to the Corps Commander. I could only reply I had followed my official channels through MG. He then explained at length the difficulty of the military situation, which had necessitated the clearance of a certain area without delay. Under such circumstances, hasty decisions and injustices were bound to occur. But my main thesis he accepted and regretted. He gave me his assurance. There will be no more forcible repatriation, and no repatriation at all without proper screening by qualified MG officers.

So the Commander of the 8th Army had acceded to 50 rebellious relief workers, half of whom were pacifists (John Corsellis was one of the protesters). Selby-Bigge returned to Klagenfurt and his workers were delighted at the success of his démarche.

What Selby-Bigge did *not* mention was that earlier, on 30 May, he *had* in fact had the whole matter out with the Commander of 5th Corps, General Keightley. He was summoned by the general and ordered to persuade the Slovenes to go peacefully, but refused to do so. He concealed this from McCreery and omitted it from his later memoirs, perhaps in order to shield Keightley from blame for an unethical order. He did, however, confide it to a Red Cross colleague,

---

* Selby-Bigge described Pearson, a Welsh school teacher who tragically died young, as 'having considerable experience and a sound imagination – his simple frankness made him an easy partner'.

Lady Falmouth, who 40 years later recounted it to Nikolai Tolstoy in these words:

> This man had escaped and said to his friends, 'Now, whatever you do, don't go.' So when the next lot were due to go, they refused. There was a good deal of difficulty in the camp. Nobody more was sent, but [the camp commandant] reported back to Keightley that they didn't want to go. He saw Selby-Bigge, who was the Red Cross representative, who got on very well with them [the people being repatriated] who evidently accepted his advice. [Keightley] said he wanted him to encourage them to go. To which he replied he didn't think he could, because this report had come back, which appeared to be authentic, and the Red Cross couldn't do that. They couldn't encourage people to do a thing they didn't want to do, when it was obviously difficult.

> Keightley was very insistent, saying it was an order from higher up, and on Selby-Bigge's refusing he said: 'Well, this is an order.' To which Selby-Bigge said, 'I'm sorry sir, but I'm not under your command: I'm an official of the Red Cross, and I'm afraid I can't do this.' So Keightley said: 'Very well, you must go,' and sent him back to England. To which Selby-Bigge said: 'Of course I quite understand. I'll go back and report to my people. I can't do it.' That was the end of the interview. As he went out of the door, Keightley said: 'It's all right, they won't go.' And they didn't.[39]

Selby-Bigge's intervention with top British generals came too late to save the *domobranci*, the last of whom were in fact sent back on the day after his meeting with Keightley. On that day, however, 31 May, Major Barre and Dr Meršol were able to persuade Major Johnson to revoke the order to repatriate the civilians.

Selby-Bigge presumably decided to take the matter higher, to General McCreery, because he realised the repatriations were continuing on 31 May despite General Keightley's assurance to him the day before.

On 16 June, Selby-Bigge received a letter of confirmation from the Chief-of-Staff in Udine, Sir Henry Floyd:

> Dear Bigge,

> The Army Commander has asked me to write you a line to tell you that he has personally gone into the difficult problem of the repatriation of displaced persons in Austria. A letter has been sent from these Headquarters to 5 Corps with instructions that in future no repatriation of anyone will take place without full classification by the Displaced Persons Branch of AMG [Allied Military Government]...

The Army Commander has given instructions that on no account is any force to be used in connection with any repatriation scheme. I think it is fair to remember that 5 Corps have been faced with a colossal problem, and that on the whole, the situation has been well handled.

I think that you can rest assured that matters will improve, but if you have any further cause for anxiety, I hope you will not hesitate to contact General Keightley, Commander 5 Corps, who is fully conversant with the full facts…

Yours sincerely,

Henry Floyd.[40]

This instruction confirmed the reprieve not only of the 6,000 remaining civilian Slovenes but also of tens of thousands of other Yugoslavs, in and out of uniform, who were now protected. In the days after Major Johnson had told them they could stay, however, the shaken Slovene civilians shivered in their field, wondering what was going to happen next. The repatriations had been stopped at the eleventh hour, but for how long?

On 4 June, Viktring, the film-set shantytown sprawling among the ploughed furrows, received an unannounced visit by Field Marshal Alexander. The 5th Corps had disregarded his order for the anti-Tito Yugoslavs to be sent to Distone in Italy, but he had not dropped the matter. On the same day as that order, he had sent a note to General Staff in London asking for urgent instructions on final disposal of the surrendered personnel, because 'to return them to their country of origin might be fatal for their health'.[41] Now only the civilians remained, but he had come belatedly to assert his authority on the spot.

Fourteen-year-old Marian Loboda remembered children waving white handkerchiefs in a courtyard as a 'huge, magnificent car' drove up with the Field Marshal. Pernišek was on hand to witness it:

At 11 a.m. a large number of soldiers and military police surrounded the camp. People were very apprehensive. At 12.30 six cars with English officers drove into the camp. In the third was Field Marshal Alexander. He made it stop in front of the administrative personnel including Dr Meršol, who were waiting for him outside the camp office.

A powerful figure alighted. Major Barre saluted him and introduced the group. The Field Marshal shook hands with everyone in a dignified manner and at once started to talk with the camp leader Dr Meršol. In the exchange which lasted about 20 minutes he was very kind. It was evident that he was very well informed about all aspects of our situation.

Dr Meršol went straight to the point:

We ask you for your kind protection and assistance, for the Slovenes as also for the other Yugoslavs in the camp. We particularly ask you kindly to order that the Slovene and Yugoslav civilian and military refugees should not be sent back to Yugoslavia, for prison, torture and death awaits them there.

We have been told that it is so by our soldiers who were returned to Yugoslavia last week but escaped from concentration camps where they were being beaten and tortured and in most cases killed without any hearing, judgment or sentence. Those who escaped crossed the mountains and reported to us. Some had open wounds, having been shot but not mortally wounded, and had climbed out of the mass execution pits under cover of darkness. These *domobranci* didn't fight against the Allies: on the contrary they saved Allied pilots and helped the Allies whenever they could. They fought only against the Communists, who in Slovenia and other parts of Yugoslavia behaved like robbers and murderers.[42]

The Field Marshal listened, asked a few questions, and then put his hand on Meršol's chest and said: 'As far as I am concerned, you can remain here. Rest assured that we will help you and your people.' A quick tour of the camp, and then he was gone.

That same evening Lieutenant Ames received a new order from his superiors:

*New army policy respective Yugoslavs effective forthwith:*

1.   No Yugoslavs will be returned to Yugoslavia or handed over to Yugoslav troops against their will.
2.   Yugoslavs who bore arms against Tito will be treated as surrendered personnel and sent to Viktring Camp at disposal: further instructions awaited.
3.   All this personnel will be regarded as displaced personnel and ultimately routed via Italy.
4.   No evacuation from Viktring TFO [till further orders].

Pernišek concluded in his diary: 'Thus did God help us in those terrible days. We prayed much and our prayers were heard.'

British Red Cross Nurse Balding was more down to earth in hers: 'Camp in high spirits 'cos FM said they wouldn't be sent back Yugo.'

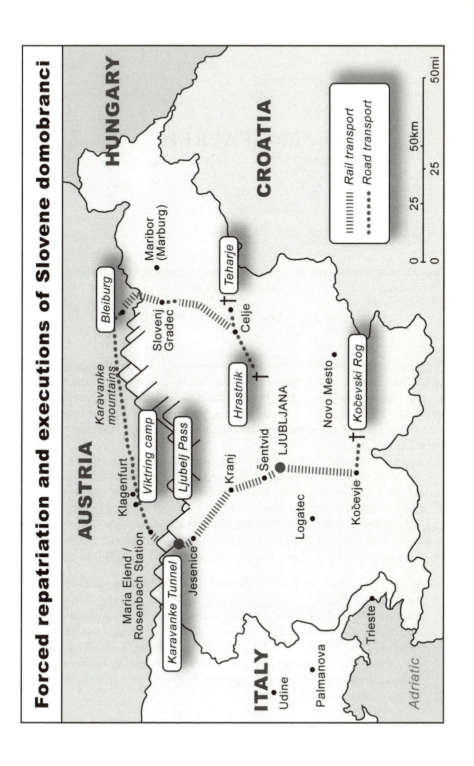

# Forced repatriation and executions of Slovene domobranci

**AUSTRIA**

**HUNGARY**

**CROATIA**

**ITALY**

*Adriatic*

Karavanke mountains

Maria Elend / Rosenbach Station

Klagenfurt

Bleiburg

Viktring camp

Ljubelj Pass

Karavanke Tunnel

Jesenice

Kranj

Šentvid

LJUBLJANA

Logatec

Udine

Palmanova

Trieste

Maribor (Marburg)

Slovenj Gradec

Celje

Teharje

Hrastnik

Novo Mesto

Kočevje

Kočevski Rog

|||||||| Rail transport
•••••• Road transport

0    25    50km
0    25    50mi

# 4 MASSACRED

*All the soldiers taken must be cared for with magnanimity and sincerity, so that they may be used by us.*

*Sun Tzu, 4th century BC*, The Art of War[1]

Max Rak should not be enjoying his retirement now in Naples, Florida. If life had been normal, he would have followed his father into a career on the Slovene railways. But by the time he was 20, that prospect was gone. On 29 May 1945, he was on his way to die with the rest of his *domobranci* comrades, locked by the British into a train wending its way back into Slovenia.

It came to a halt in Slovenj Gradec just over the border, and he and the rest of his *domobranci* comrades were herded into a second-floor room in a school, packed tightly so that they could scarcely sit. Out of the window, he and two friends saw Partisans walking by and a thought struck him: the only difference between his uniform and theirs was the red star they wore. He had concealed a pair of nail scissors, and he cut out red stars from a red-white-and-blue Slovene flag he begged off a fellow-prisoner:

> We put ourselves in line to go to the bathroom and waited half an hour. We went in, hiding the red stars in our pockets. When we stepped out, we had pinned the red stars on our caps. I walked past a number of guards to the stairway, went down and crossed the courtyard. Somebody was repairing a truck there, and as I knew something about motors I started working with him on the truck. I looked around, spotted the main gate and passed through it, saluting to the sentry. I was free!

His friend Ludve Potokar, a distinguished writer and poet, had gone ahead of him, pretending to be a Partisan officer looking for a prisoner, shouting foul language and ordering Partisans to open doors for him. He walked out of the building, rounded a corner, hid behind a tree and slipped into the woodland. Rak met him a kilometre away by following signs of broken branches.

They walked over the mountains towards Viktring but decided not to return to the camp for fear of being loaded by the British back on to the death transports. In exchange for food, they tended sheep for a farmer on a mountain overlooking the Drava valley, which Rak had crossed on his military courier's motor-cycle in his flight from Slovenia. A few weeks later, Slovene women scouts sent out from Viktring made contact with them. It was safe to go back. The repatriation orders had been cancelled.

So instead of working the railways or dying with a bullet in the back of the neck, Rak ended up a successful doctor in Cleveland, USA. 'I had enough guts and courage to escape. I am happy. America gave us all a chance to succeed. I could not have achieved as much if I had stayed at home,' he says contentedly.

It was a happy end for Rak. Ludve Potokar emigrated to Canada and continued writing, though it was 50 years before his work was celebrated in Slovenia.[2] He took to drink and committed suicide 20 years later, his last job being tending a level crossing. The third friend never emerged from the school in Slovenj Gradec. He lost his nerve at the last moment or was caught. Either way he was rapidly put to death.

Janez Dernulc, now living in Wales, also escaped. He was with a group of *domobranci* the Partisans were marching across the countryside at night from Slovenj Gradec to Mislinje. He and three friends decided to make a break for it when the right moment came:

> We started talking quietly among ourselves as we marched six abreast. 'Are you going to jump? Are we going to escape?' 'Not yet, not yet.' Then all of a sudden Vinko said, 'Now or never,' and we jumped. The road was just going past a house, and on the other side of the house was forest. In 20 metres we were inside the forest.

> Nothing happened. Probably a Partisan saw us running away, but no doubt he had an order not to do anything, because if they started shooting the whole lot would escape. He never shot at us and we were free.

They roamed through the countryside for several days trying to find their way out of Slovenia, and ran into a Partisan patrol, which arrested them. While waiting, Janez saw a concave slope leading down into a valley and reckoned his guard would not be able to shoot him if he ran down it crouching low. He bolted again, and reached the forest unharmed amid a hail of bullets.

Those who did not escape had little chance of mercy. The new Communist authorities could in theory have removed the *domobranci* from circulation by putting them on trial or dispersing them to labour camps. However, bridges and railways were destroyed, and there were severe shortages of trains, road vehicles, petrol and food. Historian Božo Repe, whose father was a Partisan, maintains the new regime decided against this because it feared a war with the West.[3] They did not want *domobranci* around to join forces possibly with an invading enemy.

There were two stronger motives. The *domobranci* had been fighting the Partisans for two years, and were responsible for at least 4,000 of the names standing today on memorials to Partisan dead across Slovenia.* The Partisans had personal scores to settle; memories of comrades cut down by *domobranci* gunfire were still fresh. They had an opportunity for revenge, and they took it.

The new hard-line Communist leaders were also determined to consolidate their power, and they chose a particularly bloody way of doing so. In an interview in 1979, the former Yugoslav Communist leader Milovan Djilas put it frankly: 'We were an entirely new, brash, revolutionary force without a properly elected leadership, courts and all the rest. Indeed, in 1945 we still went about detaining and executing people quite arbitrarily either for political reasons or for anything else we decided could be culpable. Our basis of legitimacy was even thinner than that of the Soviet government.'[4]

For the youthful new leaders of Slovenia, the way seemed open to finish off their enemies, carry out a socialist revolution, and implement their vision of a new people and a new society. Rather than conventional rule of law, they installed People's Courts, dealing out justice according to ideological principles. The *domobranci* were to enjoy neither old nor new processes of law. They were killed without trials, at the culmination of a long process of terror and humiliation. They were the victims of revenge, a desire for power and the harsh practicalities of wartime.

Tito, a handful of his fellow leaders at the Yugoslav federal level, and the trio who took power in Slovenia, Edvard Kardelj, Boris Kidrič and Ivan Matija-Maček, were all party to the decision to kill the *domobranci*, according to Repe. Local commanders also certainly settled personal scores – Slovenes were few in number and everybody knew each other. Tito showed his hand in a speech in Ljubljana on 26 May 1945, saying: 'Regarding those traitors who were within the country itself…this is now a matter of the past. The hand of justice, the avenging hand of our nation has already reached a great majority; only a minority of traitors have managed to escape and be taken under the wing of patrons abroad. This minority will never again see our beautiful mountains and flowering fields, and even if this did happen, it would only last for a very short time.'[5]

---

\*    Silvo Grgič, writing for the Partisan Book Club in 1997, estimated the number that the *domobranci* killed during the war was considerably higher at 10–11,000, of which some 3,000 were civilians and the rest Partisans.

The *Slovenski poročevalec* newspaper wrote on the same day: 'We have imprinted revenge in our hearts as a programme and a core, in order to shatter and destroy this company of traitors and executioners...Victims must be avenged. Revenge must reach down to the deepest roots. We shall not only cut down the rotten tree, we shall dig up its roots and burn them, and the soil in which they grew we shall plough ten feet deep, so that not the least sprout remains of the tree.'[6]

One of the victims who lived to describe this process was a civilian, Pavči Maček, 16-year-old daughter of a timber exporter and flourmill owner from Logatec, southwest of Ljubljana. She and her 17-year-old sister Polonca were in a Ljubljana convent school, and were separated from their parents, who had fled earlier to Italy. The girls arrived later in Viktring, heard the *domobranci* were going to Italy, and asked them for a lift to rejoin their parents.

Instead of a family reunion in Italy, the two sisters found themselves crammed into a filthy, suffocating cattle wagon, heading back to Slovenia. The *domobranci* started tearing up identity cards and photos. A young lieutenant wrote a message on the back of a photo and said to Pavči: 'My dear, would you do a favour, possibly a last one? As you're a child, they won't do anything to you. When you get back, give this picture to my fiancée.' She nodded and promised to guard it as if it were a holy relic.

'It seemed impossible our troops were here. Was I dreaming? I can't describe the horror, grief and disgust on their faces. I felt I was looking into the dark eyes of the mortally wounded deer my father once shot. Although they weren't crying, it was as if tears were flowing down their cheeks,' wrote Pavči later.

First stop was the same school in Slovenj Gradec from which Rak escaped. Partisan women took some of their shoes and mountain boots, and she saw several groups of *domobranci* being led away:

On the third day we left with the remaining *domobranci*, after Slovene Partisans had taken us over from Serbs. We waited in line in a passage and listened to footsteps and screaming. *Domobranci* were running down the stairs with Partisans chasing, jeering and beating them with belts and guns so that they stumbled, fell, picked themselves up and rushed on again. My sister burst into convulsive sobs but the girls quietened her, saying, 'Don't cry! We mustn't show it hurts or let them enjoy our suffering.' We controlled ourselves and passed our tormentors calmly and proudly. We waited a long time at the station, wretched and miserable, hunched on knapsacks and cases, and they again interrogated us, jeered and took photos. It was dark when we left.

We got down from the wagons at Mislinje, where the railway ended, and marched up the valley in darkness. I slipped and fell on the damp grass. A fire burned at the edge of the meadow and cast ghastly shadows. I thought we were going to die there. In the darkness someone shrieked the command 'On the road!' and we ran uphill, but another Partisan chased us back. We huddled together like lost sheep terrified by wolves. The guard barked 'In ranks of eight!' and we got ourselves in order somehow as the road narrowed.

I slipped unexpectedly over the edge of the road and just saved myself from falling, but had to stop and caused confusion in the ranks. A guard cursed. My legs trembled from exhaustion and terror as if filled with lead, so that I simply couldn't move. I cried to my sister, 'I'm finished!' 'You must continue,' she said, 'you can't stop here or they'll kill you! Give me your bundle. Keep going, you can do it!' This spurred me on; I clenched my teeth and forced myself forward.

The straps of my rucksack were cutting my shoulders and the road never seemed to end. The moon shone through the clouds and lit up a ruined bridge. I stumbled on the sharp stones, almost fell and saw dark stains on the ground. Oh horror, it was the blood of our wretched sufferers. We were so tired I would have sat on the road and slept forever. At three in the morning we reached a railway station and found we'd walked 18 kilometres. That was the most terrible night for me. Soon I was relieved to climb into a wagon, put my head on my rucksack and fall instantly asleep.

We were woken by shrieks and frenzied beatings on the door. They were opened and the sun poured in, blinding us. My sister whispered in my ear, 'Do your contrition, our end has come!' We were made to stand on one side of the road and the *domobranci* on the other, while Partisans, with bloodthirsty grins on their faces and riding high-spirited horses, chased our lads back and forth. They beat them over the head and ordered them to throw away their belts and lie on the ground. Then they had them get up and run forward, all the time flogging them. When a disabled boy was too slow, they drew their revolvers and shot him.

We reached Teharje that evening after being made to run forward, go back, stop and go forward again. We were worn down by our rucksacks and staggered. We started throwing away food, clothes and then whole rucksacks and suitcases...A fellow villager, his forehead streaked with strands of hair glued down by sweat and clotted blood, came to my aid. Parched, cracked lips begged for water.

The Teharje concentration camp was a last staging post before the execution pits. Some of the *domobranci* were already stripped of most of their clothes. By the time they reached the killing zone, they were all down to just a shirt or underpants. On the first day nobody got any food. Then there was beetroot soup, followed on the sixth day by a thin slice of bread. In spite of her hunger, Pavči says she could not eat and was continually weeping. They were only allowed short moments at fixed times in lavatories, and soon their room was filled with a stench. They lay on the ground, covered with itching lice. Every day they were questioned, threatened and mocked by the Partisans, until they became faint from weakness:

> They took the children under 14 away from their mothers to send to a boarding school, saying they were innocent. The mothers wept and begged, and the children even more, especially the smaller ones. It would have melted a stone, but not those people. That was nothing to what the *domobranci* suffered. There was no pity for them. They sat for three weeks on the hard stone with the sun burning them mercilessly. At night, poorly dressed and without other covering, they were stiff with cold. They got up and lay down in response to commands, and if a guard saw one of them talking with us, a terrible punishment followed. I don't know how they survived.

> They came shouting each night with a list of names. They didn't call my sister or me so we remained. One day they said, 'Those with a brother, fiancée or father in the *domobranci*, come here,' and I told my sister I'd go because it was so terrible there, but she said, 'We stay here, just be quiet.' So we remained, while the civilians were murdered too… Late at night I heard the cries of the lads who'd gone mad, probably because he'd been beaten so brutally.

Then, after six weeks, they and other civilians were told they were being sent home for trial by People's Courts. Pavči did not believe it and decided to try to escape:

> Our train halted outside Ljubljana station. During the stop, girls from Moste [part of Ljubljana] and the two of us got down from the open wagon cautiously and, because there didn't seem to be any guards around, we crossed the railway lines step by step. We reached the first gardens and houses quickly and then started running as fast as we could. We were feeble and half-starved, but fear and the hope of escape gave us strength. Out of breath, we reached our fellow-sufferers' home and fell asleep at once.

The two sisters made their way to an aunt, who de-loused them and nursed them back to health. Eventually, they were able to get travel documents to the Italian seaside, on the grounds that Pavči was a convalescent minor. They were reunited with their parents at the Monigo refugee camp near Treviso.

The tribulations of the others continued, and death was steadily approaching. The tormented journeys ended for most at one of two mass execution sites, in Hrastnik in eastern Slovenia and at Kočevski Rog in the wooded hills of the south. There the battered remnants of the 11,000 *domobranci* were dispatched with a shot in the back on the edge of a pit. Three men reached the edge of the pit, evaded the fatal bullet, and crawled out to live into the 21st century. Their stories portray how human beings can endure the grimmest of ordeals, maintain the will to live in the face of imminent death, and emerge from trauma to resume normal lives.

France Kozina, former inmate of the Italian concentration camp on Rab, involuntary Partisan and finally a *domobranec*, was one of these men. Another was France Dejak, unwilling Partisan, twice deserter, and later policeman in Ljubljana and Kočevje. Both Kozina and Dejak were interviewed for this book, while Milan Zajec recorded his own account when he walked into a British refugee camp near Trieste, Italy, two years after scrambling from the pit. While he crouched among the hundreds of rotting corpses, Zajec was consumed by a desire to live to tell what happened. The 90 pages he subsequently wrote,[7] with the help of a Captain Bentley, no doubt served as a therapy and helped him return to sanity.

All three came from the vicinity of the small town of Ribnica near the Kočevski Rog heights. Near to their homes, they were practically the only ones to stand a chance after their escape of hiding from the Partisans and secret police, who were scouring the countryside for enemies of the new regime.

Kozina, Dejak and Zajec were sent back to Slovenia through the Karavanke rail tunnel in the west, and their first staging post was a former German barracks in Kranj, half way to Ljubljana. From there they went to Šentvid on the outskirts of the capital, ending up at the town of Kočevje further to the south, their last stopover before the massacre. For those sent back from Bleiburg further to the east, including Pavči Maček, Tine Velikonja and Justin Stanovnik, the first staging posts were Slovenj Gradec and then Teharje, and the main killing ground was Hrastnik. In these staging posts, they were interrogated, identified, sorted into categories and subjected to first rounds of beatings, executions, pillaging and humiliations. It was at this stage that civilians such as the Mačeks and *domobranci* under the age of 18 such as Velikonja and Stanovnik were released – after a few weeks of this gruelling treatment. Velikonja, now a doctor, was freed after 70 days during which he believes his rations were carefully calculated to bring him to the verge of death from starvation. During his imprisonment, his writer father was sentenced to death by a People's Court and executed.

When Kozina, Dejak and Zajec arrived in Kranj, guards forced them out of the wagons and beat them. Money, clothes and gold objects were stolen, and a number were taken off and shot right there. In one wagon, two Partisan guards were found murdered, and so all the other occupants were shot. A large group were kept in a chilly theatre with two open oil drums by the stage as latrines. Kozina remembers they had to parade in front of a Partisan commander on a horse, who told them to throw any remaining possessions on to a cape on the ground. A student owned up to a weapon he had been concealing.

'He was beaten until he was covered in blood. The commander ordered him to lie down. "Which way?" "On your stomach." The commander put his foot on him, took his rifle, put it against the student's ear and fired. "You, you and you, go over there!" I had to dig his grave, half a metre deep, drag him over and roll him over into it,' says Kozina. The scene was witnessed by Milan Zajec, who also saw a Partisan push a gun into the mouth of an elderly *domobranec* and smash his teeth. Another Partisan ripped off a rosary, smashed it and knocked two teeth out of the owner.

All the time the Partisans were questioning them to find out how old they were, whether they had earlier served with the Partisans, how long they had been with the *domobranci*, what rank they held, which village they came from, and which engagements they had taken part in against Partisans. They looked for those they knew and asked for people by name. Usually the victims of these selections were led away to be executed immediately. Kozina recognised a young Partisan who was dividing out those as under-age. The brother of France and Ciril Markež, now in Argentina, fell victim to this filtering. The interrogators realised his father had been a prominent personality in the town of Jesenice, and he was taken away to be executed even though he was young enough normally to be spared. He swallowed his medallion of the Virgin Mary and its chain as he was taken away, an eyewitness told his brothers later.

Across the country in Celje, the detained *domobranci* faced the hostility of a civilian population fêting the victorious Partisans. They were forced to parade through the streets shouting: 'We are traitors, we killed women and children and fought against our nation.' Women, children and youths ran alongside spitting and jeering at them. Just a few gave them pitying glances.[8]

Zajec and his brother kept their heads down and said nothing, hoping to avoid notice. 'It started raining, and the Partisans pushed us out into the rain. Some people were black with beating and begged to be killed. The Partisans laughed and ordered those who had not yet been beaten to raise their hands.' There was a little soup, but scarcely any water, and thirst began to take its toll. Zajec's elder brother whispered to him: 'Pray and be ready for death. Maybe we will see each other in another world. Don't be afraid, we go together.'

Re-embarking at Kranj railway station, they saw flowers, flags and joyful faces as the population celebrated liberation from German rule. The happy scenes from the outside world deepened their misery. Then they were off, crammed 60 or 80 to a cattle truck, to the next marshalling point at Šentvid. The Catholic 'Bishop's School' where they were held has a chequered history. When built in 1904, it was one of the largest buildings in South East Europe. During the war, it was used by the Gestapo as an interrogation centre. It later served as a barracks of the Yugoslav People's Army until Slovene independence in 1991. Now it is a Catholic school again, and at the end of a long dark corridor, it houses a remarkable and comprehensive archive on the 1945 refugees. Its contents were imported from Argentina, the US and Canada by Janez Arnež, a Slovene who taught economics in New York, and is now its elderly, unpaid curator.

By the end of May 1945, the building had been vacated by the Gestapo and commandeered by the Partisans as a relay for the captured *domobranci*. Some stayed there for a few hours, others for weeks. Once more they were subjected to beatings and humiliations aimed at weakening their physical and mental resistance. On descending from the train, they were whipped with belts and had to exchange their remaining clothes for thin, unwashed garments riddled with lice. Some had their shoes taken away. Zajec remembers thirst becoming unbearable.

Then it was back on the trucks again, this time only as far as a broken railway bridge across the Ljubljanica River. There they disembarked and made their way over a canal bridge, and Zajec remembers running another gauntlet of Partisans raining blows. A few present-day inhabitants of Ljubljana still remember cries and shouts coming from the ruined bridge in the middle of the night as the prisoners were forced across to a train waiting on the other side.

Then it was off on the final leg to Kočevje, just 60 kilometres to the south, but it took them until dawn. There was only one train, which chugged to and fro with its cargoes of death. They began praying and a Partisan shouted: 'Pray, you white dogs who listen to priests, soon Mathilda [death] will come for you.' They overheard Partisans saying they would be killed at Kočevje. *Domobranci* pointed at brightly-lit houses glimpsed through the cracks in the trucks. Peering through a grating, Kozina saw his home village of Sušje just a quarter of an hour's walk away, and felt a pang at the sight of warm, comfortable homes. Many clung to the hope that they were being sent to labour camps. As he neared his own home village of Dolenji Lazi, Dejak scribbled 'Going to Kočevje hungry' on a scrap of paper addressed to his mother and slipped it out through a crack. He asked her to send food. Several others did likewise, and for weeks afterwards women wandered up and down the line picking up news of their loved ones.

In Kočevje, they were taken to a former home for the blind and searched again for valuables. Dejak traded a second watch he had been hiding on his upper arm for a piece of bread from a Partisan. It was the first food he had had for days. Some of the rest got a thin soup made of pine-needles. Zajec spotted one of his brothers stumbling barefoot over a wet bridge and tried to talk to him, but was driven away. They passed bloodied *domobranci* uniforms on the ground. 'We saw death in front of us. It was the only thing in our minds,' wrote Zajec.

They knew what their fate was, and the Partisans knew that they knew it. The final crescendo of violence appears to have been motivated not just by a desire to torture. It was also a deterrent against last-minute attacks or escape attempts by desperate men. They were tied tightly together in pairs by wire lashed around their upper arms. Zajec caught sight of his three brothers bound up in the same way. 'Our eyes met for the last time. We said good-bye with our eyes, and embraced each other in our spirits.'

The Partisans had only one train, four lorries and little petrol. But they devised a killing process that dispatched 700 *domobranci* per day. They forced their captives to climb in pairs into trucks, their limbs turning black and blue as circulation failed. They had to kneel face downwards, densely packed, with four guards at each corner of the truck. The trucks each took 40 men. The journey up into the hills took two hours, there and back, making a total of 700 executions per day. Zajec described the last approach to death:

It was a beautiful day, clear as glass. Dew was glittering in the sun-rays. I could not understand that we were going to be killed when we had only just started to live. We were all between 18 and 24 years old. The wire cut into our flesh. We were beaten by the Partisans at the corners of the truck. I started to sob. If I moved, everybody was hurt, and we all fell on top of each other... We started to pray aloud and get ready for death. We had been preparing for death ever since the Partisans got hold of us... I was afraid I would be sick and I could not get off the truck at Kočevski Rog. The sun was strong and I was thirsty.

We approached the killing site in a valley. We heard shooting and screaming of *domobranci* being killed. Nobody cried yet. We were just waiting. I could not feel my legs any more. They cut my shoe-straps and removed my shoes. The knife went into my flesh and it bled. I saw an 18-year-old boy with his eyes gouged out and his skull smashed. He was still conscious, sitting quietly, not moaning, just sighing... We had to walk along a path from the road through lines of Partisans slashing us with curved knives tied to sticks. We were forced to sit down and stand up, still tied together with wire that cut into our flesh. We had to walk several metres and then back again. It seemed to take about an hour. We were made to sing Communist songs. Some had their heads cut by the knives and were dragged along unconscious behind.

The Partisans were singing and shouting. When we came to the pit, we were all beaten, untied and each had to take off his upper clothes and some also their underwear. When I was untied I started taking my clothes off but could hardly feel my arms and hands and could scarcely pull them off. I kept my shirt, and hid a medallion of Holy Mary of Carmel under it. I commended myself to Holy Mary and an easy death. A Partisan shouted and pushed me to start running. I didn't know where I was going, but I saw another desperate man being beaten by clubs and knives and disappearing around a bend. I saw a deep pit in front of me with bloody corpses lying around. I heard a voice saying: 'Take care of him' to two men who were shooting at each individual in front of me. I was calm and I only wanted death. When I reached the pit I didn't stop. I jumped over the dead bodies and into the pit. At the same time a Partisan shot at me. I shrieked: 'Jesus have pity on me.' There were two shots and I fell over the precipice.

Kozina was driven along the same path:

In a clearing they untied us and made us take off our clothes. I was down to my underwear and another had just a shirt. We had to stand in line. It was the point of no return. A guy asked me where my home was and how long I'd been in the *domobranci*. I looked down into the pit, bent down and saw the guy put fresh bullets into his Luger. He was Francelj Karl – I knew him. He was a tailor, older than me. When he fired I jumped. My hair was thrown forward by the shot. I figured out: that's the end of me. When I landed, my thigh was gashed open and I cut my foot on a rock.

Dejak saw Partisans tear gold teeth out of the jaws of living *domobranci*. He noted they spoke Slovene and wore British uniforms supplied as aid to Tito:

When we came to the pit, the guard said: 'Stop'. He asked where I came from and how old I was. He looked at my face, all bloody and swollen, and said: 'Beat him! He's a Ribnica devil.' He was from the village next to mine. I knew his voice. I looked at him. The man who had been tied to me, just before he was cut down by bullets, called out to me: 'See you again above the stars!' The other Partisan was ready to shoot. I jumped. He fired and hit me in the flesh of my left thigh. It was 10 a.m. on 8 June when I fell on to the bodies below. It felt like a cushion, they were so soft.

The three men had survived the mass execution but their chances of remaining alive were close to nil. Sprawling on a heap of dead and dying in the pit, they had to avoid death from hunger, thirst or wounds, find a way out of the chasm 15 metres deep, and evade the enemies who swarmed above.

They were not all in the pit at the same time, but their stories are similar. A few other soldiers were alive in the pits. Figures at the side beckoned them away from the middle. Velikonja, drawing on his medical knowledge, speculates that the executioners shirked from standing close to their victims to deliver a shot to the back of the neck because of the powerful spray of blood this causes. They stood a bit further away, but were inexperienced and either missed the neck or aimed at the larger target of the back. Kozina narrowly evaded the next body 'descending just like an eagle'. It bounced on the heap and blood sprayed around the sides of the pit. A 19-year-old student with a wound in his neck asked, 'Is that France Kozina?' Another man with a bullet hole through his cheek called out France Dejak's name. In the middle of the mayhem they introduced themselves to each other, and exchanged messages for their families in case they got out. When Zajec landed at the bottom, he did not know whether he was alive or dead:

> I saw I was lying on a heap of naked bloody corpses. There was a terrible moaning under me, and new victims were falling over me. Blood flowed over me and into my mouth. I shouted out to those at the top that they should shoot me. I wanted to die, but death would not come. I decided to crawl under the corpses and suffocate, but then somebody at the edge called and it was as if I awoke from a sleep…I had blood all over me but I was not seriously injured. I knew I had been saved by my medallion of Holy Mary of Carmel. I took it from my shirt pocket and thanked her for her mercy. I showed it to a friend and he asked to kiss it because he felt he was about to die.

Dejak too found he was only lightly wounded, but they all felt terribly cold. Dejak's teeth began chattering and Zajec shivered with terror as the wounded moaned and slowly died. They tore clothes off corpses and pulled them on. Both heard dying *domobranci* pray for their enemies, and a priest chanted in Latin. At intervals, Partisans above fired bursts of machine-gun fire into the pit and tossed grenades. One wounded *domobranec* whose nerve broke pulled himself into the middle and shouted, 'Kill me, kill me.' He was blown to pieces.

Then they heard the sound of digging. 'We knew what that meant. They were going to blast the pit with explosives. After an hour there was a detonation and huge rocks came tumbling down in a cloud of dust, causing total darkness. Four more explosions sent more rocks down with hollow thuds. Then they threw lime powder, and we couldn't see half a metre in front of us and almost suffocated. I fainted and vomited dust. When I recovered, I prayed, looked at my medallion and calmed myself,' said Zajec.

Dejak had a sudden fear the Partisans would lower men down on ropes to finish them off, and he crept on to a ledge and blackened his face with soot to avoid notice. But nobody came.

The slaughter stopped at nightfall, and the handful of survivors looked for a way of escape. Tunnels extended away from the bottom of the pit, but they led nowhere. Eventually they noticed that the blasts had brought a beech tree-trunk down into the chasm. Kozina climbed to the surface to scout out the prospects. The top of the tree was in the middle of the opening, but by swinging he could bring it to just below the edge. The next night, he decided to make a break with three others, Karel Turk, Janko Svete and Ivan Jančar. Turk went up first and Kozina followed him. 'When I was young I was really strong. He stepped on my shoulder and I said: "When I say jump, you go." He made it.' Svete followed, and then Jančar tried. Kozina got underneath him, but Jančar was too weak and gave up, saying: 'I'm never going to make it.' Kozina himself got to the top of the tree but could not reach the edge. His comrades held a branch down, and he hauled himself out. Jančar stayed.

A *domobranec* near Dejak also scaled the tree, but came back saying it was impossible to get out as it had shifted leaving several metres of sheer rock to climb to the surface. Dejak recalled: 'I decided to try my luck too, although my comrades doubted I could make it, especially since I was wounded. I said to myself I must at least try. My friends helped me as far up the tree as they could, then I climbed up, little by little, all the way to the tree stump. How I managed to climb a further five metres of steep rock, I will never understand. I feel that there was a higher force – the help of God Himself – that sustained me in this desperate effort. He alone knows why He saved me.'[9]

Nursing a right hand injured by the wire, he scrambled out of the pit, and found himself 50 metres from a burning log fire surrounded by Partisans. He edged round to the other side of the pit, moving silently close to the ground, and then broke a dry twig. 'All the Partisans turned in my direction and someone yelled, "Stop!" I stopped, looked towards them and waited. But after a few moments they turned back to the fire. They probably couldn't see anything as the light of the fire blinded them, while I saw them distinctly. They must have thought it was a wild animal or a branch falling.' He gradually moved away, stood up and stole off into the woods.

Zajec spent the longest time in the pit, five days and five nights without food or water. *Domobranci* bodies continued to rain down out of the hot June sun, forming a steaming heap from which he heard the constant trickle of blood. He tore strips of clothing, wetted them with urine and covered his mouth against the stench. He licked damp stalagmites to quench his thirst. By the fourth day, the shooting stopped. He estimated the pit must now contain around 1,000 corpses. One of the survivors took courage, clambered painfully to the top over an outcrop of rock eroded by rain-water and was promptly seized by a waiting Partisan. Half an hour later his stabbed body tumbled back into the pit.

After four days, only five could move around, and then only one besides Zajec remained alive. 'He was restless. I soothed him. Our lips and mouths could hardly speak. He had a knife he had taken from a corpse. I took it and cut into a dead comrade. I gave the first bit to him. He ate it and I asked him what it was like. He said it was good and asked for more. I started too. It was fat, greasy and tasteless and I couldn't eat more than two small pieces. I gave him five pieces,' wrote Zajec. According to Velikonja, hypothermia was the most likely cause of death for those who survived the executioner's shot.

On the fifth day, stinking, lice-ridden and dangerously weak from hunger and thirst, Zajec, sustained by his religious belief, felt as if a voice was calling him. He had a sudden passion to save himself:

> I asked my friend if he wanted to try to get out. He said, 'I have no strength. I feel I will die soon. If you can manage, save yourself. God will help you. You can tell people where we rest.' I said good-bye and began climbing the rocks but got only a few metres. I looked around and saw the beech tree. I thought it was a trap, but it was the last chance, so I tried. I was shaking so much I almost fell off. I used my last strength to get to the top. The tree was only just attached to the rock. My heart was pounding. I thought it would break, and I was afraid the Partisans would be waiting for me, torture me and throw me back into the pit. I sat for a while on the edge of the pit. Big flies flew into my face, as if they were trying to push me back in. I saw stars, a new moon and clear skies. I felt the sky was giving me new life. After five days amongst death, I sucked in the fresh air.

In their terribly weakened state, the escapers were still far from safe. They needed to evade detection, find sustenance after a week or more without food or water, and discover a way out of the forested hills. The odds remained heavily stacked against them. Partisans and secret police were fanning out to track down political opponents and eliminate them. Until a few weeks before, large swathes of Slovenia were ruled by the Communists' enemies. Some of the predominantly Catholic population welcomed the Partisans' arrival in power, but others did not. As Communists, they felt justified in imposing dictatorship to achieve their ends. No village was safe. Homes were under observation, spies abounded and fear spread through a rural population reeling from three years of occupation and civil war.

Kozina was a strong country boy, used to rough terrain, and had good local knowledge:

> Without me the two other guys would never have made it to safety. We needed to go west, so I waited close to the pit until the sun rose, and then we moved off. We heard trucks heading for the pit again. We took cloths from dead people and wound them round our feet. At one point, we came on a patch of wild strawberries and ate them all. We walked 35 kilometres in two days and two nights and eventually arrived at my village.

I left the two other guys by the barn and crept over to my house. I knocked on the door. My mother asked, 'Who are you?' 'I am France, your son.' – 'Keep quiet, wait until the moon has gone.' When there was no more light, my mother opened the door and said, 'I was waiting for you.' I can cry about this now, but I could not cry then.

His mother and three sisters made beds for the men in the attic, washed them and gave them food. Apart from the wild strawberries, it was the first time they had eaten for 16 days. His mother washed his wound with spirits and he was appalled to see his legs swollen like potatoes.

They had to keep their presence secret. France's brother was with the Partisans during the war and had been captured by the Germans. When the brother later returned home, France told his mother not to say a word about his own escape. They reckoned the Communists would do their best to ensure no survivors stayed alive to tell the tale. It was not a vain assumption. Karel Turk, one of the two who escaped with Kozina, returned to his home three and a half hours away, and his father felt it prudent to report his presence to the authorities. Karel was promptly arrested and killed. Janko Svete hid in his mother's house near the Italian border for two years, and was then arrested, released and volunteered for a labour brigade in Croatia. On his return in 1952, he drowned; Kozina claims it was not an accident.

Dejak was acquainted with the area around Kočevski Rog from his time as a policeman, and was able to orientate himself by the sun as he moved away from the pit. After walking all night and most of the next day, he knew he was close to home. He sipped dew from grass and sucked up puddles of muddy water. Then he came across a man with a hay-wagon and a small boy. A keg of water was tied to the back, and Dejak could not resist the temptation to ask for a drink. He explained he had escaped from a jail in Kočevje, but the man guessed he was a *domobranec*, making Dejak uneasy. The man took him on the cart, and gave him corn bread, which he had to spit out because his throat was too inflamed to swallow. The man dropped him at the house of a woman, who gave him a full glass of slivovitz (plum brandy) and an old pair of trousers from the inter-war Yugoslav army. Dejak recalled:

I felt so good. The slivovitz freed up my throat. I had not been drinking or eating for four days. Then suddenly the daughter of a neighbour came in, looked at me and said, 'I know you. You are a policeman from Ribnica.' I was alarmed and went off into the forest again. It got darker. Suddenly I spotted a Partisan with a rifle and I carefully made my way round him. There was another, but it turned into a bush, and then another. I ran around for one and a half hours and became exhausted. I sat down under a tree and realised something was wrong with me. I had started hallucinating through the slivovitz, and all my deep fears of the Partisans came flooding up.

He spotted his village five minutes' walk away, but stumbled and slid head-first down a gully, remaining unconscious for three or four hours. He crawled through back gardens into his mother's house at day-break and collapsed on to a bed and slept. An hour later his mother returned and found him. She had received his message thrown from the death train. A woman had found it and brought it to her.

A few weeks later he narrowly escaped arrest, when soldiers and police searching for concealed food went through his hiding place in a hay-loft with bayonets. His mother was called in for questioning by secret police, who told her they knew he had escaped and was roaming the woods. She should urge him to give himself up. After he got away to Austria, she was arrested and spent 22 months in jail for helping him.

One of Kozina's sisters confided to her priest that she was sheltering survivors from the Kočevski Rog pit. He asked who they were and told her of Dejak's escape too. After an exchange of letters, Kozina got together with Dejak and his brother, and the three spent the next two and a half years together, living in tents on hillsides in the summer and moving from place to place in the winter. They whiled away the time by knitting, mending socks, weaving baskets, making rugs from corn husks – and Kozina wrote poetry.

Dejak and Kozina had decided to make a break for Italy already in winter 1946. They made their way on foot towards the frontier, carefully assessing the reliability of anybody who gave them shelter, quickly moving on if there seemed the slightest risk of betrayal, and worrying about their footsteps in the snow. Dejak recalled: 'We had Partisan uniforms with red stars and weapons. Suddenly we came across a Partisan coming towards us. He saluted me because I was wearing a lieutenant's overcoat. I asked him for his identity card to maintain the pretence. He moved on, but I was afraid he was suspicious because I had a long beard and my hair had grown long. We came across a Partisan hut and they started shooting towards us. We decided it was too dangerous, gave up and made our way home.'

They eventually escaped in 1948 with the help of Slovene couriers sent secretly by Dejak's sister in Austria. They walked 40 kilometres to Ljubljana overnight, skirted the city and took a train to the border town of Jesenice, sitting apart from each other. On nearing the border, they passed a couple of militiamen pushing their bikes with rifles over their shoulders. Nobody said anything. They dived down towards the nearby Sava River. As their guide crossed a footbridge, they heard someone shout 'Stop!' and there was a burst of fire.

'We took off our shoes and rolled up our pants, grabbed each other's hands and started to wade the river,' said Dejak. 'The current at that point was so swift and strong it could bring down an individual wader.

Reaching the other bank, we continued walking barefoot in total silence. It was by then 11 p.m. We kept walking barefoot all night and at daybreak we crossed the Austrian–Yugoslav border. We reached precious freedom.'[10]

As Zajec scrambled clear of the pit edge, he saw a human being in front of him. Shocked and turning to flee, he realised the man was dead, strung up naked on a tree. He turned in another direction and fell down a slope on to logs. 'Pus was oozing from my wounds. The wire had cut me to the bone when I fell into the pit. Everything was painful. Each pine needle was excruciating to my feet. My arms were swollen. I was thirsty and had a burning pain in my mouth and throat right down to my stomach. My tongue swelled and I could hardly breathe.' Just when he thought he could crawl no further, he came upon a meadow full of dew. He lay down and sipped the water from the grass and flowers, and it tasted like honey spirit. He lay resting there until evening, until he felt his 'guardian angel' urging him to move on. The next day he ate clover and grass. Apart from his tentative nibble at human remains, it was the first food he had had since a thin soup in the barracks in Kranj eight days ago. But he still could not find water. He tried vainly to draw up water with a broken pot from a well infested with dead cats and rats. He was worried he would go mad.

Then he came on a farm and observed an old man bringing water for animals in a stable:

> I could hardly keep myself from shouting. I waited until it was dark, crept into the stable and there was a bucket of water in the middle. I fell upon the bucket and drank. The man was frightened. My shirt and pants were bloodied and my face was black. He came back with a woman and children. They shouted at me like at a criminal and accused me of being a *domobranec*. I suspected a trap when I saw the little girl had disappeared. I took some eggs and two potatoes and made off into the woods. On the way I swallowed the eggs, but I couldn't eat the potatoes.

His home was still three days away, and he decided to make for the nearby village of Krušnice, where he knew people likely to be friendly. He began shaking and his heart beat irregularly. From his experience in the pit, he recognised this as a sign of approaching death. He began talking to God and preparing to die. Then he saw the light of a house 50 metres in front. He crawled up to a window and knocked, begging for help. The woman inside thought it was a Communist trick and told him to go away. Then she opened, and realised he was a *domobranec*:

> I fell into the middle of the kitchen, and she gave me milk and a raw egg. Weeping, she took me by the hand and led me up to the attic. She changed my clothes and I lost consciousness. When I

woke the next morning, she told me she was afraid I would die. She nursed and bandaged me like a mother. The only thing I wanted was water, but I couldn't quench my thirst. I felt a burning pain in my mouth and stomach, and my mouth and lips were one big scab. With neighbours, the woman treated my wounds with home-made medicines and in a few days I recovered a bit.

She and her husband concealed him in an underground hiding place, from where he saw Partisans pass discussing how many hiding people they found. By now, it was a capital offence to conceal enemies of the regime. The woman took him to a cave in the woods for three days, each day bringing him bread, apples, pears, nuts, milk and slivovitz wrapped in a cloth.

It was too risky to stay longer. With his feet still swollen and his hands and arms infected, he hobbled onwards to the house of an uncle and cousins. On his arrival, they laid him down on a mattress and washed his wounds with spirit and home-made medicines. He went to sleep, dreaming of Communists beating him, heaps of corpses, and wounded men reaching up their hands to be saved. He told his story to his incredulous relatives, who thought he had lost his mind. They hid him the whole summer in a remote cottage in the woods, bringing him food while he lay for two months recuperating. Zajec tamed robins so that they ate crumbs from his hand. When winter came, he was afraid Partisans would see tracks to his cottage, and he moved into a barn in the village. He heard that the villagers were being told that he and all the other *domobranci* had been sent to forced labour in Serbia and would not be coming back.

'One day I heard a loud noise in the barn. It was on fire. I was afraid and began to shiver. I had no time to take my gun. I opened a hole, jumped from the burning straw with a blanket wrapped round me and walked slowly towards the woods trying not to attract attention. Somebody must have seen me, because the village was immediately full of OZNA [secret police]. They came back several times looking for me.'

He decided to stay in the woods, but was becoming more confident. Armed with a gun, ammunition and hand grenades, he had no trouble evading patrols. In spring 1947, he decided to attempt an escape from Slovenia. He took a bicycle and rode to Ljubljana, giving clenched fist salutes to Partisan patrols on the road. In the capital, he found buildings festooned with red stars and portraits of Tito, children singing Partisan songs – and empty shops.

He and another man headed for the Italian frontier, joining up with two others who knew the border region:

We gave each other fake names. Near Gorizia [an Italian border town] we ran out of water and became very thirsty. We waited until night, put cloth around our shoes to make them silent and tried to find the border. We thought we had passed it when one of the other men nudged me that something was moving. A Yugoslav border guard cried 'Stop!' and we scattered and ran on. We heard him screaming insults and going to fetch reinforcements. We ran for several kilometres until we saw Gorizia in front of us.

At dawn I entered the town and visited the church of the Holy Virgin to thank her for her protection. I went to the commander of the British refugee camp, and described in detail what I had been through. I had no papers. They interrogated me for five hours. They were kind and nice.

# 5 DISPLACED PERSONS

*You mustn't demand anything, but you can ask and it will be granted so far as possible.*

## June–October 1945

Back in Viktring, the surviving Slovene civilians knew within days much of what had befallen the *domobranci*. Diarist France Pernišek quotes escapees describing the scene at Kočevski Rog and further killings at Hrastnik, Teharje and Škofja Loka, and at Podutik near Ljubljana, where 800 *domobranci* and civilians who had not fled to Austria were killed. He picked up a Ljubljana radio report that 'the reactionaries have been poisoning the wells around Podutik', which he interpreted to mean corpses thrown in ravines were contaminating the water. He was right. Djilas subsequently wrote: 'A year or two later, there was grumbling in the Slovenian Central Committee that they had trouble with peasants from those areas, because underground rivers were casting up bodies. They also said piles of corpses were heaving up as they rotted in shallow mass graves, so that the very earth seemed to breathe.'[1]

Refugees who had fled to the woods around Viktring trickled back. But the lives of all of them had fundamentally changed. They knew that most if not all the *domobranci* – husbands, brothers, sons and friends – had died. Practically every family was bereaved, and they had come close to extinction themselves. The British, on whom they had counted, had betrayed them. Going home, which most had assumed would be possible within a few weeks, now just offered the prospect of oppression or death. There was no foreseeable hope of building new homes in another land. Still deep in shock, they felt abandoned, miserable and hopeless.

The British authorities allocated them a new status as Displaced Persons (DPs). This at least implicitly acknowledged a right to protection and care. However it also suggested finality – that there was no way back – as well as a sense of limbo and belonging nowhere. They came to feel it as a stigma. Pernišek, DP Index Card A.01533419, wrote:

> What now? Mr Corsellis answered this question briefly: 'Now we'll have to register you as Displaced Persons. When you get your registration card you'll be just a DP number, stateless and without rights. You mustn't demand anything, but you can ask and it will be granted as far as possible. Among us English there's a firm will to help you and make easier the hard life of the stateless person without rights.'

> These frank words have had a very calming effect on us though not pleasant to the ear. We're serfs without rights, small change in the hands of international brokers and speculators to settle their accounts, and cheap labour for the locals.

The distraught people needed help in coming to terms with their trauma. The relief workers were one source of support. The Catholic religion, with its priests, churches, ceremonies and rituals, represented another. Priests were well placed to act as bereavement counsellors, since this was one of their traditional peacetime roles. The Viktring camp was so full of priests that Mass was being said practically every hour.

Others used their personal faith without the intermediation of priests. Zajec has described the touching scenes among the *domobranci*, many simple country-boys, heading for extinction at the pit and quietly praying and encouraging each other with promises to see each other 'over the stars'. Zajec gained strength from his medallion of Holy Mary of Carmel, believing in its power literally. Even if one does not share his belief in the supernatural, one can understand in psychological terms that he saw the human countenance looking up from the medallion as a protection. It helped him pull himself together, focus on what he had to do and envision the goal of a normal life beyond his torment.

Pernišek must have had more pressing things to do than fill his diary each day. But he gave it priority, and it seems clear that recounting this turbulent period of his life in writing served as a means of digesting it and making it bearable. He related the events to his Catholic faith, endowing otherwise senseless and distressing happenings with a spiritual meaning. Thus, when he and his children had no food, the comparison with the baby Jesus gave a positive slant to their hunger. When disaster struck and they seemed abandoned to their fates, they could rely on the love and protection of God. And when lives were saved, thanks were due to God and the Holy Mary.

Throughout the four years the refugees spent in the Austrian camps, church services, prayers, singing, processions and calendars figured prominently in their communal life. Slovene Catholicism, nurtured in the Catholic heartlands of the Habsburg Empire, is full of elaborate rituals strange to British and American Catholics brought up in the more austere traditions of Irish Catholicism. Milči Lekan felt goose-pimples as she heard the Slovene choir echoing among the lofty arches of Viktring Abbey. A Welsh Guard told her the singing was better than at his own country's song festival, the Eisteddfod. The interactive nature of their prayers and singing encouraged mutual solidarity and comfort. Ember Day on 19 May, a day of fasting and prayer occurring at a tense moment just before the repatriations, produced the following entry in Pernišek's diary:

> The church is full to the last small corner from seven in the morning. A different priest delivers a sermon each day, followed by sung mass. People are very composed and all receive Holy Communion, while the singing is from the heart and most beautiful. The confessionals are also permanently besieged. Wherever one looks one sees tears in people's eyes. We are all suffering under the cross we put on our own shoulders. We only ask that God does not try us beyond our

Catholic rituals were an important part of camp life. 'The young girls have decorated the altar with garlands. Our hearts are filled with unshakeable confidence, hope and consolation,' wrote Pernišek.

strength. Afternoon and evening services are also beautiful. *Šmarnice* – a sung holy rosary and sung litanies of Our Lady – are offered at six before a large framed canvas painting of Marija Pomagaj [Mary Help Us].* The *domobranci* have their own *šmarnice*, the special attraction being the mighty male choir.

The Feast of the Sacred Heart on 8 June occurred when the Slovene civilians just realised the *domobranci* were dead, and were stunned at their own narrow escape. Pernišek is already viewing destiny with new courage: 'The atmosphere at mass is very festive. The young girls had decorated the altar, a massive and beautiful piece of ancient art, with garlands. Our hearts are filled with unshakeable confidence, hope and consolation. If everyone abandons us, Jesus will never close his heart and we'll never be ashamed of trusting in Him.'

Vida Rosenberg, who was in an Austrian mountain village when she heard the fate of her *domobranec* brother, described how she dealt with the trauma: 'So many people were in the same position that the shock was lessened, we shared each other's burdens and I went to Mass every day, which was an enormous support. I was able to verbalise and share my fears. Blind trust protected us and the prayers with the priests helped us. I was praying as a member of a group, conscious of people

Geometry class in Lienz camp. The grammar school set exacting standards. Headmaster Marko Bajuk walked into classes and popped questions, in Latin to the younger pupils, and in Greek to the older ones.

---

* Literally, *šmarnice* means a bouquet of lilies of the valley. Marija Pomagaj is the most venerated Catholic shrine in Slovenia.

who had to face losses greater than mine praying all around me. The Mass itself was very helpful and the Austrian priest Schuchter was a marvellous person.'

If there was no church, the Slovenes built one. In one of the next camps, Lienz, they converted a wooden barrack-hut into a chapel and improvised bells from whatever came to hand. Director Bajuk recorded in his memoirs: 'We had everything superbly organised for the life of the spirit: a lovely chapel and a tall bell tower from which hung lengths of railway track which gave a most harmonious ringing sound. The lads rang the "bells" so well, really in tune [Gaber had a bell-ringing course under his belt] that it was a pleasure to listen to them on Slivnica* – you could hear their beautiful strong booming sound even up there.'

## Slovenska begunska gimnazija
### Lienz-Peggez

The Slovene refugee camp grammar school. Front row: Headmaster Marko Bajuk; John Strachan, FAU; Major Richards, camp commandant; John Corsellis, FAU; Prof. Kajetan Gantar. 2nd row: first left, Ivo Kermavner, sports teacher; penultimate right with glasses, Dr Valentin Meršol. 3rd row: first left, hat and glasses, Prof. Jeglič. 4th row: first left, white shirt and open collar, Marko Sfiligoj; dark suit and glasses, Prof. Žagar; last right, hat and glasses, Prof. Božidar Bajuk. Back row: glasses, Prof. Majcen; exact centre, glasses, Prof. Drago Zudenigo.

---

\*    A nearby mountain.

Young Val Meršol admired the bells but regretted he had to hear them each day at 6.30 a.m. For him religion had another more practical consequence. He found members of the Marian Congregation, a select group of devout worshippers, had privileged access to the camp football. He found another ball, which he named 'the devil's ball'.

Back in the camp in the field at Viktring, the Slovenes' camp administration was moving into top gear at the secular level too. Its committee announced it would open a grammar school, in addition to the elementary school which had been operating since the fourth day of their arrival. It decided to arrange talks, issue bulletins, and organise a choir, gymnastics, sports, technical courses and foreign-language instruction. Photos of the camps rarely show anyone standing around doing nothing. They did not have time. Industriousness, a quality of which Slovenes are proud, filled a void which could have otherwise made way for gloom and despair.

Director Marko Bajuk, appointed 'Head of Culture', set academic expectations which would cause present generations to cringe. Eleven-year-old Val Meršol described his routine: 'Prof. Bajuk was a short, portly man with a goatee beard. He'd a habit of walking into classes and popping surprise questions in Latin at the younger boys, and in Greek to the older ones. We'd have a spy keeping look-out who'd yell: "Hannibal ante portas" when he was on the rampage.'

Welfare officer John Corsellis was given responsibility for sanitation and education, and himself taught two classes of English. That was half his day. The other half was spent trying to breathe a sense of urgency into the director and staff of a 700-person 'enemy national' refugee camp in nearby Klagenfurt. Pernišek classified Corsellis as 'an unassuming youngster, a law student by background, very hard-working, conscientious and always kind and patient'. The prickly Director Bajuk noted that Corsellis lacked proper academic qualifications and stated: 'If he wanted to interfere in my school work, I firmly took the position that he does not understand our rules and I continued to do things my way.' He found Corsellis 'mean with every pencil', but acknowledged the young aid worker was good to the Slovenes and understood their circumstances.

Food was a constant problem. For fast-growing boys and girls, gnawing hunger was among their strongest memories of camp life. Aloysius Ambrožič, then in his mid-teens and now a Cardinal, says: 'We got used to just about everything in the camps, except that we often went hungry. I felt I could have eaten a horse.' Six-year-old Marko Bajuk (the Director's grandson) received a large piece of white bread on his first communion, and because it was such a rarity he hid it under his shirt and took it home to share with his brothers and parents. As young Frank Jeglič continued his diary, 50% of the entries concerned food. Maria Suhadolc had cravings for macaroni and potatoes, while Marija Jančar recalls painful moments in front of a Graz shop window displaying succulent buns she could not afford. Little orphaned Anica Guden jumped on biscuits and jam sandwiches British soldiers occasionally tossed to her. She squirrelled away scraps of chocolate and soap and traded them for her first pair of real shoes from the camp shoemaker.

Young Val Meršol took an enterprising approach: 'Food was very scarce even for the Austrians and there was a brisk barter and black market trade. We were quite hungry. I remember the British mess had just had roast beef and they were clearing the scraps into the garbage; I tried to take some, and the British cook yelled at me and chased me away with a meat cleaver.'

That was not the only prank Val and his friends got up to:

The old abbey had a real treasure trove: an ammunition and weapons depot with rather inadequate fencing, irresistible to any 11-year-old. We'd sneak in and steal ammunition, the bigger the better; there were flat doughnut-shaped rings of mortar-propellant and machine-gun and small cannon ammo. The shells could be wedged open and the powder used for fun; and to really bug the British we learned how to shoot the mortars. All you did was pop a shell into the hills and the British would play their sirens, roar away in their trucks and be generally annoyed and ineffective.

The days of the shantytown in the Viktring field were numbered. Military Government was in place, and policy dictated that refugees should be housed in camps designated for the purpose, and suitable for winter occupation. Major Barre took leave of them on 18 June with tears in his eyes as the Slovenes gathered in his castle courtyard to bid him farewell.* His successor announced they would be moving.

The Slovenes' camp committee determined how the refugees should be organised in the four camps to which they were to be sent:

• People to be kept together where possible following regional groupings (people from Gorenjska, Dolenjska, Notranjska and from Ljubljana and surroundings);

• Each community to be as homogeneous as possible, already now choosing its own leadership;

• High school and grammar school pupils to stay together in the camp with the biggest population, which should be the central camp, and their parents to go to this camp;

---

* A three-column 'Tribute to Major Barre' in the Ljubljana Catholic newspaper *Slovenec* of 9 May 1996 recorded: 'In celebration of his 90th birthday Toronto Slovenes gave him a letter of thanks with 300 signatures and a banquet in his honour...When asked why he had acted as he did 50 years ago, he answered: "From humanity," adding quietly, "I am of course a Christian."'

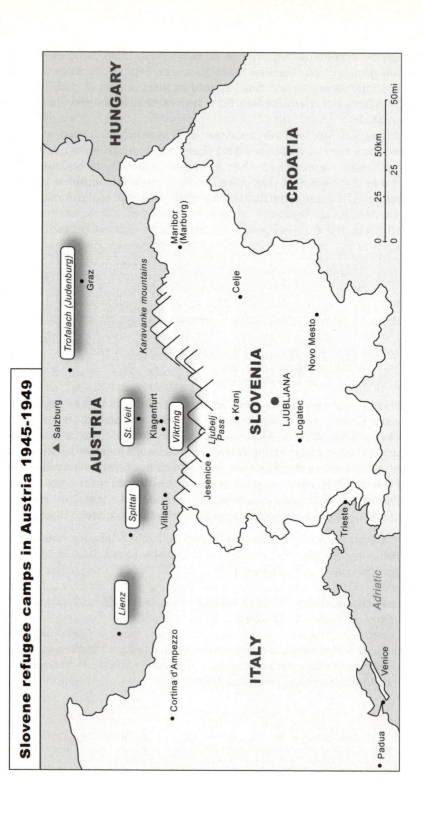

Slovene refugee camps in Austria 1945-1949

• Ditto for grammar school teachers and a proportion of secondary teachers;

• Primary school pupils don't need to go to the central camp, because each camp will have its own primary and nursery schools;

• Each camp should have sufficient male and female teachers and some intelligentsia;

• Individual wishes should wherever possible be respected, including teachers and priests, the first priority being to keep families together. Priests should go with the people and Chancellor Dr Jože Jagodič should allocate those unable to choose for themselves.

The new British commandant, Major Bell, who ruled the camp for only ten days, assented to this exercise in self-governance. The framework preserved natural community structures, helped families keep together, maintained education, optimised use of scarce resources, ensured a broad spread of leadership, and made room for democratic choice. It was an enlightened concept that enhanced the refugees' sense of self-respect and their chances of later successful re-insertion into society. Despite considerable buffeting over the next four years, the framework stood the test of time.

On 29 June, less than two months after the first dazed refugees stumbled into the field, the Viktring camp was evacuated. British soldiers shepherded their charges on to lorries. With the tacit consent of Major Bell, men hid axes, ready to smash open doors if there was any sign they were heading for 'Palmanova in Italy'. They arrived instead in Lienz, east Tyrol, and in three smaller camps in Spittal, St Veit and Judenburg. The Viktring episode was closed.

John Corsellis accompanied the Slovenes to Lienz and they quickly ran into trouble. It looked as if the system of self-government was going to unravel at its first test. Corsellis wrote to his mother:

> The position in the Lienz camp is delicate and complex. It holds 3,500 and has over 4,400 and so is somewhat overcrowded! 1,600 are Russians and Yugoslavs who were here before the Slovenes arrived and thus occupy all the jobs in the office, kitchens, stores and workshops. Then arrived the 2,600 Slovenes, who had virtually run their own camp at Viktring. The camp director (Captain Martyn) is not nearly as imaginative or liberal as the two we had at Viktring, and reacted strongly to the overtures made by the Slovenes who are in an absolute majority. At Viktring the one thing the majors were keen on was that the refugees should run their own camp, while here the captain is determined that if the refugees realise only one thing, it's that the British Army are running the camp. Thus

the over-enthusiastic Slovenes were severely snubbed and the Russians remain in virtual monopoly of camp jobs, which leads to ugly results. The food is undoubtedly poor in quantity and quality and the Slovenes are convinced the Russians in the kitchen put water into the soup doled out to the Slovene barracks. The only solution is a mixed kitchen staff but the powers that be resist the idea...

The real thing we're sent to do is to help and encourage the refugees start their own carpenters', tinsmiths', boot-makers' and tailors' shops, train apprentices in them, get schools going, adult education and lectures, gymnastics, sports and recreations, concert parties and gardening and many such-like activities so that they don't fall into the all too common apathy and later 'unemployableness' to be found in camps.* But the captain has more limited ideas and has shown mistrust of the two meddlesome Red Cross men who disturb the quiet of his camp and give him more work to do. So one has the delicate task of going slow to overcome his mistrust and wait till he gets to know one better and has more confidence in one before pressing too many new ideas, and on the other hand dealing with the not unnaturally dissatisfied Slovenes, trying to temper their enthusiasm which will only make things worse with the Officer Commanding, who will be strengthened in his conviction that these so-and-sos are trying to run his camp.

Soon however, Corsellis was reporting progress. He and his colleague, James Strachan, got gym and football going, scrounged medical supplies from a bombed-out school and persuaded Russian and Slovene doctors to share them. He started a lending library with Penguin paperbacks he received from his mother.

At the St Veit camp, the refugees found only tents and bare barracks with no furniture. Those in Lienz were delighted with their new quarters, but discovered an ugly secret. Marian Loboda, 15 years old at the time, felt 'we had arrived at the best hotel: wooden huts were luxury after Viktring's rickety hovels. My mother and I settled in with two other families, ten of us in a room 4 x 5 metres. With double-decker beds we each had our own bed.'

Next day he and other boys discovered bullet holes in the wooden walls and mounds of fresh earth with Orthodox crosses close to the camp, and learned from Russians about the repatriation of the Cossacks and Ukrainians who had been there before. The British had brought up tanks and loaded them at gunpoint on to trucks taking them to the

---

* FAU training for field workers was influenced by Quaker experience in areas of mass unemployment in Wales in the depression of the 1920s and 1930s.

Soviet zone, some reportedly committing suicide by disembowelling themselves with bayonets. Others drowned themselves in the nearby river Drava. Seventeen-year-old Milči Lekan found bloodstains on the walls of her barracks.

The teenage Loboda was 'never so hungry as in those first weeks' and he blamed the Russian cooks. The affair was coming to a head and led to another scathing entry in Pernišek's diary:

*Friday 25th August.* Food is scant: some days only green boiled water. People who've been in Gonars concentration camp tell us they were given more food there and it was more sustaining. Today it was decided to campaign for a separate Slovene kitchen and end the theft of food supplies. The Russians resist handing over control although they could easily keep the barrack 25 kitchen for themselves; but they're in an absolute minority in the camp and obviously if they hand the kitchen over they'll have no one to steal from! There were angry exchanges at a joint meeting when the self-styled Superintendent K called the Slovenes 'filthy swine' and said the Russians would never eat what the Slovenes cooked. But we won the argument and took over the kitchen for the whole camp.

First round to the Slovenes, but there were other problems with the Russians. On 11 September, Corsellis wrote to his mother: 'They have no idea of organisation and, while you can tell the Slovenes what you want done and leave them to get on with it, you have to keep a continual eye on the Russians. Also they have no feeling of solidarity – you may speak at length with a Russian spokesman, only next day for streams of them to say he was not speaking for them! Compared to them the Slovenes are ideal.'

Another Russian trait that annoyed the Slovenes was a readiness to deploy sex to gain advantage. Pernišek got to know some of them and found them an intriguing lot:

The majority are Russian emigrants who lived in Yugoslavia for more than twenty years and speak Serbian well. Most are proficient in slander, lies, swindle and theft, but there are some highly educated, refined, noble individuals who are ashamed to belong to the group, and with whom we get on well. Many are deeply religious and ecumenically minded, and we talk about the need for more unity among Christians, especially after the intense suffering we're undergoing. The Russians from the Soviet Union include labour camp people and soldiers of the Vlasov army* who escaped into the woods during the repatriations. Some believe in Bolshevik doctrine and are morally less scrupulous, addicted to vodka

---

* Who fought on the German side.

and quite poor. There is intense hatred between the old and new Russians.

> There's a difficult battle to be fought on very unequal terms because we've no 'women for sale' while the Russians use them to open all doors. They've dances and merry-making till the early hours and competitions presided over by former dancers from Belgrade night-clubs and cabarets and less reputable women. One has a great influence over the camp commandant, a British Major; her room is the centre of intrigues and activities and the Major spends long hours there. When they've a celebration or marriage the camp immediately suffers a shortage of bread – today we only got one loaf for 16 people.

The Catholic upbringing of the Slovenes emphasised chastity, and contact with the opposite sex was limited. For them, modesty was important and there was no chance that their women would be offered up 'for sale'. Schoolboy Franc Rode, the future Archbishop of Ljubljana, found it 'terribly strange' to see the British female commandant of the Judenburg camp go around in shorts. She signed his schoolbook – and that was that. Schoolboy Val Meršol wanted to attend a performance of Franz Lehar's *Merry Widow*, but was banned as too young. Schoolboy Frank Jeglič found puppy-love with Helen, and they played the accordion together. By the middle of October, most of the Russians were gone.

The Slovenes next crossed swords with the British over censorship. More so than the Americans, who were taking an anti-Communist stance under President Truman, the British leaned over backwards to avoid antagonising their wartime Yugoslav comrades. The regime in Yugoslavia would later tolerate greater freedom of opinion, but at that time, it was a tyranny modelled on the Soviet Union of the 1930s, set on unifying public opinion by force. The 6,000 embittered Slovenes in Austria held views which the Communists were stamping out at home. Their vociferous presence just across the border could have developed into a major irritant, and the British authorities wanted no such trouble. Britain had voted out Churchill in favour of a Labour government that was nationalising industry and continued to provide military supplies to Tito as well as the Soviet Union. The British electorate had swung to the left.

The Slovene refugees were well aware of this, but were determined to write in their camp publications with whatever frankness they thought appropriate, and set out to circumvent British censorship. They were permitted to publish one daily called *Novice* [*News*], appearing in Russian and Slovene. A Sergeant Shany, who spoke Russian and could understand Slovene, was detailed to censor it. He underlined, in red, articles in the Austrian newspaper *Kärntner Nachrichten* [*Carinthian News*], and editors were allowed to publish only those. Anything on religious, ideological or national subjects was forbidden, and of course these were precisely the topics that the Slovenes wanted to write about.

Soon the sergeant ceded his censor's pen to John Corsellis, who favoured self-restraint over repression. He wrote to his mother: 'I'm beginning to sympathise with the censors. I'm now one myself. On the one hand I want to encourage the Slovenes to extend their journalistic efforts – they produce a daily paper in Russian and Slovene, as well as a weekly children's newspaper and a weekly cultural, educational and political review – on the other hand I must make them tone down their anti-Communist material: they have every reason to be anti-Communist, but HQ in Klagenfurt or the Yugoslav attaché may not think so. So there I sit solemnly with [Franc Kremžar], a man three times my age who was chairman of a group of papers in Ljubljana and one of Slovenia's foremost journalists, and try to suggest tactfully that while it would be all right to print that letter describing conditions in Slovenia, it might be wiser to cover oneself in the editorial!'

The Slovenes clandestinely began publishing a parallel newspaper called *Domači Glasovi* [*Voices from Home*], which vigorously laid into Tito and his regime. They wrote and duplicated the underground newspaper in the camp but gave its place of publication as Klagenfurt. They distributed it at 3 p.m. to give the impression that it had been sent up on the afternoon train, and circulated it in all the Slovene camps. Somehow, it seemed to them, the British never caught on.

One day the editor, Father Franc Blatnik, was invited by Corsellis and his fellow welfare officer to accompany them on a day's excursion, and he smelled a rat. Sure enough, as soon as they left the camp, the lecture began. Father Blatnik recalled afterwards:

> We admire your people's high culture, deep religious faith, love of cleanliness and order, excellent way of bringing up your young people, honesty and high moral standards; but we can't understand your attitude to Communism. You fly into a passion like turkeycocks at the sight of the colour red, but they are human beings like us. One has to adjust to them and talk things over with them democratically, but you flare up at the very word Communism. This is the only issue we don't agree on. We find you kind, friendly and appreciative, but on this point you don't trust us.

Blatnik politely retorted that what happened to the *domobranci* when returned to Yugoslavia was a legitimate topic of interest. Arriving at the mountain village of Anras, they paid a call to the vicarage of a Slovene priest, Vladimir Kozina. On his desk, Corsellis noticed *Voices from Home* and remarked to Blatnik, 'Your writings travel far. I congratulate you.'

Blatnik denied he had anything to do with it, and pointed to Klagenfurt on the title page. 'Herr Doktor, halten Sie mich bitte nicht für so dumm [Doctor, please don't think I'm that stupid],' Corsellis replied. Blatnik was startled that his deception was laid bare: the censor knew all along what was going on. But his consternation was rapidly mollified by the realisation that Corsellis was not going to make difficulties. If he were, he would have stepped in before. Blatnik stammered, 'Thank you,' and the matter was closed.[2]

Of Blatnik, Corsellis wrote in another letter home:

> He is a Salesian priest but always wears lay clothes (the Salesians are a very active Catholic order who work mainly for orphans and youth generally: they have colleges in London and Oxford and all over the continent). During the war he was doing welfare and liaison work with Slovenes deported by the Germans to Serbia and interned in concentration camps in Italy, cooperating on this with the Vatican. At the same time he smuggled information for use by the British out of Yugoslavia via the British Minister to the Vatican and got shoved into jail in Rome for three months by the Italians – in the notorious Regina Coeli.

The Catholic Slovenes benefited from two protestant organisations, the Young Men's Christian Association (YMCA) and Young Women's Christian Association (YWCA). Fifty-five years later, Catholic Archbishop Rode spoke warmly of the lakeside vacations they organised for the camp children. Rode took to writing poetry and composing music. He declaimed a Royalist poem when the BBC's Slovene service announced the birth of a daughter to Yugoslavia's King Peter, living in exile in London. 'We all got up and cheered. That's how naïve we were,' says Rode. He too was mourning two *domobranci* brothers sent back to Slovenia.

While the adults often felt depressed that they could not exercise their professions or make meaningful plans for the future, the children found their camp life was charming in a spot of outstanding beauty. Among the boys – including Rode – one of the most popular activities was the scout troop, which had a camp on the bank of a nearby lake. Val Meršol, the troop's cook and trumpeter, found the American scouts he joined after emigration were soft in comparison: 'They didn't even have knives or matches,' he snorted. Marian Loboda recalls his pride when swearing the scout's oath of honour. Together with the football, Sunday excursions, religious meetings and studies, he experienced these as the happiest years of his youth. For Joseph Plevnik, it was a life of fellowship, swimming, shows in the camp theatre and roaming the surrounding hills. Franci Markež, now in Argentina, speaks of choirs, Shakespeare, Molière, religious life, playing truant and learning to swim in the Millstatt lake. They stole fruit on the way there because they were so hungry, and were sick on the way back.

Milči Lekan recalled: 'We loved the mountains and walked a lot. We were young, foolish and full of hope. Things were taken care of and we were never fearful how things would turn out.' Marija Jančar (née Hribar) lived from day to day, adapting easily to ups and downs.

Frank Jeglič added: 'There were lots of kids and we had games and fun, running around barefoot. I was a keen berry-picker, picking 4–5 litres at a time and trading them at farms for potatoes and butter. We had no sense of worry. Any anxiety of our parents was not transmitted downwards. There was never any need for counselling.'

Perni²ek described the strange mixture of pain and joy in another eloquent entry in his diary:

*Friday 18th August.* The banks of the river Drava are one big garden. The dark green pine trees, bent and broken by the storm, lord it over the slender alders whose leaves are turned to silver by the glaring sun. A light breeze makes the leaves quiver and the barberry bushes, covered with a thousand rubies, shimmer while swallows circle overhead in large circles. The Drava rushes through this garden.

I stand with my little daughter and we tell the river to carry heartfelt greetings to our lovely Slovenian homeland and dear family and friends. Walking along the shore we come across the untended graves of the [Cossack] disaster victims...

We pick barberries. As we gather the red clusters I feel myself to be in our Slovenian woods, and the bushes are sprinkled with the blood of our fathers, sons and brothers. Dear brother Jože, which bush in Rog is sprinkled with your blood? We pick but my fingers feel sticky, smeared with blood. Dear girl, let's stop picking the barberries and go away. They remind me of our slaughtered heroes.

Scattered around the surrounding mountains were other Slovenes who had left before the main group went over the Ljubelj. In the village of Anras lived Vladimir Kozina, who during the war had hidden in the loft of his family home in Slovenia and listened, powerless to intervene, as Communists killed his father, mother and crippled brother below. He had been ordained as a priest in Anras by Slovene Bishop Rožman, who had left for Klagenfurt before the *domobranci* were repatriated, and was now tormented by fears of being perceived as having abandoned his flock.[3] Vladimir took a jaundiced view of the British Army's arrival in Lienz:

My first impression of them was disappointing. I expected to meet tall, neatly dressed men and officers, armed to the hilt. Back home we Slovenes pictured them as a nation of martial giants, blindly placing our faith and trust and destiny into the hands of these Tommies, whose arrival we had desired so much. Now they had come, squat, dusty and slovenly. My former admiration vanished. I was appalled by their loose conduct and shabby appearance. Had the English really come to free us? Or brought us more misery and suffering?[4]

Vida Rosenberg was taken in by a farming family near Anras headed by Herr Meyerhof, father of 16 children. Many of the Austrian families had their own dramas, since their sons had served in Nazi armies and had yet to return. The Meyerhofs were waiting for three of their sons,

The Slovenes used metal from German warplanes and any other scraps they could lay their hands on to fashion bowls, kitchen pots, sieves, wooden utensils, shoes, Hallowe'en masks and altar monstrances.

Sewing thread was a vital but scarce commodity in the camps. John Corsellis arranged with his mother to buy large quantities at Woolworth's in England and send it over to him.

not knowing whether they were alive or not. The other students on the farm had to work, but when Vida turned up, Herr Meyerhof refused to let her do anything, declaring: 'If I help somebody, God will help me, God will help my children.'

Vida said: 'They just fed me and every day I was a little bigger. The impressive old man would cut me bread and some of that delicious smoked bacon. Never was I so fat, every day half a kilo more: I came with 50 kilos and ended with 66. They did it so that somebody would help their sons. While I was there two returned, and in Graz I received a huge parcel from them with thanks, since their third son had meanwhile returned home safe and sound.'

Gustl Kuk, a law student, had a similar experience: 'Local farmers received us and kept saying, if we are good to you, maybe our boys will return, for most were still on the Russian front. We were helping them with chores, collecting hay and were part of the family. They were friendly, humane, very good people.'

Back in the camps, the Slovenes were making the most of whatever meagre materials they could lay their hands on, setting up workshops to produce objects unavailable due to wartime shortages. They discovered fields where the Germans had dumped unserviceable warplanes, dismantled the wings and transported them piece by piece to the workshops, where they fashioned them into bowls, kitchen pots, sieves, wooden utensils, shoes, Hallowe'en masks and altar monstrances. They supplied all the surrounding refugee camps and did a roaring trade with the locals.[5] An engineer who previously ran a building firm in Ljubljana managed the workshops. Examples of their production can be seen today in the archive in the Šentvid Catholic school in Ljubljana. When the bridge over the river Drava outside the Lienz camp was swept away in floods, engineers and carpenters among the refugees replaced it within a day.

John Corsellis specialised in the provision of sewing thread. This may seem trivial, but it was not. Cotton thread was either unavailable, or if it was, only at exorbitant black market prices the refugees could not afford. Availability of thread was decisive. With it, the Slovenes could turn out a broad range of essential household objects. Without it, the dependent workshops came grinding to a halt. So he persuaded his mother back in Britain to buy supplies of thread from Woolworth's store. When the first dispatch arrived, he wrote to her:

> The cotton has been absolutely marvellous, beyond my wildest dreams! It goes through the camp central stores to five different recipients – 1) two shifts of tailors in the main workshops (we are very short of machines and have to get all the work out of them we can) – 2) a special shop salvaging clothes and making slippers out of rags (we made our 1,200th pair recently: they are most useful as people can save their precious shoes) – 3) an arts and

crafts shop, where we make children's toys, knit, embroider, make lace etc. – 4) the cobblers' shop, and 5) the hospital, where a sewing machine is used full-time mending hospital linen and making baby clothes.

Within a few weeks of founding the grammar school, the time for summer exams was upon them, and Director Bajuk informed HQ in Klagenfurt that he was holding baccalaureate exams. He asked Klagenfurt to send someone to head an exam commission. He got Colonel Baty, the head of education in the British Military Government, who turned up at 11 p.m. one evening to start a full-scale school inspection. Director Bajuk, himself former Inspector of Slovene secondary schools, recognised one of his kind. As Baty peppered him with expert questions, Bajuk guessed that the Colonel must have been a grammar school headmaster in civilian life, which he was. Baty scoured the timetable of lessons and remarked to Corsellis, 'Just like ours'. The next day he visited the classes, and later wrote a glowing report that Bajuk admitted he could not have written better himself:

> Dr Bajuk is a man of outstanding personality and energy. Both from the reports of the camp authorities and from direct observation it was clear that his leadership was the most vital factor in the school. His experience as a scholar, administrator and student of music is invaluable, Baty wrote.

> The other 17 members of staff (some part-time) are understood to be qualified according to the requirements for Yugoslav secondary schools. So far as an outsider not speaking Slovene can judge, their ability as teachers is undoubted and their personal relations with one another, the camp management and their pupils appeared natural and happy. The role of the camp commandant corresponds to that of a friendly and well-informed chairman of governors. He is greatly helped by Mr John Corsellis of the Friends Ambulance Unit, who makes the educational side of the camp his special business...

> A systematic time-table, much on English lines, was shown and corresponded exactly with what was in fact carried out. All classes were orderly, punctual and well disciplined. The manners of pupils were rather more formal than usual in England, but it was abundantly clear that their good external behaviour proceeded from natural courtesy and a determination to make the best possible use of their opportunities.

Baty found Greek reached a standard higher than in most schools in England where it was taught, reading in Latin was excellent, the geography class was exemplary in its attention and manners, and Italian lessons were lively and responsive.

GENERAL CONCLUSION: The school is maintaining, under very great difficulties, the best traditions of European education and culture. In the circumstances the venture can fairly be called heroic, and deserves all possible recognition and support. The courtesy and appreciation showed by the Slovenes is a high testimonial to their work and understanding.

He recommended the Military Government should sanction issue of Abitur certificates (the equivalent of baccalaureate), as well as teacher training certificates. He urged the Slovenes to seek Vatican help in arranging university admissions: 'The greatest possible care should be taken not to disperse this very homogeneous unit. For the cultural future of these Slovenes, the continuation of this school is vital...The potential loss of doctors, lawyers, teachers and educated men generally is very disturbing, if these persons cannot get in touch with [universities] which are willing and able to help them.'[6]

The report was a resounding endorsement of Bajuk's early insistence on restoring high-quality schooling and of the policy of self-government. It recognised the importance of the school in maintaining Slovene culture, warned of the dangers of dispersal, and acknowledged the potential contribution well-educated refugees could make to society.

The Slovene camp committee. Sitting: Lojze Ambrožič (his Cardinal son is Archbishop of Toronto), Dr Valentin Meršol, Monsignor Matija Škrbec, Dr Franc Puc. Standing: Valentin Markež, Jože Lekan, France Pernišek, Jože Mavrič, Father Ciril Petelin.

After the treachery of the *domobranci* episode, British civic values were beginning to make a positive contribution. Practically all Baty's recommendations were implemented.

Bajuk's regime was a tough one, but some of his pupils were just as tough. Franc Jerman, a young *domobranec* who had escaped from the repatriation trains, got into hot water with Director Bajuk because he could not answer a question in class. Asked why, he replied he did not have the right book. Bajuk told him he did not care how he did it, but he had to know the subject. Frank was absent for a week and then reappeared with the book, together with a few others. He had crossed the frontier to his home in Slovenia, loaded a haversack with schoolbooks and returned, risking his life to get the right answer in class. If the Partisans had caught him, he would doubtless have been executed. Marian Loboda, his friend, added, however: 'He always blamed himself for his rashness, because the Communists heard of his visit and held his sister in prison for years for failing to denounce him, and by the time she was released she was half paralysed.'

The future Archbishop Rode remembers how excited he was when he took his examination for enrolment into the grammar school. 'I felt I was bound to fail, but I passed,' he said. School for him was full of choirs, concerts, Salesian fathers organising sports, and history lessons from a Serbian monarchist.

Director Bajuk was strict about admission of new students to the grammar school. Miroslav Odar travelled from Spittal to Lienz by train to take the exams, but was turned away at the gate. He crawled through a gap in the fence, hid in a barracks for two weeks, was fed by a trainee priest – and passed.

Paula Hribovšek, who had left Slovenia on her own in May 1945, made the same journey to seek admission, showing her school certificate from Kranj. She was the sister of a young poet who had been killed after being sent back with the *domobranci*. Bajuk turned her down, saying: 'This certificate is worthless; you can't study here.' Her studies had followed a different curriculum. She was spotted crying by Professor Jeglič, who besides teaching maths in the camp was a former head of Slovene primary schools, and had a wife from her home village, Radovljica. He intervened with Bajuk and she was allowed to enter the school, but two classes below her level. Afterwards she was glad Bajuk's gruffness provoked her tears and Jeglič's intervention.

The university issue was much harder to crack, not least because refugees were forbidden to travel between the British, American, French and Russian zones of Austria, and to neighbouring Italy. Jože Jančar did not let this put him off, and with Corsellis' encouragement set off with a Cistercian monk towards Merano in Italian South Tyrol. His goal was to gain admission to the University of Padua for all qualified Slovene students. They walked on both sides of the road, so that if the British

Field Security Service (FSS) drove past they could dive into woods on both sides. They walked 170 kilometres, mingling with Germans, Hungarians and smugglers as they slipped across the frontier. Then on to a train, where Jančar realised he had neither ticket nor money, so he offered his Displaced Person card to the conductor, who clipped it.

Near Cortina d'Ampezzo the line was bombed so they had to leave the train. Jančar hitched a lift on a lorry full of singing young men. To his horror, he realised the song was the Italian Partisans' Bandiera Rossa [Red Flag]. He mumbled something about looking for colleagues and they invited him to their headquarters to check names. He hid in a lavatory, and waited until they lost interest and moved on.

In Padua, he persuaded Father Anton Prešeren, a Slovene who was second-in-command of Jesuits worldwide, to get him an appointment with the University Director. Prešeren offered the Secretary, but Jančar insisted, and the senior churchman put in a personal call to the Director.

'He asked me where I was studying. I said "Ljubljana." "Oh, Provincia di Lubiana. Any documents?" "Yes, I have four indexes recording completed studies." "That's exactly what I want. I'll accept you and your wife and sister." Jančar added that there were 80 others, and the Director replied, "All right, anyone who can produce a document from Ljubljana University will be accepted, provided they find their own money and accommodation." I nearly jumped through the window with joy and went off to Prešeren, who said: "I can't believe it, because he's God Almighty, you know."'

God Almighty might have agreed, but the logistic challenges of sending refugees based in Austria to university in Italy proved too much for the mortals administering the camps amid the ruins of war. The project was too complicated and expensive. Another Slovene gained admission at Padua after pleading his case in Latin with the pro-Rector, but could find no funding. The Padua option collapsed.

Graz, just to the east in Austria, had a well-established university, but it was in the Russian zone. Then news came that the Russians were pulling out, and Graz became the best bet. Corsellis and Jančar, who had been working together since Viktring, began an offensive to find places for 145 students from three camps in the two months before the academic year began. Missing the deadline would mean losing the chance of a university education, perhaps forever. Corsellis, aged 22, drew on all the skills of pestering, persuasion and diplomacy that he had developed over the last three years, telephoning and writing to every authority he could think of. Finally, he was summoned to a meeting in Graz with the Military Government, the UN and the Red Cross. All the principles were settled quickly. The only remaining stumbling block was accommodation. Graz was badly bombed.

Jože Jančar meanwhile set out with a letter from Corsellis, arriving at the bombed-out station of Graz in the dark and sleeping in a siding under a train, worrying that someone might steal the bread Corsellis had given him. He charged in to the Dean's office pretending to have an appointment and was welcomed in fluent Slovene. The Dean reacted favourably to the idea, a Military Government officer found a disused school as accommodation, and the way seemed clear.

Unfortunately, Austrian universities did not recognise Director Bajuk's baccalaureate certificates. In 1944, the government in Vienna decreed that all refugee students would have to re-sit exams before an Austrian commission, which would have effectively ruled out the Slovenes for that year.

'I took my courage in both hands and went to Graz,' Bajuk wrote in his memoirs:

> I was in the office by 8 a.m. and found the Vice-Chancellor had just got back from a three-week conference in Vienna. At 9 a.m. after a lecture he received me very kindly, quickly understood the issue and promised to put it on the agenda of the 11 a.m. Deans' meeting, so that I would know the result at 12. I returned at 11.30 to enquire. He spotted me through the half-open door of his office as the Deans were putting on their gowns for a graduation ceremony. He beckoned me in, introduced me and said:

'We have decided unanimously that:

Slovene students in their Displaced Persons camp at Graz University. Created in 1945, this was the only such facility anywhere in post-war Western Europe. Iris Murdoch worked there as a welfare officer. Left to right: Jože Jančar, Ludve Potokar, Blaž Korošec, Leo Čop, Jože Opara.

a) you are trustworthy and we accept your report;

b) you know which students have passed the baccalaureate exam, in your capacity as headmaster and schools inspector responsible for the baccalaureate exams;

c) your reliability is also confirmed by your pupils who are now our students, who are all hard-working, conscientious and well behaved, so much so that we point them out as examples to others, and therefore

d) baccalaureate certificates for any of your students issued by you are acceptable substitutes for authentic baccalaureate certificates.'

My head swam. How had we secured such a miraculous decision from the university, which went against the directives of its government – a university which used to be known for its nationalistic chauvinism? I wanted to thank them, but was so taken aback I only managed to stutter... This was a generous broad-mindedness of the first degree.

Thus was created, under the auspices of the British authorities, the only post-war refugee camp reserved exclusively for university students in the Western occupation zones of Europe. Food supplies to start with were minimal and enrolment was hair-raising. Riko Ziernfeld, now living in Canada, described how he set about studying mechanical engineering:

I spent two days in the train going from Lienz to Graz. It stopped for a whole night in Klagenfurt. In Graz we were [first] lodged in the Keplerschule, a bombed-out school. It had bed frames but no bedding. I had an inferiority complex as I had no shoes, only wooden clogs with a leather strap, and I wore a green jacket typical of the camps. Everybody knew you were a Displaced Person. I knew no German. The first month I went to the lectures and tried to write down as many words as possible, looking them up in the dictionary at the end of the day.

Metod Milač, echoing many others, nevertheless described his opportunity to pursue university studies in Graz as one of the crucial events of his life. Soon they moved to more agreeable accommodation in the Hochsteingasse on the edge of the city, 'on a small hill under an appealing vineyard, in a small barrack camp'. The Slovenes were always in the majority, but they were soon sharing their good fortune with refugee students from 11 other countries.

Once more, luck put a character unstinting in her generosity in charge of them, a British officer named Margaret Jaboor. Milač, still appalled by the callous British treatment of the *domobranci*, paid tribute to her as a caring and altruistic officer: 'Our relationship with Miss Jaboor was on the highest level. We had no doubts she did everything in her power for us and more. She truly deserved our gratitude and thanks.'

She had plenty to put up with, but had a sense of humour. Jože Jančar, the first student representative, remembers one of several incidents:

> Miss Jaboor called me in. 'I have a complaint,' she said. 'I have the Abbot here, this morning. He's very concerned.' I said, 'What's happened?' keeping my face straight, but at the same time nearly bursting out laughing. And she did too, you know; we had a rapport. 'He complained your students are pinching apples in our garden in the monastery in the back. And he put one of the monks in charge to protect it – they built a little hut. And the monk was sleeping in it. Last night somebody came along and rolled the monk down the hill.'[7]

At a theatre evening, one of them hailed her as 'unsere Mutter [our mother]' and the whole audience gave her a standing ovation.[8]

Back in the Lienz camp, Director Bajuk built up a lending library of over 1,000 books, mostly in Slovene. Corsellis helped him obtain 16 second-hand volumes of a German lexicon from a British Red Cross store. Bajuk supplemented these with 700 volumes from the estate of a former Vienna university professor. He acquired three pianos and a pianino, and started a music school which, besides piano and violin, featured singing lessons by a Russian ballerina. The choir numbered over 120 voices, and an ex-Olympic athlete organised sports. Bajuk wrote:

> There wasn't a single evening without a lecture covering all sorts of subjects, politics, social, philosophy, theology etc. We barely managed to find space for all the lectures and meetings. People found it difficult to get hold of the more popular books, so I thought of 'reading evenings'... People loved to come; usually 200 or more attended. [My son] Božidar did the reading, by sections and chapters – one per week – of selected novels. He explained literary language peculiarities, other points of interest and the lifework of the author. After these readings Professor Dr Mihelčič talked on an interesting topic from the past week, especially politics from as far around the world as we could reach.

The camp newspaper announced the refugees could go free to English film shows for the troops in Lienz, adding however that 'conditions are that they turn up punctually, do not occupy the better seats, behave in an orderly manner and if the cinema should be full give up their seats to the English'.

It was in many respects an idyll. The camp was purring along smoothly, nature was heavenly, schooling was settled, children were happy, and the community was strong. The only problem was the fundamental question every refugee has to face sooner or later: where would they eventually go? The camp could never be more than a temporary stage in their lives. What country would accept them as immigrants? Was it really so dangerous to return home?

The last question became more persistent as spring came. Many refugees were farmers with roots in their native soil. They sat disconsolately outside their barracks hearing their pastures, orchards and vineyards calling out for attention. Archbishop Rode, then a small boy, remembers the question whether to return was always to the forefront in his farming family. It raised sensitive issues, as France Pernišek recorded in his diary on 9 April 1946:

> Many are unable to hold out, and prepare to leave for home. But they're worried what'll happen. Will they be left in peace or face prison and suffering? If spared that, how will their neighbours treat them? Will they be received with hatred and abuse, spat upon and taunted like some who returned earlier? Many have family at home; a daughter stayed or a son returned from the army or POW camp. They tell them to come home as they can't manage the work on their own. Thus are they torn between a passionate longing and utter uncertainty and forebodings of evil and fear.
>
> From our barracks a few are returning. Many can't understand their decision, accuse them of betrayal, say they're victims of the Communists' propaganda. Poor people! They don't deserve the scornful looks and sarcastic comments. The barrack leader is going back and is the first target, even though he was very wise and scrupulously fair. Some elderly women are going as well: honest, devout, thoroughly good women, who walk around with tear-stained faces because of the spiteful remarks. It's not the other farmers that are hostile, but insensitive, selfish townspeople.
>
> It's incredible the loathing some of our people still feel towards anyone they suspect of contact with the Communists back home. It's impossible to get them to understand that in spring country people feel the powerful call to return to their fields. We should understand this mysterious inner process...Many prayed long before they made the decision.

In autumn 1945, this was still some way away. The camp held a commemoration service for the *domobranci*. Such services at the expiry of a set time can act as a rite of passage for the bereaved. It helps set them free from the dead and encourages them to undertake new commitments.[9] Jože Jančar and Marija Hribar, who bicycled away together after abandoning a birthday tea, did just that: they decided to get married. Marija, now in her 80s, remembers the occasion: 'It was not bad. We wed in the chapel in the camp. We had a party, and everybody got drunk on coffee. Our presents included half a calf, Austrian wood sculptures, a gold pen from Dr Meršol, and four lovely damask serviettes that I still have. Now I am left with them. Jože was lovely. He always knew what to say to people. He helped me to cope. He was a very kind person.'
Jože died in 2000, aged 80, in Bristol, England.

# 6 GO HOME

*What are you Yugoslavs doing staying on here anyway?*

## October 1945–March 1947

A tug-of-war was developing as to how the refugees should be handled. The hard-line approach consisted of making their lives more uncomfortable so that they would return home. John Corsellis represented the more compassionate line and was increasingly seen by the Slovene refugees as their champion. He and others of like mind tried to improve material conditions and sustain their self-confidence as a group. Already in a report in August 1945, Corsellis argued that the Slovenes deserved to be treated with more latitude than other nationalities:

> At Viktring, under exceptionally difficult conditions, the refugees ran the camp themselves with the minimum of equipment, and ran it well enough for its inmates to compare life favourably with that at the camps to which they were later sent...The Slovenes have a high degree of social consciousness and form a close-knit and cohesive community. They have shown a marked leaning towards and aptitude for democratic methods. Their leaders work hard for those in need and oppose any preferential treatment for themselves or their friends...
>
> Conclusion: the administration of the Slovenes of Viktring and Lienz shows that they have enough competent leaders and skilled workers and are a unified enough community to run their camp by themselves. If they are concentrated in a camp in which they would be in a majority, the most satisfactory course would be to attach a liaison officer in an advisory rather than directory capacity. This would contribute greatly to the preservation of that individual and

communal self-respect which is usually the first casualty in the refugee camp.

This radical proposal got nowhere. The one liaison officer would have replaced a major and 12 other military men. Coming from a 22-year-old pacifist, it went too far. Rather than lose their jobs and authority, the soldiers saw all sorts of reasons why they needed to be on hand and govern. The British Army continued in charge, in a muddled way. On 5 September, Corsellis wrote to his mother: 'Supplies promised months ago still have not turned up... A considerable proportion of the barrack roofs leak and while the Army find no difficulty in roofing new camps, material for mending our roofs has been promised for two months now. The same applies to elementary things like straw palliasses, glass,

The Slovene camp newspaper published this cartoon of welfare officers John Corsellis (right) and John Strachan, with thanks for defending a Slovene refugee from a false court charge.

blankets, etc., all or most of which are available if only the right person would wake up.'

The Slovenes sent their schoolchildren into the hills to collect moss for the palliasses in place of the missing straw. Two weeks later, Corsellis again despaired:

> What a life! It is hardly possible to believe that an Army that un-doubtedly was very efficient and successful at waging war could be quite such a failure at dealing with civilian problems... Neither the major nor the captain have had any refugee camp or other admin experience, except in the army where the organisation is ready-made and foolproof, and neither shows any signs of wanting to learn. Even on practical matters where I thought I was pretty dense, they leave me miles behind in stupidity... The strain of having to make the most obvious suggestions in spheres of work quite outside our own without giving the impression that we are trying to run the camp is pretty colossal.

Corsellis had to defend seven refugees against roughshod military justice. They had been picked up for allegedly assaulting two pro-Tito Yugoslavs, but Corsellis was 90% sure they were innocent, and was shocked how dilatory the British authorities were. The case was first in the hands of an unpleasant military police lieutenant; who handed it to a friendly sergeant, who passed it on to a corporal – with still no charges being laid. An Austrian policewoman told him: 'I've been feeling rather worried about that recently – there never seems to be a defence at the court here: they just go up and are sentenced.' This hardly seemed the way for the British to teach the Austrians democratic justice after years of Nazism. Corsellis arranged for a Slovene high court judge to visit the detainees to prepare their defence, and the case was subsequently dismissed with no evidence offered.

In October 1945, it was decided the United Nations Relief and Rehabilitation Administration (UNRRA) would take over the camps. But the British Army dragged its feet, and the transition was drawn out. 'It is very galling seeing personnel keen to take over who could clear up the incredible muddle, but not allowed to because officers refuse to give up some cushy jobs,' Corsellis wrote.

A cultural clash between the young aid workers and the military, used to the disciplined life of military messes, was inevitable. Corsellis conceded: 'It must be a considerable strain to have to live with two youthful, highbrow, non-smoking, non-drinking, non-card-playing, non-swearing conchies* who seldom even dress in the correct way and haven't even got any uniforms smarter than battledress.'

---

\* Conscientious objectors.

The advent of UNRRA promised a fillip to the liberal line promoted by Corsellis and other aid workers. The British Zone director of UNRRA, Australian Major C.D. Chapman, told staff they were there in an advisory capacity and the refugees should run their own groups and elect their own leaders. 'These people have faced great disaster and must be given hope, courage and retraining to face normal life again. They must be helped to help themselves as rapidly as possible,' he declared.

UNRRA had a more sinister side as far as the refugees were concerned. As a UN body, the Soviets had influence over its activities. The Kremlin was not interested in making life agreeable for anti-Communist refugees spreading views hostile to their home regimes. From the Soviet point of view, it would be better if they all went home, where they would come under the same controls as their compatriots. So despite the liberal words of Major Chapman, UNRRA also had a hard edge. They wanted not just to help, but also to persuade their charges to return.

UNRRA finally took over just before Christmas 1945, but the confusion if anything increased, and nothing much came of the major's talk of encouragement and retraining. Corsellis, who transferred to the new body, found that the refugees flocked to his office when they wanted something done, since the new team took an inordinate time to settle in. None of the UNRRA officials spoke the refugees' languages and there were hardly any interpreters.

'This morning, I had a two-hour conference on housing with a Slovene who only spoke Serbo-Croat and Italian, a Latvian who only spoke Russian and German (plus their mother tongues) and a Russian who only spoke Russian and Serbo-Croat, and while I understand most of what is said in Serbo-Croat I can only speak satisfactorily in Italian and German,' Corsellis wrote to his mother. He did not say whether anybody got housed as a result, but Corsellis was later to head a language school back in England.

He was not impressed with the new UNRRA people and felt the staff was becoming unnecessarily large:

> The frustrating thing is that there are plenty of honest and able men in the camp, often considerably more capable than the UNRRA personnel. The latter are in fact in some cases doing damage by interfering tactlessly in well-established departments. Surprisingly pervasive in UNRRA is the idea that refugees are inferior beings that can be patronised or ordered about, while in many cases they are superior to UNRRA personnel in capability, intelligence, manners, civilisation and honesty and morality.

He noticed how readily British and American personnel gave vent to instinctive anti-Catholic sentiments. After a bit, however, a few jewels emerged, including nurse Dara Lieven, described by Corsellis to his mother as an aristocratic Russian émigrée, trained at St Thomas's Hospital in London, with a superb Slav face. Also a female American Chief Welfare Officer for the British Zone, whom 'I took under my wing in fatherly fashion'.

Best of all was a new camp director, a tall British Air Force Group Captain called Ryder Young, who in 1938 piloted the plane carrying British Prime Minister Neville Chamberlain to his appeasement meeting with Hitler in Munich. Ryder Young won the affection of the refugees through his warmth, joviality and kindness. Director Bajuk remembered him thus:

> He was a bachelor, and all heart... He really was a tall man. You saw him immediately, walking with long strides between the barracks, always kind and with a smile. Little Dr Meršol was dancing around him like a little dwarf, because Young was always turning round and Meršol wanted to be on his left side. Raising his head, he was always on the lookout for the camp inmates, returning greetings and greeting them. He liked us Slovenes especially because he said we were so clean, conscientious in our work and polite. The grammar school was especially close to his heart. How often he just stuck his head round my door, greeted me, closed the door and walked off: but always smiling like a naughty boy.

Val Meršol, then a schoolboy, thought likewise: 'Ryder Young was a remarkable, warm, caring man. He helped people with extra food, housing problems and finding work. In the English classes, he taught us how to pronounce "th" and he started the scouts, which were unknown to us Slovenes.'

One-legged farmer Franc Cenkar remembers him more directly. Franc lost his leg fighting with the *domobranci* and was treated in Lienz hospital. On release he was sent to the refugee camp, but was told by the receptionist the camp was full and he could not come in:

> I go out and cry, and Valentin Meršol and that English officer Ryder Young come up. Meršol asks me, 'What happened with you?' and I cry: 'I've got nothing. I've crutches, I don't have a leg, I've got no place to go.' He asks me what happened and I tell him: 'They don't want to take me in.' That English officer says: 'Go back right away.' I go back and that English officer says to [the receptionist] Pleško: 'Take him in right away,' and he takes me in.

Ryder Young arrived on 10 May 1946, and by 4 September he was dead, killed in a car crash after a heart attack. The Slovene scout troop he fostered turned out en bloc at his funeral in Klagenfurt. Corsellis wrote to his mother:

> The DPs were deeply distressed, as he had worked wholeheartedly for and was much loved by them. I got to know him very closely. The

relationship was peculiarly close, with him a senior RAF officer of 32 years in the service and me a very youthful and junior camp worker. From the start he recognised my adequate experience in camp administration and specialised knowledge, and time and again would change a decision if he saw I was unhappy. I was continually amazed at the readiness with which he'd take advice from his juniors; at the same time he held very decided views and had strong principles.

Former scout Jože Tomažević, now in Buenos Aires, commented: 'The British betrayed our army and I was suspicious of them. But then I saw John Corsellis and Ryder Young were not such people. They both really tried to help us, and put a lot of effort into organisation on our behalf.'

Things, however, were taking a turn for the worse. Easter 1946 gave cause for another fervent entry in Pernišek's diary:

The priests' choir sings psalms while the people pray and await the moment of the Resurrection. The Risen Saviour starts on his first triumphant procession through the camp. Paths which for many years heard only the harsh tramp of soldiers, the clatter of their weapons, curses and profanity, today resound with mighty hymns of Christian triumph. The magnificent Easter procession encircles the camp with devout prayer, harmonious chimes and victorious Slovene Easter hymns. Surely for the first time today the Lord Jesus walks through this camp in majesty.

Six days later, armed British soldiers surrounded the barracks; Pernišek found a gun pointing at him and an announcement was made over loudspeakers that military police were searching for 'war criminals, political criminals, collaborators, quislings and SS'. They searched in cupboards, roof spaces and underneath floorboards. Pernišek, grimly recalling Italian raids in Ljubljana, was hauled off for interrogation by the Field Security Service (FSS), the British military and political police. As a member of the camp committee, he was questioned for 15 days.

The FSS was responsible for security in areas under British Military Government, which included the camps even though they were administered by UNRRA. It was considered to be under Communist influence. The war had brought an upswing of left-wing sentiment in Britain, and some British soldiers were attracted by the political system of their wartime Allies. It is now known that Churchill's decision to switch support to Tito during the war was partly based on deliberately distorted reports about Yugoslavia from Captain James Klugman, a British officer in Cairo who was an under-cover Communist agent.[1] The FSS had friendly contacts with local Austrian Communists.

Also, there were a number of Jews of various nationalities with the FSS, brought in as linguists familiar with conditions on the continent.

At that time, a fair number of Jews held leading positions in Communist parties of the Soviet Union and Eastern Europe. For a Catholic Central European such as Pernišek, the link between Jews and Communists was all too easy to make and aroused fears and prejudices. His diaries recounting his brushes with the FSS made clear he did not think Jews were on his side. This may well have been true, since the Slovene refugees were associated with an armed force that had collaborated with the Germans.

At first, he was assured he would be back in two days, but the questioning was drawn out and he had to share a cell with haughty German SS officers and a sentimental, womanising Austrian doctor. He feared the interrogation was a prelude to being sent back to Slovenia, but a young air force sergeant promised he would not be repatriated, and told him he was not a prisoner, just being kept in a cell because there was nowhere else to put him. Pernišek relaxed because the conversation turned into an interesting discussion. They wanted to know about Catholic activities in Slovenia during the war, the internal organisation of the camps and why people did not want to return:

> *11 May 1946*. The interrogation finished. One soldier on his own questioned me calmly and politely for 11 hours today and yesterday. He kept on apologising and asking me to be patient because he'd so many questions. He gave me cigarettes and liqueur. I gather from the many questions on our organisation and camp institutions and the relationship between our priests and the people, that the Yugoslav government has been accusing us of having our own rebel federal government and organising our own army.

He was freed and returned to the camp, not quite knowing what to make of it. He had been treated politely and felt half flattered by compliments and the interest shown. But it was clear the British were looking for supposed war criminals on behalf of the Yugoslavs. This cooperation would be formalised later in a Bled Agreement between the two countries. It was a none too friendly game of cat and mouse – and once more at the hands of the British. Pernišek wrote: 'Prison has exhausted me and badly affected my nerves.'

Six weeks later, the screw was given another turn. Two UNRRA officers conducted lengthy interviews with the Slovene camp leaders about repatriation. Pernišek was involved again:

> Both spoke most politely and calmly … they wanted to know our views on the possibility of repatriating Slovene refugees. Why didn't we go home and what were the obstacles – political, economic or religious? They understood the intelligentsia couldn't go back, but not why the small people, farmers and workers couldn't; they certainly weren't politically active and didn't present a danger to the present regime. And why didn't the old people go? Would there be any sense

in a commission of UNRRA staff and refugees visiting Yugoslavia and calling on refugees who'd returned to find out whether they'd been left in peace, how they'd been received and the present situation? Were we carrying out propaganda against repatriation, and aware of the difficulties we'd face as emigrants? UNRRA has no money to pay for transport. Where would we get money for travel? They told us UNRRA didn't have long to live and a new body to look after refugees was a long way off.

On the one hand, the visitors were urging the refugees to think realistically about their situation. But they were also making clear that repatriation was now a priority issue, taking precedence over more liberal concerns such as welfare. 'No money to pay' represented a veiled threat: better to choose the cheap solution of going home rather than aspire to emigrate abroad.

Ten days later, on 12 July 1946, an UNRRA Repatriation Commission led by a Hungarian Dr Bedo turned up, again trying to find war criminals. The refugees experienced this as harassment, but it was not an unusual process for the times. This was the epoch of the Nuremberg War Crimes Tribunals, and public opinion was primed to expect justice and punishment for the wartime guilty.

Dr Bedo did not over-step the mark, however. Again, it was more a scare than a real threat. Pernišek was among those summoned: 'Everyone above 18 has to report to the commission. Dr Bedo asked my wife and me whether we believed in God and Jesus crucified. When we answered yes, he asked if we'd been members of any German organisation and if we'd fought against the British and Americans. When we answered no, he gave us a certificate to that effect and the matter was ended.'

A Soviet Mission turned up in Klagenfurt asking for records about Russian refugees, who became terrified because they were afraid of repatriation or reprisals against their families at home. John Corsellis and his camp director felt the Soviet Mission had no business poking around in these records, and eventually reached a satisfactory compromise with a Colonel Hall, second-in-command of the Displaced Persons Section of the British Military Government, who had taken a fatherly liking to the young pacifist.

In mid-July 1946, Pernišek recorded another enormous religious celebration by the Slovene refugees:

> The Slovene camp community moves slowly in a penitential procession praying aloud against background music of chirping swallows and quails. A simple wooden cross made by a peasant is carried at the head of the procession, followed by the elementary and middle school children, their faces glowing like red poppies in contentment and delight. After them march the young lads and men with bowed heads and rosaries held in their hands, praying devoutly. Everyone

sends his own prayer to heaven, but all are united in one petition: Good God, shorten our days of exile, send Your holy angels to take us home! But if it's not Your will, then let it be what You will. We are in Your hands, we trust in Your Goodness, Providence and Wisdom.

The girls and women follow a banner of Our Lady of Fatima and sing Marian hymns. All along the road, huge stacks of wheat sheaves placed in the fields serve as silent sentinel witnesses to the procession. On the hill by the chapel of Our Lady the people come to a halt and gather round an outdoor altar under the blue sky to hear the Mass. In front of the picture of Our Lady the Slovene camp community renews its promise to live a good life, to honour, and abstain from manual work on holy days, not to swear or use foul language, and to be temperate in food and drink. In this way the community hopes to obtain from the Lord the graces needed for such a life and also the possibility to return to their homeland freed from Communist terror and injustice.

In spite of this act of penitence, food rations deteriorated drastically, falling to around 400 calories a day, not much above starvation level. Much of Europe was short of food at this time. But under the military directly after the war's end, the daily minimum in the camps had never fallen below 850. By comparison, the average German diet during the war until the winter of 1944–1945 was never less than 1,800 calories.[2] According to Maria Suhadolc, now living in Canada, she and other teenage girls stopped having periods because of malnutrition. They did not return until they reached their countries of emigration. Breakfast for adults and children alike consisted of a mushy coffee mixture. At midday, there was a watery soup with a few morsels of macaroni, beans or potato or meat fibres, followed by unsweetened coffee for supper. A loaf of bread was shared between five or ten people.

The Slovenes concluded this was a deliberate strategy to persuade them to return. Some indeed did go, saying if they had to die they preferred to be buried at home. But the growing solidarity of the Slovene refugees in the face of adversity also pulled in the opposite direction. Some children felt so safe and fulfilled in the camp community that they refused to accompany their parents returning home. Pernišek gave vent to growing bitterness and despair:

Day after day we're disillusioned anew by the allies. In the place of compassion and respect for human rights we see the selfishness of petty tradesmen. They'd sell their own souls to the devil for profit, so why not their friends and allies? All the talk of humanitarian ideals is a cover-up for loathsome selfishness. And we risked our lives for these allies, lost everything we had and are now to be robbed of our basic human rights...

We're often overwhelmed by despair. Dear Lord, in the midst of all disappointments help me to continue to trust in Your limitless love, faithfulness and justice. With Your grace prevent me from sinking into despair. I ask this not only for myself but for all my fellow Slovenes. I ask that You don't count it as a sin when I feel full of doubts and despair.

Either the Lord answered his prayer, or writing the last paragraph helped Pernišek pull himself together. He co-authored a petition to UNRRA headquarters in Klagenfurt laying out the refugees' forward-looking strategy. They made it clear that the leadership was not against refugees returning home, and encouraged this for those who were old, ill or had no reason to fear retribution. However, they offered for inspection scores of letters from people who returned and wrote to warn against doing likewise. The petition asked that all Slovenes in Austria and Italy be allowed to emigrate as a group.

The camp director forwarded the petition to UNRRA headquarters with a covering letter drafted by John Corsellis, which confirmed that the refugees were not indulging in any widespread agitation against returning home. Although the Slovenes still had many tough fights ahead of them, what they asked for in the petition they eventually achieved. They did not know it, but they were on a winning path.

When Lieutenant-General Sir James Steele, Commander-in-Chief of the British Military Government in Austria, made a tour of inspection, Corsellis latched on to the only non-uniformed character in his retinue. He chattered away to the young Foreign Office official for 20 minutes about repatriation and migration. Years later, he received from his visitor, by that time Sir Michael Cullis, a copy of a 19-page 'Report on Visit to Displaced Persons Camps in British Zone of Austria' drafted on his return.

Cullis noticed that in the Lienz camp the Slovenes, Croats and Serbs kept strictly separate. Anticipating the break-up of Yugoslavia 45 years later, he observed 'striking evidence of the lack of sympathy existing between the constituent nationalities of Yugoslavia whom even their recent misfortunes do not seem to have brought together into anything like harmony'.

Cullis took the view that, despite all their misadventures, the refugees appreciated that they were being taken care of. He recommended that this potentially pro-British and pro-Western element should not be squandered. They should not be abandoned to their fate in return for a hypothetical political advantage in terms of good relations with Tito. The British should retain responsibility for them, since the Austrian Government, with the Soviets still occupying part of their land, could not be trusted to resist outside pressure to hand dissidents over to claimant countries.

His report was useful to the Slovenes since it supported their status as a community and portrayed them as assets rather than nuisances. It was a counter-balance to hard-line attempts to determine their fate through interrogations, detentions and hardship.

John Corsellis, besides looking after camp admissions, registrations, housing, clothing, welfare, supplies of cotton and smoothing over other people's quarrels, started lobbying on behalf of the Slovenes. In spring 1947, just before returning to England for good, he sent Cullis a full-scale report. He copied it to the Foreign Office, the headquarters of UNRRA, the International Refugee Organisation (IRO), the DP branch of the British High Commission in Austria, and Members of Parliament in London who had shown an interest in refugees, including Winston Churchill, who acknowledged receipt. Corsellis wrote:

> The number of refugees that will return to Yugoslavia in the near future is dependent on political developments there: the number that will require resettlement cannot therefore be assessed immediately with any confidence. Their conduct in and out of DP camps during the last 21 months has however shown clearly that given the minimum of outside help they are more than capable and ready to help themselves, and would form excellent immigrants to any country offering them reasonable conditions of entry.

Cullis told Corsellis his memo was useful in negotiations on Displaced Persons with the Soviets, who had been holding out against an Austrian Treaty because of the presence of anti-Communist refugees. Major Blake, military attaché to the Commander-in-Chief of British Forces in Austria, acknowledged: 'As there are likely to be DP developments in the near future it may be of great value.'

But for Pernišek, All Saints' Day 1946 brought renewed misery:

> It's a grey day. Mist covers the valley and it drizzles all day. My thoughts are at home. My father is alone in the cemetery of St Peter in Radece. There's no one to light a candle on his grave. My mother wrote that she won't visit it until I return home. So I don't know if she'll ever see it again.

> Jože, unhappy brother, where are you resting and sleeping your eternal sleep? Is your grave in the cold waters of the Sava, or do you await the day of resurrection somewhere in our beautiful but blood-soaked Slovene soil? My heart today feels a profound grief. But you have already passed through your own suffering: God knows what's waiting for us, what dreadful trials and suffering God is preparing for us. Fear of the unknown dark future is worse than death itself.

Before Corsellis left, the refugees suffered a new blow: UNRRA decided in autumn 1946 to close down the flourishing Lienz camp and move the occupants to Spittal, 60 kilometres to the southeast. Numbers of refugees were by this time declining in Austria, and it was logical for

UNRRA to reduce the number of camps and economise on transport by moving refugees closer to headquarters in Klagenfurt. However, the move caused no end of trouble.

Corsellis was appalled, writing in his letter-diary:

*10 November 1946.* Today is Monday. On Thursday, Friday and Saturday we're sending our 2,000 Yugoslavs by train to a camp three hours' journey away. The organisational side of the transfer is exacting and the director is excelling himself in stupidity. The DPs are being transported with all luggage, furniture, stoves, beds etc., 700 at a time, in 20 covered and 20 open goods wagons over three days and will arrive at the other camp in the dark. There is a 50% chance at least that it will rain or snow and we will have little over six hours each day to load the train, which will be no small feat, demanding careful organisation and all our transport resources...

Good planning will mean a lot to these 2,000 wretches – it is anyhow criminal to move them in November – and the least we can do is avoid as much suffering as possible. If properly packed, there will be room for all the little furniture they have, but if loading is done in a hurry the family may have to leave behind the one small cupboard they have had up till now.

As it was, the weather held, but the camp which awaited them in Spittal was shabbier than the one they left in Lienz – lavatories and washrooms were outside rather than in the barracks. The rooms were cold, they were riddled with bed bugs, and there was so little wood they had to burn pinecones. Pernišek wrote:

For the time being we're crammed ten to a room and it's difficult to put things in order in such a crush. I'm walking by the railway line; luggage and furniture are scattered around in all directions. To find one's belongings one has to rummage everywhere; we won't be looking for our bones at the day of judgment as eagerly as we're searching today...

The food is poor here as well: this morning unsweetened black coffee with a little bread of very poor quality...At midday we get a soup which is appetizing but thin and the portions are small. The same in the evening. There are no special supplements and they don't issue any tinned food.

The Slovene leaders of the Lienz camp paid a courtesy call on the UNRRA camp director at Spittal. He requested that they refrain from political activity, criticism of the situation in whatever country, and harassment or resentment towards those who decided to return home. They departed promising good behaviour, though it was a vain hope that the issues would go away.

They ran into trouble with their compatriots in Spittal. Lienz was the largest camp, and so the grammar school and most of the intelligentsia and community leaders went there. This had its merits, but it led under-privileged Spittal to resent 'their lordships' of Lienz. Now the tables were turned, and the Lienz group were the poor relations in Spittal.

The move almost torpedoed the grammar school. The Lienz director allowed the refugees to transport with them the chapel, two scout huts and one barrack large enough for the school and accommodation for teachers. No sooner had the dismounted planking been stacked in a dark place in Spittal than the local Slovene refugees made off with it to burn in stoves and re-furbish their own miserable quarters. The Lienz arrivals were allotted ten more cubic metres of wood, but that was stolen too. Eventually, the school started up again in an abandoned Russian stable at the far end of the camp.

Then the Australian camp director told Director Bajuk that grammar school studies took too long and they should just teach the pupils to read and write and then send them out to work. Many of the Slovenes' flourishing careers in countries of emigration could have been killed off if this had gone through. The camp welfare officer, Miss Michell, ordered Director Bajuk to produce overnight a plan for a secondary technical school in place of his beloved grammar school. He had other ideas: 'I said I would need three days and she conceded this. At the teachers' meeting we decided to play a trick, sketching an elaborate plan which covered everything but said nothing. She read it through, her face shone and she nodded, "Excellent, excellent." On 29 January the new school opened. We only altered the time-table a little to make room for a new subject, descriptive geometry, for two hours a week.' Within a few weeks, the grammar school curriculum was back in full force.

The last wretched remnants to move from Lienz were a group of Russian émigrés, including old people, sick, children and mothers with newborn babies, who were sent off in the depths of winter. Corsellis, who accompanied them wrapped in a blanket in a freezing cattle wagon, sent the following complaint to his mother for the New Year:

> On 16th December our last train-load of people left the camp. Over 400 people, 60 of them over sixty years old, Russian émigrés, weak and miserable, had to spend 11 hours exposed, either in the open or in cattle trucks. We had a stove in each truck, but it only heated eight of the 30 people. And they knew they were going to very bad accommodation – they were to be sent to a camp with enough room, but then Klagenfurt changed its mind and they went where the Slovenes went, which was full. So they got the very leavings.

> It certainly made one bitter – this was UNRRA's idea of 'relief and rehabilitation.' It was criminal transferring the people gratuitously

in mid-winter. The official reason was that UNRRA had no money left and had to cut down camps to economise and reduce staff. But HQ should have tumbled to that in the autumn or, if they could not see beyond the ends of their noses, should have waited till the spring. The move was made largely from the cynical point of view that the DPs were so comfortable they didn't want to go home and a little discomfort would do them good and encourage repatriation. I'd like to make someone from HQ live in a DP camp for even a fortnight under average DP rations and conditions. Then perhaps they'd revise their ideas of DPs living in comfort.

Their courage and patience continually astonishes me. Everyone must have spent hours of work getting their rooms liveable-in for the winter, saving a reserve of food and fuel. And then just at the start of the most difficult three months of the year they were uprooted and dumped in a camp, of which the best rooms were worse than the worst in Lienz; and dumped when it was too late to do much in the way of preparation against the cold. And still they remain not too uncheerful.

There were about two feet of snow on the ground on the 16th. We left Lienz at 1.30 in the afternoon and were told we'd get to Spittal soon after 6 – we arrived eventually at 10, 8–1/2 hours for a trip that should take 1–1/2 hours. It wasn't the fault of the Austrians, but of HQ, who decided we were to be taken not by a special train, but hitched to the daily goods train. At every station we stopped and the engine was uncoupled and did half an hour's shunting. The old, women and children meanwhile were shivering, taking turns round the stoves until the coal ran out. I was well dressed, swathed myself in a blanket and was reasonably comfortable, except that one of my feet froze and, stamp as I did, I could not restore circulation. Eventually everything was unloaded from the train and in the camp by two next morning.

Pernišek, together with his family and a priest, toured the down-at-heel barracks on Christmas Eve 1946, blessing rooms, sprinkling holy water and swinging a burning censer. 'Then the good Mr Corsellis came to wish us a happy Christmas. This lad doesn't forget us. He told us Lienz had been the best-run camp not only in the British zone, but in the whole of Austria, and they closed it down so that the refugees shouldn't have too comfortable a life.'

As for the good Mr Corsellis, he spent Christmas with three rearguard Displaced Persons in Lienz, eating pork and tinned turkey, drinking a lone bottle of spumante and playing games that made their sides ache with laughing. On New Year's Eve Pernišek looked back on 1946. By now they had been more than 18 months away from home:

1946 brought us many sufferings and disappointments. We watched UNRRA change from a humanitarian aid agency into an institution for pushing repatriation. They frustrated our initiatives and industriousness whenever they could. They starved us and dislodged us from a well-organised camp where some people could have achieved self-sufficiency in caring for their families. But the order was to persuade as many as possible to return home. This fury for repatriation claimed a victim on 24 December: Cerar, the father of four young children, caught a severe chill in his unheated and otherwise totally inadequate room and died of an infection of the inner ear brought on by hypothermia. When people asked the supply officer why there wasn't enough fuel for heating he answered briskly, 'And what are you Yugoslavs doing staying on here anyway?'

To herald the New Year of 1947 the refugees sang the Triglav March celebrating their land's highest mountain, and shivered as freezing storms swept down from the mountains on their under-heated camp. Pernišek made a New Year's wish:

O dear family home, you are the one real happiness in our life! A man recognises your priceless worth when he loses you! I desire nothing more than to possess the smallest and humblest home of my own. Every day I pray God to grant me this, the most coveted good on this earth. I'll forgo my profession and take on hard labour, so as to become a free man again delivered from this appalling welfare! I've enough of this always-reproachful charity, reminding me I'm a DP, a being without rights, a number: DP A 01533419.

By the end of January, he detected 'a tiny, tiny shining and warm ray of hope lit up the cold darkness.' Pernišek, as one of the camp committee, knew that contacts to enable the whole block of refugees to emigrate to Argentina were beginning to bear fruit.

Back in the first days of Viktring, the Slovene camp committee had established links with Dr Miha Krek, former leader of the Catholic Slovene People's Party and Vice-Premier of the Yugoslav Royal Government in Exile in London, who now headed a Yugoslav Welfare Society in Rome, working closely with the Vatican. A later Slovene account[3] described how Dr Krek set about finding a new home for his stranded compatriots:

The agonising days after the Viktring tragedy left our people ready to go anywhere. Our eyes were turned towards Rome and Dr Krek. He was planning, searching for contacts, lobbying and sending letters in every direction, convinced we had to find a new homeland where we could earn an existence through our own efforts, staying together to preserve our way of life towards the day we returned home.

He scanned the atlas and explored the situation in: <u>Australia</u> – their bishops in Rome promised to do everything for us to emigrate there, but having got nowhere with the problem of transport after three whole years the situation was now urgent. <u>South Africa</u> – a rich and cultured country, but only accepting skilled personnel. <u>France</u> – not willing to consider a single refugee in spite of unpopulated areas in its south. <u>Ecuador</u> – obviously rich, but culturally and economically underdeveloped and only offering uncultivated land. How would we live before the fields were tilled for the first time? <u>Peru</u> – no one is showing any interest in emigration, the same for <u>Brazil</u>. <u>Venezuela</u> – prepared to accept refugees but would send them to climatically difficult regions and pay them poorly. There remained <u>Argentina</u>, the country most ready to receive refugees, understand their situation and offer the best conditions.

As luck had it, there was a Slovene priest in Argentina, Father Janez Hladnik, who was well connected and had travelled the length and breadth of the country. Krek appealed to Hladnik, but after several weeks of lobbying he was getting nowhere. Then, says Cirila Pernišek-Žužek, he came across a Slovene girl who worked for the sister-in-law of a minister. He obtained an interview with the minister, and a few days later he had an appointment with General Juan Peron, Argentina's dictator. Peron met him at the door to his office and said: 'I know about your problem. The Slovenes can all come. Here is my aide-de-camp. He will help you.'

That was the end of the interview and from then on all doors were open. Peron, a right-wing populist, was engaged in a battle for public opinion and power against the Communists. He was delighted at the prospect of receiving a group of immigrants who were Catholic, hard working, had large families and were anti-Communist. Whether out of political calculation or generosity, he asked for 10,000 to be sent without delay, including families and children. Trained workers would get jobs in industry and the rest should work on the land. Argentina took the old, the unemployable and the sick with no questions asked. No other government extended a welcome on anything approaching such a large scale.

A canvas of Slovene refugees in Italy and Austria showed 95% were interested. A Slovene Emigration Committee was set up in Rome to collect applications, compile a card index, provide movement papers and passports, negotiate visa procedures with Argentinian consulates and fund the journeys. These were all tall tasks. In the world immediately after World War II, travel for large groups of people was a ponderous and bureaucratic process. As Displaced Persons, the refugees had no rights, legal representation or money, and most had no personal documents. The Slovenes persuaded the Argentinians to reduce the number of documents required for visas from eight to three and to recognise the International Red Cross passport. They also arranged group movement permits – the first time this was done. Consular officials issued five visas a day. Eventually, the first list of 500 Slovenes was certified with the Direccion de Migraciones in Buenos Aires on 6 February 1947. The Inter-Governmental Committee for Refugees was approached for money, but turned the request down, apparently due to the influence of Tito representatives on it.

Dr Krek dispatched Slovene Father Jože Košiček to Buenos Aires to help Hladnik, who was struggling to cope single-handed. Košiček wrote a practical guide for the emigrants:

1. The Argentinian Government gave permission in principle for the settlement of 10,000 Slovenes in Argentina. This is to the merit of Mr Hladnik who has excellent connections with the Government and the Church authorities. Special permission was issued to 500 refugees in Italy to emigrate at once. As further lists arrive, others will receive permission.

2. The International Welfare Organisation, with which the American Catholics and the Vatican collaborate, can pay for the transport of the refugees, for the present only to South America.

3. Argentina is a very rich country. The climate is hot, but not insupportable. The fertility of the soil is three times better than in the Banat.* Everything can be sold. Those prepared to work cannot starve. The Government is looking for settlers. Do not worry about the payment of the assigned land. Should anyone be able to return home he will receive the money for the investments and work. People who ten years ago paid 10,000 pesos in instalments for land can sell it today for 40,000. No manure is needed. After lunch the farmers sleep here some hours. One cannot imagine how easy the work is. Certainly the first months will be bad. It will be necessary to plough fresh land. I am only afraid the refugees will not want to return home if the possibility arises. I regret that today there are no indications for return.

4. I know the great difficulties you have with the mail with Rome. Therefore you yourself should prepare everything necessary for emigration, lists of people who are unconditionally determined to go. Put them together by hundreds! Put first persons who are in direct danger there. The Allies want to solve the question of refugees in Italy first, and then will be your turn. Have everything prepared. Advise people who cannot decide on emigration to return home as soon as possible. If they think they will only go through purgatory, they should return. A special problem

---

*   The richest agricultural area of ex-Yugoslavia.

is the small number of bad people. Think carefully whether to take them with you.

5. I am concerned about the intelligentsia: there is no possibility they could all find jobs in their professions. Intelligentsia are in abundance in Argentina. There are 5,000 students in the medical faculty at Buenos Aires. Rich farmers – and that means all of them – are pushing their children to different schools and the countryside remains empty. The intelligentsia must be prepared for manual work, as must the students. If somebody has completed some exams, he has to repeat them in good Spanish language. They look with mistrust at foreigners, as scamps or people more diligent and capable than the general population.

6. Argentina is a Christian country although in many places morals and the practical Christian life are not very high. All evil – together with Communism – was brought into the country by foreigners.

7. Prices are high, wages also. There is no black market. There is a great demand for workers, especially masons. Today in the newspaper 'La Prensa' there are about 2,500 advertisements asking for workers and less than 100 offers. There is an especially large demand for cooks, housemaids, seamstresses etc., and foreigners are welcome.

8. We are now setting up a small office because Mr Hladnik, a saint and an extremely unselfish soul, cannot do everything. Ask your people to pray for him, because it will probably be due only to him if we in our misery get a modest home and a piece of bread.

So the funding was settled, but there was a problem over intellectuals. The camp leaders included former school inspectors, a newspaper owner and other academics. The Graz University students would soon be matriculating and hoping for careers corresponding to their qualifications, and that was far from assured.

Back in the camps, not everybody was happy that the Slovenes should sail off to Argentina. The regime in Yugoslavia did not want anti-Communist compatriots propagating hostile attitudes around the world. They were still pulling all the strings they could to have them sent home. On top of that, UNRRA really was running out of money, its funds ever more limited by a recalcitrant Soviet Union.

Delegation after delegation turned up to assess what was best for the refugees. A British parliamentary group came in February 1947, and the Slovene camp committee petitioned them for renewed guarantees that nobody would be sent back by force, and that Slovene refugees in Austria and Italy should be allowed to emigrate together as early as possible.

A month later a Yugoslav Repatriation Commission appeared consisting of a young major and a Yugoslav Professor Kunc, who went out of his way to be friendly, asking all the people whom he met what the Yugoslav government could do to attract more people home. Director Bajuk, indignant that they were interrupting school lessons with questions to the pupils, received them gruffly in his office: 'I gave them my point of view. I did not introduce myself, didn't offer my hand although they reached out with theirs. I stood tall behind my desk and did not move a pace. They wanted to be pleasant and obliging. I either answered their questions as briskly as possible or not at all. Several times I refused to answer and simply shrugged my shoulders instead of giving an answer. I declined everything by asserting that we have enough.'

When Professor Kunc questioned the operator of the camp printing press, the latter replied: 'You know what, Mr Professor? Open up the frontier! We'll go to Ljubelj [on the border] and our relatives will meet us there and we'll talk together. We'll see which direction the majority will choose: for Austria or Yugoslavia.' The Professor smiled wanly and moved on.

Major Chapman, chief of the UNRRA mission in Carinthia, spent a fortnight in Yugoslavia trying to see for himself what conditions were like. He wanted to visit 14 of the people in the camp who had returned to Slovenia but could not find any of them at home. On his return, he lectured the refugee leaders on their grim prospects if they did not return home, but faced undiminished scepticism.

By now, the refugees had the camp director, Jarvie, and his chief welfare officer, Miss Michell, on their side. The two officers were so pleased with the Slovenes' comportment during the British parliamentary delegation's visit that they had tears in their eyes when they thanked them, and Miss Michell said she wouldn't leave the Slovenes until she could see them happy again. Only a few weeks ago they had been trying to break up their grammar school.

At the beginning of March 1947, Jarvie was transferred and Miss Michell made redundant. The Yugoslav government had complained to UNRRA that Jarvie was an obstacle to repatriation. Once more, the Slovene refugees lined up in front of their barracks to say good-bye to officials who had become their friends. Only Director Bajuk disapproved: he suspected the pair of having an affair,* and he had the doors of the grammar school locked so that the pupils could not take part. As their jeep drove off, the Slovenes buried a sixth-form pupil from the grammar school who had died of tuberculosis.

John Corsellis was detailed to the camp's TB centre and came in for blustering from UNRRA's chief medical officer on a visit of inspection:

I started by explaining the difficulties of being dependent on the neighbouring camp for certain services and the very difficult

---

* On their return to Australia, they married, and for some time ran a reception camp for European refugee immigrants, many of them Slovenes.

supply situation, and Colonel Cottrell, interrupting me in mid-sentence, expressed the impression I was resigning myself to the difficulties, and if so he'd no use for me. His remark was pretty strongly worded and got my goat. I denied his assumption energetically and a little later, when he again cut in and complained he wasn't informed on what we were doing, I was able to counter-attack, producing my monthly report, which dealt clearly with the point and gave full information. Things cheered up then, and I found he appreciated people who stood up to him. The zone senior medical officer, my immediate chief, was clearly pleased at the colonel's discomfiture.

One of his tasks was to help TB patients resume activity to avert depression and emptiness that could delay recovery – occupational therapy. It was impossible to find a single welfare officer who was intellectual enough to make an impression on the educated, or practical enough to work with workers and farmers. He found a Latvian, a former senior Health Ministry official who was also a competent painter, to deal with the educated, while a Slovene who ran workshops producing nails and brushes concentrated on the others.

As spring came in 1947, a few more farmers returned to tend their fields in Slovenia and more families split up. Among them were the Oblak family – father, mother, daughter and six sons who had fled to Viktring in May 1945. A seventh son had died earlier fighting the Partisans. One of the six sons returned to the family farm in Slovenia and wrote saying he could not cope on his own and asking the rest to come back. The father, mother and four sons answered his call, leaving behind Anton, aged 22 and missing one eye lost fighting with the domobranci, and his sister, aged 15. The two of them stayed in the camps and later emigrated to Cleveland, USA.

Stane Snoj's father also went back, lured by a promise of housing, leaving his wife and son behind in the camp. Six months later, the father was sentenced to 20 years' imprisonment. Just before Stane emigrated to Argentina in 1948, he learned his father was dead. In 1990 the family obtained court papers showing he had been executed. Relating this 50 years later in Buenos Aires, Stane said: 'When my father went back to Slovenia, I felt as if I died.'

One who hesitated was Edvard Vračko, the judge, who departed on foot with his 16-year-old daughter in May 1945. Corsellis remembers him in the camp as a short man with a sharp nose and always several days of stubble, who was caring, articulate, and aggressive. Vračko left behind his wife, who was recovering from an operation, and two younger daughters, and now he was missing them. At the same time, he was a member of the Slovene camp committee, and they resented contacts he made with a Yugoslav Communist agent who hung around the camp. They themselves were accused of agitating against a return to Slovenia, but they felt he was doing the opposite, encouraging people to go home. Eventually they excluded him from their body. Vračko did not follow the others into emigration, and did not go back either, settling in Klagenfurt.

The refugees had arrived seemingly at a dead end. The Cold War was in full swing. They were afraid to go back, and the Yugoslav regime was obsessed with the presence of thousands of anti-Communists just across the frontier. The UN and the British were at their wits' end and ever tempted by the hope that the refugees would travel the 50 kilometres back to their homeland. A solution in Argentina seemed in the offing, but had tantalisingly failed to crystallise. The same old arguments were being brought out each time their future was broached. In the meantime, lives were slipping past in no man's land.

John Corsellis noted in his letter-diary that the endless camp life was taking its toll on relationships among the refugees, who were becoming ultra-sensitive, succumbing to jealousies, scandal-mongering and distrust. Director Bajuk's memoirs, while at times generous in praise, are also riddled with scornful comments.

Pernišek, similarly frustrated, summed up the prevailing gloom in his diary on 9 March 1947:

> Most discuss Argentina and prepare themselves for a long, long journey, but the boat isn't ready yet and God knows when it will be. Meanwhile we'll rot in the camp as the English won't let us leave Europe, but rather deport us home or carry us off somewhere in their Empire where again we'll be doomed to live in refugee camps. In what way have we sinned so grievously to deserve this fate? It's understandable the Germans should suffer. Be done by as they did! Yet the victors are interested in them, strive to get them on their side and might even fight for them! And they handle the Jews with kid gloves, even though the Jews detest them. And they want to provide the Balts with new, well-ordered lives as quickly as possible.

> It's only against us, who gave up everything for them, trusting them blindly and believing their promises, that they discriminate, scold and obstruct. It's true; it's only a few kilometres from here to our homes. That's why they urge us to return. Miss Lieven* only recently said no Yugoslavs will be allowed to emigrate across the ocean while there's a possibility a single one will go home. She is from HQ in Vienna and she certainly meant it.

---

* Dara Lieven, the 'aristocratic Russian émigrée' who had worked as a nurse at the camp in Lienz, had now transferred to the UNRRA HQ working on repatriation.

# 7 DARKNESS BEFORE DAWN

*I dreamed of a beautiful home and a happy family life, now only a brief struggle for survival and then the end.*

## March 1947–June 1949

So Pernišek went out to pick potatoes. The refugees were allowed to seek employment in the vicinity. There was not much to be found in the war-damaged economy around the camps. But it was better than sitting around hopelessly, and although money wages were rare, there were opportunities to supplement the meagre rations in the camps.

At first he went into the forests, gathering firewood, pine cones and dandelion leaves. But he felt he was just killing time by wandering the woods like a hungry wild animal, and decided to become a day-labourer on a farm belonging to Tangerner, an Austrian who had just returned from a prisoner-of-war camp and was assembling a polyglot crew of refugees to put his neglected fields in order. One of them, fellow Slovene Tone, who was a good-natured, experienced farm worker, told Pernišek: 'Don't be in too much of a hurry; whoever overworks as a day-labourer is a blockhead.' A Ukrainian ploughed with the horses, and Pernišek's wife did sewing. They were allowed to eat as much as they wanted, and townsman Pernišek was soon able to graduate from picking potatoes to handling horses and cattle. He wrote in his diary: 'I go home and sleep soundly. I feel better among cows and horses than among some of our people. I forget completely the troubles of camp life and feel really free, but when I leave the fields and catch sight of the camp I experience a pressure on my heart.'

When Tangerner's fields were back to normal, Pernišek moved on to farmer Guggenberg, who needed labourers to help with hoeing, cultivating and mowing. The farmer could only pay in food, since he had inherited the property with debt. Mowing the rich grass in the middle of June was hot and tiring work, leaving Perniŝek's fingers stiff and numb for days on end. He preferred leading the slow, heavy farm-horse, with Guggenberg tending the plough behind. But the food was wonderful:

> So all's well. Food more than enough, appetising and nourishing. Before we start work there's a wheat, rye and maize flour porridge boiled in milk. While it's warm the mistress of the house puts in large chunks of butter, and the butter melts all over and forms a lovely coating. The master prays and we all dig in. The porridge is thick; we cut it and put pieces into our mouths. It's delicious and sustaining, and I think of the slush in the camp and the morsel of bread made of anything except real flour.

> During the morning the mistress brings us lovely smoked ham, bread and cider. At midday there's vegetable or potato soup and ham dumplings made of bread. They're very tasty because they're full of crackling and as large as the cockroaches which creep around the fireplace. In the afternoon we've the same food as for the morning break, and in the evening maize cakes immersed in warm milk. The bread itself is flat and hard. The people in Tyrol don't grow much wheat so they use it very sparingly. The mistress only bakes bread once a fortnight and locks it up in a chest so it doesn't get eaten too quickly. We get meat or chicken often, and dried meat or mutton. At haymaking or the harvest season a lamb is sometimes sacrificed.

> Early each Saturday the mistress of the house fills my rucksack with food to take to the dairymaid up on the alp. The road is steep, the knapsack heavy. I enjoy the magnificent view of the valley below. Breathless, I reach the farm on the alp and greet the dairymaid. Before midday I start off towards the valley carrying my rucksack of cheese and butter, lighter than the morning load. I reach the farmstead in record time, hand over the goods, bathe in the rivulet nearby, change my clothes and go to the station, very happy with a rucksack of food.

Perniŝek's ten-year-old daughter Cirila, thin as a rake, made a similar coup. Together with a friend, she asked farmers digging up potatoes in a field if they could buy some. The farmers filled their rucksacks up and refused payment. The girls proudly brought back enough to keep two families going through the winter.

While Perniŝek boosted his spirits and his belly with the best of Austrian farm cooking, John Corsellis was completing organisation of the treatment centre for tuberculosis. The unit comprised 11 barracks for up to 120 patients. The staff were specialised in TB, and it was equipped with X-ray, clinical and laboratory equipment not available in other camps. By early June 1947 it was running smoothly with a minimum of supervision, with the refugees providing most of the staff. That was one of Corsellis' main objectives: to prove that they were capable of administering themselves. It was also his swansong.

UNRRA finally ran out of money and support. Refugee care was taken over by a new International Refugee Organisation (IRO), later to become the UN High Commission for Refugees (UNHCR). But it was in its infancy, and Western powers were struggling to force through its creation in the face of Soviet opposition. So the occupying British Army resumed responsibility for the camps in July 1947. This meant John Corsellis' work came to an end. The Friends Ambulance Unit, with which he had first come to Austria, and his subsequent employer, UNRRA, were disbanded. He headed home and the Slovenes lost a champion.

Another blow struck. The Labour government in Britain signed an agreement with the Yugoslav government in the Slovene resort of Bled responding to the Tito government's pressure to lay hands on Yugoslav nationals considered as war criminals, traitors or collaborators. This formalisation of existing cooperation terrified the Slovene refugees. Wild rumours swept through the camp. An Austrian newspaper, *Die Neue Zeit*, reported they would be repatriated shortly. A few days later, the Vienna newspaper *Welt-Presse* denied it. Father Blatnik said he had been told by a British Field Security Service sergeant that 'now a wild hunt is beginning...for teachers, doctors, priests and intelligentsia'. A refugee woman claimed a Yugoslav agent told her she should return to Slovenia immediately as 'in this camp you'll see terrible things in a few days'.

Although the November gloom was making for cold, damp nights, many of the men started sleeping outside the camp, in barns of friendly farmers or in the forests. They had good reason to, since the British were once again hunting down individuals to interrogate. The British Field Security Service (FSS) turned up looking for elderly newspaper editor Franc Kremžar. It was threatening, but had a comic side as well. According to several Slovenes involved, John Corsellis had contacts among the British police and, while he was still there, he tipped refugee leaders off about imminent raids. Kremžar had been pre-warned in this case too, and he was not at home. When the armed soldiers entered the barrack where he lived, they barged by mistake into the next-door cubicle inhabited by the Pernišek family. The soldiers became embarrassed as only the British can, and there were many exclamations of 'Sorry! Sorry! What nice children you have. *Sorry!*', and they departed empty-handed.

A few weeks later the FSS were back again looking for Kremžar. They had him called to the kitchen to fetch his ration card and waited for him on the road outside. The ruse did not work: Kremžar and his friend Pernišek were watching from a hillside above. Another made a hideaway with a table and chair underneath the stage of the camp theatre. The Slovenes were wising up to the game of cat and mouse.

Kremžar had by this time smuggled his 18-year-old son Marko out of Slovenia. Marko, a *domobranec*, was sent back to Slovenia on 27 May 1945. Two of his brothers had already died at the hands of the Partisans during the war. Kremžar senior was an editor on the daily *Slovenec* before the war. During the war he edited the *Domoljub* weekly. Its editorial policy was decided by the Italians and Germans, and any Slovene holding a senior position on it was deemed a collaborator by the Communists. More importantly, he was President of the non-Communist Slovene National Parliament, which met only once, on 3 May 1945.

Marko was held first in Kranj and then for two months in Šentvid near Ljubljana, where he watched fellow-prisoners starve and be taken away for execution. Despite having a prominent Catholic father, Marko was spared from execution in Kočevski Rog because he was only 17 when he joined the *domobranci*. However, he was put on a mass trial in March 1946, and sent to a youth re-education centre.

He was allowed to study, and as a result made contact with somebody who brought him a letter from his father in the Austrian refugee camp. 'I absconded and took a train on 27 October 1946. It was a dangerous journey, but I had a lot of luck. As this was Election Day there were no controls on the train. I rendezvoused with a clandestine courier, who took me over the mountains to rejoin my family in Austria,' said Marko.

The Bled Agreement sounded menacing. Yugoslav government officials, together with international representatives from a Special Commission in Vienna, could interrogate any Yugoslav refugees they wanted. The declared purpose was to procure information concerning organisations of Yugoslavs opposed to the interests of the UN and the repatriation of refugees. In practice, the Yugoslavs were after their political enemies, and the British government was ready to go along with them – to a certain extent. It defined its policy thus:

> The British Government will move to Germany all Yugoslavs in the camps suspected of having actively assisted the enemy during the war, or of being members of organisations trying to overthrow by force of arms the government of their native country; or who are trying to dissuade their compatriots from returning home. It will hand over all Yugoslavs against whom the Yugoslav government prepares authenticated cases of active and deliberate collaboration with Axis forces where established prima facie. But if a *prima facie* case has not been established, the individual will be released.

So mere suspicion of such deeds would lead to transfer to Germany, and prima facie evidence of active and deliberate collaboration during the war would lead to forced repatriation, trial by a people's court and most probably execution. It all depended how the British were to interpret 'prima facie'. This was the procedure for establishing whether there was enough preliminary evidence to bring a case to court. With some justification, the British considered the practice provided strong safeguards against wrongful prosecution. The Slovene refugees, still traumatised by the 1945 deceit of the British, had little confidence that they were set on anything but betraying them once again. As Pernišek put it: 'Naturally enough our people in and outside the camps were terrified of the deal. We are of no account, rubbish in the foreigners' backyard which they want to clean up. This constant pressure to return home was bad enough so far. Now it'll be intensified. We'll be starved even more: more discrimination, disdain and oppression.'

However, the repatriation of the *domobranci* took place in the immediate aftermath of a brutal war. Since June 1945, scarcely anybody had been forced to go back. The Bled Agreement would be a test to see how fair British justice could be. The British government set up a commission to fulfil its side of the agreement. Its head was a person calculated to confirm the worst suspicions of the Slovene Catholics – Brigadier Fitzroy Maclean, the liaison officer parachuted into Yugoslavia in 1943 to cooperate with Tito's Communist Partisans. He had influenced Churchill's decision to abandon rival guerrilla leader Dragoljub Mihailović and build up the strength of the Partisans with arms and supplies. Mihailović led the Chetniks, who waged resistance with the aim of restoring the monarchy. Although Maclean did warn Churchill that Tito was likely to install a dictatorial Communist regime, to most of the Slovenes he was the instigator of the British alliance with their Communist enemies. Pernišek watched angrily when he appeared in the camp:

> The well-known Major Maclean, the principal British liaison officer with Tito's Partisans during the war, speaks Serbo-Croat and is asking where and who are the *domobranci* and the Chetniks. He comes across as an absolute cynic, going round the camp hunting young lads and men and asking if they were with the *domobranci*. When they say no, he asks if they are anti-Communists; when they say yes, he asks why they didn't join the *domobranci*. The man's a cad.

> ... Then three weeks later...

> Maclean is back asking where the *domobranci* are. Why does this interest him so much? If anyone knows where they are, he does. Can't he leave the dead in peace? Or rather, is his conscience pricking him?

> ... A month later Pernišek himself was questioned...

> My turn to be interrogated by the Maclean Commission, by a civilian who seemed a decent sort of fellow and spoke poor Serbo-Croat.

'Your surname and Christian names?' I give them.

'Do you have any document?' I show them. He can't believe I've so many, because most people have none.

'Did you live all the time at your birthplace?' I say no, because I studied at various places and lived longest in Ljubljana. I show him my Ljubljana municipal identity card.

'Did you have a job in Ljubljana? Where?' I show him my certificate of appointment at OUZD* and of my professional examination.

'Was OUZD a German agency?' I answer briefly no.

'Are you married?' I show him my marriage certificate.

'Any children?' I show him both children's birth certificates.

'Where do you plan to emigrate?'

'To England.' He winces but says nothing.

'Did you serve in the Yugoslav Army?'

'Yes.'

'Were you called up? Where? Became a POW?'†

'I was called up at Slavonski Brod, but I wasn't made a POW.'

'Do you have relatives at home?'

'I've a mother and sister in Ljubljana.'

'Did anyone threaten you?'

'Personally, no. But in general, yes, like everyone else.'

'Are you in contact with your mother and sister?'

'We write to each other, but that's the only contact.'

'Are they happy at home?'

---

*   Slovene social security organisation for workers.
†   Prisoner of war.

'My mother was put in prison, they ransacked the flat. They shot her son, took everything from my mother and my sister, and she had to do forced labour for very many months. I think they're not happy in view of all they had to undergo.'

He promised I'd get a certificate and the result of the interrogation. We rose and bowed to each other, and on 12th September this gentleman personally gave me a white card with Maclean's signature, so I'm white!

According to other witnesses, Maclean had more understanding for the Slovene refugees than it seemed. However, there was no let-up. As snow moved down the surrounding mountains, rumours surfaced that the refugees were about to be sent to Germany. It never happened, but on All Saints' Day, 1 November 1947, British police began rummaging through the camp registration office card index. Fearing a new raid, 150 of the men again slept out in the cold of the surrounding fields and woods for the next week. In early mornings, a long snake of frozen and bedraggled men crept cautiously back to the camp, led by a scout making signs to stop or advance as he checked whether soldiers or police were around. Yugoslav agents roamed the camp, stopping to chat, mixing veiled threats with hints at benefits awaiting people who returned home. A number of the refugees, wondering if there would ever be any other outcome, were grateful to grasp at the straws and welcomed the chance to talk. For others it was counter-productive, since they reckoned if they were pressured like this in the camps, it could only be worse at home. Few actually went back. Again, Pernišek was the voice of a growing animosity to all things British:

The Bled Agreement has started a severe war of nerves. The fears are justified because the British have committed injustices in the past: they've done this to us already, and they'll use hidden force in the future. What do a few thousand Yugoslav refugees matter if wiped out in Britain's interests? They didn't care about millions of Armenians, Boers, Indians and Red Indians. They're used to it. Every page of British history is marked with the blood and tears of subjugated and betrayed peoples.

This was strong stuff, prompted by the bitterness of the refugees on account of their wretched conditions. Nevertheless, two and a half years after the end of the war, the refugees were still waking up to armed British soldiers entering their barracks at dawn with lists of people for questioning. On 10 November 1947, the British Army raided the camp again, and the radio announced they were looking for 'British deserters, black marketers and some other people'. Pernišek was picked up for another bout of questioning. Then a greater disaster struck:

*11th November.* A last bomb has gone off. The camp director announced over the public address system that the Military Government has decided that 54 individuals (with their families) must leave the camp for St Martin camp at Villach.* They are suspected by the Yugoslav government of obstructing repatriation and spreading anti-repatriation propaganda. They listed everyone, and I was there with my family, so we must move to a worse place with greater insecurity. St Martin is a den of thieves and I'm not going! They'll banish us to Germany and then where?

The Bled Agreement is being put into effect. I'll seek refuge with the farmers; it won't be easy as there isn't any more work on the land and winter is arriving. God will help, as this is surely the last of our Stations of the Cross. It's an appalling shock for me and the family. I fear for my health: every autumn and spring I suffer pains in the stomach and duodenum, of nervous origin but very severe, and they started up during the last weeks of mental strain.

The order, which in fact originated from UNRRA rather than the British, removed most of the Slovene refugee leaders. They were told they must reside in St Martin camp or privately until transfer to Germany. Out went Judge Edvard Vračko, Director Bajuk of the grammar school and Franc Kremžar. Bajuk's grandson recalls armed British soldiers throwing a cordon around the camp with soldiers stationed every two or three metres. They searched the huts one by one with lists of people they were looking for. His grandmother however attended Mass at 6 a.m. She spotted the soldiers gathering and tipped off her family. His father and uncle hid in the attics, while grandfather Bajuk stayed below with the women and children. His grandson recalls: 'I remember the shining boots of an officer who pointed his revolver at my mother and asked where my father was – he was listening from his hiding place above the room's wooden ceiling. Again we saw our parents weep! The officer repeated his threat the next day, and my brother Marko and I threw ourselves against the boots of the officer, trying to drag him to the ground – our first intervention in defence of our family.'

Director Bajuk strode over to the camp commandant and protested that the captain had behaved rudely. The commandant agreed, ordered the captain to apologise, and sent the whole Bajuk family out of the camp all the same.

Pernišek's family briefly broke up. His wife moved to the hospitable Tangerners in the mountains, while his daughter Cirila, now 12, stayed on in the camp clandestinely. Every morning, to maintain the pretence she

---

* According to Dr Gabriela Stieber (*Nachkriegsflüchtlinge in Kärnten und der Steiermark*, Leykam, Graz, 1997, pp 278–280) St Martin was one of the worst camps in the British Zone, having been built extremely cheaply, with no double-glazing and single-thickness wooden walls.

lived outside, she wriggled through a hole in the wire fence, walked round to the main entrance and went back in to her school classes. Pernišek collapsed as the ulcerous pains got the better of him. He took to his bed and Dr Meršol admitted him to the camp hospital. But he could not stay there because of the ban, so he was transferred to the male ward of the general hospital in nearby Seeboden. Seriously ill patients were on one side, and the rest talked and smoked until 11 p.m. on the other:

> My fortieth birthday in hospital! Good-bye forever to the good times
> we had. Not much good awaits me in the future: a few years in a cold
> foreign country, probably a few hard years. I dreamt of a beautiful
> home and a happy family life, now only a brief struggle for survival
> and then the end.

Meanwhile his nine-year-old son fell seriously ill and was put in the camp hospital. Doctors advised his wife not to move to St Martin with their daughter on account of the son's condition, so the whole family settled with the Tangerners.

Dr Meršol, who had saved the refugees through his leadership in May 1945, was also in a bad way. He had been badly injured in the car accident in which camp director Ryder Young died and never recovered his full health. His wife had an operation for cancer in 1947, and the doctor had his hands full looking after their four children. Pernišek observed him working through the night drafting memoranda and petitions or translating documents into English. Meršol's nerves were run raw and he frequently dreamed of meeting and talking with dead *domobranci*. John Corsellis earlier noticed his children were among the poorest clad, with holes all over their jackets. He admired the doctor for not taking advantage of his position as leader of the camp committee.

Pernišek's wife heard of a secret plan by the banished leaders to make for the American Zone of Germany, where they believed they would be treated more humanely. She begged to accompany them, but her husband asked her not to go. He could not leave hospital yet.

The Bajuks decided to make a break for the part of Austria controlled by the Americans. They were not allowed to leave the British Zone, but friendly railway staff smuggled Božidar the classics teacher and his brother among logs on a train heading north with lumber from Yugoslavia. Grandfather Bajuk, the women and children travelled on a passenger train, equipped with false identity papers in German, English, French and Russian. The grown-ups forbade the children to speak Slovene while on the train. However, the two-year-old grand-daughter managed to take a swig from a bottle of schnapps and burst into loud Slovene conversation, stifled only by an elder brother putting a cushion over her face.

On arrival in Salzburg, Director Bajuk, the venerable intellectual of pre-war Slovenia, spent the next few days living with his family on benches in the station. The two brothers hiding on the log train were arrested and handed over to the American authorities, who re-assembled the family and dispatched them to a camp on the Danube opposite Mauthausen.

Grandfather Bajuk made contact with a Catholic vicar in Salzburg who was an old seminary schoolmate and asked him to help them emigrate. The vicar promised to take it up with a Catholic American commander who came to see him once a week. It worked. The Bajuks were able to leave directly for Argentina without returning to the camp in the British Zone.

Bajuk's grandson Marko, now living in Mendoza, Argentina, remembers a mysterious episode before they left. When they said good-bye, the Austrian vicar told them: 'You had a narrow escape. I didn't want to worry you at the time, but authorities in Vienna found out you were about to become victims of a trade between British officers and the Yugoslav secret police. In exchange for a large bribe of Egyptian cigarettes, you were to be sent back to Slovenia. Somebody found out at the last moment, and it was stopped.'

Down at the TB treatment centre in the Spittal camp, things started going wrong as soon as John Corsellis left. A quarrel broke out between his successor, British former hospital matron Violetta Thurstan, and one of the doctors, Franc Puc. She considered Puc a fool, uncooperative and out of date. He found her sour-faced and rude and claimed she threatened to block his emigration to the US. They quarrelled over medicines prescribed to patients. A protest was sent to International Refugee Organisation headquarters. Nerves frayed, despair deepened.

However, on 1 July 1947 a first handful of Slovene refugees did actually emigrate, to Venezuela. Six days later another group left for the same destination. Venezuela's work prospects and climate ruled it out as a choice for more than a few, but it was a sign of movement. Pernišek's diary, miserable as it was, also showed a growing realisation that the night is coldest when dawn is imminent, that the worst trials are often those before relief comes.

Among the refugees, the split between the people from Lienz and Spittal was healing and the renewed cohesion helped strengthen morale. The Swiss Catholic aid organisation Caritas sent 38 cases and six sacks of food, all beautifully packed and accompanied by warm letters. A Swiss Catholic delegate toured the camp and went away appalled at the poverty and promising to do more. The refugees felt somebody out there cared. Young Cirila Pernišek took up a pen-friendship with Rita Müller in Switzerland, who sent woollen stockings, chocolate, powdered milk and Ovomaltine. Forty years later, Cirila met Rita for the first time in her home near Zürich and the two women talked until 3 a.m. Cirila also visited a pen-friend of her father, Helena Brendel in St Gallen, Switzerland, who told her: 'Today is the first time I have seen you, but I feel I have known you my whole life long.'

Pernišek, having daily injections for his ulcer and waiting for a decision whether to operate, was told by the consultant: 'Taking into account your situation and that of your family right now, I won't operate. I can see you can bear pain and discomfort: you're an undemanding patient. You'll be going to somewhere in America, where you'll quieten down, live well and in peace and get cured without the knife, and all the physical symptoms will disappear.' As he left, the doctor added he would be able to return to the camp 'as the Yugoslav mission has left'.

Indeed it had. The explanation appeared in an Austrian newspaper two days later on 11 December 1947: the Yugoslav government had abrogated the Bled Agreement. No reason was given, but it appears that it was because the desired results were not forthcoming. Every person the Communists asked for was vetted by the British authorities, and the British justice system this time held fast. Chris Mayhew, later Lord Mayhew and a British Labour minister, told John Corsellis in 1996 that the Maclean Commission was his idea, and that it had returned very few individuals to Yugoslavia, and then only when there was strong evidence to justify it. So, while the refugees considered the Bled Agreement an instrument to harass them, it did protect them from false accusations and repatriation. Although hard times still lay ahead, abrogation was clearly a step in the right direction.

Even the TB centre was seeing better days. Violetta Thurstan turned her fire on the British military, persuading them to move the centre from a dusty roadside in the foggy valley to a heavenly spot at Seeboden by a pine forest and a trout stream, with glorious views of snowy mountains, facing south and bathed in sunshine. It was an old Messerschmidt factory, with central heating and a kitchen that could cook for 400 people.

A final test of British justice was still to come, and in the meantime camp life remained grim despite the glimmers of hope. Cirila remembers gnawing hunger, with a daily ration of one piece of black bread, peas and a thin soup. Their Christmas meal at the end of 1947 was polenta with black coffee. The bed-bound Pernišek heard himself being personally attacked on Ljubljana radio by one of the refugees who returned home. In his diary, he wrote:

*24 December*. There was a little Christmas party in the women's ward for those able to walk. The boys and girls with Rudi Knez as conductor sang some carols beautifully, and we all had tears in our eyes. Mr Knez accompanied on the accordion. I lived through some sad Christmases but this was the worst, and my wife and daughter were crying the whole evening in their cold room.

On 3 January 1948, despite abrogation of the Bled Agreement, British soldiers rang in the New Year with new raids on the camps. Four Slovenes were taken away to another camp. Pernišek was warned he was on the list for arrest. He assumed a false identity as Franjo Perme, occupation care-taker, and took up clandestine residence in Barrack 36, which was not his own. Lojze Ambrožič, father of the future Cardinal and an old friend from the Orel (Eagle) Catholic youth movement, kept him supplied with ration cards, and a Slovene woman brought him food to his hiding place.

In March, Pernišek moved with his family into a former autobahn barrack in the village of St Peter in Edling. One of the British camp staff, a Miss Meredith, surprised him by kindly lending him her official car for the day so that he could transport wardrobe, bed and chairs. He called her 'a dour Anglican, but infinitely better than her Catholic colleague in Seeboden'. The local authorities initially refused them ration cards, but after telling his life story to the mayor, the latter shrugged and said, 'Na ja, you're a political refugee.' Pernišek still felt a followed man. When he took a trip to Feld am See to see his brother-in-law, a gendarme stopped him as he got off the bus and asked him where he was going and why.

The only way out was forwards. As a member of the camp committee, Pernišek was responsible for drawing up lists of emigrants to Argentina. The months were dragging by, and he decided to go with a Father Cyril to International Refugee Organisation headquarters in Klagenfurt to shake them up. The woman official he met, speaking through an interpreter, asked if they were the people who kept on writing to the IRO. They replied yes, and she urged them to desist. They requested that procedures be speeded up. She asked if they had money for the trip. They said no, and she said the IRO had none either. Although the Catholic International Welfare Organisation was paying for the boat passages to Argentina, they needed funds to travel to a port. Also, refugees heading for other destinations needed funding for their whole journeys. It was stalemate, so they decided to handle as much of the arrangements as they could themselves.

Despite the obstacles, small groups were leaving for a variety of destinations. In a letter to an IRO friend in July 1948, Corsellis noted that 100 Displaced Persons were leaving the Spittal camp every week. Pernišek noticed there were fewer people at Mass on Easter Sunday 1948.

Besides Argentina, opportunities were opening up elsewhere. Canada was the first to open its doors to the Slovenes, and it moved faster than Argentina. The first few emigrants left for Canada in October 1947, and by October 1948 it had taken more of the Slovenes than the rest of the world put together. However, the Canadian total then stood at 624, little more than a tenth of all the Slovenes in the camps. The Canadians only wanted strong, healthy, single young people. Leo Čop, now living near Toronto, said: 'They were measuring people and feeling their muscles and didn't allow you to have one filled tooth or scar. Only physically perfect specimens. Then the Swedes at the UN said: "Are you selecting bulls for your country, or what?" and they became a bit ashamed.'

Pernišek noted: 'Like slaves in the market, [the women] were examined from teeth to nails and measured, weighed, scrutinised and sifted to guard against defect or deficiency. They were looking for the fittest.'

Those who went to Canada had to sign a one-year work contract. For the men, the jobs were as lumberjacks in the north of Canada, building new railways, or for a few, working on farms. The women were sent to farms, hospitals or domestic work. After the year was up, they were free to bid for whatever job they wanted and marry and set up families.

Britain started taking Slovenes from December 1947, and 600 had settled there by 1949. The British Government created a 'Westward Ho' scheme for Displaced Persons camps in Germany and Austria. Post-war Britain was short of labour in certain sectors of the economy and the immigrants had specified jobs to go to: 50% were destined for coalmines, 20% to work on the land, and 20% to factories.[1] No other European country took more than a handful.

The United States also began taking wartime refugees from Europe, but only from 1949. President Truman launched a scheme to take 200,000 'European democrats who have become victims of totalitarianism'. With the Cold War at its height, the Americans realised the value of anti-Communists with expert knowledge of languages and countries behind the Iron Curtain. A number were whisked straight back to Europe as US military intelligence operatives, receiving their security clearance before their naturalisation papers. However, emigrants to the US had to have local sponsors who vouched for them financially. For many, this was an insurmountable obstacle, since they knew nobody. Big families had little chance since few Americans were likely to under-write such a large financial risk.

So emigration was under way by mid-1948, but only Argentina was going to take any sizeable number. The way there was still blocked as endless formalities were worked through.

It seemed just a question of a few more months waiting, but the Yugoslav Communists mounted last-gasp attempts to disrupt the emigration process. Cominform, the organisation which coordinated Communist activities throughout the world, was located briefly in Belgrade. Pernišek claimed to have laid hands on one of its directives concerning subversion in refugee camps. Although he is not an objective source, there is no particular reason to doubt its authenticity. The fact that the Communists resorted to such tactics in the Cold War is not in doubt, and its style corresponds to similar documents of the time. It read:

> They [Communists] should foment and continue divisions between differing political groups, to exploit the refugees in pursuit of Communist objectives. Disputes between refugee newspapers, in the private lives of refugees and in their workplaces should be fomented. Conflict should be promoted between old and new émigrés, within their upper classes and especially among the

politically active. Rivalry should be caused between the more and the less able, so that the latter feel discriminated against. The refugees' fight against the Communists must be transformed into one among themselves. All kinds of malcontents must be used, and quarrels stirred up. The growth of positive and constructive activities must be prevented.

Frictions must be identified between the refugees and the Allied authorities, and between them and the camp administrations, so that they begin to hate their protectors. Disorders must be fostered between them, the occupiers and the local police, so that they always appear the villains of the piece, criminals, work-shy and ungrateful. The world, and in particular the countries where they have applied for emigration, should end up with the most unfavourable estimation. Cultural activities among the refugees should be destroyed, and they should be discredited in the eyes of potential employers. To achieve this, use should be made of ideological fellow travellers and individuals of low mentality, not excluding criminals. Local newspapers have already carried reports of refugees attacking isolated mountain farms and taking away goods, horses and cattle and even killing farmers who tried to stop them.

The Slovene camp leaders were tipped off about a supposed plot by the Yugoslav secret police (OZNA) to kidnap them. They were warned not to go out alone, or travel west in the direction of Lienz or south towards Villach near the Slovene frontier. When Pernišek went into town with his small son he was followed into a shop by an OZNA agent named Rak who had been waiting outside the town gate.

Emigration commissions became cautious about the risk of Communist infiltration among the refugees heading for new countries. None of the host countries wished to import a Fifth Column at the height of the Cold War. At first, Rak was accepted to go to the United Kingdom, but before his group left he was imprisoned, and although subsequently released did not accompany them. Another refugee named Breznik became violent when turned down. He broke all the windows and the door in his room, and then attacked another refugee, shouting, 'It's you who keep on saying I'm a member of OZNA.' He too was locked up. The Slovene camp committee became uneasy: this was the sort of bad publicity the Communists seemed to be intending to foster.

Another thunderbolt struck. John Corsellis, now back in Oxford, received a desperate appeal for help from Marija Jančar: her husband Jože had been arrested in their student quarters in Graz. The British Field Security Service (FSS) took him away handcuffed at 4 a.m. She was told they were acting on behalf of the Maclean Commission. The Yugoslav government had demanded him as a supposed collaborator.

Jančar, who had chaired the Slovene Students Group in Graz, had left Slovenia in May 1945 because he was a Communist assassination target. One of the relief workers who looked after the student group in 1946 was English writer (later Dame) Iris Murdoch. She befriended the Jančars and helped them with encouragement and financial aid later as new immigrants to Britain. But she had left Graz by the time Jože was arrested and could be of no help.

So it was to John Corsellis that Marija turned, since he and her husband had worked together to bring the students to Graz. She wrote:

> This is the worst that can happen to me as I'm left without support or protection. You knew my husband well, that he was always honest and a good man who could never harm anyone. You also know his attitude to politics, that he would never have been a Fascist, still less deserved to be taken into handcuffs like a criminal…I ask you to help me. I've limitless confidence in you and believe that you alone can help my husband and me, if anyone at all can. Before all I ask you to see he is given a hearing as quickly as possible. He's seriously ill with tuberculosis, and a prolonged imprisonment could lead to a worsening of his health.

Corsellis wrote to his Member of Parliament, the Conservative Colonel Douglas Dodds-Parker, who sent the letter on to Chris Mayhew, then Under-Secretary of State for Foreign Affairs in the British Labour government. The latter replied:

> Jančar is one of those men whose surrender has been demanded by the Yugoslav Government on charges of collaboration. Our international commitments oblige us to look into such allegations, but in order to ensure that no man is handed back unless a prima facie case of wilful and active collaboration has been established to the satisfaction of English Legal opinion, we have set up a threefold screening procedure. A man is first interrogated by a member of the Special Refugee Commission to see whether he is identical with the man whose surrender has been demanded, and to allow him to give an account of his wartime actions. He is also informed of the Yugoslav charges against him. [The case] is then reviewed by a legal panel who decide whether a prima facie case has been established. The case is then referred here and again carefully scrutinised to see whether any relevant considerations have been overlooked, and the final decision is taken whether to hand him back…You may be certain that Mr Corsellis' testimony on his behalf will be considered in his favour.

A month later, following representations also by the student camp's British head, Margaret Jaboor, John Corsellis received a telegram from Jože that he had been released. A moving letter in German followed: 'Dear Brother! Excuse the form of address, but in my most difficult days and hours you showed yourself more than a brother.' British justice had held firm. However, by that time, the couple were too frightened to continue their studies in Graz and emigrated to Britain as European Voluntary Workers. Initially, they had to go to separate parts of the country, as the scheme did not cater for couples. Jože eventually obtained his doctor's qualifications, but Marija's medical studies were finished forever.

Back in the Spittal camp, spirits were picking up with the summer sunshine and rising prospects of leaving the drudgery of refugee life. There was a sports festival, with soccer, volleyball, athletics, table tennis, chess and gymnastics. Food was suddenly more abundant, and stalls at the festival offered sausages, pastry, fancy bread and bonbons. The threat to transfer the camp occupants to Germany was never carried out. In September, Dara Lieven of the IRO told them Argentina would give precedence to families who could not go elsewhere, including those with many children and some of the intelligentsia. Pernišek got confirmation from the IRO on 9 September that his own family's application to Argentina was accepted. Now he set himself to the administrative tasks with gusto, making a trip to a nearby camp to help with the procedures:

> We're enjoying an Indian summer and I've been attacked by the latest camp disease, travel fever. I went for a travel permit. The district council people were very friendly and gave me one for the whole British Zone. I went to the station and asked for a ticket to Trofaiach. The clerk was polite although I didn't have change. The ticket collector greeted me effusively, 'Good morning, sir, ticket please,' and returned my greeting in a manner I never experienced before the war...

> I reached Trofaiach and after walking twenty minutes found myself in the camp. It's beautifully situated in woodlands surrounded by high mountains and is well kept and clean, even if it houses twenty different nationalities. The 300 Slovenes have their own area, conspicuous features being the flower beds in front of the barracks, including tobacco with its wide palm-like leaves, and lots of small children wearing short-sleeve shirts. Thank God we have lots of children. This year there's hope of a good harvest. Our people are still full of vitality and healthy in body and soul.

On 30 September 1948, the first Slovenes left for Argentina, with one last kick in the pants from bureaucracy. They were told at midday they would leave at 3 a.m. the next morning. At 2 p.m., they were told they were off at 5 p.m. The emigrants finally passed the camp in a train at 7.30 a.m. the next day after spending all night in the station waiting room.

Now they were off on a voyage to new homes, new lives and new hopes, but it was to a far-away country of which they knew little, to a fate which was as uncertain and risky as anything they had encountered. And they were going forever, leaving the community life of the camps that was one of the few solaces of the past three years. Pernišek captured the mood in his diary when the first young Slovene women left for Canada:

*9th September*. Some of our girls left for Canada. They should have left in July, but it was obvious they wanted to stay longer with us and parting had come too early, so there were a lot of tears. It was difficult looking at them, healthy and beautiful in body and soul, like blossom being strewn by the wind…We gave them a lovely farewell party.

…Then a few weeks later…

*17th October*. The camp choir gave a lovely concert, singing songs we'd often heard before, but which today left us with really deep feelings. Everyone knew this was the last performance for many singers as the camp is beginning to empty. This gave an added dimension.

*23rd October*. 148 are off to Argentina, leftovers from the last transport. There was Holy Mass at 6. When the song 'Marija skoz življenje' ('Mary throughout our life') was finished there wasn't a dry eye. They gathered in front of the garages. It's getting harder and harder to say good-bye!

*24th October*. Feast day of Archangel Raphael, patron saint of émigrés. Many took part in an all-night vigil in the chapel before the Blessed Sacrament.

After four years in the refugee camps, the Slovenes forged a strong community. There were heartbreaks when groups left for countries of asylum.

Everybody had to go through a medical, not always easy with the dark shadow of TB occasionally showing up on a lung. Some refugees managed to slip a relative or friend in their place into the X-ray session. A few doctors gave a helping hand. When a refugee named Nace Jeriha gave a blood sample, the doctor turned it upside down, shook it, added a bit of white fluid, shook his head and said, 'Please get your son and let him give his blood again for you. What we have here is mainly spirit.' Nace grumbled but brought his son Lado. The Argentinian consul, Señor Virasoro, approved even handicapped people. He positively welcomed the families with numerous children which other countries shied clear of. The grandson of Director Bajuk recalls:

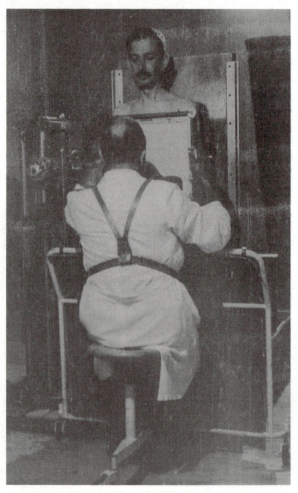

Dr Franc Puc carries out a chest X-ray examination on diarist France Pernišek. His health broke down from malnutrition and despair.

Every so often families left the camp for the Americas and Australia.* How can I forget the blackboards which appeared with host country details and conditions for emigrants? In 1947 and 1948 we saw father return home sad and worried; having four children and being a classics teacher were not qualifications. Our friends went off and we stayed, burdened by the fear we'd not be able to leave. But the day came even for us. The Argentinian consul looked at uncle, aunt, parents and four children forming a perfect human staircase and said, 'My country needs lots of people, lots of children – there's lots of work!' How happy we were! The next day he escorted us personally to the train.

Single men over 45 heading for Argentina had to secure the agreement of another family that they could live with them. After years of deprivation and making do with scraps and rags, families were sent down to the local store to receive new clothing, linen and footwear. Pernišek's birthday came round again, a year after he marked his 40th anniversary with laments over his hopeless future:

*23rd November.* I'm celebrating my own birthday in excellent spirits. How hard it was last year! Today I've an assured departure to a better future: there'll still be great difficulties to overcome with patience, but the green light is shining. With God's help we'll start a new life in our new homeland. The consul says it's a large and rich country with enough work and food for everyone; he's delighted with our lovely healthy families and many children, who are our hope and joy and also the hope and joy of Argentina, a country ruled by a man with a great heart.

*25th December.* A holy day. Everyone joyfully wished each other a happy Christmas. Next year we'll be celebrating it in our new homeland, Argentina. We hope God will continue to bless us and we'll find a land of peace, the most important things being health and work. God was with us up till now, and will be in the future. They regaled us with potica,† white bread and sausages.

As he and his family packed their belongings into wooden boxes, Pernišek went down to Spittal town to buy tools. The ironmonger said the other Slovenes had practically bought up the whole store, and the diary

---

\* Around 200 emigrated to Australia. A correspondent writing to the *Free Slovenia Almanac* in Buenos Aires in 1950 (pp 227–229) wrote: 'We are distributed across the continent from Perth to Sydney and Darwin. Each lives on his own, almost without links to others, as there are thousands and thousands of miles between us. The most active and with best contact with one another are those in New South Wales…Some already have their own land and are building new homes…We Slovenes will only live as a family when we have our own Slovene priest.'

† A Slovene festive cake.

quoted him as saying: 'We'll miss you. You were hard working, honest people. All the years you were around we had peace, no theft or assaults; you never pestered us. You were ready to do any housework, and we could leave you alone in a house because you people are honest and not demanding in any way. On the other hand you were good customers and brought us profitable business. We're already feeling the pinch from your departure, and in future we'll feel it even more...We wish you a safe journey: we're sure you'll all do well because you're industrious, capable, gifted, honest and very religious. The whole town and surrounding countryside are talking of nothing but your departure, especially the farmers you helped so much.' They shook hands and said good-bye.

On New Year's Day, 1949, the Pernišek family made their last preparations for the journey. As when he left his home in Ljubljana in May 1945, he realised that a deep change was taking place:

*1st January.* A New Year, threshold of a new life in the new world. We're leaving our wooden town where we've lived four long, hard years as third-class citizens without the most basic human rights. We were numbers in the long, long list of displaced persons brought about by World War II. But still we're sorry to leave and I've feelings I can't describe: something is gripping my soul, my throat and my heart, and no words are coming from my mouth.

We're leaving the old world still in ruins. Our homeland is close, just beyond the Karavanke mountains. I keep looking at them and remembering my mother, sister, nephews and other relatives and good friends there, whose hands I couldn't shake and say good-bye. I'm restless from hearing so many conflicting reports, and I've nightmares of being persecuted and hunted like a wild animal. We're taking leave of our fellow camp-dwellers, of our unforgettable, good Dr Meršol, the parish priests and curates and the other good people still remaining.

*2nd January.* Those leaving for Argentina had a 6 a.m. Mass said by the Rev. Klopčič. We hand in our heavy baggage. My heart feels heavy and others feel the same: the nearer the departure, the heavier the heart. Even my wife and children are silent. We climb into the lorries. 'God be with you, safe journey' is heard again and again. Good-bye, good-bye.

At the station we were put straight into comfortable second-class carriages. The train moved slowly and almost silently. Strange. We're leaving behind four years of anxiety, bitter disappointments and sad memories, yet the transition from refugee to free person isn't easy. We didn't cry when we departed on 5 May 1945, leaving behind everything – home, possessions, loved parents, brothers and sisters. We didn't know if we'd be alive next day, and if alive where we'd spend the night, what we'd eat. We departed into the totally unknown – and left as if on a Mayday spring excursion. Perhaps fear took the place of sadness or we were given a special grace. Personally, I'm sure it was a special grace.

# 8 INVITED BY PERON

*Very slowly the ship slides through the water, and the grey hill falls further and further behind and becomes ever greyer.*

That the Slovenes were finally able to emigrate was due much to their own initiative. However, they were far from being masters of their own destiny. They could only go to a country that operated an emigration scheme for Displaced Persons. The schemes ran for a certain time, and then the doors closed again. The receiving countries decided who came and when. Documents and travel were arranged by others. They were still in a no man's land of dependency. Only in their new homelands would they be able to take full responsibility for their lives. When this happened, it would be like a bracing shower of cold water.

They found it hard to realise the grey regimentation was coming to an end, and at the same time they were anxious. Departure meant breaking up the tight-knit community that kept them going through the dark days. Would they be able to maintain this fellowship in their new environments, or would they suffer unfriendliness and isolation? Many were feeling homesick even before they set off.

The camp elders were encouraging everybody to go to Argentina in order to preserve cohesion as a Slovene group. An ulterior motive, rarely stated openly, was to preserve a Slovene non-Communist political movement capable one day of resuming influence in the home country. The rank-and-file could see the safety there would be in numbers, but worried whether there would really be prosperity and jobs for all. Would it not be preferable to try more familiar countries of emigration, such as the United States or Canada? The educated ones also questioned, correctly for many, whether their certificates would count for much in Argentina. Would they end up as unskilled labourers?

In the end, the answer for most had to be Argentina. Other countries set conditions which disqualified the majority. What they also did not know was that unexpected acts of human kindness, which they had already encountered at times in the camps, were also awaiting them in their new homelands.

Leo Čop took the royal path to his destination. Not for him mass organisation or a ship slowly wallowing across the ocean. He took a plane, or rather several planes. Čop was set on Canada, but a phone call came through saying there was a job for him in Bolivia. 'I swore I wouldn't go to South America, but I had to swallow my words as it was a chemical job in my profession. I had to ask a Dutchman at the refugee office where Bolivia was. I was so confused, I got on the wrong train,' he said.

He flew to Bolivia via Shannon, Gander, New York, Miami and Peru. On one aircraft an engine caught fire and they had to return to the airport, while the plane taking him to Lima almost ran out of fuel before it could land in dense fog. In the meantime, his girlfriend Maria emigrated with her mother and sister to Canada, where regulations allowed a woman to arrange for a male partner to join her as long as they married. 'The three women were quite a force. I caved in, and went to Canada and we married there,' said Leo.

For the others there were just trains and converted troopships. The Pernišek family crossed the Alps over the Brenner Pass in mid-winter in an unheated railway carriage. They shivered in their coats as their train trundled through the snow-covered countryside of Italy under dark overcast skies. The train stopped for long periods in stations, but Italian police refused to let them descend to find food or hot drinks. Frozen and thirsty after travelling through the night, they arrived on 4 January 1949 at the Grugliasco transit centre for Displaced Persons near Turin. They made their way from the train through a snowstorm and settled down to wait. Their last dismal lodging in war-stricken Europe was a former mental hospital previously used by German soldiers and Jewish refugees. Food was macaroni and potatoes smelling of paraffin, and the washrooms were dirty and broken. Pernišek felt bored wandering around the nearby park with its bare trees. They waited 12 days. On the day they left for Genoa, his wife fell ill. In his diary, he described the sadness of leaving Europe, balanced by a realisation that better times were starting:

> *Monday 17th January.* We reach Genoa. The harbour police checked our passports and our hearts almost stopped beating at this last police check on European soil. Everyone was very polite; they had no list of wanted people. We boarded the ship *Holbrook*. They separated the men from the women, the men to the male section and the women to large communal dormitories with comfortable beds and clean, new, fresh linen. People's faces have turned serious and sad and most are crying. Good-bye, homeland, good-bye our beloved parents. Very slowly the ship slides through the water and the grey hill falls further and further behind and grows ever greyer.

We are summoned to the restaurant, huge, spotlessly clean, elegantly furnished with beautiful, clean tables and chairs and fine cutlery. We are attentively waited on and plenty of nourishing, savoury food is served on metal platters, just what we need after a day without warm food and an exhausting journey. After four years of grim starvation we're given a really well served good supper.

The boat was a converted US troopship, and the refugees discovered that American soldiers travelling to fight the war enjoyed levels of comfort unheard of in the refugee camps. They were entering another world, with the living standards of an economy running in top gear.

What kind of boat is our SS *Holbrook*? It's an American Liberty ship transporting American soldiers across the Atlantic during the war, a very large, very comfortable ship with mess decks for the sleeping and living quarters of the soldiers, a very large kitchen, huge cold stores, a most modern well-equipped hospital and separate dining rooms for officers and crew. On deck there are plenty of comfortable easy chairs, so there's no need to fight for one. The food is simply ideal for half-starved refugees.

Two days out to sea, Pernišek's wife became seriously ill, wracked by stomach cramps that spread to her fingers, hands and feet. A Russian doctor who cared for her in the camps briefed the ship's American doctor. The young American listened carefully, took her in his arms, carried her into the sickbay, and gave her a morphine injection and two litres of intravenous transfusion. He told the family she was jaundiced, severely under-nourished and very weak. Four years in the camps had taken their toll, but the doctor reassured them it would not be long before she recovered. A Slovene Catholic priest, as usual on hand to bring comfort to his flock, said a Mass for her recovery in the officers' saloon.

*Friday 21st January*. I went to see my wife in the sick bay; the children aren't admitted...In the bed opposite there was a Russian woman seriously ill with pneumonia. The doctors are afraid of this disease because patients can't stand the night dampness and sea air: that's why they're warning us not to stay on deck at night. The poor Russian woman died during the night. At 5 p.m. all the passengers gathered to pay their last respects. A funeral at sea is deeply moving. The children and I were gripped with a chilly fear as we thought of our own dear gravely ill mum in the sickbay.

The ship's hospital filled up with refugees who had caught 'flu on the unheated train journey across Italy or in the ramshackle transit camp. Pernišek's wife got over the worst in a few days, but then he himself was rushed to the sickbay with poisoning from contaminated ice. These illnesses were the last disagreeable relics of the Europe they were leaving behind; soon the sun became warmer as they sailed into tropical waters. On the way, they stopped in Dakar in West Africa and traders came alongside selling bananas. For many it was the first time they had seen a banana or a black person. Marian Loboda, 15, painted the ship's railings, and was paid ten packets of Lucky Strike cigarettes which he sold on arrival. When they reached Buenos Aires in early February 1949, Pernišek's diary recorded a relaxed South American reception:

> *Friday 4th February.* The ship stopped at 8 a.m. We're waiting for medical and immigration check-ups. I was very pleasantly surprised when I received the Immigration Commission's living and ration cards for 14 days for the Immigrants' Hotel: it'll help us over the worst initial difficulties. The police will issue us with identity cards entitling us to the same rights as any other Argentinian citizen.

The medical checks were none too drastic. X-ray examinations showed a few had tuberculosis, but they were allowed to stay. Handicapped people were checked through without problems. Pernišek witnessed one of the first gratuitous acts of human kindness. As a gesture, it was elegant and discreet. The examining doctor asked all the refugees to raise their hands. One Slovene next to him had a paralysed arm. The doctor seized both his arms and raised them, as if it were a demonstration to the others. The invalid passed with everybody else.

The Rode family, lacking two sons repatriated with the *domobranci*, had to wait over Christmas until 27 December 1948 because nobody worked in the harbour during the festive period. The Pernišeks, arriving a little later, were welcomed by fellow-countrymen who had gone ahead:

> *Saturday 5th February.* Disembarkation. There are Slovenes on the pier waiting for us, waving handkerchiefs. We go to the customs. They open our poor bags and let us go to the Immigrants' Hotel... Well, here we are! The end of the life of a refugee wandering the world. We're starting a completely new chapter. Every beginning is difficult, but let's confront any new difficulties with courage. We're fully free, in a rich country, they're offering us work, and prosperity can be seen all around us. With God's help, if we persevere and don't demand too much, we'll succeed in organising a good life for ourselves.

His daughter Cirila celebrated her 14th birthday that day, sitting on a gangway on the ship. A friend from the kitchen brought her a couple of oranges as a present, and a group of refugees sang 'Happy Birthday'. She was happy surrounded by friends, and felt as if she were on holiday. Her mother felt otherwise, confiding: 'If there was no sea, I would walk back.'

Pernišek did not like the negative attitude of the Slovenes who had arrived earlier. He wrote in his diary that they had nothing nice to say, only complaints that they found it hard to find anywhere to live, and so on. Some were already talking of returning home (he did not mention his wife was one of them). He found they had an upsetting influence.

The disembarking Slovenes were now on their own. The paternalism of the camp regime lay in the past, but now they had to take responsibility for their destinies. Rich though the country might be, it offered them few gifts. Father Košiček's reports of prosperous farms so fertile that the farmers could sleep during the afternoon turned out to be a fantasy. The farms were in the hands of big landowners who only offered poorly paid unskilled jobs. The newcomers wondered why some of the Slovene refugee leaders, who urged people to go as a group to preserve Slovene values, themselves ended up in the United States.

New arrivals were as a rule allowed to stay for two weeks at the Immigrants' Hotel on the Buenos Aires harbour-front, receiving two dollars a day. The Perniseks were turned out after ten days with their luggage placed in front of the door, since space was needed for a group coming in from Calabria. They moved with 12 other families into an empty warehouse, where there was just room for everybody to lie down and sleep on the floor. They had blankets, a kerosene cooker, their luggage and nothing else. After three months, the family of four moved to a single room of their own, sharing a kitchen with two other families. Educated, cultivated and trained as a senior civil servant, Pernišek took a first job as a carpenter. His daughter Cirila was sent to a convent school to learn Spanish. She had to wash clothes, iron, serve at meals, and for four hours a day she could attend school, but not speak in class. She described it as 'like a prison'. She then went to work in a stocking factory. It was a typical experience. They were starting life again at the bottom of the ladder.

Initially, many went off to live in Lanus, one of the poorest areas of Buenos Aires, where a visitor described their first dwellings as 'clapperboard houses and streets, just a sea of mud'. Later they built a modern Slovene 'village' alongside.

Despite the warnings there would be few opportunities in Argentina for the intelligentsia, the Bajuk family was among those disembarking in Buenos Aires. Director Marko Bajuk retired from his headmaster's career just before emigrating, having completed his statutory 35 years of service. He wrote in his memoirs:

> It was not easy to say good-bye to my young people. If I had to choose my profession again, I would be a teacher again. This radiant youth is extremely interesting; every day brings something new. It would be a fool who tried to put together a recipe for education and upbringing at this stage. You cannot automate it or make it uniform. You can lay down directives and make guesses here and there, but it is your heart that is indispensable – with that you can achieve everything, without it you can do nothing. When at the end of the year they wanted to take a photograph, Professors Luskar and Jeglič came to

me and said: 'Pupils and teachers are waiting with the photographer, can you come and take the empty chair which is waiting for you?' They came twice. No, I couldn't do it. I wept and among them I would have wept even more. I couldn't. The photograph was taken with my empty chair in it.

All my life with young people is full of happy memories...The work at our refugee grammar school gave me especially happy memories and feelings of satisfaction. How many boys who would have otherwise spent their time loitering about God knows where were directed along the right path, ending up on all continents as decent men, in particular in North America?

In later life, his pupils warmly endorsed his feeling of achievement. His strict regime of schooling, applied from the first days in the Viktring field, was a key element in keeping the refugee community together. As refugees hanging on tenuously in camps, they could have received just basic schooling or none at all. In the event, many emerged with solid academic qualifications enabling them to compete for the best jobs. The school was, in Milči Lekan's words, 'my passport to the wide world'. As a musician and composer, Bajuk was a driving force behind the camps' extraordinarily rich cultural life. As the son of a peasant, he was a self-made man and an all-rounder in the renaissance style.

His son Božidar was a classics teacher and like his father a widely cultivated man. For a family with this background, the United States seemed a better proposition. While still in the camps, they found a potential sponsor in California. But his readiness to accept financial responsibility stopped short at the family members who were too old to work. So it had to be Argentina.

The first question the Bajuks asked on arrival in Buenos Aires was: where are the mountains? Slovenia is full of beautiful mountains, and there is a saying that every Slovene worth his salt climbs its highest peak, the Triglav, at least once. A local pointed them towards Mendoza at the foot of the Andes. They did not realise it was 1,100 kilometres away, but off they set. They found a room, three metres by four, and the family set about assembling wooden crates for the local wine. With the earnings they bought their first kerosene cooker, winter overcoats and a mattress for the grandmother, who was ill with rheumatism. As the crate production got into swing, they could afford folding bedsteads. It was better than the camps, but a harsh test for the 63-year-old Director Bajuk and his family of intellectuals. For months, the grandchildren remember their grandparents as 'all dressed up ready to go home to Slovenia'. However, like other mountain folk, the Slovenes were tough, and the Bajuks were no exception.

Grandson, Božidar Bajuk junior, eight years old at the time, remembers his first day at an Argentinian school, six months after arrival in Mendoza:

On 15th March classes started and for the first time they dressed me in a white dustcoat, the primary school uniform. At eight one adapts quickly to new ways of learning and those years of primary school are a mass of beautiful memories, of happiness and enthusiasm. As children we always felt 'different'. I didn't like this at first, but it became more bearable as time passed and in the end it changed into pride... Five or six boys would wait for me at the bus stop to copy my Latin homework.

For his father, also called Božidar, the change was radical. The son's first recollections of him are sitting in his study in Ljubljana, with just a chair and table in one corner, the walls surrounded by books. The fateful days of May 1945 put paid to the status and recognition which he would normally have enjoyed as a classics teacher in Slovenia. As he staggered through the Ljubelj tunnel to the Viktring encampment, he was on the verge of a nervous breakdown, his home and library abandoned. In Mendoza, instead of teaching Latin and Greek as he still did in the camps, his first jobs were as a bricklayer and a carpenter. The new foothold in life was precarious and lowly for him too.

It was the same for the family of Franc Kremžar, a former Ljubljana newspaper editor and parliamentary deputy. His son Marko was one of the Graz University students and could have emigrated to the US if he had been on his own. But his father, mother and aunt were all over 60 and had no chance of being admitted. Marko did not want to go without them, so they all emigrated to Argentina. Marko describes how he started his working career:

> I looked for a job and father searched for somewhere to live, while mother and aunt sat on a bench in the park. I couldn't find work until we'd a permanent address, and my father couldn't find accommodation without the guarantee of a job. Most families split up, the men to public construction jobs and the women to domestic work. A few found employment and accommodation in factories, while some with several children travelled into the interior.

> Our two weeks were up and we still hadn't anywhere to live. They let us stay another week, and a fellow Slovene who'd been in Argentina since before the war and knew my father suggested a solution. He lived in a suburb with two sons and a daughter who boarded in a college during the school year, so that they had two rooms free. He proposed that my mother and aunt should look after the house and garden so that his wife, also a Slovene, could return to work.

> I started in the Goodyear factory as a cleaner. At last we had a roof and I earned enough for us to eat... My father, a journalist, found a job as a cleaner in a sanatorium and I progressed to assembling the cabins of heavy lorries, exhausting but better-paid work.

As luck had it, the union at Marko's workplace called a strike. He took a job as a building labourer while waiting for the dispute to be solved. Eventually, the workers got their pay increases, but Marko and other newcomers were made redundant. Marko was entitled to compensation and was already settled in a new job. It was his breakthrough:

> Never had I had so much money, almost two months' pay. We bought a plot of land, in an uninhabited area with planning permission, got a 'National Mortgage Bank' loan and, with the help of bricklayer friends, built and moved into a pretty little house, while growing inflation made loan repayments easier.

He applied to a local university on the strength of his European certificates. He had to send them to the Argentinian Interior Ministry, which passed them to the Foreign Ministry, which sent them on to the Austrian Foreign Ministry. From there, they went to the Austrian Interior Ministry, which dispatched them to the University of Graz. The rector certified their authenticity and sent them back by the same route. Marko was able to enrol.

The Kavčičes, a grocer family with two daughters, took along Paula Hribovšek, whom Director Bajuk tried in vain to bar from the camp grammar school. They spent the first two weeks in the Immigrants Hotel, and a Slovene priest then helped her find a job. It was in a knitting factory run by a Serb and a Croat, who also provided lodgings for Paula with nine other Slovene girls. Among aspiring Slovene men, it became known as Babji Grad – Girls' Castle. Paula recounts:

> I first met Marko in Spittal. I didn't know him well; he was just one of many students. Our established pattern was for girls to limit their circle of friends to girls, and boys to boys, until the boys started work and earned enough to contemplate marriage. And every Sunday we went to church and had Mass, meetings and games. The girls felt secure, knowing it was probable they'd marry: they wanted to marry and have their own families, but didn't feel any urgency in finding a man; in the natural course of events they would meet the right man!

In the natural course of events, Marko and Paula came together 10,000 kilometres from their homeland. They married in 1957. Marko took a job in a Swiss-owned textile factory, claiming to be an apprentice weaver. This was not true, but the Swiss mechanic allowed him to practise on a new machine awaiting installation. Soon he was making cloth for suits and overcoats, and he still has a union card as a cashmere weaver. Kremžar later made a career as an executive in various international firms and as an author on Slovene issues.

The Kremžar family too had taken a single person with them: 16-year-old Stanko Jerebič. Like Marko Kremžar, he lacked the right job qualifications but fell upon an employer who decided to give him a chance:

> I applied to a firm advertising for a bookkeeper, as by that time I'd completed eight lessons. I'll never forget the accountant's guffaws when I told my professional skills, but there's another thing I'll never forget: how the good man stayed behind every day to teach me, then let me take over the books and praised the quality of my work. I stayed five years and learned enough to justify my existence.

Argentina was not quite the 'melting pot' of North America, where newcomers swiftly adopted the local culture. The Slovenes in Argentina continued to nurture a community spirit based on Slovene identity, religious faith and family life. Every Sunday, they congregated before and after Mass in the courtyard of the church and on the pavement, exchanging news, advice and assistance. They published Slovene periodicals, reviews and schoolbooks. They found each other jobs, helped build each other's houses, and began sending parcels of food and second-hand clothing back to their relatives in Slovenia. Always in the back of the minds of the community leaders was the belief that they represented the real Slovenia. Exiled, but upholding the true values of the nation. 'In these early times, we lived as in our own republic. We were not much interested in anything to do with Argentina then,' said one.

Marko Kremžar described how they cherished the spirit of the refugee camps:

> Our teachers gathered the children of school age together as soon as we arrived and, although they'd the same difficulties over jobs and food as we had, taught them every Saturday as in the refugee camps. Some families with a little money sacrificed it for the school, and the teachers taught without any kind of payment – a tradition that persists until today.

> Small cooperatives were soon buying land in the suburbs and so 'Slovene hearths' started, and often families without houses of their own helped set them up. They provided bases for the Saturday schools with classrooms, a chapel and a multi-purpose hall for theatre, athletics and dances. Then we built a Slovene Cultural Centre which brought all the 'hearths' together, and the teachers combined their study programmes and adapted them to new needs. Later we started secondary education and then a university. So we divided our lives between work and study during the week; and between study, family and community at the weekends.

As his compatriot Stane Snoj put it: 'We simply started up again and adapted to our new circumstances the customs and activities we'd brought with us from Slovenia and from the camps. Today a Slovenia in miniature exists which has become famous abroad.'

The Slovene community in Argentina however, was not homogeneous. The Catholic newcomers found 25,000 Slovenes already living in Argentina, and the two groups did not get on well. The earlier arrivals lost their homes in 1920 when western Slovenia was ceded to Italy by the Treaty of Rapallo. These people were naturally anti-Fascist, and were happy that Slovenia regained part of the lost territory at the end of World War II. They gave credit to the Partisans. For many years, this older community cold-shouldered the Catholic refugees – and vice versa. When the Catholics were disembarking in 1949, a number of the previous refugees were heading in the other direction, returning to Slovenia to reclaim their homes on the Adriatic.

Within seven or eight years the refugees had a footing in their new homeland. They had gone through a stage of their lives which was unique in its intensity and drama and which they would never forget. They had been exposed to shock, misery and despair. But they had pulled themselves up by their bootstraps, fortified by their community spirit fostered in the camps.

Slovenia was now half a world away, and their concerns and ambitions had changed. The refugees' lives became agreeably ordinary. They were earning the wherewithal to support families and enjoy a rising standard of living. They found the Argentinians relaxed and easy-going. Their hosts saw how they had to work hard at the beginning and accepted them as fellow citizens.

The immigrants were helped by peace and a robust economy. Argentina, though later to slide into economic collapse, was a well-to-do country in the early years. There were jobs and plenty of easy credit to build homes. It was a more favourable environment than post-war Slovenia, which was held back by rigid state planning and a disastrous collectivisation of farming.

Even elders such as Marko Bajuk, former Director of the camp grammar school, found a dignified occupation eventually. When he first arrived in Mendoza, he took work scraping weeds from paving stone cracks in the town park. However, when the Argentinians realised his academic background, the park authorities made him assistant to the library botanist, cataloguing Latin descriptions of plants.

His son Božidar benefited likewise. The Argentinian teacher of Božidar's two older boys noticed that, although they were only just mastering Spanish, they were achieving good results at school. She asked about their family background, and intervened with the Dean of Mendoza University to arrange Božidar a job handling its foreign-language correspondence with overseas institutes. He also worked as a choir director and teacher in Slovene schools, thus in the end achieving his goal of living as a Christian intellectual.

Most of Božidar's lost library miraculously turned up again. One of his sons remembers as a small boy being shocked by the sight of the Gestapo burning piles of the books in a courtyard where an anti-aircraft gun was mounted. The library was abandoned when they fled in 1945. In later years, on trips to Buenos Aires, the son regularly visited a book importer to fetch Slovene books his father ordered from Mendoza to replenish his shelves. Then, 30 years after their flight, a woman in the block where they used to live in Ljubljana discovered most of Božidar's original library hidden in an attic. Now the books are all in the son's home in Mendoza. A few days before the father died, Božidar junior recalls him telling the children:

> You're sorry I'll soon be departing to the Kingdom, but I tell you I'm happy! You can't imagine the clarity with which I take leave of life. All the things I've lost and suffered have led to one result: I can review the outcome of my life, and I've won! I've saved my family; I've four children in professions and 18 grandchildren all well launched. I've preserved faith and freedom and, above everything, I've handed on all the values to you – my children. Thanks be to God!'

France Pernišek, who despaired on his 40th birthday whether he had anything to look forward to in life, lived on into his nineties, dying in Argentina just before the end of the century. For a few heady days in May 1945, he was appointed to a high position in a non-Communist government of Slovenia. This was never to be, though other refugees always felt the sense of authority he derived from this short-lived status. His diary ceased soon after he settled into his new homeland. He had recorded the refugees' Odyssey with an eye for colourful detail and a poetic touch. History owes a debt, in that he sensed the epic nature of their struggle and was determined to capture it even at the most desperate moments. He wrote intensely of the Catholic faith and vision which drove the refugees forward and kept them together, and also of their bitterness, resentment and despair when the world turned against them. Objective he was not, but his diary has the immediacy of real life.

After a spell as a carpenter in Argentina, his life moved into calmer waters. He devoted his spare time to the newly established Slovenian Association, helping his country-people find accommodation, jobs and schools and deal with the local bureaucracy. Many years later, when he was interviewed for this book, he looked back on his life as a proud father with a long career of meticulous office work behind him. His matter-of-fact tone then contrasted with the dramatic and impassioned entries in his refugee's diary:

> I got a job in a textile factory office and worked there 25 years until I retired at 74 on full pension. My son studied at the State University and has worked as an architect since 1966, is married and has four children. My daughter started work at 14, first in a stocking factory and later as a secretary. She is married to a lawyer and has three children; their daughter has just qualified at university as a biochemist while their two sons are still studying engineering.

As for Julia Bohinc, fate posed one obstacle too many for her:

At 65, father became a bricklayer's mate, something he'd never done before. With 60% of the locals he had to travel two or three hours to work. My oldest brother was found a job nearby. One of my sisters worked for a family in the capital, while another sister and I found some sewing near home in a workshop making slippers, where the pay was very low. We placed our younger brothers aged 13 and 15 in a college where they had to study for five years, as this was the only way they could obtain admission. We resolved to build a house of our own near Buenos Aires, where the job prospects were better. Father bought a plot of land by instalments...We fed modestly as we were used to a simple diet, spent the minimum on clothes and there was no question of any kind of entertainment.

I still dreamed that once I lived near the capital and knew the language better I could take up my beloved books again and continue with my studies, for I'd completed secondary school at the camp in Spittal. By mid-1950 everything seemed to be going well and father was very happy with a better job as night watchman. One morning he got home, lay down, exchanged a couple of words and went to sleep – forever. His heart, which had suffered so much from all we'd experienced and now seemed about to enjoy happiness and the fruits of his labours, could manage no more. The day we buried him I buried my own plans for the future.

# 9 INTO THE MELTING POT

*I thank God he kicked me out of Slovenia in 1945, because he opened the door for me.*

If it was hard going to start with in Argentina, life had an even tougher edge in Canada, but prospects in the long term were better and there was a sense of adventure. For their one-year labour contracts, the men were mostly sent to areas where winter lasted five months and temperatures fell to minus 40° centigrade. They had to build railways or fell trees in the 'bush'. The young men who had moved heaven and earth to get into Graz University found muscles were required, not intellect. And come single please: couples spent the first year separated.

Riko Ziernfeld, who saved his life in 1945 by taking off his military tunic and joining the civilians, studied mechanical engineering at Graz for three years. But there was no point in writing 'student' on his application to Canada, so he put himself down as 'labourer'. Before he could complete his degree, he was off to the Canadian wilderness:

> We went to southern Saskatchewan, where we stayed five months, exchanging old rails for new ones. I was pulling the spikes with a big crowbar and then nailing the rails again, and the first two weeks we broke so many hammers you wouldn't believe! They'd have two guys just bringing new hammers from the store; because if you missed the spike, you hit the hammer across the rail and it just broke off. But after two weeks we became experts; you just looked at the spike and could drive it in with two, three hits. There were 80 people, Slovenes, Croats and Latvians, mostly from Graz, 20 from the university and 60 from the city.

> After that they sent us to the bush; to Northern Ontario, between Nipigon and Bildmore, a camp from which we went every day to cut

wood. With the railway I wasn't too tired, but the bush was terrible!
For five weeks I was so tired I didn't have the strength to eat: I just
flopped down on my bunk bed and fell asleep. We were cutting spruces
with bow saws into eight-foot lengths, each a foot and a half in
diameter. We piled them on to sledges and pushed them down
tracks bulldozed through the forests on which we sprayed water to
freeze them solid. When it thawed, we floated the logs down to the
paper factories. Even when it was minus 10° centigrade, I got so hot
I worked without a shirt. It was hard but I enjoyed it, and with my
wages I bought myself a fancy suit.

Tone Suhadolc, who got the commendation for saving a shot-down
US pilot, had a law degree from Ljubljana University. But like Ziernfeld
he registered as a farm boy in his application, claiming he had no
education. He slipped somebody else into the X-ray test because of a
shadow on his lung. When he went to see the Canadian consul in Graz, he
met a German girl he knew at the International Refugee Organisation.
She brightly greeted him with 'Hallo, Herr Doktor.' He thought that
blew his cover as an illiterate, but somehow the consul did not hear:

> In Canada, I had to sign a contract for half a year on the railway
> and half in the bush, cutting pulpwood. The railways were tough,
> but we were young and out in the country and had fun really and
> good food. In the bush it was harder because if you didn't work you
> didn't make money. I left early because I still had that excuse that
> my lungs were bad. So I came to Hamilton to a steel company, and,
> boy, that was hard work…

> I never used my law doctorate because here it's completely different.
> I'd have had to start all over again. It took me 12 years to qualify in
> accountancy. The first few years I never even thought I'd be able to
> change, especially when I married after two years. I bought a house
> and then it took me five years to get through the course. It was
> tough. In the steelworks I was doing some of the hardest physical
> work. Oh! That was hot! Then you move up a bit, and it's a bit
> better. I started steel work at the age of 29 and did it for 12 years to
> 41, but I was a farmer's son and so basically strong. There were a
> few fellow students from Graz in the same steel-works.

Ivan Kukovica, who jumped from a moving train taking him back to
Slovenia in 1945, put down 'student' on his form because he had
studied civil engineering for four years. He was rejected but asked to be
re-considered. Next time he gave his occupation as lumberjack, and
nobody questioned the discrepancy. He did his first year on the Canadian
railway and felling trees, and then found work cooking soup in a pickle
factory. He married, his wife became pregnant, and they had nowhere
to live: 'In despair I said we had to do something. By that time we'd

saved $400 and with that I bought a double lot and started to build my house myself with cement blocks, and moved in when I had the roof and partitions inside. I didn't have any plaster; I could see from the kitchen and the bathroom into the living room! Life was very difficult for the first ten years, with only $2,000 to look after nine kids.'

Some found their studies were not in vain. Vida Rosenberg walked down Toronto's Bloor Street on her arrival, saw a beautiful building with a wrought-iron fence and an English lawn at number 200, and thought: 'If I could ever work there I'd be the happiest person on earth!' A year later, the employment office told her the Manufacturers' Life Insurance Company might have an opening:

> The employment office gave the address, 200 Bloor Street, and I came to it. It can't be true! I was shaking, I was so nervous. I gave them my papers. They set me an exam, but the department manager came and said, 'No, we really can't give a test to somebody with that education' and I thanked God for all those papers! So my five semesters of law studies were worthwhile.

Gloria Bratina was not going to be stuck in a lowly job for long. As a 19-year-old girl she fought her way through the Ljubelj tunnel, mounted guard at night on the road, and forcibly prevented her *domobranci* brothers from joining the trains back to Slovenia. This gritty individual was soon out of the Alberta sugar beet farm to which she was sent. Having done several semesters of medical studies in Graz, she wrote to the University to ask if she could return. They agreed, and thus scarcely had she been accepted as an immigrant in Canada than she was back in Austria. This time her status was different; she was not a Displaced Person but had right of abode in Canada:

> I got married here in Canada first and then went back and qualified as a doctor. I had to repeat one semester. It was much easier to study because when we were first there we were very insecure, but now there was a certain security. I'd my husband to support me, I'd good friends there and we studied like crazy. I had some of the same professors and colleagues.

Peter Pavlin got academic qualifications through the sweat of his brow in Canada. After a year wielding a sledgehammer in an all-immigrant railroad gang of Slovenes, Ukrainians and Serbs, he had saved $1,000, which got him a scholarship at the University of Western Ontario in London, Ontario. Together with a Polish immigrant, he found lodgings in a girls' college run by Ursuline Sisters. Pastoral care by the Sisters included providing the boys with blind dates among the college girls to escort to dances.

His future wife, Stefania, worked her one-year contract as a maid with a French-Canadian family in Quebec. She got her break through the generosity of students performing Gilbert and Sullivan: 'A priest helped us, writing to Catholic universities through the bishops to see if they could assist these European students. Few replies came, but some did, one from Mount St Vincent College in Halifax. The students put on a play, *HMS Pinafore*, and the proceeds went for the tuition of a student. I was asked if I wanted to go and said yes. I was there till I graduated in 1952, and that gave me a Bachelor of Arts degree, majoring in philosophy!'

Leo Čop, who had a good job in Bolivia, found himself back on the bottom rung of the ladder in Canada:

> I applied to 53 companies and the reply was always 'No vacancies available', even though they were advertising for staff, including chemists such as me. After a bit the wife of an Irish chemist whom I had approached let it out: his boss had told him they didn't hire foreigners or Catholics. But Shell in Montreal were strapped; they were doubling their refinery's capacity and were desperate to find chemical engineers. I got the job because Anglo-Saxon Canadians did not want to go to French Canada.

The family of Aloysius Ambrožič, the future Cardinal, found a sponsor who was prepared to stand as guarantor for all of them. He remembers they were among the few large families to get in to Canada:

> We were lucky, together all the way through, my parents and five boys and two girls, seven kids aged 7 to 19. I have to take my hat off to the Canadians. And the way our neighbours helped us. A year later two friends, who were *domobranci* and had been sent back, escaped into Austria. They wanted to come to Canada and we went to our neighbour, a Mr Keeler, an Anglican I think. So we said: 'Look, somebody has to sponsor these two young guys. We can't, we're not Canadian citizens yet.' He signed on the dotted line without any questions! No question. That's the kind of thing I find so extraordinary.

Ambrožič senior owned a small farm and grocery in Gabrje back in Slovenia, and had been a village community leader. In Canada, aged over 50, he threw himself back into farm work to prove, in the words of his Cardinal son, that he could still hack it. He suffered because none of his sons wanted to follow him into farming. The whole family sold chickens and eggs by the thousands on a farm outside Toronto. They lived modestly, but the Cardinal remembers two big improvements from the camps: they were never hungry and they were free from material fears and anxieties.

Food was one of the greatest joys. Maria Suhadolc, wife of Tone, says that as a teenage girl in the camps she was never ill enough to seek medical help and there were few infectious diseases, but everybody was under-nourished. When they got to Canada, they could indulge in a healthy, balanced diet which eliminated the effects of years of deprivation. She said it took a while to get used to food being plentiful.

Riko Ziernfeld took time to adapt too: 'The first two weeks after we came to Canada we couldn't eat more than normal...Then we ate whatever they brought us. They were bringing piles of food and we were gobbling up everything. I asked if I could get some more canned peaches, which I liked very much, and the guy brought me five cans and I finished them without any problem.'

Professor Joseph Plevnik, starting work as a farmhand, described it thus: 'I had the first decent meal after four years and was able to recover what had been drained from my system. Not overnight. I was raised on a farm back home and I worked as I used to as a teenager, but my bones ached and I couldn't sleep and I thought I was getting rheumatism. It wasn't that at all, it was just the whole bone structure was soft – not enough food for four years. I was a growing boy. Calcium deficiency, but by Christmas it disappeared.'

Homesickness was another matter, and that was not so easy to deal with, as Cardinal Ambrožič testified:

> I finished high school in the camp. I enjoyed it. When I came to Canada I was homesick for the camp; I had no friends and couldn't speak English. Moving from Slovenia to Austria was not such a cultural change. It was all Central Europe. But the Anglo-Saxon world was quite different. It was a cultural shock.

Maria Suhadolc had been thinking of returning home even before she emigrated, because her parents and sister had stayed in Slovenia. She too felt homesick in Canada, and it took her a long time to write a letter back home saying she had decided to stay for good. Her family was disappointed.

Plevnik, who was Maria's brother, remembers the panic among the Slovenes when their ship docked in Halifax and they realised they were locked on board for the night. The old distrust from the refugee camps rose again. The next morning they realised the authorities just wanted to keep them together so they did not get lost. Plevnik found domestic work for Maria with a rich family of lawyers in Halifax, the Daleys. They were her cure for homesickness, showing kindness which went beyond the call of any normal obligations. Like the doctor lifting the paralysed arm of the Slovene in Buenos Aires harbour, these bursts of kindness contrast with the cruelty, indifference and dogmatic rigidity which form a large part of this tale. The memory of these benefactors who passed briefly through their lives stays etched in the minds of those who benefited. Years later Maria said: 'When I went to Halifax, I found this wonderful family waiting for me. It was my first home in Canada. They helped me take English courses in Halifax and prepare for the future. I was away from people I knew on the boat coming over, and the Daleys drove me to see my brother.'

The Daleys gave Joseph a job washing cars, shovelling snow and bringing in firewood. They helped him enrol in the nearby Jesuit College. He got top marks and stayed with the Jesuits for the rest of his life.

The need for sponsorship was frequently a sticking point. The father of the Markež family refused in principle to ask anyone for an affidavit, so they all went to Argentina. Stanko Grebenc and his sister received US visas on the basis of a pledge from an uncle in Minnesota who was interested in the sister as a future bride for his son. However, the sister had fallen in love with a Slovene in the refugee camp and said she could not go. Stanko realised he could not ask to go without his sister, so he too headed for Argentina.

The bureaucracy in the US, described in 1949 by the *Free Slovenia Almanac*, was daunting:

> Work and accommodation for every refugee must be guaranteed by a sponsor. This is splendid for the individual – whoever comes has a roof and employment – but makes emigration more difficult, as time is taken up in the search for sponsors. Three parties cooperate: the government, the IRO and private organisations, denominational, humanitarian and national. The government is involved in (a) the commission, which screens candidates' past, especially political, (b) the consul, who only gives visas to candidates who satisfy the regulations on health, ability to earn a living and moral antecedents, and (c) the immigration inspectorate, which checks all documents and pre-embarkation tests.

Matej Roessmann's sponsor turned out to be another of the lurking guardian angels. He survived as a *domobranec* in 1945 by changing into civilian clothes, and was already a qualified lawyer. He set off with his wife Pepca for Cleveland, Ohio. On the troopship going over, there were not enough crew, so male passengers were asked to help. Matej became a kitchen help. One of the black sailors asked him where he was going, and told him: 'Cleveland, no good. New York good. Chicago good.'

But Cleveland was good. Their sponsors, a rich family called Armstrong, took them in as domestic help, and became their friends and confidants. Pepca cooked while Matej cut grass, raked leaves, cared for horses and picked up apples so the horses could not eat them.

Arthur Armstrong told them: 'Don't throw anything away, but you will never go hungry in my house.' Matej's law degree was invalid in the US, so Armstrong helped him enrol in Western Reserve University, let him off work for half days and lent him an Oldsmobile to commute to the campus. Picking up English as he went along, Matej graduated, but had to wait until he got US citizenship before passing his final Bar exams. He qualified to practise law in the United States some 15 years after first opening his law books in Ljubljana.

Matej's brother Uroš needed 22 years to complete his qualifications as a doctor. Back in 1943, he enrolled in Ljubljana's medical school, but it was closed down and he joined the *domobranci* as a medic. After avoiding repatriation, he was admitted to medical studies at Graz, but first had to learn German. He sailed in 1949 to New York and took a bus to Columbus, Ohio, where he had a scholarship at the university:

> A Catholic student group found me accommodation with a very nice family, who came to pick me up at the bus station. It was heaven on earth. The fall was so gorgeous. There were 50,000 students on the campus. It was a totally different world. There was no more hunger and I was given clothing.

Uroš passed out of under-graduate school after two years, went to the medical school in Cleveland, then on to internships, to the US Army Medical Corps, marriage and finally his first pay-cheque as a doctor in 1965.

Dr Franc Puc, who had been recruited by Corsellis to work in the Spittal camp's TB centre, likewise struggled long and hard to resume his medical career in the US. On arrival in New York the family had to split up. They had already had to leave two daughters and a son in Slovenia.

Franc took a job in New York City, while his wife was a domestic help on the outskirts. Daughter Marija worked with a Slovene diplomat family on Long Island, and the 17-year-old son had a job on a turkey farm. Every one or two weeks, they could get together, usually at church but sometimes in parks or riding subways. Marija described the challenge:

> Dad had a tough time for maybe five years. He became a hospital orderly and then wanted to get to schooling again. So he studied and worked and studied and studied and took the advanced exams as a physician and passed first time. He was born in 1903, so he was 50 when he took his medical board. He had to learn English and first had to be an intern and then a resident. Then life became not marvellous, but OK.

Marko Sfilogoj, who made a lucky escape with the *domobranci* headquarters staff, described how his 50-year-old father Franc, a banker, worked in the US as a lift operator, then as a quality control technician in a factory. Marko soon found himself back in military uniform: he was drafted with his younger brother into the US Army to fight the Korean War.

Albina Loboda's *domobranec* brother, who jumped off a British Army truck in 1945, burned to death in a US tank in Korea. He originally planned to emigrate with his family to Argentina, but stayed on to wait for an elder sister who served in the camps as a cook. By the time she was ready to go, emigration to Argentina had closed, so they went to the US. The benefit of military conscription was that on their return they got grants to resume their studies. One of those was Miroslav Odar, who arrived hoping to complete the mechanical engineering studies he started in Graz:

> I came to the US before I finished and was drafted to Korea, where the war was still on, and saw active service. The fighting was terrible.

I went through two wars, and that's enough for anybody! I was lucky and wasn't wounded. I wasn't even an American citizen and complained because the US is the only country that takes non-citizens into the army. You served or went back to Europe. Quite a choice! So I lost two years. I wasn't ready for school and two more years went by. Then I went back to study and got my degree after five years at Case University in Cleveland under the GI system, which helped financially.

Rudy Kolarič, who walked up the Ljubelj Pass in 1945 as a teenager with a bucket over his head, was drafted into military intelligence for two years during the Korean War. He too was able to finance a scholarship to university. Military intelligence was the obvious role for refugees from behind the Iron Curtain. Former *domobranec* Jože Lekan did service translating Soviet broadcasts in Europe and interviewing people coming out of Siberian prison camps.

Frank Jeglič, son of the former head of Slovene primary schools, volunteered for the draft since he ran out of money studying engineering at Notre Dame University. He was sent to the US Signal Corps in Germany. When he first emigrated in January 1950, it was to Minnesota, where the temperature was minus 40° centigrade. His father dug graves when the thaw came, and then went to work in iron ore mines with Frank's brother. Frank remembered how his schoolteacher, 72-year-old Miss Keefe, bought comic books so that he could learn English by associating words with pictures. The principal, Miss Sharp, whom he described as 'a wonderful benefactor, all heart and encouragement', prompted Jeglič senior to apply for a new teaching licence. Then they moved south to Illinois, where Frank dropped out of school at 16 to become a garbage collector. Later, the father resumed maths teaching and Frank completed his university degree with his GI money.

Dr Valentin Meršol, leader of the Slovenes' camp committee, had connections in the US because he had studied at Johns Hopkins University. He and his family found a sponsor who ran a telephone company in Rock Creek, Ohio, and subsequently moved to Cleveland. They found it difficult at first to convince the existing Slovene population that they were not Nazis. American public opinion considered Tito as their ally and assumed any enemy of his must be bad. But after a bit the mood swung to anti-Communism and the newcomers were welcomed.

The doctor's youngest son Val found the standard of his American school well below that set by Director Bajuk in the refugee camp. The geometry tests were no challenge. He took time to rid himself of the insecurity of his refugee life, so he carried a knife to school for the first year. Then he went to work on a turkey farm, picked vegetables for pickles, milked cows and finally went to medical school. He no longer carried the knife, but until he completed medical school he kept a toy dog that he brought with him when he fled Ljubljana as a boy.

Anton Oblak came to Cleveland with his 15-year-old sister. The rest of their large farming family had returned to Slovenia before emigration started. Anton lost an eye fighting with the *domobranci*, and enrolled in the first class of the camp grammar school at the age of 22. When not in class, he was a camp policeman. In America, they were sponsored by an uncle who ran a Cleveland furniture store. The store no longer exists, but the name Oblak is still on the street front. Anton told one of the authors how he started:

> First it was hard to get work so I helped my uncle with deliveries. Then I started different jobs: at Fisher Body and then in a cafeteria, cleaning the floors and toilets and all kind of things and staying there about three months. In the evenings we went to school for English, and I got a job at a brickyard – heavy, dirty work. Then I went to machine shop evening school and started machine shop work. I was making pretty good money during the Korean and Vietnam Wars, working ten hours a day. The owners were Slovenes, here before the War, and they were pretty good to me…My sister and I earned enough to be independent within three months. In 1953 I bought a house.

Another with humble origins was France Dejak, one of the three who escaped from the execution pits. When he reached Austria, he joined courier bands smuggling people out of Slovenia. He emigrated to the United States since he had an aunt in Cleveland. After five weeks he found a job in a foundry, where he said he worked like a horse. His German-born foreman told him the work was 'fit only for niggers' and advised him to leave when he could.

France Kozina, who like Dejak escaped from the pits, found satisfaction through procreation. What better response to death than to create life? As he huddled in the pit in 1945, Kozina swore that if he ever got out he would marry before the age of 28, or failing that become a priest. Later, he wooed his future wife with 94 letters over six months, and married her the day before his 28th birthday. Through the windows of his house in the town of Niagara Falls, he points proudly at surrounding dwellings occupied by his 32 children, grandchildren and great-grandchildren.

He married a Slovene with a background almost as dark as his own. Back in Slovenia, Partisans seized her father from their home, locked the rest of the family in the wine cellar and set the building on fire. They lifted the door off its hinges just in time. The father was tortured by the Partisans and then released after being spotted by a Partisan who knew him.

If you visit the Niagara Falls before going to Kozina's house, it is hard not to draw comparisons between his own terrible experiences and the turbulent waters that plunge over the precipice. In his home near this troubled nature, he recounts his story slowly and deliberately over several hours. The mental effort is enormous. Every truck window, every door-frame, every room, every path, even the face of his would-be executioner, remains fixed in his memory at the age of 81.

For 40 years Kozina told hardly anybody about his escape. He was scared the Yugoslav secret service would try to silence him. He retired in 1985 from 'a beautiful job' in General Motors. Their house is full of landscapes of Slovenia from 60 years ago. But their wartime experiences hang heavily on their minds: every day they talk about them and go to church. At the end of his interview, he sighs wearily: 'I have frequent nightmares. I won't sleep well again tonight.'

As they moved on in their lives, some of the refugees had to resign themselves to careers that were not of their choice. Riko Ziernfeld, who did three years of mechanical engineering studies in Graz, tried to do a Canadian degree in electrical engineering. He found the strain of studying and working factory nightshifts too much and gave up: 'I got a job in 1956 with a consulting engineering firm where I stayed until I retired. It was a very satisfying and interesting job, as draughtsman and then as technical designer. My wife also worked, for General Electric on the assembly line. With our joint income we lived very comfortably and could visit Europe often, twice a year if we wanted to.'

Tone Suhadolc moved from tree felling and forging steel to accountancy, and never regretted leaving Slovenia. His *domobranec* elder brother chided him just before repatriation to Slovenia: 'You will be sorry if you don't go with us.' Tone was with the *domobranci* too, but disliked them:

> My sister back in Slovenia is probably right that I would have been killed if I had gone back. In Canada it was tough for quite a while but in the end I was happy in my job and lucky in marriage. We feel Canadians now more than anything else. My children all live in Hamilton so we're all together at least once a week. It's beautiful. In the end it worked out for most of us. It's funny. The newcomers from Yugoslavia who immigrate now were lazy at home but when they come here they work like hell. Now at least when they come they're helped, but when we came there was nothing.

Tone's wife Maria says:

> I am a Canadian, but I have a special spot in my heart for Slovenia. When we first came we were still thinking of saving the money and returning to Slovenia when the opportunity came. We didn't intend staying here…When you're single you've mixed feelings and your heart is where your home was. Then you marry and sort out your feelings. We became Canadians when we married and the first child was born and we bought a house. You begin to feel part of this

country. It is interesting how many married fellow Slovenes and how few Canadians.

Cardinal Ambrožič, who rose to the peak of his vocation from being young Aloysius on a modest farm in Slovenia and then a Displaced Person, brims with willpower. The nightmares he had of being sent back to Slovenia stopped after five years because, he says, he eliminated the fear from his subconscious. He respects the Slovene emigrants' material achievements:

> Canada is a wide-open land. I was ambitious, but I never thought I would become a bishop. This would not happen in many other countries. If we had remained we would have been second-class citizens... Of my brothers, one has done well. He's rich, really rich, not from his law practice but from his investments. But the others are all well situated. Because – and I say this without envy – there are some people who really make themselves rich. In the old country they'd be caught in the social web and not be able to rise above it, whereas the new country does offer that possibility, and some of these people have done extremely well...

> The people themselves are responsible for their success. They were ideological not economic refugees. They showed leadership qualities and exposed themselves to danger and risked quite a lot. People like that will always land on their feet. Some of the families were highly educated. There's a Slovene millionaire here, who would have been a labourer for the rest of his life if he had stayed in Slovenia. He came here and got an education and succeeded. If one lets refugees do as much as they can for themselves, some people will always emerge to fill the vacuum as leaders. Often it is those who would not otherwise be prominent who take over.

Wherever they settled, a preoccupation was to bring family members over to join them from Slovenia. After a number of years, Yugoslav authorities relaxed restrictions on emigration, and there was a steady outflow to the States. Once they acquired US citizenship, the Slovenes who came in the first wave could stand sponsor for their relatives. Ivan Kukovica, who had nine children, sponsored two sisters to emigrate from Slovenia to Canada after 12 years: 'The two girls and their husbands are living now close to me in Guelph. Nobody is starving; we're all well off. Traditionally with nine children, one should have gone into the church, but nothing happened this time, not even a nun! However, one is very religious, maybe too much.'

Dr Franc Puc applied for all the three children he left behind in Slovenia to emigrate, but the Yugoslav authorities said the son had to do his military service first. So the two sisters came first, and the son arrived once he had learned how to fight for the state he was leaving. Puc's daughter Marija recalled:

> It was awfully hard for my parents to have three children back home. For me, somehow, it was hard to get used to having brothers and sisters again. We're really close now but it took several years, because the three were close to each other, and I was like an outsider...My father-in-law settled here all right. He lied about his age, made himself ten years younger and got a job. He was fairly high-powered in Slovenia. Here, no, but he was happy and cheerful. It was a lot harder for my mother-in-law. She came over later and was very bitter about having to leave everything.
>
> By the time my dad died the whole family was well established. We all went through college and made it. My dad never had much money-wise, but all the time he was sending packages and money back to Yugoslavia to take care of my two younger sisters and brother. My mother was 91 when she died. They both ended up reasonably comfortable and very thankful for everything they had. They were happy; my mother was never moaning about what she had left back home; she had to work hard and didn't mind that. Well before the end, they had thoroughly fulfilled lives – 17 grandchildren!

Most felt quickly at home in the American melting pot. Marko Sfilogoj, who narrowly escaped death as a *domobranec*, is overjoyed at the cards destiny dealt him. He met his future Slovene wife in the refugee camps when he was designated to pump DDT on the inmates to protect against lice, a process which involved ruffling among the clothes of both sexes. She accused him of never ceasing pestering her thereafter, and they married in the US in 1953. Marko recounted:

> I thank God he kicked me out of Slovenia in 1945, because he opened the door for me, otherwise...a lot of people don't agree and my wife's mad at me! She says we left a beautiful country – yes, we would personally, both of us, have had very nice, soft lives if this hadn't happened, but we wouldn't have all these opportunities, such interesting careers...We're much happier our children have been brought up here and not in Slovenia. I can see even with my brother's and my sister's children [in Slovenia], our kids have more to go on, and it's much easier for them to do what they want and choose.
>
> Never from the day I left home have I felt defeated. I never felt down in Lienz or the other places, I never felt defeated or miserable or that I'd be crying and envying other people. For some reason it was almost like a challenge or fun, going through all these experiences! Even in the army or my profession here, I never felt I

was downed or my background was against me...We've a very happy family life, strongly flavoured Slovene, but completely integrated in the American way of life. We've absolutely no problems with living in American society. Why should we? We are superior! We're from two continents!

Dr Valentin Meršol set out to re-qualify to practise medicine. His years as Yugoslav King Alexander's personal physician and as head of the infectious diseases department in Ljubljana were not recognised. The State of Ohio, where they settled, did not even allow foreigners to take the medical licence exam. Governor Lausche, a Slovenian from a previous emigration, helped him clear this legal hurdle. He passed the exam, and with his experience of treating polio in Austria was enrolled to combat the last American polio epidemic before a vaccine was found. In his mid-fifties, having bought a house for his family, he opened a practice in a Slovene neighbourhood of Cleveland and was swamped by patients. According to his son, he did a lot of work for free and quite a few refugees walked out of his office with prescriptions and $10 to help them. He died in 1981 a week short of his 88th birthday. His wife died in the mid-1950s, worn out by the cancer she already had when she fled.

Val Meršol junior established a successful ear-nose-and-throat practice in Cleveland, and married a nurse whom he met while they were tending a dying patient in intensive care. Once, he was responsible for treating an aged émigré Serb suffering from an ailment neither he nor his colleagues could diagnose. He described it to his father, who asked which part of Serbia he came from, smiled and replied: 'He's a shepherd with liver flukes.' Young Val ran the tests, found he was right and proudly proclaimed the diagnosis of this rare affliction to his colleagues, omitting to reveal that it was not his own. They were duly impressed. Val now has his own large family and lives in a rambling country house at nearby Chagrin Falls. He is still the tearaway mischief-maker of his youth, describing himself in his mid-sixties as the oldest nine-year-old of the neighbourhood: 'I could never have done all this if I had stayed at home. One has more independence here. When I grew up as a kid there was more class-consciousness than you experience here. My parents did a super job and kept us from feeling anxious during those refugee years. My father was like a rock.'

Frank Jeglič was among several Slovenes who worked at NASA on the American space programme. He then worked with the Babcock and Willcox engineering company for 30 years, married and had two children. Director Bajuk praised Frank's father, who was one of the camp community leaders, as 'lively, sincere, straightforward, conscientious, reliable and full of character'. The son admired him for the sense of calm and security he created in adversity:

> I have had a wonderful life. Although there was always fear of Communists coming into the refugee camp, there was a tremendous

feeling of togetherness and people were able to laugh. My father taught maths in the schools but also stage-managed plays and musicals. People felt a common cause. Nobody needed counselling, as they do nowadays.

I am grateful for what I have. I have no needs. I still do consulting. I travel. I do volunteer work. I want to give back. I have never forgotten how good people have been. I want to concentrate less on material things now.

One-legged farmer Franc Cenkar had particular reason to feel satisfied at the way his life panned out. Cenkar wanted to work as a mechanic, but the Lienz camp authorities decided a cripple should be a tailor. He was taught the job in the camp tailors' shop, along with 20 other invalids:

When I arrived in America I could speak no English, not one word. A little German. It takes me five years to learn enough English to survive and then I make citizen papers. I work for 33 years as a tailor for a Slovenian firm. When I started I got 75 cents per hour and when I quit $8 per hour.

Cenkar never forgot his original ambition. When he retired, there was at last nobody to boss him around about his career plans, and he did what he always planned to do, invalid or not: 'I worked all my life as a tailor, but now when I go on pension I quit. I never liked tailoring! I go to school for three winters and now I fix motors...I'm now enjoying myself as a mechanic. Not before.'

# *10* AN UNEASY CONSCIENCE

*Our alleged surrender of 10,000 Slovenes [is] a canard which has been refuted on more than one occasion.*

Britain, the only European country to open its doors to the Slovene refugees, was a more humdrum proposition than the New World. Its economy had been severely damaged, and living standards had fallen even lower than they were during the war. The European Voluntary Worker scheme required the immigrants to go to specified jobs for two years, during which time they needed official permission to move from one place to another. The 1949 *Free Slovenia Almanac* wrote gloomily:

> Some have found private accommodation but most have stayed in hostels run by the National Service Hostel Corporation, living with Serbs, Poles and Balts. Conditions are difficult because they are paid less than the English, but have to pay just the same social insurance contributions. They find the environment unfriendly and feel strangers amongst the cold English. Dr Kuhar cares for their spiritual life and celebrates Mass three times a week. They await the curate Father Ignacij Kunstelj. They feel exploited and would be glad to move elsewhere.

In view of the lethal treatment they suffered at British hands, it was surprising that the Slovenes wanted to go to England at all. But there was still a lingering admiration for Britain and its values. Besides, they had to emigrate somewhere, and the choice was narrow. By 1950, a land worker living in a hostel was giving a more positive view to the newly arrived Father Kunstelj: 'I'm getting on quite well. Work is variable, the people the same: some friendly, others show clearly they're the bosses. You're seldom invited into a home, and then mostly for a cup of English tea, the cure of all ailments. I earn more on piecework but have to work harder. Those who moved on to farms say they're doing well: enough to do but also enough to eat. Generally they like us because we're used to hard work. I won't change in a hurry.'[1]

Others were unreservedly happy with Britain. It was not as raw and demanding as the New World, and less volatile than Latin countries. They were attracted by Britain's welfare state. Franjo and Bernarda Sekolec spoke appreciatively of the controls which kept the rent of their pleasant flat in London's Holland Park artificially low at £2.50 a week. They did not even have to find it themselves; they got the address through a welfare officer at Franjo's employer, the British Broadcasting Corporation (BBC).

Franjo and Bernarda came to Britain together because they had fallen in love. Their first two spouses were killed by military action in Slovenia. Bernarda could be admitted to Britain because she was a doctor and Franjo decided to go with her. He began work as an employee in refugee hostels, and then moved to dish-washing and a job as a porter in a chemical factory.

Franjo went to a lecture in London in 1954 by the UN High Commissioner for Refugees, who told him Tito had promised to let children join their parents. He immediately set about arranging for the couple's children from previous marriages to move to the UK. A few months later they arrived, both aged ten. The daughter emigrated again to Australia when she married, while the son married a Slovene au pair. There were not enough girls among the post-war refugees, so the Slovene community in the UK. filled gaps with young women from home. Bernarda Sekolec had to study for another 18 months before she could take a job as a hospital dietician:

> It was difficult for the children because they didn't speak English. But they soon learned, especially the daughter because she was talkative, and that's how you learn languages. For the boy it was harder. We've lived 28 years in this house and have marvellous neighbours. They've accepted us as a matter of course...

> In a hospital I was drinking tea with a colleague one day when he asked me: 'And who are you really?' and I said, 'I'm a DP, a Displaced Person', and he looked astonished. 'So you're DPs? And I thought DPs were half savages!'

Janez Dernulc, who escaped from a marching column of captured *domobranci*, was sent to the Welsh coal pits. One of his brothers was killed after being sent back by the British, and another died in Buchenwald concentration camp. With 20 other Slovenes, he was dispatched to the village of Ogden in Wales and immediately took to the place:

> Coming to Britain was very nice; everything was so quiet and calm. Italy was noisy. We talked to people here and they were treating us very, very nicely; we were here like one of them straightaway. Some

said, 'It's better in America, or we go to Canada,' but somehow I never really wanted to go...

My plan was to work in the pit, but first to learn English. I had an afternoon shift, and in the mornings I wrote and read and wrote and read for two hours every day. At weekends I went and had a dance, relaxation and a good meal. I got on very well with the miners... The minimum wage was £6.50 but the top was £17 a week and I was already knocking £23. I worked seven days a week and nights and Sunday afternoons, and they called me 'John the Pole the Madman' and never showed any resentment. They said we're cleaner and tidier than anybody else... We were one of them at once. In the pit union, the Communist secretary always wanted to talk with me – no problems.

The secret of adapting to another country is hard work, being tolerant and using your savings to bring you a little reward. There are no poor Slovenes here; they've all got their houses and are well off with a pension, most of them with supplementary pensions. One or two have gone back and they're disappointed: one went because there was a family there and he was by himself. I know of only two really. Most of our people here are really happy.

Dernulc got together with another Slovene in the mines and started fashioning household objects in a garage. They wrote to British Home Stores offering one of their objects and were invited to London. Their product was rejected but they were asked instead to produce 1,200 barrel table lamps. By 1976, their firm employed 128 people.

The partners married Anica and Marija Guden, two of the most traumatised refugees. Anica witnessed the Partisans slaughtering her parents and three brothers, and only survived by feigning death. Her sister Marija escaped because an Italian patrol appeared when she was showing the livestock to the Partisans. The youngsters stayed on their farm, half paralysed by fear, and joined the exodus to Austria in May 1945.

In Spittal camp, the welfare officer took special pains to find a supportive family where they could stay together. Again, guardian angels appeared who soothed the girls' trauma with exceptional kindness. The girls came to England under the European Voluntary Workers scheme as domestic helps, aged 16 and 19. Anica and Marija related their story years later:

We were told we were going to Cambridge to Professor and Mrs Steers. She sent us German, Swiss, French and British money to spend on the way over on the train. His subject was geography and she was a lecturer at St Catherine's College. They had James aged three and Gracie aged one, a professional nanny, two gardeners, a woman to clean and a special woman only to do the silver; eventually I took over the children. When we arrive, Mrs Steers says: 'Anica and Marija, we know all your tragedy. This is your home. We're your new mother and father, and you can address us as such.' They give us the front door key, we go anywhere we like. But we make a good impression because we don't go out. We don't get into any mischief, we stay at home. Mrs Steers sent me to learn to drive and I then drove the Professor to the station when he went to meetings in London. The children by then went to school and I took them, so I did a lot of driving...

We had the most wonderful life there; Mrs Steers was a proper mother to us, a most marvellous woman. Life really started there, because we were for such a long time in such poor, humble circumstances, and when we came to a house where the table was covered with a tablecloth and all things were there for the breakfast, I cried, I cried. For three weeks I cried because I couldn't think this could be true. And then I think, why do I have such a good life here when my brother and sister at home, what do they have? We have visitors every Sunday and they come in the kitchen and she says, 'This is our Marija and this is our Anica'. She was always calling us down, you know, to have a glass of sherry. She was really more than a mother to us.

One day Mrs Steers brought a uniformed guest into the kitchen to introduce him to the girls. It was Field Marshal Lord Alexander. As the Supreme Commander of the Mediterranean area, he was responsible for the British Army troops who sent the *domobranci* back to their deaths in Slovenia. On the 4 June 1945, when they had already been dispatched, he visited the Viktring camp and ordered that no more be sent back against their will. Anica and Marija were among the civilians who were reprieved by this order. Mrs Steers just said, 'This is Anica and this is Marija.' The girls knew Mrs Steers always told her guests their background, so they assumed the Field Marshal knew the poignancy of the encounter. He greeted them and left.

Anica and Marija basked in this kind and prosperous environment. Every year, the family joined four of Mrs Steers' married sisters on holiday in a castle in Scotland. Each family brought its own cook. It was, as Anica said, 'a dream life we had in Cambridge'.

For refugees such as the Gudens, however, the dreams were often nightmares. Sleep summoned up painful visions of their persecution – often scenes of being chased. Anica described it thus:

I was afraid in the night. I had nightmares that the Partisans come in and they want to...When we heard a dog barking, we was both shaking. Mrs Steers always comes and she say, don't worry, you're in a safe place here, no harm will come to you two. It was the fear which grew into us, you know. Once the family went away for a few days, and I was afraid again in the night. I thought I have nobody now to tell about a noise, to protect me. The nightmares were very, very, very strong when we were in Austria; in Cambridge they were still very, very, very strong. Now they declined, but they are part of the inner life of me and my husband. Sometimes the nightmares come, he come down in the morning and he said, 'You know, I was dreaming that the Partisans are after me'. And I'm still frightened, I'm still very frightened if I'm by myself at home.

Jože Jančar, who fled with his bride-to-be on bicycles, was another who suffered nightmares for the rest of his life, despite the fact that as a psychiatrist he had privileged insights into the workings of the human mind. In some of the other refugee immigrants, he saw the nightmares lead to mental collapse or even suicide:

Why have suicides happened? Because if you are carrying a problem you suppress it very strongly and it doesn't surface, but you have nightmares. I still have nightmares regularly. You reach the point of no return when you have another problem which is so grave that the original one comes to the surface and then things burst. There were two Slovenes who committed suicide, both very nice people, very sensitive, very creative, one a poet and one a painter. First they took to alcohol, but alcohol could not save them. In a psychiatric ward we have a lot of problems with post-war traumas. Going round the hospitals, I often find Polish and Ukrainian refugees who have been in mental hospitals for years because they experienced trauma and then suddenly something else happened, either bereavement or some other tragedy and they just disintegrated.

Jože and Marija came to England because they decided it was too risky to stay in Graz after Jože's arrest in 1947. Marija, whom Anica Guden described as an extraordinarily beautiful young woman, had an uncle in the US, but she found it too far and she was not attracted to the American way of life. The immigration rules stated they had to be single, which was not too difficult to simulate, since they had no civil papers for their marriage, only a certificate from the church in the refugee camp. They travelled to England separately, and Marija was sent to a camp on an airfield between Lancaster and Preston. Jože had been studying to become a doctor, but in England the first jobs had to be in mines, factories or agriculture. Jože recalled:

I had to get out of these jobs if I was to continue medicine. I went into Gloucester one day looking for a Catholic church, hoping somebody would know a language other than English. A young priest spoke Italian, and I asked him if I could get a job as a nurse in Gloucester. He said no but when he added, 'I know a doctor near

Bristol in charge of mentally handicapped people, would you like to work with them?' I said I would. We went to see the medical superintendent at Hortham Hospital near Bristol. This was the longest interview I've had, nearly three hours. He wanted to know all about the war and what was happening in Europe; his wife knew a bit of German and the priest translated into Italian. Then he said, 'I'll take you,' and I was appointed to the highest possible grade, nursing assistant Grade 1. I then asked Dr Lyons if he'd give my wife a job. He asked, 'Does she speak better English than you?' I said she did and he accepted us.

Later Jože continued his medical studies at Galway University in Ireland. Marija, who had just learned she was pregnant, saw him off at Bristol railway station. The Irish professor, who studied at Heidelberg, allowed him to write some of the exams in German. The Franciscan priest teaching him philosophy and psychology permitted him to write papers in Latin: 'Then came a crisis. I remember vividly it was St Patrick's Day when I walked along Galway Bay wondering what to do. My landlady was asking for money and I already owed her two weeks' rent. I thought of asking the police to deport me; I didn't know anybody to borrow money from, and there seemed nothing else I could do. The next day Iris Murdoch sent me £100 and this saw me through.'

Iris Murdoch, later a distinguished English novelist, befriended the couple as a welfare officer in the Graz student camp in 1946. She kept in touch and became godmother to their daughter. 'Iris was very nice. She was a quiet person, less lively than in the recent film of her life. She came to visit our family and was always probing, asking: "What do you think?"' said Marija.

Jože pondered emigrating to Australia, but Marija vetoed it, saying two countries were enough for a lifetime. In England, Jože reached the peak of his profession. He wrote over 100 learned papers, and was joint author of *Clinical Pathology in Mental Retardation*. In 1981–1983 he was senior vice president of the Royal College of Psychiatrists. A citation on his appointment praised him for putting psychiatry of mental handicap on a firm footing.

The Jančars' three children wanted to be 'normal' like British schoolchildren, and they only learned to speak a little Slovene. The 600 Slovene refugees in Britain were scattered around the country, and although there were meeting places in London, Rochdale and Bedford, community life was less intense than in Argentina. Marija says it was only when they grew up that her children became interested in their parents' past – and then they were astonished by what they heard.

For many years, hardly anyone in Britain would have wanted to tell the Jančar children what happened in Austria in 1945. Many hundreds of British soldiers were directly involved in dispatching the Cossacks,

Slovenes and other Yugoslavs back to their enemies. Yet until the mid-1970s, the events were practically unknown. Those involved kept quiet after they returned to civilian life. Many returning soldiers wanted to look forward to new lives rather than dwell on wartime hardships. Besides this innocent psychological reaction, however, uneasy consciences must have contributed to the silence.

This may have been the case with General Charles Keightley, who commanded the 5th Corps of the 8th Army, which sent the refugees back. Even though he must have known what happened, and possibly commanded the operation, he gave the following reply in June 1945 when questioned about the matter by Field Marshal Alexander:

> On 24 May, orders were received from AFHQ [Allied Forces Headquarters] that no Yugoslav nationals would be handed over to Tito if this involved the use of force. By this date, the evacuation of those who had borne arms against Tito was complete. This order was rigorously applied in evacuating Yugoslav Displaced Personnel, whose evacuation succeeded the evacuation of the Military Personnel.[2]

This was false. The evacuation was not complete on 24 May. Keightley's 5th Corps continued sending the Serb, Croat and Slovene soldiers back until 31 May. One of his Divisional commanders, General Horatius Murray, also wrote a note at the time:

> No members of the Slovene National Army or any other Yugoslav forces hostile to [Tito] have been handed over to the Partisans. On the other hand, on instructions from 5 Corps, numerous nations who have been fighting the Allied Yugoslav troops under the command of Marshal Tito were handed over to the latter forces.

As author Ian Mitchell, who catalogued the cover-up in *The Cost of a Reputation*[3] points out, the first sentence of this statement is false, and the second contradicts it.

In 1947, General Keightley, then Military Secretary to the Secretary of State for War, had to draft a reply to a Parliamentary question about reports of forcible repatriations and mass killings. He wrote:

> It can be categorically stated that...no Yugoslav displaced persons were ever sent back to Yugoslavia against their will or under false pretences, nor were any Yugoslav prisoners once they came into British hands. It is understood that a certain number of Yugoslavs did return to Yugoslavia shortly after the ceasefire entirely of their own free will. Whether any of these were killed in Yugoslavia cannot be found out for certain, but it is certain that no mass killing as described ever took place.[4]

Early in 1948, Catholic delegates in London questioned the government why silence was being maintained about the affair. The answer was that British troops disarmed about 600 fleeing Yugoslav collaborators at the end of May 1945 and returned them to their native country in compliance with international law.

This too bore little relationship with the truth, and the continuing deceit contributed to the Slovenes' feeling of insecurity in the camps run by the British in Austria. So in May 1948, while the surviving Slovene civilians made a pilgrimage to the scene of the catastrophe in Viktring, Corsellis wrote to the British Foreign Office. Geoffrey (later Sir Geoffrey, GBE, KCMG) Wallinger, a counsellor dealing with refugee questions, invited him to meet one Saturday early in June. The meeting is described in a booklet written by Father Blatnik based on a letter he received afterwards from Corsellis. According to the Blatnik account, the encounter ran like this:

> In view of the answer quoted earlier, John Corsellis wrote to the Foreign Office, astonished that the government could give an answer which was untrue. He told them he had been at Viktring at the time and seen with his own eyes how many had been sent back, and these were no collaborators. The Foreign Office wrote that they would be very interested to hear from him in greater detail and invited him to visit them. When he arrived, they started by asking what he had personally witnessed and then said, 'Thank you for such a detailed account. It may have been as you describe but we have different reports. These speak of only 600 Yugoslav collaborators being repatriated. Perhaps the figures are not completely accurate. You must understand that our troops in Austria had a precise objective at the time: to organise a defence in the event of any attack by Tito or the Soviet Union. So they were not prepared for these collaborators to turn up, nor did they want to have much to do with them. That is why their report was perhaps here and there inaccurate or insufficient, but it's the only one we have. The officers who signed it have returned to civilian life, and the War Office cannot trace them to get them to give a fuller account of the whole affair, so that we are limited to what we have. You maintain that over 10,000 were repatriated. We do not dispute this, but all the same 600 remains the official figure for us because that is the one that appeared in the reports made at the time. Thank you very much for the interest you have taken in the matter, and goodbye.'[5]

In other words, the official account may be wrong, but it did not seem important enough to check further. The official history of the British Army's Mediterranean Campaigns, written by General Sir William Jackson, blandly stated, in referring to the handling of the refugees, that 'the outcome was entirely satisfactory to the Allied side'.[6]

Geoffrey Stuttard, formerly with the British Army on the Allied Control Commission for Austria, also took up arms to find the truth. He was married to a Slovene refugee, Anka Žebot, whose father had been deputy mayor of Maribor and a member of Yugoslavia's inter-war parliament. Stuttard lobbied the Foreign Office through Major Tufton Beamish, a Member of Parliament who had visited the camps in Austria. Beamish received a reply, sent under the name of Chris Mayhew, the Under-Secretary. While Mayhew's previous missive to Corsellis about Jančar was reassuringly correct, this one, no doubt drafted by civil servants, was remarkable for its condescension and denial of the truth:

> I am very much afraid that these unhappy people have been the victims of provocateurs who are constantly trying to drive a wedge between the refugees and their British protectors, since it has been explained to refugees in our zones on many occasions that nobody with a clear conscience need fear lest he be forcibly repatriated. This impression is heightened by the reference to *our alleged surrender of 10,000 Slovenes – a canard which has been refuted* on more than one occasion, but which reappears with conspicuous frequency in allegations purporting to come from displaced persons [emphasis added].[7]

If there were guilty consciences, in this respect they were on the British side. It was only in the 1970s and the 1980s that historians such as Nicholas Bethell and Nikolai Tolstoy began to question what really happened. In *The Last Secret* published in 1974, Bethell described the forcible repatriation of the Cossacks, and the British Army's role in forcing fleeing Croats back into the hands of the Partisans at Bleiburg. Tolstoy went further into the Cossacks affair in the best-seller *Victims of Yalta* in 1976, and ten years later published *The Minister and the Massacres*, which claimed Harold Macmillan was the guiding hand. In a pamphlet, Tolstoy in particular criticised Lord Aldington, a former Conservative government minister, for the role he played in his capacity as Chief-of-Staff of 5th Corps. Aldington, who was Brigadier Toby Low at the time and has since died, denied Tolstoy's allegations, sued him for libel in 1989 and won record damages. Aldington's lawyers wrote to publishers, bookshops and public libraries throughout Britain threatening further legal action if they continued to make available *The Minister and the Massacres*. Even today, the book is virtually unobtainable in Britain, but it can be found on the shelves of Slovene and other emigrants around the world.

However, the broad public debate that followed implicitly acknowledged the British responsibility for the acts of May 1945. The British tradition of free speech and a free press, once it got into gear, performed the salutary role of revealing an uncomfortable truth. In February 1978, *The Times* wrote an editorial criticising 'the cold blindness of the British politicians and officials' who took 'wrong decisions which were then carried out with heartless and unnecessary rigidity'.[8]

A wholesale condemnation of the British would be unfair. Some of the British officers and soldiers who carried out these orders tried to make amends.

Nigel Nicolson, then an officer in the Grenadier Guards, acknowledged that he carried out the order to tell the Slovenes the lie about Italy. At the time, he wrote a critical military situation report: 'The whole business is most unsavoury, and British troops have the utmost distaste in carrying out their orders.'[9] His military superior was furious and ordered him to write it again. He did, removing all suggestions of wrongdoing in a new report, which stated untruthfully, but with intentional irony, that those repatriated were received kindly and efficiently and given light refreshments.

Nicolson in later years openly admitted he did wrong, contributed to the revelations in his autobiography *Long Life*, and for years waged a campaign for the British government to make an official apology. Nicolson's public acknowledgement stands up well when compared with others who have remained silent or refuse to concede they did anything wrong.*

A number of British soldiers protested to their superiors at the time. They included officers as senior as Major-Generals Robert Arbuthnott and Sir Horatius Murray, as well as rank-and-file.[10] Their objections failed to save the Cossacks and the Yugoslav soldiers. But by making their views known, they implicitly gave strength to the relief workers' rebellion which led to the last-minute reprieve of the civilians.

The civilian refugees also partly owe their lives to the alacrity with which the British 8th Army high command reacted. Officers at HQ were flexible and informal enough to listen to Selby-Bigge of the British Red Cross and David Pearson of the Friends Ambulance Unit (FAU), despite their lack of status as civilians, and had the humanity to recognise the strength of their case.

Despite his disgust at the repatriations, Selby-Bigge still wrote of the 8th Army in his memoirs: 'From the desert days, it had been a privileged army, with a frankness of speech and a lack of formality which in no way impaired its discipline. It was remarkable that long years of fighting had not brutalised them. They would flood to hear classical music or opera.'[11]

It should be remembered that the civilian relief workers who rebelled were British too. Their language skills enabled them to listen to the refugees, and they recognised the urgency of what was happening. Not only were they principled and independent, but their high level of professionalism led the Army to listen to their protests.

It was not easy for the FAU to make such a stand. They were in a morally delicate position themselves. As conscientious objectors, they had refused to serve in the armed forces because their beliefs forbade them to take another human being's life. They were vulnerable to accusations of cowardice, and many did their utmost to disprove this by conspicuous bravery. Until D-Day in June 1944, an FAU relief worker was statistically more likely than a soldier to become a casualty.

---

* Nigel Nicolson died on 23 September 2004, at 87.

The FAU workers faced other awkward questions of conscience. A number felt a little ashamed of their gung-ho eagerness to ride with advancing tanks in the thick of battle. Some of the FAU males, hardened by warfare and bonding with soldiers, objected to a decision to send out FAU women. Others, when they experienced the horrors of war, decided their pacifism was irresponsible and joined the Army. The worst moral dilemma was suffered by Tom Haley, who stayed on nursing seriously wounded soldiers after the British Army retreated before the Japanese in Burma. Many could not be transported and were certain to meet a horrible death if captured. There was one solution – mercy killing – but that was abhorrent to a pacifist. Confronted with this choice between two evils, Haley said: 'As a pacifist, this was the most horrible and distressing thing for me in the whole of the war and it has lived with me ever since. I backed up the doctor and surgeon. I was in a cleft stick which there was no escape from: there was no way in which I could reconcile what was necessary to help these men die with dignity with what was in accordance with my belief as a pacifist in the sacredness of human life.' The wounded soldiers were not alive when the Japanese arrived.[12]

Some military personnel could never accept the pacifists. British Army nurse Jane Balding wrote in her diary how ashamed she was to walk around the Viktring camp with John Corsellis beside her. She recalled having 'a very wet FAU wished on me', and later referred to him as the WYM – Wet Young Man. .

Other serving soldiers went out of their way to express appreciation of the FAU's work. When John Corsellis lobbied for the release of Jože Jančar in 1947, he received a reply from his Member of Parliament, Colonel Douglas Dodds-Parker, who had served in the Grenadier Guards. Dodds-Parker (despatches, French Legion of Honour, Croix de Guerre) added at the end of his letter: 'P.S. What magnificent, and unadvertised* work 'the Friends' do – they were always first on the scene with help in the various crises before the war.'

Churchill also admitted erring, though only in private. He told friends in December 1945 that believing he could trust Tito was one of his worst mistakes of the war.[13] He took the decision personally, against the advice of the Foreign Office and part of his military. As in France, he over-estimated the ability of Special Operations Executive (SOE) units to 'set Europe ablaze' by organising and supporting local resistance fighters. In hindsight, some historians have doubted whether such exploits had much impact on the outcome of the war, which was won largely by regular forces.[14]

---

* The FAU has indeed kept a low profile. Its 1,300 members, drawn from all walks of life, included rebels from the Coldstream Guards and those other historic pillars of the establishment, Eton, Harrow, Winchester and Westminster schools, the latter contributing four members, including John Corsellis and Donald Swann of the Flanders and Swann comedy series. Several ex-FAU later achieved eminence – Gerald Gardiner, Lord Chancellor 1964–1970, Richard Wainwright, MP and Chairman of the Liberal Party, and Sydney Carter, composer of *The Lord of the Dance*, to mention a few.

Churchill was, however, receiving misleading reports about the activities of Tito and the Chetnik leader Mihailović from a Communist infiltrator among British authorities.[15] He also had an underlying logic in switching from Mihailović. Roosevelt, Stalin and he had agreed they must stay united in their goal of defeating Hitler. They did not wish the enemy to play one ally off against the other. In such circumstances, it is logical that Churchill should choose the more combative Tito over Mihailović, who took a lower profile in order to minimise reprisals among the Serb population. The fact that Tito was also fighting to gain power in post-war Yugoslavia was to him irrelevant. When his liaison officer with Tito, Fitzroy Maclean, explained that Tito intended to set up a Soviet-style regime in Yugoslavia after the war, Churchill retorted:

Do you intend to make Yugoslavia your home after the war?

No, Sir.

Nor do I. And, that being so, the less you and I worry about the form of Government they set up, the better. That is for them to decide. What interests us is which of them is doing most harm to the Germans.[16]

Some historians have viewed this remark as cynical, but it reflected the single-minded strategy of concentrating on total defeat of the Germans. In the circumstances of Britain's near-isolation in Europe, as country after country had collapsed under the Wehrmacht invasion, it reflected the need to be decisive. It was tough for the citizens of Yugoslavia, but the British Prime Minister had warned in the British House of Commons in 1940 that he had 'nothing to offer but blood, toil, tears and sweat'.[17] Opening the doors to a Communist regime in Yugoslavia may have been a mistake over the longer term, but it was not an act of deliberate dishonour. As far as the Slovene *domobranci* were concerned, his instructions were that they should not be sent back.[18]

When the British Army's action in Austria in 1945 became known 30 years later, a number of British Members of Parliament erected a memorial plaque in London. It stands discreetly in a small green reservation at Thurloe Place on Cromwell Road opposite the Victoria and Albert Museum. Those who stop to read it amid the whirl of traffic find this inscription:

This Memorial was placed by members of all parties and both Houses of Parliament and many other sympathisers as a memorial of the countless innocent men, women and children from the Soviet Union and other Eastern European states who were imprisoned and died at the hands of Communist governments after being repatriated at the conclusion of the Second World War.

May they rest in peace.

Only cognoscenti would understand why such a monument should be found in London. It makes no mention that it was the British Army who sent them back. The issue of British moral responsibility is evaded. It is a gesture, but expressed in weasel words. The Labour British government of the time (1978), reluctant to stir an old controversy, refused to associate itself with the initiative. Margaret Thatcher, then leader of the Conservative opposition and later Prime Minister, contributed £10 from her own purse to the fund-raising. But the government she headed from 1979 vetoed a proposal by Nicholas Bethell that the inscription should say the people were 'delivered against their will by Britain and her allies to imprisonment and death'.[19]

Nigel Nicolson's appeal for an official British apology has fallen on deaf ears. Likewise, his protest to General Jackson about the cynical treatment of the affair in the official military history 'failed to elicit a word of pity or remorse'.[20]

Some Slovene refugees such as Jože Lekan, a *domobranec* who escaped at the last moment, still give vent to their resentment: 'I hate the British guts... Little did I know we were not even zeros at the conference tables of the big powers. These politicians are a bunch of liars. And God damn their souls for it.'

Cardinal Ambrožič in Toronto says: 'The British did not have much sympathy for us. There was a certain war-weariness. They were allied with Russia and Tito. I am not sure how much Toby Low knew about Stalinist methods.'

For Marian Loboda, a leader of the Slovene community in Argentina, Britain should do a *mea culpa*. 'They were a big disappointment. I told John Corsellis he had to be a very good person for us to accept him as a friend after what happened.'

Ex-*domobranec* Matej Roessmann, now in Cleveland, comments: 'In the camps we could not trust the British any more. Roosevelt's view of the organisation of the world was deeply different from Churchill's. I realised when I was in the camps that the US and the USSR were only the two world powers left. Britain, France and Italy were de-classified. It is sad that we had to suffer that from the British.'

For his sister-in-law, Milči Roessmann (née Lekan), the British deceit stems from their imperialist outlook. 'The Empire was their objective. Everything else was just pieces. Individuals did not matter. It was a typical British mentality.'

However, few work up much of a head of steam about the British. They are more equivocal than towards their fellow Slovenes. As Colonel Emil Cof put it: 'We were blinded by their gentlemanly behaviour, and by the dream of an alliance with the British we had during the whole war. It was difficult to accept in a moment that it had all changed.'

The overall British record is thus mixed. The British have been hard-hearted, but ashamed; ready to reverse mistakes, but also subsequently to cover them up; open to discussing the issue in the late 1980s in a glare of publicity, but only sporadically ready to admit wrongdoing.

In spring 2002, the Dutch government resigned en bloc to take collective responsibility for the inadvertent connivance of Dutch UN troops in the Serb massacre of over 7,500 Bosnian Muslims in Srebrenica in 1993. Tine Velikonja wrote on behalf of the 'New Slovenian Covenant' Catholic association to the British Ambassador in Ljubljana seeking to draw a parallel with the repatriation and massacre of the Slovene *domobranci* in 1945:[21]

> From 26 to 31 May 1945, things happened [in Austria], incredibly similar – similar sometimes even in details – to those taking place at Srebrenica almost exactly half a century later...As Mladić lied to the Bosnians that nothing would happen to them and that they need not worry, so the British officers lied to the officers of the Slovene *domobranci* that nothing would happen to them and that they were going to Italy; and as the Dutch commander Karremans drank plum brandy with Mladić after the event, the British officers fraternized before and after the event with the military and political officers of the Slovene and Yugoslav Communist army...
>
> The British however have not admitted and do not admit a parallel development concerning Viktring and the Slovenes. Some strong attempts have been made...but they were stifled. With such a good example coming from the continent now, it is hardly possible that you could not see your role clearly at last...Do not think that we do not know your merits for the freedom of Europe! It is also said that the only crime committed by the British Army during World War II was that at the Viktring field...Our question is: why did you choose us, why was it us?
>
> He received no reply.

# 11 DEALING WITH HISTORY

*The actions of these leaders were national betrayal and collaboration, for which we Slovenes suffered much more cruel anguish than was brought by the world war itself.*

*– Milan Kučan, President of Slovenia, 1990–2002*

In July 1991, Stanko Grebenc fled for a second time from Slovenia across the Ljubelj Pass into Austria to escape attack. The first time was in May 1945. After 40 years as an emigrant in Argentina, he could not believe it was happening to him again. Grebenc was taking part in a conference in Ljubljana to seek reconciliation between the emigrants and their home country. It was just when Slovenia was becoming independent. The Communists had been replaced in government by a Catholic-led coalition, but still exerted influence through the Yugoslav People's Army.

The day independence was declared, Slovene Television asked the local commander of the Serb-dominated Yugoslav People's Army if he intended to withdraw from Slovenia. 'One doesn't withdraw from one's own country,' he shot back. The next day, his tanks rumbled from their barracks and fanned out along roads to quash Slovenia's autonomy. Once again Slovenia was under occupation, this time by an army which was supposed to defend it. In many respects, the Yugoslav People's Army was the heir of the Partisans who fought in World War II. Now they could no longer claim to be national liberators. They invoked Yugoslavia's national integrity, but in practice they were acting on behalf of the Belgrade regime of nationalist Slobodan Milošević.

Yugoslav People's Army jets bombed a television station on the Nanos mountain near the Adriatic Sea, killing several occupants. Grebenc felt it was time to get out of Ljubljana. As he drove over the Ljubelj Pass, jets swooped to attack another TV transmitter on the

Karavanke Mountains. When he trudged up the road on foot at the age of 14, it was packed with people. This time at least he had a car, but the road was deserted. He headed for Vienna and decided to sit the war out.

It lasted ten days. Shooting echoed by night in the Mostec woods in the middle of Ljubljana, and a new generation rushed to underground shelters when air raid sirens sounded. However, the Yugoslav People's Army included Slovenes among its ranks, so the leaders of the secession were pre-warned of its strategy for bringing the republic back to heel. The Army got bogged down and started suffering casualties and desertions. The Slovenes cut off electricity and water supplies to its barracks. There were tense negotiations involving European Union intermediaries in Tito's former palace on the island of Brioni, and Belgrade gave way. In October 1991, the Yugoslav People's Army left Slovenia, never to return.

Stanko Grebenc drove back to Klagenfurt and looked for a place to spend the night. It was the middle of the summer holidays and everything was booked up. Everything, the tourist office said, except a hotel in a village called Viktring. Grebenc was staggered. He lodged overlooking the same field where he and 17,000 other Slovenes had collapsed exhausted to the ground after fleeing in 1945.

Over in Argentina, the Slovene community went wild with enthusiasm and celebrated in the Plaza de Mayo in the centre of Buenos Aires. They interpreted independence as confirming the collapse of Communism and setting Slovenes free to decide their destiny.

But what destiny? By the logic of the Slovenes in emigration, it was the moment for their compatriots at home to re-embrace the ideals that they had preserved abroad. They hoped society would return to Catholic family values. But the people and the country the refugees had left 45 years earlier were no longer the same. Many Slovenes at home had different aspirations and concerns from those who left then. The newfound freedom only served to highlight the divisions between them. For the Slovene emigrants, the joy of independence soon turned sour.

The first non-Communist government, headed by Christian Democrat Lojze Peterle, set about introducing a market economy. However, the transition led to a near-collapse of economic activity. Inflation soared to 1,000%, the new tolar currency slumped, companies went bankrupt, unemployment rocketed and Slovenia lost its lucrative markets in other parts of Yugoslavia. After a time the situation stabilised, but the new government, inevitably run by people with little government experience, got blamed for the mess and did not last long. It was replaced by a coalition headed by Janez Drnovšek, who had other priorities. He had been one of the rotating Presidents of the old Yugoslavia. His party included the liberal wing of the ex-Communists, but was also heir to the free-thinking pre-war Liberal Democrat Party, which opposed the Catholics as backward and authoritarian. Communism may have died, but liberal anti-clericalism continued unabated, and the ancient conflict took on a new shape.

The Drnovšek administration faced the same challenges of consolidating democratic institutions, making the market economy viable and preparing to join the European Union and NATO. But for a party of ex-Communists, self-preservation appeared to be a higher priority than restoring a society based on traditional religious values. Alongside them was Milan Kučan, former leader of the Slovene League of Communists and newly elected President. His post was non-executive but carried prestige and influence. As the son of a slain wartime resistance fighter – his father was killed when he was a few years old – Kučan's heart was still with the Partisans. He knew he must be President of all the Slovenes, including the Catholics, and made several gestures of reconciliation. But his sympathies were elsewhere, and the Catholic Church and its supporters soon found him an obstacle to their revived ambitions.

Back in the late 1940s, while the surviving *domobranci* and their families were suffering in the Austrian camps, Slovenes at home were going through worse. Many were mourning dead relatives. The Communists moved faster and more rigorously to impose socialism than any of the East European countries modelled on the Soviet Union. Starvation and disintegration were threatening much of Europe, and the doctrinaire policies of the new regime initially made things worse. The state nationalised everything it could lay its hands on and began a breakneck process of industrialisation. Forced collectivisation of farming proved a disaster, and was abandoned in the early 1950s, but only after severely depleting basic food supplies.

Slovene historian Žarko Lazarevič recently described how the Communist authorities threw whatever resources they had into restoring manufacturing capacity in the war-torn country and forcing the pace of industrialisation: 'It was necessary to transform Slovenia into an industrial country in a very short time, and irrespective of the cost and casualties...The state took into its hands all economic mechanisms; it became the factor that determined, in both the short and the long term, the form of companies, their location, the extent and manner of financing their investments, the extent of production and precise shares of distribution of products.'[1]

The Catholic Church was a principal target of repression. Many churches were destroyed, and in 1952 a group of Communists set the Archbishop of Ljubljana, Anton Vovk, alight with petrol, inflicting severe burns.[2] People's Courts eliminated real or suspected enemies of the new regime as it imposed a dictatorship. Suspected collaborators continued to be imprisoned or executed without trial into 1946. In the Adriatic ports of the Primorska area, Slovene Communists as early as 1943 started killing several thousand Italians and others in an exercise of ethnic cleansing and revenge lasting until 1947. They threw corpses into rocky chasms (foibe) much as they did at Kočevski Rog.[3] General

Rupnik, leader of the wartime *domobranci*, was extradited by the British from Italy and paraded around the capital in a cage. After brain-washing, he made confessions in court denying everything he had stood for. Scarcely able to stand from weakness, he pulled himself together to cry 'Long live the Slovene nation' before a firing squad executed him.[4] It was a time of high drama in Slovene history, in which soaring hopes of justice and equality mingled with shocking cruelty. According to one estimate, 220,000 Slovenes, or 15% of the nation, were either in prison or in exile at this time.[5]

Marija Jančar heard in England that her father, brother and 16-year-old sister were all sentenced to prison terms. 'There was no special reason,' she said. 'It was enough that they were the relatives of a refugee in the Austrian camps.' Rudy Kolarič, who wore a bucket on the Ljubelj Pass road and later emigrated to the US, left a father who was imprisoned twice. His uncle was put on trial and executed in 1946.

Similar fates befell the families of those who emigrated to Argentina. The uncle of Franci and Ciril Markež was imprisoned until 1952 and his wife did not recognise him when he was released. He weighed 38 kilograms. Their cousins spent 15 years in prison.

Ciril's neighbour in the Argentinian town of Bariloche, Dinko Bertoncelj, remembers a cousin returning from conscription in the German Army after the war to find Dinko's mother lying on her bed half starving. Dinko and his sister had fled to Austria. The sister decided to go home, but was sentenced to two years' forced labour building roads.

The grandmother of Vera Aršič-Bajuk, now in Argentina, was evicted from her home and made to walk through snow to a truck, which took her to a detention centre. She had to leave all her possessions except a few cushions. The authorities knew her family had fled to Austria, and that made her an enemy of the people. During the war, the Germans forced Leo Čop's father to disinherit his son for being a nationalist agitator. After the war, the Communist authorities obliged the old man to disinherit his son again because he had fled to Austria. 'In the end, I inherited some land after all, after 1991,' says Leo, laughing.

Modern Slovene historian Nataša Urbanc describes how industrial-isation caused a mass migration to the towns, resulting in a severe housing shortage. 'The elite occupied seized villas and apartments, but the majority of people lived in very modest apartments without bathrooms, with one common tap and a toilet in an outhouse. Many had only a single room with no kitchen, or a kitchen shared with other residents.'[6] Tone Mizerit, who was ten when his family emigrated in the 1950s to Argentina, was one of those who had to share one room with his mother and three siblings. His father had been forcibly conscripted into the Partisans, deserted, and fled in 1945. This stigmatised the whole family. At school one day, the teacher told the class in which Tone's brother Marko was sitting: 'Marko's father is a traitor.' Only after their arrival in Argentina did his mother tell the children that two of her brothers were slaughtered *domobranci*. It was not safe to talk about it while still in Slovenia.

The regime forced workers to perform extra 'shock work' in factories and fields. Then it emulated the Soviets in prosecuting Communists who had been in the West during the war. It staged show trials of comrades who had been in Dachau concentration camp, executing 11 of them.[7] In 1948, the split between Tito and Stalin made life even more depressing. It raised fears of Soviet invasion and led to further shortages and another wave of imprisonments, this time of pro-Moscow loyalists. The people felt isolated in the world, their will to work sagged, and by the early 1950s the Communist regime had lost much of its initial support. In the early post-war years, it had enjoyed a measure of popular approval as a victorious resistance movement promising a fairer society. Now it faced outright dissent.

Alarmed by its unpopularity, the government gave up its more extreme dogmas. By the mid-1950s, it had abandoned collectivisation of agriculture and introduced economic policies geared to raising living standards. Slovene industry produced its first bicycle in 1954, refrigerator in 1957, and washing machine and television set two years later. The economy reaped the benefits of peace, showing good rates of growth. Aid began to flow, not only from international organisations, but also from the US, Britain and France, who realised that the break with Stalin made Yugoslavia a potential ally.

The post-war persecutions faded into the past. A system of workers' participation in decision-making gave the people at least the impression of having more say, even if in practice the Communists still called the shots. Emigration was permitted from the mid-1950s. As a boy, Kučan realised that the wire fence and watchtowers he could see from his home on the frontier with Hungary were to stop the Hungarians leaving their country, not the Slovenes theirs. Young men emigrated in droves to avoid military service or seek better living standards in the West.

The emigrants who left in 1945 were glad to keep well away from the post-war turmoil. After a time, they began by sending parcels of meat, jam, chocolate, sweets, cigarettes, toothpaste and soap to their families in Slovenia. Then they were able to bring relatives over to join them in their new homelands. For a long time, however, few emigrants dared return to Slovenia. Too many of their relatives and friends had been killed in the frenzy of revenge and class warfare after 1945. Slovene politicians and media consistently denigrated them as traitors who had become foreigners. They were stripped of their citizenship, often as a prelude to seizure of their property.

As political pressures eased, some of the emigrants put their toes carefully in the water again. Cirila Pernišek-Žužek returned briefly in 1958 and 1959 and established friendly relations with her uncle, a

Partisan, and his wife, a dedicated Communist. But she was scared and glad to get out again. The first time Marija Jančar returned, her young daughter took fright when uniformed men came aboard their train at the frontier station of Villach. One of the grandsons of Director Bajuk found he had to fill out a five-page visa application in 1975 to re-enter the land of his birth. His relatives in Slovenia asked him to avoid mentioning he would stay with them. Maria Suhadolc mixed easily with her relatives when she went for a visit about the same time, but a Partisan woman on the radio alarmed her with a diatribe against the political emigrants. When Marian Loboda visited in the early 1990s from Argentina, he found people astonished he could still speak Slovene. Nobody seemed aware that Slovene families in Argentina had been nurturing their language for all those years by obliging their children to study Slovene poets on Saturday mornings while their Argentinian classmates played football.

When Slovenia became independent in 1991, the emigrants could finally return without fear. Jernej Markež had tears of joy, not fear, when he crossed the border on his first visit. So did Marija Jančar's daughter when she set eyes on the island church in Lake Bled.

'When I went back three years ago, I found people nicer and they no longer avoided me. I have become an honorary member of two Slovenian ski clubs,' said Dinko Bertoncelj in Argentina. However, he found the place had changed. Modern Slovenia, like anywhere else in Europe, bore little resemblance to the country they had left.

Val Meršol, who left Ljubljana as a schoolboy and practises medicine in Cleveland, says: 'The first time I went back, I noticed Ljubljana had far more houses. The traffic was impossible, and I was afraid of getting lost in the city where I grew up. Everything seemed smaller than I remembered. The language had become flat. There were no dialects any more.'

They found society had become more materialistic, a phenomenon which they blamed on 40 years of Communism, but which follows an overall trend in Europe.

Cirila Pernišek-Žužek, who was taken aback to find Ljubljana railway station full of Bosnians in 2000, said: 'We had a vision of Slovenia, but the reality is different. There is something broken in these people. Their backbone has gone. Slovenes still have their Catholic belief, but they don't seem totally convinced. In Argentina I have become used to people showing their feelings. The Slovenes are warm but they don't express their feelings. The Slovenes don't *feel* God any more.'

Max Rak, who walked out of a detention centre in 1945 wearing a fake Partisan star, went back many times but felt apprehensive until 1991. 'Until then, I still saw too many red stars around. Now there is no fear any more. I am pretty much ignored. Nobody pays much attention to me. They are sentimental journeys: I go to look at the grave of my father. I am not bitter, but I am happy to leave again,' he says from his home in Florida.

Frank Jeglič in Cleveland says: 'I went back in 1998 for a long trip with my grown-up daughters in a rented car. We had a reunion with my family. I find them nice and they say there are more opportunities for their children now. I felt safe, but we don't have a lot in common.' Val Meršol says he has no axe to grind, but he has little contact with the ex-Partisan side of his family in Slovenia, who include a long-serving editor of the main daily newspaper.

France Dejak, who scrambled out of the execution pit in 1945 and emigrated to Cleveland, returned to Slovenia three times after independence, but said stiffly in 2002: 'I was not well received. I was disappointed by many things. I will not go again.' He died in Cleveland 18 months later, having cheated death for 58 years. His fellow-escapee France Kozina says a court interrogated him when he went back in 1993.

Some, like Marija Hirschegger, found people suspicious that they had come to reclaim property. Some have indeed got their houses back. Others have received only their land, or been offered financial compensation. It is a tricky question. Once they fled, the houses were unoccupied and, with housing in short supply, the post-war regime took over the property and made it available to locals. Now many of the houses are occupied by families who have been there for decades and do not see why they should move out. The emigrants grumble about procrastination, but some realise the potential wrong in penalising innocent occupants. 'I have no intention to request back any property which is occupied by somebody else, but the occupants are still afraid as they know they got it from the state. My grandfather's house is falling apart and the roof leaks, but a man still lives in one corner,' Hirschegger says.

Dinko Bertoncelj's brother decided to buy back the house where he was born rather than await the outcome of legal proceedings. He had been conscripted into the German Army and ended the war as a prisoner of the Soviets, a fate which for most meant death. He survived by convincing his captors that he was a fellow-Slav. They sent him back to Slovenia, where he had to serve another two years with the Yugoslav People's Army.

Those stripped of their Yugoslav citizenship received formal acknowledgements after 1991 that this was null and void under international law. On that basis, they have got Slovene passports. Second-generation children borne of Slovene parents abroad have also received Slovene papers, which is useful in view of Slovenia's accession to the European Union in 2004.

Ex-*domobranec* Uroš Roessmann, who became a neuropathologist in America, decided he should help independent Slovenia by sharing his medical knowledge. For three consecutive years, he spent three months back in the country of his birth in an attempt to do so. After years in America, however, he found the ways of the Slovenian medical profession too stuffy:

Slowly depression set in because it became clear that nothing was really going to change. The same people remained in charge, and they were not going to let go of their privileges and power. The universities are still run on the old Austrian system of hierarchy, with the Herr Professor still high and mighty. They are the same species as our fathers and grandfathers experienced. Young people have no chance. There is too much personal politics. Here in America there are far more opportunities. I have lost interest in going back to Slovenia for any prolonged period of time.

Roessmann invited Slovenes to train in American medical schools. 'A young lady came over for 16 months, did some nice work and published a doctoral dissertation. Back in Slovenia they gave her masses of work for which she was not trained and refused her an appointment in the faculty. So she abandoned her career in Slovenia and came back to work at the hospital in Cleveland. A smart young lady has been lost forever to the Slovene medical profession.'

The daughter of Božidar Fink, now in his eighties in Buenos Aires, returned to make a successful career as a musician in Slovenia. When she accepted an award in Ljubljana recently, she began her speech by announcing: 'My father was a *domobranec*.' Nobody commented.

Marija Jančar returned to Slovenia in May 2002 with her three grown-up children and four grandchildren to celebrate her 80th birthday. After a gap of 57 years, she was able to make up for the birthday tea she missed when she fled by bicycle with the children's father.

But the mother of Ciril Tekavec, now living in Argentina, found the experience all too sad. A native of the Primorska region near the Adriatic, she said: 'I am like a flower which will never produce the fresh scent of the Primorska again.'

All are deeply offended by what they see as the failure of their fellow Slovenes to acknowledge what really happened to them in the war. One, who could never bring herself to go back, said: 'I feel ashamed of those Slovenes. I wish them no good. It should be hallowed ground, but it is cursed ground, saturated with bodies.'

The emigrants have plenty of friends back home in Slovenia. Their story is just one round in a century-old tussle pitting the traditional forces of the Catholic Church against modernising anti-clericalists and Communist revolutionaries. During the 45 years of Communism, the Catholics had to keep their heads down. The *domobranci*, the emigrants and the post-war massacres could not be discussed. Now the Communist Party, which suppressed and distorted important parts of the history, has been dissolved. The Catholic establishment wants to regain lost ground, but its political opponents remain strong. The arguments go on and on, with no quarter given.

How, for example, should the new Slovene state commemorate those who died in the war and immediately after it? For a young nation which went through bloody tumult only half a century ago, this is an issue impossible to avoid. Many families concerned are still alive. Britain commemorates its dead as soldiers who died defending their country against a foreign threat, without anybody contesting such a statement. Modern Germans largely agree that their wartime dead resulted from a fatal mistake, never to be repeated. But what was the meaning of such huge numbers of deaths in Slovenia? Were they heroes, villains or victims?

In Slovenia, some 400 mass graves have been discovered. They were largely unmarked because they mostly contain victims of the Communists, who had an interest in keeping them secret as long as they ruled. When a motorway was built recently near Maribor, construction workers came upon an anti-tank ditch stretching several kilometres on either side. The strip excavated for the motorway contained over 600 corpses (probably Croats) dating from the post-war period.

A multi-party parliamentary commission charged with marking the graves tried to find a common wording for years. Those sympathising with the Partisans jibbed at the idea of giving equal honours to those who fought alongside the enemy. The Catholics wanted their own dead to be designated as counter-revolutionaries, to show that they were not fighting for the occupiers but against Communist revolution. They wanted the inscriptions to indicate that the victims had been illegally put to death without trial. In the end, it was decided in 2003 that the grave monuments should commemorate 'victims of wartime and post-war executions'. The Catholics were not happy.

Besides marking graves, the commission decided to erect a monument to all the victims and create memorial parks at Kočevski Rog and Teharje. Names are to be listed in a Book of the Dead, the state is to issue death certificates, and state prosecutors have been told to examine whether prosecutions should be brought for the post-war executions. This is a comprehensive plan, but after ten years, little progress had been made.

It is not that Slovenia *lacks* war memorials. In almost every Slovene village stands a memorial to local Partisans who died. These are much like war memorials in France and Britain, except that the Catholic Slovenes who were killed fighting against the Communists are excluded. Since independence, Catholics have erected their own separate memorials listing *domobranci* killed. Monument stands against monument, and the conflict is literally carved in stone. One of the basic purposes of a war memorial, encouraging peace, is unfulfilled.

Several memorials with different messages stand at Poljana on the border with Austria, where Partisans killed several hundred German and Croat soldiers on 15 May 1945. This was nearly a week after hostilities ended everywhere else in Europe and was Germany's last defeat of the war. The Germans and Croats were trying to give themselves up to the British at Bleiburg in Austria rather than to the Partisans. One memorial carries a standard tribute to the Partisans:

You loved freedom as your own mother.
You gave your lives because you did not want to be slaves.

Fine words, except that by then the victors were already free from enemy rule. Another stone celebrates the capture of a high German commander; the Partisans were looking for commanders to execute as war criminals. A third memorial, put up much later in 1985, at a time when the one-sided Partisan attitude to history was beginning to be questioned, states cryptically:

To Freedom and Peace

That at least is something to which both sides can subscribe. The trouble is it is so vague that few people in later ages would have any idea why a column carrying these four words had to be put up just there. Like the British memorial in London, imprecision serves to dodge an awkward issue.

Slovene war memorials extend into Austria. At Borovlje (Ferlach), a stone marks the final battle at which *domobranci* pushed aside Partisans blocking the road leading from the Ljubelj Pass. The Partisans, said Slovene President Kučan in May 2000, were there to 'liberate the Slovene part of Carinthia'. No conciliation there either: the remark was not calculated to please local Austrians.

On All Saints' Day, Slovenia's leaders have so many memorials to venerate that they cannot do it all in one day. They spread it over two days, and television gives them prime coverage. Citizens scrutinise carefully who goes where and what they say. President Kučan made visits to countless Partisan monuments during his 12-year term of office, but according to the Catholics, who had been counting, he only ever went to two *domobranci* sites.

Take a journey up the rough roads into the wooded hills of Kočevski Rog and you will see little patches of candles flickering if you know where to look. Go there on a weekday and feel the quiet charm of trees, flowers and fresh air far from the hustle of everyday life. It inspires reflection, and for good reason. Nature created rocky pits and chasms among these rolling hills. Mankind has filled many of them up, with dead bodies. This is where half the *domobranci* repatriated by the British in 1945 were killed in the space of a couple of weeks. These are killing grounds.

Once the domain of an Austrian nobleman, Kočevski Rog still has the feel of Partisan country. Wind your way through the woods, and you may come on the preserved remains of a Partisan encampment. Tens of thousands of factory workers and schoolchildren were ferried up to see 'Baza 20' for 45 years after the war. Many of the hutments are labelled as offices of the Communist Party, just in case you should miss the point that wartime heroism and Communism were one and the same thing. In its wartime heyday, 'Baza 20' was a hive of clandestine activity. Kitchens had special chimneys to conceal smoke. Some 100 couriers came and went each day, and the British Royal Air Force flew supplies into a nearby airstrip. It had a radio station, a printing press and workshops. The huge post-war car park and cafeteria nowadays see few visitors, and the site is slipping gently into neglect. The incipient dilapidation of 'Baza 20' symbolises the declining power of the Partisan myth. The message is beginning to ring hollow.

For 35 years, the existence of the mass graves was a subject too dangerous to raise.* Former *domobranci* such as Tine Velikonja and Justin Stanovnik, freed because they were under age, kept quiet for two decades. Many of the families knew what had happened to their men-folk, but said nothing. The women wore black shawls as a sign of bereavement, and priests said Masses for the dead, but they could not be announced in advance. Accounts of the slaughter written by emigrants abroad found their way into the Slovene National Library, but they were locked away from all but a handful of approved readers. Then relatives began laying candles in the places where the *domobranci* were buried, marking the way with discreet crosses carved on trees. In the 1980s, a few brave Slovene writers began writing about the affair and demanding explanations from the Communist regime. From then on, families could visit the pits more openly. Just a small wooden cross and a circle of flickering candles mark many of them. One pit contains the remains of wounded *domobranci* whom Partisans rounded up in hospitals. They were forced to stumble along forest paths to their execution in a gully. Those who could not walk were carried on stretchers.

Many Partisans dispatching the *domobranci* came from other republics of Yugoslavia, but escapees testify that a number were Slovenes whom they recognised personally. The executioners were organised in a People's Defence Corps of Yugoslavia (KNOJ), formed to consolidate the Communists' grasp on power. Most of the executioners must now be dead, but not all. Some were unable to cope with the trauma of the killings and are reported to have taken to drink, gone mad or committed suicide. Who these people were however, remains largely a mystery.[8]

---

\*    Edvard Kocbek, a Slovene Christian Socialist (left-wing Catholic) poet and leader who cooperated with the Partisans during the war, received in his letter-box in 1946 an account of the escape of one of the *domobranci* survivors. At a meeting of the Slovene Communist Party Central Committee in October that year, he demanded an answer as to what happened to the *domobranci*. He was told they were mostly in labour camps and would gradually be allowed home. When he received more reports about their execution, he wrote about them and offered his resignation. He was then excluded from political life, attacked as a writer for being 'politically negative' and barred from publishing for the next ten years. His full account of his attempt to uncover the truth was published in 1975 in a Slovene periodical in Trieste, Italy.

After the killings were finished, the Partisans filled the pits with rocks and earth blown up by explosions that sent clouds of dust 50 metres into the air. They were then made level with the landscape, though a sharp eye can notice that the acacias planted on top are different from the trees on the edges. In one, the bodies were covered with rubbish from a garage. Subsidence has set in and now the main pit at Jama pod Macesnovo gorico is clearly visible again. You can clamber down, peer into a fissure and see a human thighbone lying on a ledge 15 metres below. Potholers have descended into several of the pits and established the presence of large numbers of human remains. Along the path leading from the road, there are small stone defensive structures, apparently where Partisans stood guard to prevent any last-minute breakout by *domobranci*.

But whose remains lie where? For many of the surviving families, this is a source of distress. On All Saints' Day, Slovene television has for some years interviewed people walking around the Kočevski Rog woods bewailing that they did not know which pit their relative was in. In other European countries, in both world wars, families accepted that the whereabouts of their lost ones could never be known. For Central European Catholics such as the Slovenes, however, cherishing the grave of a dead loved one is an important part of their spiritual life. Catholics have considered exhuming the remains. But this would be a huge excavation and not all the pits have been located. The main site at Jama pod Macesnovo gorico has become a shrine, with a place of worship and plaques laid by Slovenes, Serbs and Croats. A Via Dolorosa of hewn wooden images lines the track leading to it, assimilating the death of the *domobranci* to the killing of Christ. A cult of martyrdom is taking shape, furthered by the continued presence of the bodies.

The Catholics on the parliamentary commission calculate that altogether about 12,000 *domobranci* were killed. By 2002, they had established the names of 9,000 of them, mostly by going round knocking on doors. The British Army in Austria sent back about 11,850 Slovenes, of whom just over 11,000 were *domobranci*. Those under-aged were released, though some later died of their harsh treatment or just disappeared. The *domobranci* who were executed also include several hundred captured in Slovenia.

Some 4,000 to 5,000 *domobranci* lie in Kočevski Rog, with another 5,000 in disused mineshafts at Hrastnik in the east, close to the Teharje concentration camp. The rest were killed at various sites elsewhere in the country, in Teharje, Slovenj Gradec, Slovenska Bistrica, Crngrob, Žančane, Škofja Loka, Radovljica, Šentvid, Podutik and Brezovica.

Other Yugoslavs besides Slovenes lie in these graves. In Kočevski Rog, about 1,000 Serb Chetniks and Croats are also buried; in Hrastnik, there are between 2,000 and 4,000 bodies of non-Slovenes.[9]

The Slovene Institute for Contemporary History has calculated that 68,448 Slovenes were killed during the war or directly after it.[10] This was 5.4% of the population, and compares with a death rate of 0.6% for Britain. In addition, many tens of thousands of Croat Ustashe who were turned back at the frontier with Austria by the British and the Partisans probably met their ends in Slovenia. Jože Dežman, Director of the Gorenjski Museum, Kranj and researcher into the post-war killings, has estimated that the total of Yugoslavs of all nationalities who were killed in Slovenia in the immediate post-war period was between 70,000 and 200,000 – in a country then totalling 1.2 million inhabitants.[11]

So much for the grim statistics. Kočevski Rog remains a haunting place. At a packed annual commemoration service, the recorded voices of a *domobranci* choir echo through the trees alongside their brittle bones in the pits. The air seems still impregnated with the fears, prayers and mutual solidarity of thousands of young men approaching an abrupt end to lives which had only just begun. The lingering memory of these doomed human beings is deeply moving, more so than the fading glories of Partisan resistance at 'Baza 20' further up the track.

Milan Kučan, the dominant political personality in Slovenia for the last 15 years of the 20th century, made his own pilgrimage to the *domobranci* graves on Kočevksi Rog. It was a bold move by a man who spent most of his adult life as a Communist politician. This was in July 1990, when he was riding on a wave of popularity. He had voluntarily ended the Communists' exclusive hold on political power, creating conditions for a free democracy. He was the champion of Slovenia's right to go its own way despite attempts by hard-line Communists in Belgrade to hold them back. He was President of the Slovene Republic, then still formally within Federal Yugoslavia. He was the man of the moment, but may have been wondering for how long. After all, he represented a political belief that was collapsing. One way or another, he felt it was time to make his move to end the simmering dispute over wartime events.

He stood before several thousand people, mostly Catholics, in a clearing near the pit containing the largest number of dead *domobranci*, and delivered a speech appealing for post-war wounds to be healed:

> The reconciliation with all the dead victims of war that we now have a duty to perform is a test of our nation's maturity, self-confidence and self-respect...There must not be and cannot be any kind of victory or any kind of defeat. We should close the book on all our wars and our post-war wounds – completely, without any feigned ignorance and without any final thoughts. Let us bury all the dead once and for all, with all dignity and respect. Let us leave them to the memory and judgment of history. Let all violent deaths, from a time when the demons of war raged around us, be equal in our consciousness. Let there be no more evil from wartime and post-war settling of differences...

Through this place, surrounded by the impenetrable Slovenian forest, perforated with inaccessible underground secrets, passed the most terrible winds of our recent past. Here we were put to death. Here we put each other to death, here we fought and sought shelter from violence. Here we were victorious and we concealed the evil caused by our fighting and victory. Here, victory was turned many times into defeat. Let us tell ourselves: here, where the bones of those who fought for one ideology or another are strewn about, this is the right place for that reconciliation which we need as a nation set on the future. Let us mourn sincerely what happened!

At the end, he shook hands with the then Archbishop of Ljubljana, Alojzij Šuštar, and that should have been it. Never before had a Communist leader made a public appearance at this site, which the regime had kept secret for so long. Hard though it was for him, he had spoken his words of conciliation, and the other side would hopefully acknowledge it as a break-through.

They did not. The speech went down badly with his Catholic opponents. It was no doubt sincere, but it was full of elliptical generalities. They looked in vain for any word that the Communists were responsible

President Milan Kučan, leader of the Slovene Communist Party, shakes hands with Archbishop Alojzij Šuštar at a ceremony at the *domobranci* execution pits in Kočevski Rog in 1990.

for the killings or any outright condemnation. The wounds did not heal.

Kučan went on to become a statesman respected by European leaders. They appreciated him as a factor of stability and liberalism amid the turmoil of ex-Yugoslavia. He became a friend of the Czech Republic's Václav Havel, and together they promoted the concept of a newly democratic Central Europe. Britain's Queen Elizabeth appointed him to the Order of the Grand Cross of St Michael and St George. Even Pope Paul II honoured him in 1993 as a Knight with the medal of the Order of Pope Pius. Among many of his own people in Slovenia, he was viewed as a father of the nation, a doughty fighter for its freedom and independence, and was consistently by far the most popular politician in opinion polls. They saw him as a defender of the new state's independence and dignity. At the same time, he was a man of the people, who climbed its highest mountain every year and bought his vegetables on Ljubljana's open-air market.

Failure to solve the long-standing conflict over the war, however, was one of his notable setbacks. When he met one of the authors in his Presidential office in 2002, he said: 'I wish the Slovenians could apply more human ethics to this question. I myself perhaps did not have sufficient moral authority to raise the ethical standards.' On leaving office after 12 years, just before Christmas that year, he told television viewers: 'I tried to be President for all the Slovenes. Maybe some do not agree that I achieved this, but I want them to know that I held them all in respect.'

Warming to his theme among the flowers, the microphones, the interpreter and the press secretary, he observed in the interview that his parents' occupation as schoolteachers made it natural for them to sympathise with the Communists. Because King Alexander ruled pre-war Yugoslavia for much of the time as an absolute monarch, it was not difficult to mobilise the Slovene population in support of better social conditions. His parents supported Britain and the Soviet Union when the war broke out, were shocked by the Molotov/Ribbentrop Pact between Germany and the Soviet Union in 1939, and felt relief when Moscow switched to the Allies after Hitler's attack. His father was away from home for most of the time once Yugoslavia entered the war in 1941:

I felt concerned for my mother. I had these images of bad people coming across the border from Austria to kill our people. I was four when the war finished. It was a solemn moment. The Red Army was passing through our region, and I remember people welcoming the Slovene Partisans with flowers in their hands.

My world after the war was divided into good and bad. Not much more can be expected of a child of five or six. The criteria of good and bad which you are taught by your parents remain with you.

That goes for most Slovenes of my generation. At that time, it was relatively simple to say what was good or bad...

Nowhere were people so divided after the war as in Slovenia. Everyone was bitter. I expected in 1991 it would be possible to repair what we had gone through. I expected the founders of the Slovene state would heal this wound. Where is the problem? People are saying Slovenia should be as they want to see it, or it does not exist at all. That's not possible, but it is not easy to say Slovenia is a country common to all of us and must fit us all. It means stepping out of our own traumas, of one kind or another.

What has happened is that all the frustrations, disappointments and hatreds have returned after 50 years. After the war, a certain reconciliation did take place. There was co-existence. The children of Communists and *domobranci* went to school together and built water supplies together. The unfortunate events of the war and after it were being forgotten slowly. After independence in 1991, it was quite the opposite of what was expected. The past surfaced with renewed force...

Perhaps only future generations can solve the issue, those who are not burdened. I wonder when we will have the moral wisdom to do so. I personally believe this is a moral debt of the fathers and not to be left to our children or grandchildren.

The sense of frustration was palpable. Kučan pondered why the Communists slaughtered the *domobranci* sent back from Austria: 'To this day it is not known where the decision was made to settle scores with the *domobranci* in such a bloody manner... What remains unclear is the motive for all this after the war had ended. Revenge did play a role, as did attempts to eliminate political and ideological opponents. But neither are sufficient explanations for what happened.'

In most of his utterances he used the euphemism of 'extra-judicial killings'. That is not to say he was never more forthright, but it was always clear where his sympathies lay. Take a speech he made to Partisans and Allied veterans in Slovenia in 1998:

To disregard the evils and genocidal intent of the Nazi and Fascist armies towards the Slovenian people, some of whom sadly even offered allegiance to the occupying forces, is simply an attempt at belated revision of the roles which during the war each person chose for him- or herself. And these roles can in no way be changed by the distance of more than 50 years. For this reason, you Partisans need not hang your heads before ideological accusations. You do not even need anyone to defend you from criticisms. The outcome of the war puts you in the right. The actions you took are your defence. For through your actions you responded at that time when this was required of you by your human dignity and the honour of the nation.

It is sadly true, however, that our wartime activities have several faces. It is true that the ideological divisions, which go back decades in Slovenia's political history, to the times before and during the two world wars, led in that part of Slovenia occupied by the Italians even to tragic fratricidal killing. It is true that after 9th May 1945, the victors, drunk on victory and the irrational need for revenge, conducted wicked killings in Kočevski Rog and elsewhere in Slovenia which can in no way be excused.

And yet, in spite of all of this, the truth remains that no possible ideological reason, however much it might be affirmed, can excuse the actions of those political leaders, during the war and even before it, who persuaded numerous young Slovenians to take up arms for the occupier and use them against their brothers. The actions of these leaders were national betrayal and collaboration, for which we Slovenes suffered much more cruel anguish than was brought by the world war itself.[12]

There was a clear condemnation of the executions of the *domobranci*, but it was couched between a tribute to the Partisans and a rejection of the Catholic defence. Of the emigrants, he said:

> The refugees who went to Vetrinj (Viktring) included farm-workers, poor people, and also a highly educated intelligentsia. They immediately set up educational facilities there out of a concern to preserve the Slovene identity and culture. A large part of those who went to Argentina helped maintain the essence of the Slovene nation. But they failed to understand when Slovene culture was under threat here. It remains a riddle how that should be possible. They always use the excuse that they were anti-Communist. Winston Churchill was anti-Communist too, but he still felt the need to cooperate with Stalin to protect humanity.

These words did not live up to his aspirations to be a conciliator. Kučan believes that the combativity of the Partisans and the passivity of the Catholics reflected their different ideologies. He said only the leftist parties in pre-war Slovenia were able to understand the true face of Fascism and organise resistance to it, while the bourgeois parties were incapable of making the right judgment. He told an anecdote illustrating the need to adapt. It gives an interesting insight into the workings of a family at a time when the Communists were re-ordering society:

My grandfather was a wealthy farmer – a kulak. He had 100 hectares of land, with his own inn, a brandy-making still and a store. The post-war People's Government took that away from him. He carried on always expecting that things would change back. We grandchildren used to tease him, asking: 'Granddad, when are the changes coming?' My mother was a member of the commission which determined how much property he could keep. My grandfather died still believing that things would go back to as they were.

I found it absolutely right at the time to take away property. I believed everybody should live well and have education and healthcare, and that there should be an end to exploitation. My grandfather's property was not the result of his hard work. He was still left with enough. But when the criteria change, you need to have a different judgment. I still wish for a world free of injustice, but this is not a world of dreams. You have to live with the realities.

Such is the realism of Milan Kučan, who spent the first part of his career making his way to the top of the Slovene League of Communists, and the last part leading his new nation into a market economy based, among other things, on a respect for private property.

There is a touch of cynicism and cruelty in the anecdote. Yet precisely this adaptability was his strong card. His views may be little different than those of any other leader brought up from birth as a Communist. But his actions proved anything but dogmatic. He used his position as leader of the Slovenian League of Communists to introduce democracy of a type which his party had hitherto rejected, and to preside over a change of the economy which brought far more benefits to his people than the state-controlled system he previously championed. Like Gorbachev in the Soviet Union, it needed a Communist leader to break the repressive power of a Communist party. His reward was to be the only former head of a Communist Party in Europe to remain in power into the 21st century. For the emigrants, however, he was a long-standing barrier to rehabilitation.

For many years, one of Kučan's adversaries could be found a few hundred metres away from the Presidential building, in an old baroque palace in the historical centre of Ljubljana. Its incumbent, Archbishop Franc Rode, fled on a horse-drawn farm-cart at the age of ten with his family, spent four years in the refugee camps in Austria and emigrated to Argentina. Less than 20 years later he was back, with a mission to defend the interests of the Catholic Church in one of its former heartlands.

When you push open the huge wooden door of the Archbishop's Palace, it is slightly like entering a fortress. This is the nerve centre of the Catholic Church in Slovenia. There is no receptionist. Only men are to be seen in the interior courtyard. One denies the Archbishop is there and suggests you call the next day. Then a pleasant young man in a cassock, speaking English, hurries up: it is the press secretary. He unlocks a heavy wrought-iron gate and ushers the visitor to the Archbishop's quarters upstairs. A polite enquiry whether French would be a suitable common language, a short wait in a 19th-century drawing room with lace cloths on the table, and then the prelate glides in, a charming smile on his face. The conversation proceeds smoothly and good-temperedly, like two diplomats re-arranging Europe at the Congress of Vienna, twisting the French language to cope with the rough matters under discussion.

The youngest son of a farming family with seven children, Franc Rode was brought up with the same elemental attachment to the Catholic religion that Kučan had to Communism. For both, the belief went with the milieu into which they were born. When war broke out, Rode says his family was frightened of the occupying Germans and had little sympathy for them. But they noticed the Germans restored a certain order, and the supply of food improved. They were only 15 kilometres from Ljubljana, but had no idea what was happening there since it was sealed off by barbed wire.

Then they started to hear about 'the men of the forests'. These were the Partisans, beginning to organise themselves to fight against the invader. In view of what happened subsequently, it is surprising that Rode's father was with the resistance in these early days. The Communists did not yet dominate the movement. The father left when he heard of the Partisan attacks on Catholic individuals, families and priests in the Italian zone. Soon two of young Franc's elder brothers joined the *domobranci*.

His family had to abandon their cart and horses in the pandemonium on the road up to the Ljubelj Pass. As the tunnel was blocked, they walked over the pass on foot. Two weeks later, the young Rode realised his two brothers had been handed back to the Partisans. One was released from the Teharje concentration camp because he was under-age, but the other went to his death in the pits.

In the camps, the family hesitated long about returning to their farm in Slovenia, but in the end chose to emigrate. As a large family, Argentina was their only possibility. Among the first memories of the future young Archbishop as he disembarked in Buenos Aires were posters of the dictator Juan Peron and his flamboyant wife Evita boasting their championship of Argentina's *'descamisados'* – the shirtless poor.

They stayed 15 days in the Immigrants Hotel, living on daily grants of $2 each, and then a Slovene priest found them a place in a communal dormitory. His parents found work on a farm outside Buenos Aires, the young Franc became a boarder at a Catholic school, learned Spanish in three months and began to forget his Slovene. Separated from his parents, he decided to become a priest and joined a seminary.

Rode is one of the few Slovenes who took a dislike to Argentinians right from the start. He had no interest in joining the tight-knit community of Slovene refugees maintaining the old values in a foreign land. He did not wish to stay, and in 1955 asked the Catholic authorities to allow him to continue his studies in Europe:

> I liked Argentina as a country but I did not like the people. They were not serious, they were not objective and they held foreigners in contempt, in particular Slavs. I was called 'un Polacco de merda'. I saw no future, either spiritually or intellectually, in that country. I had the national consciousness of a Slovene. I was sent to Rome for a year and then I spent eight years in Paris doing a doctorate. It was one of the best decisions of my life to leave Argentina. Their whole history is anti-European. They held us responsible for all the pain caused to them by the Spanish.

> Then I returned to Slovenia. After 20 years of exile, my deepest wish was to return to my native country. I wanted to live among my people. I was tired of being among foreigners. I wanted my word to count as much as that of others. I wanted to be equal in Slovenia as a Slovene, and not to be a foreigner any more. So on 4th January 1965 I arrived in Ljubljana and said to myself: 'So here I am behind the Iron Curtain.' In the early years I had a hard time with the secret police, but the decision was the right one.

After 16 years teaching in Ljubljana's Faculty of Theology, Rode went to the Vatican again in 1981. From 1997 he was back in the Slovene capital as Metropolitan Archbishop of Ljubljana, defending the Catholic Church against what he sees as a campaign to exclude it from public affairs. For Rode, appointment to the Archbishopric, the highest Catholic post in Slovenia, completed a remarkable circle which began with his flight as a child.

But his homecoming did not further reconciliation. He was in opposition to the establishment, not part of it. Although charming in private, in public he was a combative character, sensitive to slights. He campaigned for Catholic religious instruction to be reintroduced as an optional subject in state schools, raising the hackles of those who believe there should be a separation between church and state. His opponents were not only former Communists but also apolitical professional classes, who considered such a proposition out of place in a modern European state. He also opposed the building of a mosque for the Bosnian community on the grounds it could be used as a political centre. Slovenia's smooth transition from Communism to democracy and a market economy may seem an accomplishment to many. But for Rode (interviewed in 2002), that was precisely the problem:

> The Communists did not lose power because of a military defeat, but because of atrophy resulting from their profound mistakes. It

was an implosion. But the Communists are still there. They never suffered a historic defeat. They prepared their coup, their future.

The mass media, the banks and the big companies are still in their hands. There is a democratic framework but the political class remains the same. They changed the political system, the ideology and the economy, but not their enemy, which is the Church. Belonging to the Church has become a criterion for exclusion: if you are a believer, you can have no position of responsibility. You don't need to be a former Communist, but you mustn't be a believer.

In a declaration in September 2002, he asserted that conditions for the Church had become worse than under Communism. Inevitably, he is compared with his more conciliatory predecessor, Alojzij Šuštar, who shook hands with Kučan at Kočevski Rog. His militancy may surprise in view of the gains the Catholic Church has made over the past 20 years. Christmas, which until 1989 was a working day, is again a public holiday. Schoolbooks are becoming more balanced. Catholic chaplains have been introduced into the Slovene Army. Large tracts of land have been returned to the Church, enabling it to set up businesses such as wine cellars. In 2001, the Church successfully lobbied against in-vitro fertilisation for single women, and in 2003 against Sunday opening of supermarkets.

Supporters say it was precisely his firmer stand that brought success on these issues. 'He is personally a very cultivated man. He knows his theology and he knows exactly what he wants. It is because he does not wave to the left and right that he has trouble with the authorities. Under Šuštar, people were used to the Church giving way,' said Cirila Pernišek-Žužek, who knew Rode as a boy in the camps and later in Argentina.

His militancy is less surprising when one considers that he was appointed by Pope John Paul II. Whereas a previous Pope sought détente with Communism in the early 1970s, the Polish Pope directly confronted the Communists. When John Paul II in 2003 visited nearby Slovakia, another Central European land which was traditionally Catholic and went through 40 years of Communism, he publicly espoused the same causes which Rode pushed in Slovenia. The Pope also seemed to favour Catholic churchmen who, like himself, stayed in their countries to face the Communists. John Paul II went out of his way to uphold the reputation of the Croatian wartime cardinal, Alojzije Stepinac, despite the latter's initial support for the pro-Nazi Ustasha regime. Stepinac stayed to be tried and imprisoned by the Communists. Rode's decision to return to Slovenia as a priest in 1965 at the height of the Cold War made him a man in the Polish Pope's mould. It is no wonder he shares his mentor's combative attitude in the fight for traditional Catholic principles.

Rode's seven years as head of the Catholic Church in Slovenia came to an end in February 2004, when he was appointed Prefect of the

Congregation for Religious, a top post in the Catholic hierarchy. Based in the Vatican, he became responsible for monks and nuns around the world. The Austrian ORF television's religious commentator described the promotion as the Pope's personal reward for Rode, but also as a move to ease tensions between Church and Government in Slovenia.[13]

Tough though he has been on Church and political issues, Rode took a milder line in looking back at what the anti-Communist Catholics did during the war. Many Catholic leaders insist their side had no choice, in the face of Partisan attacks, but to collaborate with the Germans in order to fight back and save their lives. Rode was not so sure. He wondered whether the *domobranci* should have taken to the woods and fought against the enemy occupier just like the Partisans did:

> I think the political leaders on the right were badly advised. Other choices were possible. When Italy capitulated in 1943, our side had two years of experience in the struggle. The *domobranci* could have gone into the woods. They were strong enough not to be overwhelmed. But the leaders were naïve politically. They had blind faith in the British, but they had no contacts with them, only with the Germans.

Ironically, he believed that if the Germans had been in charge of the whole of Slovenia from the start, he and his family would not have had to flee, because the Germans held their areas firmly in hand. But in the Italian zone, they had no choice but to take up arms, since the Italians did not protect them from Partisan attacks. He was forgiving towards the British, even though one of his brothers died because of them, saying he blames neither the British government nor the British nation.

What about a pardon for the Communists? There was a long pause, then: 'I wonder. I would not put the question in those terms. They were more victims than executioners. Poor Communists! I pity them rather than feel any desire to foment vengeance. Poor people! God will find a solution.'

Another emigrant who completed his Odyssey in epic fashion is Andrej Bajuk, who leads the main Catholic political grouping, United Slovenia. His is another notable comeback story. Pushed over the Ljubelj Pass in a pram as a 19-month-old baby in 1945, he returned to preside as Prime Minister for five months in 2000 at the head of a conservative government, and from 2004 served as Finance Minister. Meet him in his parliamentary office and it is immediately clear he is the grandson of Director Marko Bajuk. He is friendly and convivial, but also outspoken and impatient. He left Argentina because he was ambitious and had an international career in his sights:

> When we went to Argentina, we barely knew where it was on the map. I will always be grateful to Argentina, as are all the Slovenes there. The Argentinians opened their doors and gave us the same

opportunities as they gave their own people. I never felt a stranger.
It is an open society with respect for differences among people.

The Argentina of the military dictatorships, however, did not like
him much. He studied on an Organisation of American States (OAS)
scholarship at Berkeley University and returned to teach at a university
in Argentina: 'When General Videla came to power in a coup in 1976, I
was kicked out of university as a suspicious pinko. Everybody under the
age of 35 was considered a leftist.'

He then served for 20 years in the Inter-American Development Bank
(IADB), a branch of the World Bank, and reached the senior management.
In 1994 he left Washington for an IADB post in Paris, much to the dismay
of his three children who could not understand why their father wanted
to give up the American way of life. They came, however, and two of them
settled in Paris while a daughter returned to Slovenia and married there.

Bajuk became Prime Minister almost by accident, as a post-
retirement job. Already in Washington, he was in touch with Slovene
Catholic politicians such as Lojze Peterle, Prime Minister at the time of
independence in 1991. He bought an apartment in Ljubljana after
quitting the job, and while he was there taking part in a think-tank,
the government of Liberal Democrat Janez Drnovšek collapsed. The
opposition had to find a Prime Minister within a week, and the surprise
consensus choice was Andrej Bajuk.

Bajuk and his coalition had caught the previous Liberal Democrat
government at a weak moment when they had been in power too long
and were vulnerable to accusations of patronage. The *Večer* newspaper
accused it of being an arrogant party of yuppies and cold pragmatists.
The EU complained that Slovenia was moving too slowly with economic
reforms. Bajuk spent his first Sunday in office in June 2000 taking part
alongside Archbishop Rode in a service at the Kočevski Rog execution
pits. A surviving anti-Communist fighter made a speech asserting the
country was still in a state of civil war.

Bajuk accelerated privatisations and returned the large tracts of
land which belonged to the Catholic Church before the Communists
took over. In comparison with other ex-Communist nations of Europe,
Slovenia had been slow in privatising. Slovene companies had done
better than other East European enterprises under Communism and
felt no great pressure for structural change. Claiming that 80% of elite
posts were still held by ex-Communists, Bajuk's government began
replacing them with his own supporters. A furore arose when the chief
executive of Telekom Slovenije was ousted to make way for a political
appointee. The government struggled to keep a grip on administration
as the newcomers learned the ropes, and squabbling broke out in the
coalition. Bajuk's Slovene was at that time a little rusty: it was years
since he had studied Slovene poets in Argentina on Saturday mornings.
President Kučan publicly questioned the competence of his government.

European Union governments began to be irritated. The reforms needed for Slovenia to join the EU slowed further. At a meeting with EU ambassadors, Bajuk was annoyed by a flow of questions implying he was a man of the past. True to his grandfather's spirit, he blew his top and walked out. 'I'm not a man of the past, Kučan is,' he snapped.

In August 2000, he formed his own party, New Slovenia. By October his coalition was falling apart over electoral reform, and his party plunged to defeat in an election.

Interviewed two years later, he did not give the impression of caring all that much. Like many others who take early retirement, he felt liberated to follow his own individual way at little personal risk. He had become a free spirit, released from the obligation of making craven compromises:

> I do not regret coming back to Slovenia. I am in a special position because I am financially independent and I am at a stage in my life when I can choose what I want to do. At the beginning when I was Prime Minister, I was subject to a strong media campaign. Things have changed over time. Now people have discovered the man behind the name. I never felt hostility at a personal level. I never felt aggression.

There can be few other occasions in history where a person exiled for 55 years has returned to take over his country's government, even though his brief premiership in 2000 was not a huge success. In elections in 2004, his New Slovenia party won only 9% of the vote. However in the new conservative coalition formed late that year, Bajuk was again one of its leaders. He became Finance Minister, a post for which his expert knowledge in world finance stood him in good stead.

Leaving the realms of the government and the church, it was time for an interview with a Communist militant of the wartime resistance. For an author writing about the *domobranci* and the emigrants, this is the point when shutters start coming down. For many on this side of the political divide, the subject is not something one would wish to be associated with. Excuses are made, appointments are cancelled, and telephone conversations are abruptly terminated. It is not as if what they have to say is secret. The Communists in the resistance have had the run of the history books and their wartime activities are well documented. But a feeling apparently remains that giving an interview on anything to do with the *domobranci* could create difficulties.

M. is 90 and ready to talk, but wishes to remain just M.[14] She has the sharp gaze and determined voice of the militant she has been since the first days of the war in Yugoslavia in 1941. She became a part of the Liberation Front, and joined the Communist Party in 1942, by which time the Front was under its control: 'I had no idea what Communism was when I joined the Liberation Front. I personally joined because I wanted to work for the liberation of my country. As the daughter of an engine driver, I also wanted a better standard of living. If you were loyal, active and did all the tasks which were asked of you, the other Front members proposed you to become a member of the Communist Party.'

M. was betrayed in early 1944 by a Slovene woman at her workplace who was linked to the *domobranci* and knew of her resistance activity. M. was in a house next to her flat, singing Partisan songs with friends after curfew, when there was a knock on the door, and she was told: 'Come with me.' Slovene police searched her flat in vain for Liberation Front documents – they were there but well hidden – and she was taken off to prison:

> Slovene collaborationists were active in the police and the prisons. They raped the women, stubbed cigarettes out on flesh, and poured hot water into tubes pushed up anuses. I myself was beaten, and it was always by Slovenes. I refused to say who I knew and became more resistant. People suffered a lot in such prisons. I cannot forget the horrible things.

She was taken to Šentvid, which was then a Gestapo prison and later used as a staging post for the *domobranci* on their way to their executions. From there, she and other women prisoners were sent in cattle trucks to a concentration camp in Fürstenberg in Germany, near Ravensbrück:

> We were taken to a bathroom, and had to take our clothes off and take showers. We thought we were going to be gassed. Woman guards shouted at us, we were given blue-grey camp uniforms with no under-clothes and no clogs. It was terribly cold. We slept two or three to a bed one metre wide with one blanket each. We got one loaf of bread per day to share between ten people.
>
> The next day we paraded on the 'Appellplatz' and they checked to see if we were capable of work. We were sent to work by a lake. Wagons full of human ashes were brought on a narrow-gauge railway, and we had to throw them into the lake. Then I was moved to another concentration camp at Neubrandenburg, where I had to work 12-hour night shifts in a military industrial factory.
>
> I was there for 18 months and then evacuated to Stettin. The guards were drunk on the way, and some of us escaped at night. We came to a large estate where the children's beds were still warm in the house. We camped in the stables, and the Soviets found us and took us back to the Neubrandenburg camp, where they made us carry bricks to and fro uselessly. Eventually, we hitched a lift to Prague with some Czechs, and made our way home to Slovenia.

M. remained a loyal member of the Communist Party until it was dissolved in the early 1990s, but the Party did not always give her an easy time. When she and others returned to Slovenia, they were accused of collaborating with the Germans in the camps. There was no evidence for this, just a wave of paranoid suspicion against anyone with foreign links. M. says the Yugoslav leaders were just aping the Soviets in staging show trials. Like many Yugoslav Communists, she has no liking for the Soviets. The long quarrel between the two countries has left its marks. Pondering the fate of the *domobranci* does not figure high on her priorities:

> I didn't know they had been killed. I only heard much later. I am against the killings, but punishments had to be carried out, because what we lived through under the occupation was indescribable. It was terrible. If the situation had been reversed, it would have been me in the pits.

It is time to go. It has been a brisk, businesslike interview. M. speaks rapidly and wastes no words, slipping into the discipline of a resistance militant. She is still a beautiful woman and flashes a dazzling smile as she bids farewell: 'I am 90 now, and at this age I don't think my name needs to appear in books.' The door closes. Once a clandestine, always a clandestine.

# 12 GOODBYE ARGENTINA?

*I cannot move back to Slovenia. The Slovenia we left does not exist*
*any more.*

At the end of 2001, economic disaster struck Argentina. The once rich country to which the Slovenes emigrated in 1949 collapsed into the worst crisis of its history. Years of political corruption and economic policy errors culminated in a run on the banks, during which Argentinians in one day withdrew $1.5 billion. The government defaulted on $132 billion of international debt, all but blocked bank withdrawals, devalued the Argentinian peso, and forcibly converted dollar deposits into the peso at the much lower rate. Citizens attacked banks and pillaged supermarkets in revolt against what they considered to be legalised theft. Economy Minister Jorge Remes Lenico announced: 'Our economy has totally collapsed.'[1] President Fernando Rua was forced to resign.

Over the next year, the peso devalued against the dollar by three quarters. The dollars people had been saving had been turned into pesos with only a fraction of the purchasing power. Gross Domestic Product for the first quarter was 16.3% lower than the previous year. Unemployment soared to 21.5%, while more than half of Argentinians fell below the official poverty line.

The tragedy changed the outlook of the Slovene emigrants abruptly. They had arrived in the country with nothing, fought their way to comfortable standards of living and brought up families. They felt at ease in Argentina and were proud of what they had achieved. Now they too lost much of their savings. They were living in a country gripped by poverty, racked by violence, and a pariah in the world economy. Many were mugged, had their cars stolen in daylight hold-ups, and had to barricade their homes and pay security guards. It was a body blow, and the thoughts of many began to turn to going back to Slovenia. However, instead of realising their dream of returning victoriously, as they had half hoped for so long, once more they were thinking of leaving a country under pressure. This time the threat was not from political persecution, but from social and economic collapse. It was a bitter pill to swallow.

Whether to return to Slovenia was always the big question they faced. Some refer to their departure in May 1945 as a withdrawal rather than a flight. They considered Slovenia was falling prey to an ideology of terror and materialism which it was their duty one day to put right. In the camps in Austria, the schools, singing, theatres, workshops and churchgoing all served to keep the community bound together. In the eyes of the community leaders, this cohesion and strength would one day serve their nation again. The economic debacle in Argentina now forced them to look at the question in a new light. They were no longer considering a victorious return, but more an escape from poverty.

One of those leaders who never forgot his mission to restore the old values in his country is Marko Kremžar. He is the son of the President of the Slovene Parliament which met on 3 May 1945 in an abortive attempt to take power. Father Franc was the oldest surviving Slovene deputy of the inter-war Yugoslav Parliament. Marko represents a natural line of continuity for the emigrant community and is one of its thought-leaders. Kremžar defends the right of the emigrant community to have a say in Slovene affairs. He considers that Slovenes all over the world belong to Slovenia as a nation and have a right to Slovene citizenship: 'Slovenia no longer exists within the narrow limits of its boundaries. It is the exiled who also altogether make up Slovenia in the world. Wherever you find a Slovene, there is Slovenia...Although there is only one Slovene state, Slovenia in the world also exists after independence.'[2]

Or as he put it in a poem:

> Slovenia, my home without frontiers,
> You whom I carry around with me,
> Wherever my home is, wherever your son is,
> There are you, Slovenia.

In his book *Between Death and Life*, published in 2000,[3] he calls for the Slovene state systematically to repatriate the emigrants and thereby boost the Slovene population back at home. The nation should refrain from killing its own children through abortions. The Catholic Church should regain all its nationalised lands and forests expropriated by the Communist regime. He speaks of the work the Argentinian community did behind the scenes to facilitate Slovenia's independence in 1991. They were in touch with the Prime Minister of Slovenia of the time, Christian Democrat Lojze Peterle, and also had high-level contacts with the Vatican, which was among the first states to recognise Slovenia's independence.

Kremžar feels the homeland should set greater value on the Slovene Diaspora:

> We did quite a good job here. Emigration was eventually the good consequence of a tragic event, but it was not good for us. We were always expatriates. In the 1990s it became important. Then many European states had Christian Democrat governments, and we had had regular contacts with them since 1983. We were always present. We were able to be introduced at high levels. These countries came to know what Slovenia was...

> Our countrymen in Slovenia should know more about the Diaspora and take advantage of the thousands of ambassadors it has abroad. There are a few joint ventures, but the potential is not being fulfilled. Most do not realise how the Diaspora can help a country achieve growth in the cultural and economic fields.

Another of the community leaders in Buenos Aires, Marian Loboda, remembers a German engineer friend telling him after independence in 1991 that Slovenes could now join together all over the world in making Slovenia prosperous. He too feels this opportunity has been frustrated. He helped found a Slovene/Latin American Chamber of Commerce, but it yielded few joint undertakings.

When he went back to Slovenia immediately after independence, he sailed through the frontier without showing a passport, since he was travelling in the car of Prime Minister Peterle. But he soon felt slighted. At the time of the ill-fated reconciliation conference of 1991, he went up to Kočevski Rog with Spomenka Hribar, a well-known Slovene journalist who investigated the *domobranci* killings. He says she lingered behind when they were viewing the pits, and preferred to show them the Partisan 'Baza 20'. It annoyed him and they had a row.

For these leaders, reconciliation is linked to truth, reputation and principles. Marko Kremžar says: 'I have no desire for revenge. However we should not forget our history. To forget the past is bad for personal and national identity. The only way to avoid past errors is to remember, but also to eradicate from our heart all hatred and bitterness.'

Marian Loboda adds:

> Our past has not been clarified. There has been too much blood, too many people killed. We can't agree with them in Kučan's front. Truth is truth. Our good reputation must be restored. The authorities must stop treating us as traitors. They must put us on the same footing as everybody else. We want to be rehabilitated and we want compensation for the damage done to us. I expected a lot more from

Slovenia after independence. I constantly feel kept at a distance. There is no feeling of sympathy or connection with us. They are just putting up with us.

Božidar Fink, the lawyer *domobranec* who escaped because he was too ill to mount the British lorries, knows ex-Communists who are open; some of them are his own relatives back in Slovenia. He understands it is difficult for them to kneel down and say sorry. He believes that politics is the art of the possible and compromises must be made. However, 'There is a conflict between principles, and we cannot depart from our principles. There can be no compromise between freedom and slavery. The blood is not yet dry in Slovenia. The other side makes us no offer. They do not approach us. It is mainly a question of honour. If I am being held by the neck, I am still in an inferior position.'

Fink is proud that he officially represented independent Slovenia in Argentina for three years until an ambassador was nominated. He has no contact any more with the Slovene embassy in Buenos Aires. He is over 80, and nowadays concentrates, as he puts it with lawyerly precision, on 'discovering the truth and proving it'.

Marko Bajuk, grandson of the school director in the refugee camps, says: 'Some people say we are hardened about the events in the war. It is not emotional hatred, but we feel we have a mission. We miraculously saved ourselves twice and we must bear witness to what we know. It is a prophetic mission, a fight for the truth. We lost our country which was so beautiful and is superior to Argentina. We need to find some meaning. This is our main life force, what keeps us together.'

The passage of time will inevitably lead to change. The strong characters who spent their formative years in refugee camps are now in their seventies and eighties. The next generation is likely to be less committed to maintaining a tight-knit Slovene community. That loss may be balanced by more relaxed relations with compatriots at home.

Age did not bar the last commander of the *domobranci* from having his say at the age of 90. When one of the authors visited Buenos Aires in 2002, a telephone message left in the hotel announced that a Señor Cof was ready for a meeting. Back in May 1945, Colonel Emil Cof took command of the *domobranci* briefly when General Krener departed on realising the British were repatriating them. He gave the order to the few remaining *domobranci* to disperse. At the end of a long taxi ride out to a dusty suburb, the author found a slim, upright figure dressed in a smart jacket, a tie and a military man's well-pressed trousers waiting at the entrance to the Bishop Rožman Old People's Home.

He has cleared out a communal room to meet in private and arranged for friendly Argentinian staff to bring refreshments. 'I apologise that we are unable to receive honoured guests in the right manner,' he says superfluously, in carefully phrased English learned between the wars in the Yugoslav Military Academy in Belgrade.

Cof recounts his wartime campaign in meticulous operational detail. Occasionally he strays into Spanish or Slovene, but his line of thought is precise. He concludes:

> I went back to Slovenia in 1995 for the 50th anniversary of the killings. I admired the beauties of Slovenia, but I was sad realising the situation of the Slovenes, including my own family. They were still frightened, and not prepared to say how many people were lost.
>
> I lost my country. I lost my family. I lost the future which I had foreseen for myself. I have many sad memories and few happy ones. Could I have done anything different? I mourn for my soldiers who were killed by the Communists. It is something you cannot forget. Every year, we hold the same memorial celebration. I remember my friends who fell.

A few days later, Colonel Cof approached the author again at the Slovene Cultural Centre, bowed and proffered a hand-written letter adding further details. It had taken him one and a half hours to write. He handed it over with a slightly weary smile.

There are other Slovenes in Buenos Aires who, like Cof, bear loyalty to the old inter-war Yugoslav monarchy rather than to Slovene Catholic nationalism. They are proud of the stature that Yugoslavia once enjoyed. They find Slovenia parochial. Compared with the Catholics, they are more cosmopolitan, less religious and less bound by ethnic roots. One elderly, well-born Slovene lady in Buenos Aires declared:

> Yugoslavia was well off between the wars. It was a well-to-do country and respected. It was not considered Balkan. In Slovenia, nearly everybody then spoke some German. But the Catholics were always fighting with the Liberals there. The priests forbade them to cooperate with the Liberals because they considered them godless. As for the Communists, I hate them because they ruined my life and took away my castles.

Her social circle includes upper classes around the world. She has a worldly wit and a sense of the mildly absurd: neither castle had been returned at the date of writing.

At the Slovene cultural centre in the Argentinian capital there are unmistakable signs of assimilation. Many of the adolescents heading into Saturday morning classes on Slovene history and literature have dark features revealing mixed parentage.

'It's difficult anywhere to keep a community going for more than five generations,' says United Slovenia community president Tone Mizerit. 'The young ones are brought up to speak Slovene at home, but it is getting worse now. I would call it kitchen Slovene. It's a natural process.'

The school is named after Bishop Rožman, who led the Catholic community in Slovenia during the war and died in exile, but Mizerit says many of the Slovene children there have only a hazy notion who he was. The new generation, influenced by more easy-going Argentinian ways, feel less angry about their history and their status in the world. They are intent on the opportunities life can offer them today.

So, is the way forward for the Slovenes in Argentina that of continuing assimilation and an eventual collapse of their strong identity? Not necessarily. Numbers at the Slovene school in Buenos Aires are rising, with over 500 attending at primary level and 160 in the middle school. The teachers may face a Sisyphus task, but it does not show. The continuing commitment of teachers, parents and children to preserving Slovene culture is impressive.

Despite the emigrants' complaints of indifference on the part of the mother country, cooperation is quietly underway. Most of the Slovene children attending the school here go to summer school in Slovenia – paid for by the Slovene state. According to Mizerit, they are enthusiastic about Slovenia and many talk about going to live there one day, though only a few actually do. The Slovene state also pays for teachers at the Buenos Aires school to visit the home country.

Visiting the cultural centre is Ljoba, a young woman from Slovenia who teaches children singing and story-telling. The Slovene state is sponsoring her to hold workshops in Argentina. This woman, who sang for the Dalai Lama on his birthday when he visited Slovenia in 2002, admires the family structures among Slovenes in Argentina. She finds Slovene children there have a longer attention span than at home.

Next weekend, the annual Slovene Day celebrations in Buenos Aires prove her point. Well over a thousand Slovenes pack a theatre in sweltering heat to cheer on a rustic Slovene comedy lasting four hours and roar approval for folk singing and dancing in traditional costumes. Present as a guest is the director of Slovenia's Kranj Theatre, which is giving performances paid by the Slovene state in all the Argentinian cities where Slovenes live. 'I can't think of anywhere else in the world where the Slovene culture is so well kept alive,' he says admiringly as the evening gets into full swing.

The Slovene Ambassador to Argentina, Bojan Grobovšek, finds the going heavier. Invited to give a speech, he chooses to talk about Slovenia joining the European Union. The emigrants listen politely but with no enthusiasm. The European Union is not their cup of tea. He was a nominee of the Liberal Democrat government back at home and was tolerated rather than liked.

'We in Slovenia have become more modern. Slovenia has made it. We are pragmatic and that saves us. It is sad for those who are here. Those who came over here were very ideological, even though the younger generation has changed somewhat. What do they want now? More cannot be done,' he commented to one of the authors.

For years, the Slovenes in Argentina maintained a quasi-mystical cult around the *domobranci*. A plaque at the cultural centre hails them as 'Slovene fighters for human rights, civilisation, freedom of the nation and Christian behaviour – crowned in death with the guarantee of victory, gratitude and glory'. Heady stuff, but, as with the Partisans back in Slovenia, the fervour is gradually running out of steam. Slovene homes in Argentina often have small shrines with candles around a photo of a young *domobranec* in uniform. Millions of families around Europe had such photos after the war. But time is marching on, and all the *domobranci* who went to their death in the pits would be old men now. Only the elderly now cherish their memory in sorrow. For the new generation, a *domobranec* is an ancestor they never met. A short time ago a group of ex-Communists and Liberal Democrats from the Slovene Parliament laid a wreath in front of the plaque, and one was heard to comment: 'They were not so bad really.'

Bariloche, among Argentina's lakes and mountains, is where the Slovene adventurers went. People such as Ciril Markež, who manned a geophysical station on Mount Tronador, with condors his only company. Now he manages a ski lodge in the winter and travels 300 kilometres deeper into the Andes to run a fishing lodge in the summer.

Or Franc Jerman, the *domobranec* who risked his life by walking back into post-war Slovenia to obtain school books. He introduced triathlon into the Argentinian army, became a cross-country ski champion and competed for his new country in the Squaw Valley Winter Olympics of 1960. He built chairlifts and mountain restaurants around Bariloche, which named one of its streets after him. His greatest feat was to make the first ascent of a towering peak in the Andes, which was named the Campanile Esloveno.

With Jerman on that climb was Dinko Bertoncelj, who watched a Partisan kill his father on New Year's Day 1944. In the camps, Dinko met Austrian ski guides who told him of major-domos in white gloves serving rich guests in Bariloche. On arrival in Argentina, Dinko headed straight down there, with his heart set on a life on skis. It was the start of a career as one of Argentina's best-known mountaineers and ski guides. Dinko went on the first Argentinian expedition to the Himalayas and spent a winter on a ship frozen in the Weddell Sea off the Argentinian part of the Antarctic. Eventually, he decided with six others to establish a ski school in Bariloche. The trouble was they had no idea how to teach skiing, so Dinko returned to Austria and learned it from guides in the Arlberg.

He too was selected for the Argentinian team for the 1960 Winter Olympics, but he did not yet have citizenship. Again, General Peron came to the help. Bertoncelj met the Argentinian President at a reception and told him of his problem. Peron told him not to worry; it would be fixed. The next day Dinko went to the office that had been turning him away day after day and found his passport ready.

Dinko married Romana, whose Slovene mother was eight months pregnant with her when Partisans opened fire in Jesenice. The mother, a courier for the *domobranci*, escaped with an attaché case full of bullet holes, and Romana went with her to Brazil via the Austrian camps. She married Dinko and moved, as she put it, 'from pressing a button to make a perfect cup of coffee in Rio, to shoving wood into a stove to keep warm in Bariloche'. She had never stood on skis before, and found herself the enemy of women taken by the guitar-playing charms of Dinko.

After a spell heading a ski school in upstate New York, they returned to Bariloche, where Dinko now strives to cope with a serious injury incurred late in life slipping on a simple mountain path. It is an unfortunate closing chapter to a life of daring, adventure and determination.

Dinko has no intention of moving again. But others have had enough of Argentina and are thinking of packing up and leaving. They can no longer stand the country which opened its arms to them two generations ago. Economic disaster and corruption have rendered it intolerable for many. One is former Royalist Chetnik and *domobranec* Bo Eiletz:

> Argentina has become a terrible place. I feel very bad here. It is completely different from what it was. It was a paradise when we arrived. We could get milk chocolate, white bread and meat, none of which we ever had in the refugee camps. I met my wife here and we brought up three children here. But Argentina is now insecure and the crime and corruption is tremendous. There is a lack of discipline. The people do not like order.

Before 1990, he only ventured as far as Slovenia's border, but since then he has returned for visits three times. Now Eiletz, who is 80, faces the dilemma of an expatriate who has been absent from the home country for a long time:

> Slovenia is marvellous, beautiful. I am tempted to go back there to live. But it is now a strange land for me. Our normal lives there ended 60 years ago. I have very few relations. Most of my friends were killed in the massacres at Kočevski Rog. I would not recognise old acquaintances if I saw them again. The mentality of the people has changed. For 50 years there was a regime that overturned the truth. Some people there look back to the good old days of Tito. In my old age I could not put up with that.

His wife Mary says she would go back tomorrow if she could. One of Eiletz's nephews has moved to the US and another is an architect in Italy, and is thinking of moving to Slovenia too. The trouble is their life's savings and pensions have been slashed. Eiletz, who began in Argentina lugging cement sacks and made his way up to a managerial position in a US–Argentinian firm, says he has lost a large amount of money. For Slovenes such as these, there has been no happy end. The story has turned sour. The Argentinian economic catastrophe has denied them the serenity of old age. Stane Snoj says:

> We have no money. Now in our old age we are without anything. Everything has been taken away from us. For years in Argentina we hid all our dollars. Ten years ago we put them in the bank. Then they were blocked and when we could access them again, we got pesos which were worth hardly anything. It was legal robbery. I have no work and my son lost the job he had for 15 years.
>
> My son went back to Slovenia and got a job in a food company in Ljubljana. He also got our old house back, though with a sitting tenant who has never paid anything for rent, water or electricity. I would like to go back to Slovenia too. My wife is not so much attracted, but she would come too.

Jože Tomaževič, another veteran of the Austrian camps, is also waiting to see whether he gets back his family property in Slovenia. So far he has been returned fields and woodland, but not the house. Depending on the outcome, he says he would be happy to go back, 'and in particular to leave Argentina, where we have been robbed and made poor overnight'.

Others have roots in Argentina which are too strong. Franci Markež, a successful businessman, is a leader of the Slovene community in Buenos Aires, but with an Argentinian wife he is one of the most assimilated. Franci to Slovenes, he is Francisco to his Argentinian friends. He says:

> Slovenia is my fatherland and I have never abdicated it. But Argentina is the country where I grew up, studied and brought up my family. My wife is Argentinian. I have my friends here and I have picked up local habits. I have become used to huge, wide open spaces. I never regretted coming to Argentina. It offered me everything and I never felt a foreigner here. In Slovenia, as long as institutions continue to bear the names of butchers of the Slovene nation and there are still statues of them, I have nothing to look for in my homeland.

Cirila Pernišek-Žužek, daughter of the diarist, says she feels half Slovene and half Argentinian. She misses Slovenia's mountains, but has taken a liking to the Argentinians' warm, easy-going ways:

> I love this country even if it makes me very angry. It is impossible what they have done. I always worked 10 or 12 hours a day or even the whole night. There is a Slovene saying that if you work eight hours a day you can live, but you do nine or 10 hours if you want to get further. Now these same Slovenes who worked like this are

living in poverty. The people here are lazy but good-hearted. There is incredible solidarity in the economic crisis. They have set up soup kitchens for the poor.

It would be difficult for me to return to live in Slovenia. I know nobody any more and I would not know how to start anew without money. What would I have done if I had stayed in Slovenia? I would have no doubt had a house and a job, but I can't imagine it. Here in Argentina I was able to realise my life.

The Slovenes in Mendoza, at the foot of the Andes, are well known in the local community even though they number only a few hundred. In the Slovene tradition, they established the first choir in the city and were invited by the Bishop to sing in the main church. Mendoza has a square named after the Republic of Slovenia.

Božidar Bajuk, a grandson of the refugee camp school director, is an architect, but work is hard to come by these days. Two of his six children have gone to live in Slovenia, his son training to be an orchestra conductor in Ljubljana and his daughter teaching in Grosuplje. He says:

> We left Slovenia for ideological reasons, but we always wanted dialogue and now it is starting. I went back to Slovenia again in 1999 and found it much changed. People were no longer rude in shops; they were polite. After independence, the door opened in Slovenia and two of our children went there to study and work. The children all love Slovenia. They have citizenship and all but the youngest are on the electoral rolls.

> But our other children and grandchildren – the ones who stayed – breathe here in Argentina. There is a freedom to choose and express oneself. We are not putting aside our Argentinian culture. For me, it is not easy to live two cultures, but now I have one library with [the Latin American Nobel Prize winner] Garcia Marquez and another with [the Slovene poet] Prešeren.

No doubt a few of the younger generation will follow the Bajuk offspring in their return to the land where their parents were born. But not many. Born in Argentina, they are likely to live their lives there. As for the older generation, they feel the pull of the country they left as small children. However, they too have roots in the land they now bewail, but which is nevertheless their home. Božidar's sister-in-law Vera Aršič-Bajuk says:

> When we first went back in 1994, we were looking for our roots, our identity. We re-established contact with our relatives as if 50 years had not passed in between. We can see Slovenia is working well. It

is very open, and we appreciate the culture, the food and the architecture.

But for us, the priorities are the family, education and integration, and only then our Slovene nationality. My husband was tempted to go back. He is fed up with Argentina. But we have important links here, including five sons and 12 grandchildren. If we neglect those, it would be to go to a country where we know few people.

Her husband Marko, grandson of the former inspector of Slovene schools and brother of Slovenia's Prime Minister for five months in 2000, confirms sadly: 'I cannot really move back to Slovenia. We have established our existence here. If we did, my children would have to stay here and that would mean leaving our descendants behind. The Slovenia we left does not exist any more.'

# 13

## THE LONG ROAD TO RECONCILIATION

*One must be clear about what happened. Youth does not like hating, but they want the truth to be told correctly and sincerely.*

From the middle of the 1980s, a few determined Slovenes began discovering what happened to the *domobranci*, brought it into the public domain and demanded justice. The Communists' hold on power was slipping, and the revelations were both a symptom of their loss of control and a factor accelerating their demise. These objectors, who published in the *Nova Revija* periodical, launched appeals not only for justice but also for reconciliation. Twenty years after they launched their campaign, they had achieved neither. There was little reconciliation, and nobody was charged with any offence against the anti-Communist Catholics in the period in question.*

Spomenka Hribar is the daughter of a Communist who died in 1942 as a result of Gestapo imprisonment. Her grandfather was also a Communist and died in Dachau. She loved her father and associated Communism with him – 'something bright', as she puts it. She herself was a Communist for 26 years. In 1975 she discovered and researched the *domobranci* story, and wrote a polemical pamphlet *Sin and Guilt*. It took three years for her to get it published, and it created an uproar which reverberated throughout Yugoslavia. She was expelled from the Slovene Communist Party. For her, that was the ultimate insult. The movement which her dead father had fought for had turned against her. She set out to get her own back, and stubbornly fought to persuade Slovenia's Communist authorities to admit the crime they were trying to cover up.

---

* Until one secret policeman was indicted in May 2005.

She sees the episode as a clash between two totalitarian forces, in which each side insists it is absolutely in the right. She expresses contempt for both sides:

> In one way, the Catholics were more human. They preserved lives and property. But they were too linked with the occupiers. They were not just keeping hospitals and schools going, they were also spying, betraying and killing. The Catholics gave lists of people to the occupiers. It was not just self-defence. It was active collaboration. The Communists were not innocent either. They were set on carrying out a revolution and were killing Catholic-orientated people, not all of whom were collaborators.

> The refugees were used by the Catholic Church, which incited them to flee by spreading the idea that everybody was going to be killed. When the *domobranci* were returned, they expected to be put on trial, and those not guilty of any crimes would be released. The execution of nearly all of them was the worst thing that could happen in our history.

Looking at the present, she complains privatisation is allowing the Church to recover lands that had not belonged to it since the time of Austrian Emperor Franz-Josef. She claims the Church has lost moral capital among the population because of its hostile stance, and fewer people are attending church.

Armed with these opinions, which were bound to antagonise the emigrants, Spomenka Hribar decided to organise a conference of reconciliation between the two sides in 1991. The Communists, then on their way out of power, were used to her homilies. Their strategy was to limit the damage. But the Catholics, who felt their honour should now be restored, were enraged at her attacks. The conference got nowhere. Hribar went out to Argentina to try direct contact with the emigrant leaders there: 'We were received as if we were still Communists. For four hours they barked at us in a huge hall. It was so terrible that in the end they were ashamed...I banged on the table and made the glasses jump. I told them I had done more for the *domobranci* cause than them, and asked them whether I should leave. They were surprised that a woman should bang on the table. They were not used to that from their own women.'

Spomenka Hribar has thus stood up for the *domobranci*, but is also still the daughter of a martyred Communist. Discovering a wrong in the Communist camp does not make her love the Catholics. And they have no love for her. They see Spomenka Hribar as a wolf in sheep's clothing.

This is the fist-banging approach to solving the dispute. Stimulating it is, but conciliatory it is not. Activists on both sides talk almost admiringly of the length of their conflict. Justin Stanovnik of the Catholic 'New Slovenian Covenant' recalls the warning of the Ancient Greek Aeschylus that the stain of a civil war can never be eliminated, and that the curse continues forever. He predicts at least another 100 years, while others only slightly less pessimistically go for 50 years.

Miloš Mikeln is a more affable conciliator. By profession a writer and theatre director, he joined with Spomenka Hribar and others in 1988 to form a Committee for Human Rights. Besides pressing the shaky Communist regime to open a judicial investigation into the killings of the *domobranci*, they also militated for democracy.

Mikeln wrote a historical novel called *Veliki voz (Great Bear)*, which is the story of two friends. One has sons who became a Partisan and a post-war Communist dissident. The other man, more conventional, has a son who becomes a *domobranec*. It is a typical story of how Slovene families were split asunder and did their best to cope.

Mikeln admits the book is the story of his own life. He is the dissident Communist, and the division occurred in his own family. The novel is a plea for understanding and commiseration with human beings forced against each other by cruel fate. He believes Slovenes have not fully come to terms with the post-war killings because nobody has been put on trial:

> These people who collaborated did it with the honest intention of preserving their lives. The post-war killings were just revenge. They thought: we have them all together so let's kill them and make a socialist revolution. It was the Stalinist view: human life was not important. The Soviets lost 10 million soldiers in the war. It was an Asian view of life. It's time the Slovene government made a start [with legal proceedings]. Real people killed the *domobranci*.

Mikeln was a Partisan courier during the war, carrying information about enemy troops and armaments, as well as socks and cigarettes for his fellow-Partisans. When the war ended, he was told he was now a soldier of National Protection, given a rifle and a bicycle and set to guard ten German prisoners glad to get out of their prison camp to clear up ruins. His heart is with the Partisans, but the experience of his family's dilemma has made him a champion of understanding, reconciliation and facing up to unpalatable historical facts.

As he takes leave at the Writers' Club in central Ljubljana, he smiles and expresses concern that the British authors might have too little sympathy for the role of their own people in this affair. 'Don't be too hard with the British,' he says.

Down at Ljubljana's National Museum of Contemporary History, it is hard to detect progress in taking a more open view of this painful part of Slovene history. The exhibition portrays much the same view as that of the Partisan woman M. in Chapter 11. Until a few years ago, it was called the Museum of National Liberation, which reflected its purpose of recording the wartime activities of the Communist-controlled Liberation Front. The name has changed, but inside it is much the same.

There is practically nobody in the museum. Partisan heroism is no longer in fashion. Visits by schools and factory-workers have dried up. Some of the rooms are closed. The receptionist gives a friendly welcome and is pleased he can sell the first English version of a new catalogue. He goes ahead to turn on the lights.

The museum is showing a special exhibition of Slovenia during the 20th century. It takes a mildly critical look at the revolutionary social and economic policies of the early post-war years, but gaps remain. There is a photo of a column of returned *domobranci* marching through the streets of Kranj, but its caption does not say what happened to them or what their role was in the war. A sentence several dozen pages further on mentions they were killed and says it was a crime.[1] And that is it. One of the most dramatic events in recent Slovene history remains otherwise untold. One can sense a grudging desire to be objective and factual, but the sparseness of the explanation and the minute space allotted to the subject means the truth is all but obscured.

The museum prefers to dwell on evidence of the Catholics' collaboration. Exhibits show how the Italian occupying army helped organise and arm the Slovene Village Guards (*vaške straže*) – omitting to explain their purpose was to protect Catholic villagers from Partisan attacks.

The *Slovene National Encyclopaedia*, which has been published gradually since the early 1990s, could have been an opportunity to open up Slovenia's recent history. Its first 15 volumes cloaked sensitive events in obfuscating data and scarcely took the Catholic view of history into account. In 2002, the Catholic lobby group 'New Slovenian Covenant' submitted 200 names and topics they considered should figure – John Corsellis among them. Then, in the 16th and final volume, a section entitled 'Post-war mass murders 1945–1946' appeared. It was a sign of the times that the subject should finally be broached – and in a dispassionate manner which covered the main points. The account is nevertheless sketchy. The 500 words on the subject are an afterthought rather than a serious attempt to come to grips with a momentous episode in Slovene history.

In 1998, the country's most widely read writer, Drago Jančar, felt it was time to force the pace. He wrote an article accusing the Museum of Contemporary History of concealing the dark side of Slovenia's history. To his astonishment, they offered to allow him to stage an alternative exhibition. Together with sympathisers, he mounted an exhibition called *The Dark Side of the Moon: A Short History of Totalitarianism in Slovenia, 1945–1990*. For the first time, Slovenes could see a broad range of evidence of Communist persecution.

When Jančar began publishing critical articles in the late 1970s, the secret police turned his flat upside down. They ransacked his workplace too, confiscated an article, and put him in the same Maribor prison where the Gestapo had detained his father before dispatch to a concentration camp.

'The secret police knew very well what somebody was saying and thinking...They knew I was considering going abroad. They knew just about everything about my private life. Today I know I was being observed, like a mouse in a laboratory banging against glass walls. There was no way I could fool them,' he wrote.[2]

The documents he gathered for the exhibition shocked him. He says he did not realise how far the secret police went with intimidation, imprisonment, extortion and threats. He was ashamed that he himself had believed in Communism as a youth. He saw parallels between the Communists and the Nazis, and was shocked how totalitarian practices continued right until the regime collapsed:

> An invisible network was created, one of lurking fear, opportunism and humiliation...The documents speak about everyday lives which, due to insignificant tip-offs or negative party evaluations, became a hard trial for people: sackings from jobs, loss of scholarships, no right to travel, life in poverty, dreams of young people that would never come true, escapes abroad, blocked professional ambition. The documents depict a state of total control, of interference with every life which was unable or unwilling to be subdued or adjusted.

He is appalled that Ljubljana still has monuments to the Slovene Communist leaders Edvard Kardelj and Boris Kidrič (Kidrič also still has a village named after him). 'In the name of culture and civilisation, it is impossible to defend the monuments of people who established terror and non-culture and for a long period turned Slovenia into a land of violence, fear and silence.'

He would like both sides in the dispute to do more to recognise each other's merits. The many Partisans who fought bravely for liberation and social justice should not be blamed for the post-war killings and totalitarian society. The *domobranci* should be accepted for opposing revolutionary violence according to their convictions and values, and should be absolved from what he describes as 'the political mistake of collaboration'.[3]

For the *domobranci* and other post-war victims, he wants justice, if only symbolical: 'We don't need revenge, but we need one person to go on trial, to be sentenced to one day in prison and then be pardoned. This should be done. Somebody is responsible.'

Diasporas – nationals who have emigrated abroad – often have difficult relations with the home country. They typically feel they embody the spirit of their nation better than people back home. They feel unloved by the mother country and want to influence its affairs. What is striking about the Slovenes who fled in 1945 is that animosities last so long. The quarrels and divisions described in this book date back 60 years or more and show few signs of abating.

Opponents give no quarter or pardon. They seek to dominate rather than search for truth or reconciliation. Such behaviour has little to do with the contemporary values of Central Europe, nor of the European Union that Slovenia has joined. The latter was founded on the historical reconciliation between France and Germany. Slovenia's continuation of its feud is contrary to that spirit. The French and Germans found a way to put animosities behind them. Slovenes have yet to do so.

Is such behaviour innate to the Slovene character? Ivan Cankar, a leading Slovene author 100 years ago, wrote that what remained of the Slovene people after killings and flights during the Counter Reformation was 'a stinking mob, and we are the grandchildren of our grandfathers'.[4] Slovene psychologist Janek Musek more recently diagnosed his people as introverted, depressive, rigid and conscientious, noting that Slovenia has one of the world's highest suicide rates and that one Slovene male in five is an alcoholic.[5]

Such observations are inconclusive. Jože Dežman, Director of the Gorenjski museum, Kranj, and an expert on post-war killings, says: 'Slovenes are not yet mature for reconciliation, but I believe that their capacity for forgiving and not forgetting is higher than, for example, in Austria or Italy.'[6] Other nations of diverse backgrounds have found ways of achieving reconciliation after conflict. The Swiss, who combine two religions and four ethnic language groups, underwent civil strife until the mid-19th century. They resolved it by settling on a government system of coalitions, in which politicians developed consensus-building to a fine art. The system works because the participants believe that consensus is more valuable than conflict and that concessions can be made without fear of annihilation.

After the war, Germany too faced the challenge of reconciliation with its former enemies. The solution it adopted from the 1960s was total acknowledgement of guilt. Willy Brandt went down on his knees before the monument in the former Jewish ghetto of Warsaw to make the point most dramatically. Germany's leaders have since then made no attempt to find excuses. They assumed guilt fully and openly, and Germany has been accepted back into the community of democratic nations.

South Africa demanded that all those involved in apartheid confess to a Truth and Reconciliation Commission and offered them immunity in return. This gave a higher value to truth and reconciliation than to justice and retribution. Argentina faced a similar challenge in the 1980s when the military dictatorship collapsed and was replaced by a civilian government. To avert a spiral of revenge, the government set up a commission under the motto *Nunca mais* [*never again*] to reveal how the dictatorship tortured and assassinated its Marxist and liberal opponents. This openness defused any inclination to engage in a cycle of vengeance. In recognition, former Buenos Aires prosecutor Luis Moreno Ocampo was chosen in 2003 to head the new International Criminal Court.

At the foot of the Andes in the city of Mendoza, Catholic Slovene emigrant Vera Aršič-Bajuk draws a parallel with the Slovenes' dispute. She is a student counsellor and has experience of conflicts. She puts it thus:

> We have our own experience of reconciliation in Argentina. It is not necessary to do all that much, but one must be clear about what happened. Youth does not like hating, but they want the truth to be told correctly and sincerely. The Catholic Church admitted its historical mistakes, and it gained respect for publicly acknowledging this. Whoever does this wins respect. This is what is expected nowadays.

Telling the truth correctly and sincerely implies a re-assessment of World War II. In setting out on this path, Slovenes can find themselves in good company. Other nations which ended on the winning side have started confronting unpalatable facts. France's wartime resistance image has been tempered by recent evidence of anti-Semitism and widespread collaboration. The late President François Mitterrand worked not only for the resistance but also, it subsequently turned out, for the pro-Nazi Vichy Government, which gave him its top decoration. French police deported 80,000 Jews to the German extermination camps, virtually unaided by German occupying forces. The French guards plundered and mistreated their victims. Associations of lawyers and doctors purged Jews. As author Jonathan Fenby pointed out, until recently it was close to treason in France to talk about such facts.[7] In 1995, however, President Jacques Chirac publicly acknowledged the 'inescapable guilt' of the leaders of Vichy France, something which his predecessors had denied.

Britain, in a strong moral position because it was the only power to fight against the Nazis from beginning to end, nowadays questions the ethics of burning thousands of German civilians to death in air raids in order to undermine morale. Some now see this as an unworthy emulation of the Nazi use of terror against civilians as a means of war. Recent books highlighting the wartime suffering of German civilians, such as Guenter Grass's *Crab Walk*, Joerg Fischer's *The Fire*, Norman Davies' and Roger Moorhouse's *Portrait of a Central European City* and W.G. Sebald's *On the Natural History of Destruction*, attract readerships and sympathetic critical comment in Britain.

Austrians, who had claimed they were victims rather than perpetrators of Nazi horrors, now take a more realistic tack. A report commissioned by the government and published in 2003 chronicled how Austrians seized thousands of Jewish banks, businesses, real estate, personal property and other assets during the Nazi period. It concluded Austria did too little to right the wrongs after the war ended, and that Austrians had been hiding behind the excuse that they were victims.

The Swiss long asserted that their neutrality absolved them of wartime guilt. It took threats by the Jewish lobby against Swiss banks' interests in the United States to force them to acknowledge darker truths.

A report by independent historians, commissioned by the government and published in 2002, recounted how Switzerland turned back thousands of Jews at its frontiers to certain death, bought gold looted by the Nazis from dead Jews and occupied countries, employed forced labour at Swiss-owned factories in Germany and generally entertained closer relations with Nazi Germany than strict neutrality required. Swiss banks made a sizeable payment to compensate for Jewish funds they had not returned after the war. The Swiss government made a formal apology for its treatment of the Jews.

Pope John Paul II in 1997 condemned all acts of anti-Semitism by Christians over the ages, and before the Millennium asked for forgiveness for a whole range of injustices committed by the Catholic Church, including the Inquisition. British Prime Minister Tony Blair acknowledged in 1997 that the British government 'failed their people' in doing too little to halt the Irish Potato Famine of the 1840s, which killed two million people and sent another million into emigration. The Irish Republican Army apologised in 2002 for the deaths and suffering of non-combatants resulting from its 30-year campaign to end British rule in Northern Ireland.

So examples abound of governments and organisations finding their way towards reconciliation. They have resorted variously to favouring consensus, bringing out the full truth, openly accepting guilt and offering apologies where appropriate.

Notably however, the British have omitted to make any amends for accepting the surrender of the Slovene *domobranci* in 1945, disarming them, deceiving them and sending them back to execution in Slovenia. It is 30 years since historians started bringing the facts to light. Nobody in authority however, has acknowledged any wrongdoing.

Much of the discussion in Britain has been over which British politician or commander did what. This misses the point that whoever did it was acting on behalf of Britain. Whether they were politicians or military, they represented their nation. It was Britain which sent the soldiers back.

Over in the Hague another long-running feud is being dealt with. In the hushed court-rooms of the International Criminal Tribunal for the former Yugoslavia (ICTY), Slobodan Milošević the former Serbian leader, and several dozen others are on trial for alleged war crimes during the conflicts of the 1990s. Indictments are typically for 'persecutions, cruel and inhuman treatment of civilians, beatings, tortures, deportations, wanton and extensive destruction, plundering and destruction of religious buildings'. Women witnesses talk of being starved and raped, and having to clean someone's blood from the floor every night before they could lie down in their prisons.

The Hague Tribunal seems to be on another planet from the tormented environment they describe. That is just the point: the court is 100% respectable and oozes propriety. Judges lean over backwards to be fair, deal imperturbably with disruptive manoeuvres and are clearly set on applying the law, come what may. The punishment of those convicted is not so much the prison terms, though sentences range up to 46 years. The true impact of the Hague Tribunal is that it forces men who have thrived through brute force to bow to the conventions of a civilised society. They are being processed through the same judicial system as millions of other criminals all over the world. The sentences force them to bend to the rule of law, and that probably does hurt, since it undermines the foundation of their existence.

In other territories of former Yugoslavia, the rule of law is beginning to be applied to war criminals, if only timidly. Serbia and Croatia, besides sending some of their leaders to the Hague, have convicted a few of their own nationals for war crimes in their own courts. In Bosnia, a refrigerated building near Tuzla contains thousands of remains of the Srebrenica massacre which are being examined by forensic scientists collecting evidence.

This equitable process of law is lacking in Slovenia, at least as far as post-war crimes are concerned. It is more than ten years since Parliament ordered the Slovene state prosecutor to investigate the post-war massacres of anti-Communists. Slovenia has such a small population that everybody is said to come from the same family or have gone to school together. Somebody must know who did it. Plenty of people were tried and punished after the war for offences against the Communists, but practically nobody, it seems, killed the 12,000 *domobranci*.

It may be argued there is little point in putting anybody in the dock to answer for crimes committed nearly 60 years ago. Societies have generally not sought to punish everybody who committed atrocities during a conflict. It is recognised this would be a pointless and counter-productive exercise in legal perfectionism.

Some Slovenes believe the dispute will fade with the passing of time. Many of the main actors are dead or retired. Slovenes today have many other concerns, such as jobs, money, families, relationships and travel, and shy away from reviving battles of the past. Preoccupation with mundane peaceful issues is healthy. In a new nation which has made a break with its past, it is natural to want to look forward rather than back.

Richard Wagner, a Berlin-based political author who used to be part of the German minority in Romania, argues that keeping a lid on the dispute over wartime and post-war killings shows the pragmatism which places Slovenia in Central Europe rather than the Balkans. He believes there was a tacit agreement to put the problem aside, so that Slovenia could concentrate on the more important task of preparing to join the EU.[8]

Yet, other nations generally do insist on bringing a few to justice, even years later, in what are largely symbolic acts showing the moral principles they stand for. The World War II victors tried a number of Nazi leaders in Nuremberg in 1946. Israel captured and tried Adolf Eichmann, one of the architects of the Nazis' extermination of the Jews. France imprisoned Maurice Papon in his eighties for his role in deporting Jews from Bordeaux and convicted Klaus Barbie for suppressing the resistance in Lyons. Italy extradited ex-SS officer Erich Priebke from Argentina to stand trial in Rome.

Other nations have also done more to honour their wartime dead. Carefully tended cemeteries dot the World War I battlefields of northern France. The Thiepval Arch lists the names of tens of thousands of British soldiers who were killed but never buried.

There is a risk that the conflict lingers on, ready to flare up again. This has happened elsewhere in ex-Yugoslavia, and it is dangerous for Slovenes to imagine they will be totally different. It could poison their new-found democracy and leave a doubt over what Slovenia stands for morally. Milan Kučan often told his countrymen during his 12-year presidency that reconciliation was a prerequisite for maturity as a nation.

Jože Dežman, of the Gorenjski museum, Kranj, says:

> We have to take a stand about the legacy of the 20th century and the totalitarian burden that we are carrying. We should reach a consensus that the future should be less burdened with violence, and relationships between people should be more relaxed and open. This also means a constant questioning of our consciences, in which we show our capacity for compassion, justice and honesty.[9]

Writer Drago Jančar, who was given a state order in 2004, feels reconciliation lies some way ahead:

> Maybe the over-used word 'reconciliation' could be left to some future people and times. After all, even the Gospel does not talk much about it. What I urge is neither reconciliation nor amnesia, but something more modest but at the same time terribly difficult: an attempt to understand.[10]

# *14*  NOT FINISHED YET

*God's blessing on all nations,*
*Who long and work for that bright day,*
*When o'er earth's habitations*
*No war, no strife shall hold its sway;*
*Who long to see*
*That all men free*
*No more shall foes, but neighbours be.*

*– Slovene National Anthem*[1]

Is the tale of the Slovenes' forced emigration just a tragic adventure, or does it have deeper significance? Cardinal Ambrožič of Toronto, who as a boy fled over the Ljubelj Pass, takes the latter view. He says his whole life was shaped by the amazing experiences he went through: 'The longer I live, the more keenly do I become aware of the influence that my family, education, life and its experiences have had on my attitudes in regard to everything, from my mentality and spirituality to my societal convictions, political choices and such "pedestrian" matters as food and lodging.'

His own demeanour lends weight to this. His early life was marked by bereavement, determination in the face of disaster and recovery through self-help. While some clerics impress by their gentle saintliness, he comes across as a direct-speaking man of action. Ambrožič speaks of his formative experience in terms of a transformation: 'Throughout it all there has always been one solid Rock: Jesus Christ and His Church. In the resurrection of Jesus I meet my God as totally Other, above all my powers and imagination, and as Someone who embraces me as my loving Father.'

These are the words of a Cardinal. But this sense of otherness, of transcendence, is echoed by many of the other survivors who emigrated.

They express this same marvel, that something of immense importance happened early on and fundamentally altered the meaning of their lives. Accustomed now to the normality that followed, some can scarcely believe they went through the early traumas. They talk as if they were dreams – memories with only an uncertain link to reality.

The Slovenes' Odyssey could indeed hardly leave them unchanged, and in many respects, this is a refugee success story with a happy end. Despite later troubles in Argentina, most could feel that 'all's well that ends well'. Author Mark Wyman, in a 1998 book tracing the fortunes of World War II refugees all over Europe,[2] did draw such an upbeat lesson:

> Today the DPs (Displaced Persons) are living testimonies to another truth: while the 20th century has produced enormous numbers of refugees, it has also been the century in which the international community first developed coordinated systems for protection for those forced to flee their homelands. If the DPs were once a window to the eventual break-up of the Soviet Union, then perhaps their experiences outside Europe since 1945 might also be a window to future treatment of refugees, showing what is possible when the human concerns of caring individuals and organizations become part of the law of nations…

> The DPs' experience since World War II should give heart to those seeking humane solutions to the growing world refugee crisis. Higher walls against those seeking asylum in 1949 would have destroyed or seriously damaged a generation, and would have deprived nations around the world of worthy, productive citizens. The DPs demonstrated that refugees do not need to be parasitic drags on national well-being: given the opportunities, they can become strong contributing citizens.

The experiences of a few thousand Slovene refugees from a war that is fading from memory may seem to offer only limited lessons for today. However, it is rare to be able to track a whole body of refugees over three generations – and their story taps into a rich vein of oral and family history. Many of the positive observations made by Wyman apply also to the Slovenes, but the picture is not as rosy as he paints.

The Slovenes went through all the different stages of migration. Most left thinking they would be back in their homes within a few weeks, and a small number did just that. These were never really *refugees*. They just temporarily withdrew. The large majority clearly were refugees, however, with reason to believe that their lives and freedom would be in danger if they went back. The international community then re-classified them as *Displaced Persons*. This term recognised that they were not just escaping persecution or war. The map of Europe was being redrawn, and large numbers of people – in Germany, Poland, Czechoslovakia, Hungary, Romania, Yugoslavia and elsewhere – had to find somewhere else to live. They were victims of a new constellation of power. They were displaced.

Once the initial traumas were over, the Slovenes became *asylum seekers*, looking to move from the Austrian camps to new permanent homes. When they found them, they became *emigrants*, and when they arrived they were *immigrants*.

In analysing the way they were treated at each stage, one should acknowledge firstly that it was a disaster they had to flee at all. For this, the Nazis and the Italian Fascists must take the prime blame, even more than the Communists. They invaded Slovenia, dismembered it, persecuted the population, drew some of the people into collaboration, but also harassed them and then abandoned them.

Secondly, the attitude of the British Army to what were by then refugees – people staggering into a bare field in distress – provides the modern world with a poor example. It was reasonable to expect arrangements to be made for soldiers to return to their countries and to send back a few wartime leaders for trial for war crimes. The situation in Austria was also at that time extremely confused. But it was inhuman to return a whole army of surrendered and disarmed men against their wills to their deaths. It was also inexcusable to dispatch thousands of civilians to a similar fate, which is what the British Army planned to do with the Slovenes who are the subject of this book.

The next period of their migration, as they evolved from refugees to Displaced Persons to asylum seekers, saw a battle between hardliners who asked 'What are you Yugoslavs doing staying on here anyway?' and the liberal carers who sought to help them rebuild their lives and autonomy. The hardliners kept up the pressure, allowing Communist officials access to the camps, and carrying out *razzias* aimed at hindering the refugee leadership from functioning. In today's world, this attitude takes the shape of deterrence at points of entry, refusing to let asylum seekers work, preventing families from reuniting, dispersing communities geographically, reducing rights to social security and banning schooling in the languages of the refugees. The main justification is that if life is made too easy for refugees, more will migrate.

The liberal line won in the end, partly because a deterioration of relations between Yugoslavia and the West weakened the pressure for them to go back. It was also due to determined individuals – camp commandants, relief workers, local farmers etc. – who went out of their way to help a community they admired.

The Slovenes are an example of how preserving and nurturing a refugee community can work out well. If they had been forced to go back to Slovenia, they would have lost their lives, been imprisoned or had to share in the prevailing hardship. If they had been dispersed geographically, they might never have been able to organise their emigration – for that was largely done by self-help. As it was, they were able to move on as cohesive groups, help each other in their new homelands and contribute as responsible and wealth-generating citizens. An example is Uroš Roessmann, living in Cleveland, who became a world expert in neuropathology.

Mark Wyman praised the international community's handling of European refugees in the late 1940s as the first coordinated system for protection of those forced to flee their homelands. But the Slovene experience shows no great rush to offer new homes. They had to wait up to four years. It was principally due to Argentina's readiness to take the large majority that the community could avoid disintegration.

Božo Repe, Professor of Contemporary History at Ljubljana University, believes the history of Slovenia's wartime experiences, post-war killings and emigration is now largely known. He expects few significant new facts to be discovered, the only outstanding questions being those of interpretation. However, although the Slovene emigrants have an axe to grind, their testimony represents a wealth of new knowledge. Their story goes beyond just interpretation. It is a contribution to history.

In seeking to draw lessons, one is firstly struck with awe at the dilemmas the Slovenes were forced to face. Is it right or wrong to fight for your religious faith, to oppose Communism, to fight for your country, to collaborate with the enemy occupier, to wait until the storm passes, to avenge atrocities, to fight for social justice and equality, to hold together as a community? These questions could have been answered during the war by Britons and Americans with relative ease. Not so for the Slovenes. As a small, defenceless people they had little chance to exercise their individual wills, and when they could, many courses of action available were both right and wrong. They were forced into ethical compromises for which they paid dearly.

This was the particular brutality of World War II in Eastern Europe; not only did the occupiers impose more oppressive regimes than in the West, but civilian populations were drawn in as unwilling belligerents. For the Slovenes, there was the additional burden of a civil war taking place within the wider scope of the world war. In the circumstances, it was a tremendous achievement that a considerable number did act honourably.

The story also shows the lengths to which the Catholic Church goes to support its faithful. In their moment of need, the Slovene refugees knew the Church would stand by them. Priests communicated a reassuring vision based on faith, morality and family values. Some went willingly to their deaths in the repatriations, bringing comfort to fellow-prisoners who knew their last hour was upon them. Others served as trauma counsellors to bereaved relatives, rallying them with prayers, hymns and ritual. They taught in the camp schools and helped children to find the emotional security of a solid family and community background.

The Church also left no stone unturned in seeking countries of asylum. Dr Miha Krek, a Slovene former Vice-Premier in the wartime Yugoslav government in exile, undertook diplomacy in collaboration with the Vatican. Father Košiček, from the Slovene Social Committee in Rome, toured the camps informing refugees of the prospects. Father Hladnik in Argentina, referred to by grateful Slovenes as 'saintly' and 'a tireless idealist', got the crucial interview with Peron and liaised with Argentinian authorities. Catholic priests continue to be core components of Slovene cultural communities existing today in Argentina, Canada, the United States and Britain.

In their new homelands, the emigrants today seem not so different from anybody else in the West. What many of them had in mind at the end of the war was a Slovene government along the lines of the Christian Democrats who ruled for years afterwards in Italy. They wanted a democratic parliamentary system, a market economy and respect for spiritual values and family life. If the Partisans had not been set on seizing power by revolution, one could speculate that the Catholics, who had dominated Slovenian politics before the war, could have conceivably regained power and run a government little different from that in Italy. The only difference was that, whereas Italian Christian Democrat leader Alcide de Gasperi had kept clear of the Fascists during the war, the Slovene Catholics collaborated. And collaboration is at the core of the whole dispute.

Some Catholic emigrant leaders, aware of the negative associations, deny they ever collaborated at all. They argue they took German and Italian arms and organisational support just to defend themselves against attacks by the Communist Partisans, and their hearts were never on the side of the occupiers.

Sections of the *domobranci* had to swear oaths at parades in Ljubljana, once on 20 April 1944 on Hitler's birthday, and again on 30 January 1945, the anniversary of the Nazis taking power in Germany. The oath said:

> I swear to Almighty God that I will be faithful, courageous and obedient to my superiors, and that in the common fight with German armed forces under the command of the leader of Greater Germany, with SS troops and police, against bandits and communism as well as its allies, I will conscientiously fulfil my obligations to my Slovene homeland as part of free Europe. For this fight, I am also willing to sacrifice my life. So help me God.[3]

They also had to sign a written statement, which read:

> I joined the Slovene *domobranci* of my own free will to combat and destroy Communism, which brought my country so much misery and threatens the whole of Europe. It is my firm will to contribute with all my strength to the pacification of the country and Europe under German leadership and to stake my life for this. I have confirmed this obligation today with a sacred oath. I have been informed about my duties and rights in respect to the disciplinary and economic aspects of my service.[4]

One senses a will to take a distance from the Germans, but it is hard to argue that these were not declarations of collaboration. The *domobranci* were collaborating when they mounted guard on the largest viaduct of the strategic Trieste–Ljubljana railway. This was a service on behalf of the Germans rather than protection of the Catholic community.

A book published during the Communist era in 1961, *Clandestine Ljubljana*,[5] shows Slovene Catholic politicians and churchmen being received by Mussolini in Rome on 8 June 1941. The caption describes them as thanking Mussolini for the annexation of Slovenia's Ljubljana region to Italy. The Catholic People's Party joined an advisory committee of the Italian High Commissioner, Emilio Grazioli.[6]

Bishop Rožman wrote in a pastoral letter at the time: 'We are thankful to God, who inspired the leader of Greater Italy with the thoughts of generous rightfulness and considerate wisdom with which His Highness... proposed the establishment of Ljubljana province.'[7]

In another pastoral letter on 20 April 1941, Rožman wrote: 'As regards the cooperation of the Church representative with the new Fascist Italy, Catholics accept the authority of God's words: every man shall be obedient to higher powers. From this point of view, we acknowledge the power above us and we will be pleased to cooperate according to our consciousness, for the honourable and permanent benefit of the people, among whom God's providence has put us as priests.'

So collaboration did occur, though it was largely confined to the central and southern parts of Slovenia originally occupied by the Italians (and from 1943 by the Germans), including the capital, Ljubljana. In the northern parts integrated into the German Reich, the Nazis removed Slovenes from positions of authority. Many Catholic priests were deported, and those who remained were offered no opportunity to collaborate. In May 1944, Catholic Bishop Tomažič of Štajerska in northeast Slovenia declared he wanted no *domobranci* in his bishopric because of the 'evil' they had brought to the Ljubljana area.[8] Many other Catholics served with the Partisans throughout for patriotic reasons.

Whether collaboration was *right* is another question. As far as Slovenia was concerned, 'collaboration' with the Habsburg state had been a way of life for hundreds of years. Few considered this betrayed the national identity and culture which the Slovenes nurtured at the same time.

When World War II reached Yugoslavia, enemy occupation of Slovenia made collaboration of one sort or another unavoidable for the majority. International law recognises this inevitability in accepting that civil authorities in occupied territories continue their functions in accordance with the laws in force.

The Slovene Catholics collaborated for their own purposes and not because they believed in the pagan doctrines of Nazism. In this they contrasted with the Quislings in Norway, the National Socialist Movement in the Netherlands, the Flemish National Alliance in Belgium, the British Union of Fascists and the Action Française in France, which alone had over 700,000 members. In Slovenia, there was no such political movement aligned with Nazi ideology. Unlike in Norway, Belgium and the Netherlands, there were no SS units made up of Slovenes.

When the *domobranci* were set up in 1943, their leaders bargained with the Germans to maintain their independence, with mixed results. They avoided being drawn into SS units, and won a pledge they would be deployed on the 'Adriatic littoral', which lessened their fears of being sent to fight with German forces on the Russian front. But the Germans insisted orders and documents should be in German as well as Slovene, and put SS General Rösener in overall command. Within six months, one of the *domobranci* general staff was complaining their own role was being diminished as more and more German officers were attached.

It was the oath which caused the deepest misgivings among the *domobranci*. It caused uproar among the general staff when first mooted. Many wished to avoid any specific commitment, except to their Slovene homeland. The exact wording was negotiated over weeks with the Germans, who were intent in nailing them down. Rösener threatened them with dissolution if they did not fall into line. The Slovenes obtained that they should swear allegiance to the fight against Communism rather than to Hitler. But the Germans insisted on the reference to 'German leadership' and timed the ceremony for Hitler's birthday. On the day, ten *domobranci* refused to parade and were arrested.[9]

Among the emigrants, Božidar Fink, who has spent a lifetime formulating the justification for the Catholic stance, concedes: 'Swearing the oath of loyalty did harm. It was not good, even though we could not avoid it, and one should consider the extent to which it was made under duress.' Franci Markež, another Slovenian community leader in Argentina, describes the oath as 'unfortunate', and says the pro-German faction in the *domobranci* leadership was behind it.[10] Tine Velikonja, a *domobranec* who survived because he was under-age, maintains the ceremony could have been avoided if the *domobranci* leadership had resisted.*

Only a minority of the *domobranci* ever swore the oath, but it deepened the split in its leadership between the pro-Western faction and the group around the de facto commander, General Rupnik. The latter was a charismatic Slovene patriot, but sincerely admired the Fascists for their order and anti-Communism. An officer who served with Rupnik and then moved over to the Partisans, Jaka Avšič, describes in *Clandestine Ljubljana* how the general urged his officers to sign a letter of

---

\*    The Partisans too swore an oath – to fight 'alongside the renowned Workers-Peasants-Red Army of the SOVIET UNION' (exhibit in the Museum of Contemporary History, Ljubljana – capitals in original).

loyalty to the Italian government in 1941. He told them Italy wished them well, and they should stick to him as he had good connections. A number objected and the letter was never sent.

In another conversation, Avšič describes Rupnik as strongly supporting a German victory and predicting they would win in two weeks. Other witnesses recall him speaking about an imminent German victory up to the end. He was convinced of their invincibility. Tine Velikonja wrote on the 50th anniversary of the General's execution that Rupnik was loved by his soldiers and died heroically, but he 'transgressed the border which is defined by international legislation concerning behaviour during occupation'.[11]

What is striking about the Catholics at this time, in Slovenia and elsewhere, is the extent to which anti-Communism was a top priority. Popes Pius XI and XII set the policy out in missives, and the Slovene Church and its congregations put it into practice as an obedient flock. At the time the Communist threat was real and life-threatening, and the Catholics can claim credit for opposing it consistently. However, Catholic writings of the time caricature Communists as devils and anti-Christs. Today such virulence seems overdone.

The Western Allies thought so too. The Catholics who collaborated assumed the British and Americans shared their preoccupation with the Communist threat and thought they would help them defeat the Communists at the end of the war. They themselves put resistance to Communism at the top of their priorities, but they failed to notice that the Allies had a different agenda. For the Allies, the most important thing was to defeat the Nazis and their brutal philosophy of racial dominance and extermination, and they were ready to cooperate with Stalin to achieve that. On the one hand were Catholics valuing discipline, religious ideals and anti-Communism, and on the other were the Western Allies fighting for a liberal way of life free from Nazi tyranny. They were not on the same wavelength.

The collaboration was a Faustian pact. The *domobranci* had to help the Germans defend a key railway because, as Velikonja puts it, 'the Germans wanted their pound of flesh'. But the Germans withheld the best weapons from them, and the Gestapo, suspicious of their loyalties, harassed them to the end. They continued to fear possible transfer to the Russian Front, which would have meant probable death. The Allies meanwhile continued to aid their enemies, the Partisans.

Many of those who fled over the Ljubelj Pass believe they made the noblest of choices and see no viable alternatives. Some in hindsight consider they were naïve or made political mistakes, while others feel morally squeamish regarding the oath. Even today, opinions are divided.

The Communists equated collaboration with treason. However, this seems unfounded. The Catholics who opposed them loved their country as much as anybody else, and suffered for it at the hands of the occupiers.

They just wanted a different regime from the Communists to take power at the end of the war.

The Partisans were not totally averse to collaboration themselves, though on a smaller scale. They did so for a few months at the beginning of the war. Partisan leader Milovan Djilas also described[12] how, in March 1943, he met German representatives in Yugoslavia and discussed a truce under which the Germans would cease operations, if the Partisans stopped raids on a railway in the region of Slavonia. Tito did halt the raids but Hitler stopped the collaboration going any further. Djilas justified this by the examples of Lenin making peace with Germany at Brest-Litovsk near the end of World War I, and the 1939 Ribbentrop-Molotov Pact. In other words, the end justified the means – an argument not so different from that of the anti-Communist Catholics.

The Communists asserted that their fight enabled Slovenia to regain territory. As President, former Communist leader Milan Kučan argued that Slovenia recovered its western territory ceded to Italy after World War I only because the Partisans fought on the side of the Allies. In a speech on the 50th anniversary of the return of the Primorska region to Slovenia, he said: 'Resistance was necessary. It was necessary to fight. The border with Italy – the only border of a Western country to be changed after the war – was not changed because the anti-Fascist Allies wanted to correct the wrong done to Slovenes by the earlier decision. It was changed because of the anti-Fascist and National Liberation struggle of the Primorskan Slovenes.'[13]

This is true to an extent, but Slovenia was to the east of what was then already an Iron Curtain dividing Europe, and in the east a large number of frontiers were changing, all to the benefit of the victors. Italy had gained part of Slovenia after World War I because it ended on the winning side, while Slovenia was part of the defeated Austro-Hungarian Empire. Since Italy emerged on the losing side in World War II, it may well have had to hand back the lands it gained in 1920, whether or not the Partisans fought.

The territorial outcome for Tito was in any case mixed. His Partisans' wartime exploits failed to persuade the Allies to hand over southern Carinthia, which has a Slovenian minority. Tito also lost his main prize, the harbour city of Trieste, which had a cosmopolitan population including a large number of Slovenes.

The Partisans got to Trieste in the first days of May 1945, but New Zealand troops arrived the next day. The Partisans declared Trieste an integral part of Yugoslavia, ordered a curfew, declared martial law, brought out the local Slovenes in demonstrations shouting 'Trieste is ours', shot five Italian counter-demonstrators dead and ordained that all Italian residents from after 1918 would be expelled.

It was to no avail. Churchill ordered Alexander to ensure the city did not remain in Yugoslav hands. More Allied troops arrived, three British cruisers moored in the harbour, and Tito had to withdraw his military units. Their presence had failed to swing the balance. In the years following World War II, the Yugoslav Communists adopted such a hostile attitude to the West that the Allies continued to support the Italians on border issues. In 1954, a treaty ruled that Trieste belonged to Italy.

The Slovene Communists' slaughter of political opponents, mutual blood-letting within the Party and mass show trials are shocking to the modern reader. Cruel though this frenzy was, there were parallels elsewhere in the immediate post-war period. The Soviets exacted fearful reprisals among suspected collaborators in territories occupied by the Germans, raped and brutalised their way through the German civilian populace and decimated German prisoners of war.[14] In Czechoslovakia, after the Beneš decrees, terrible vengeance was exacted on the quarter of the population who were Sudeten Germans. They were chased out of the country in an orgy of killings, lynchings and beatings of the sick and elderly.[15] Accounts were similarly settled all across Europe, avenging Nazi atrocities blow for blow. About 1.8 million Germans were killed at this time, most dying in the camps that were set up by the Communists.

It would be wrong to deny the more positive side of the Partisans. The fact that they resisted gave pride and hope to the hapless civilian populace in Yugoslavia. In no other country of Eastern Europe did Communists come to power after having themselves fought against the Germans. In the other countries, the Communists took control only after the presence of the occupying Soviet Army had made itself felt.

Many Slovenes and other Yugoslavs welcomed the prospect of social justice and a new start that the Communists offered. Amid the Communists' cynical manoeuvres for power, there was also an idealism which responded to the wishes of large sections of the populace and an urgent need for reconstruction after the infrastructure of the state had been destroyed.

The Yugoslav Communists served their people well by keeping the Soviets out. Because the Partisans were in control at the end of the war, Stalin withdrew his troops. Subsequently, he broke with Tito and tried to undermine his power, but Tito stood up to him.

By the 1970s, Communism in Yugoslavia had become more tolerable. The economy moved into higher gear, fuelled by receipts from tourism and workers abroad, as well as heavy borrowing. Living standards rose and by some economic measures the country was better off than Britain, which was racked by strikes and inflation. Slovenia made the most of this, and Slovene professionals of that era remember working on lucrative contracts all over Yugoslavia and abroad.

Yugoslavia became a leader of the non-aligned world, which was good for prestige and international business contacts. In retrospect, the dreams of a Third World bloc lacked substance. But it was Tito the

Communist* who put his country to the forefront of the world stage, and many Slovenes and other Yugoslavs felt grateful.

For the emigrants overseas, these positive aspects were meaningless. They were kept at arms' length, denigrated as traitors and foreigners, their achievements in maintaining a flourishing Slovene cultural identity going unappreciated.

It would be a pity to end on a cold analytical note. Undertaking this story has been a moving experience. The fact that the project existed prompted people in all walks of life to dig deep in their memories and feelings. Many clearly saw an opportunity to make sense out of chaos, and they rose to the challenge.

There were unforgettable moments. For example, Colonel Emil Cof summoning the best standards of smart military precision at the age of 90 to give his report in an old people's home in a tattered suburb of Buenos Aires; or Milči Roessmann in Cleveland telling with shining eyes of her adolescent sense of adventure as she set out over the Ljubelj Pass; or the lawyer Božidar Fink meticulously laying out the case for the *domobranci* but modestly asking at the end: 'Do you think we did right?' Or the oppressed spirit of France Kozina in Canada, struggling to recount the trauma of his escape from the death pit; the endless chuckles of Val Meršol, who experienced much of the war as a schoolboy prank; Frank Jeglič serenely sitting in a Cleveland garden, happy to put the traumas behind him; or the old lady, dying in a Ljubljana hospital, who gave a girlish laugh as she described how she distributed Liberation Front leaflets from her school satchel during the war. She also told how her family was involved in the 'elimination' of a fellow-Partisan suspected of betrayal. When asked afterwards if she knew about the last bit, her grown-up daughter, herself a mother, replied quietly: 'No, she never told me about that.'

Without all their efforts to recall their pasts, many of these testimonies could have been lost forever. Besides being a story of death, suffering, disputes and accusations, this is above all a tale of individual human beings, coping with adversity for better or for worse.

In Kobarid, deep in the Julian Alps, stands a museum commemorating another series of slaughters which occurred in Slovenia. Some of the fiercest fighting of World War I took place on Slovene territory. Better known by its Italian name of Caporetto, Kobarid is the site of the greatest mountain battle in history. Around the Soča (Isonzo) river, Italian and Austrian armies fought a dozen campaigns between 1915 and 1917, with a loss of some 300,000 lives. Caporetto is where the Italians suffered a calamitous defeat, fleeing as far as the hinterlands of Venice.

---

* Tito was half Croat, half Slovene.

The museum, winner of a Council of Europe award, touchingly evokes the anguish of this war. Its computer-animated emblem is a drop of bright red blood splashing on the rock of this steep range of mountains. On one side were peasants from the south of Italy. On the other were troops from all over the Austro-Hungarian Empire, including Slovenes, fighting for a faltering Empire they wanted to leave. They were killed by bullets, shrapnel and slivers of rock ricocheting around the mountain-sides. In the winter, the survivors froze in cold and snow.

It was a vast expense of life for very little, until the Italians were caught in positions too far advanced and overwhelmed by a blitzkrieg advance under cover of mist. Over a quarter of a million surrendered and the rest broke and ran.

In the middle of the computer-animated splash of blood appear the faces of young men who wrote of their ordeals in diaries and letters. Slovenes tell of huddling together with disfigured and crazed Italian soldiers, screaming and shaking as shells exploded around them.[16]

The Kobarid museum celebrates the heroism of those who did their best in the face of impossible challenges, and presents the facts straightforwardly, without animosity. For Slovenes, World War II was an even greater tragedy, since it set brother against brother. But the museum's spirit sets an example for healing those divisions. It is a monument created by Slovenes who know the value of a compassionate understanding of history, and who instinctively live the words of their national anthem:

*God's blessing on all nations,*
*Who long and work for that bright day,*
*When o'er earth's habitations*
*No war, no strife shall hold its sway;*
*Who long to see*
*That all men free*
*No more shall foes, but neighbours be.*

# Notes

**Preface**

1   Letter in the possession of John Corsellis.

**Prologue**

1   The Partisan side of wartime history is chronicled in Yugoslav official archives and a large number of memoirs by Yugoslav participants. Memoirs in English recounted from the Partisan viewpoint include:
Fitzroy Maclean, *Eastern Approaches*, Jonathan Cape, London, 1949.
Lindsay Rogers, *Guerilla Surgeon*, Collins, London, 1957.
Milovan Djilas, *Wartime*, Harcourt Brace Jovanovich, New York, 1977 – an account influenced by Djilas' later break with Tito.
John Corsellis, *Yugoslav Refugees in Camps in Egypt and Austria 1944–1947*, North Dakota Quarterly, Winter 1993, pp 40–54, and paper delivered at the 1995 International Conference on War, Exile and Everyday Life of the Zagreb Institute of Ethnology; both were based on his personal experience of and research into the 25,000 Croat, Serb and Jewish pro-Partisan refugees in El Shatt camp in Egypt in autumn 1944.

**Chapter 1**

1   France Pernišek, *Pred štiridesetimi leti: odlomki iz dnevnika slovenskega begunca (40 Years Ago: Excerpts from the Diary of a Slovene Refugee)*, published serially in *Duhovno življenje*, Buenos Aires, May 1985–February 1990.
2   Interview with Pavči Maček, October 1995; memoirs of Marko Bajuk
3   Interview with Marija Hirschegger, 18 October 2002.
4   Part of Jože Lekan's testimony was recorded by his niece, Anica Roessmann, in the United States, 16 July 1991.
5   Idem.
6   André Lacaze, *The Tunnel*, Hamish Hamilton, London, 1980.
7   Memoir by Božidar Bajuk, a copy of which is in the possession of John Corsellis.

**Chapter 2**

1   In Slovene:
Svobode naše jabolko se zlato
nam zakotalilo je v kri in blato,
in preden spet zasije v čisti slavi,
vsi bomo blatni, ah, vsi krvavi.
2   John Keegan, *A History of Warfare*, Pimlico, London, 1994, p 365.
3   Ilija Jukič, *The Fall of Yugoslavia*, Harcourt Brace Jovanovich, New York and London, 1974, p 3.

4    Janko Prunk, *A Brief History of Slovenia*, Založba Grad, Ljubljana 2000, p 146.

5    Ibid., pp 145/6.

6    *Verbale della riunione a Kočevje il 2 agosto 1942*, quoted by Jonathan Steinberg in *All or Nothing: The Axis and the Holocaust 1941–1943*, Routledge, London, 1990, p 34, and by Alojz Židar in *Il popolo sloveno ricorda e accusa*, Založba Lipa, Koper, 2001, p 189.

7    Alojz Židar, op. cit., p 127.

8    Metod M. Milač, *Resistance, Imprisonment and Forced Labor, A Slovene Student in World War II*, Peter Lang Publishing Inc., New York, 2002.

9    Janko Prunk, op. cit., p 146.

10   Lenin, *Collected Works, XVIII*, pp 44–46, quoted by Ilija Jukič, op. cit., p 95.

11   Ilija Jukič, op. cit., p 95.

12   *Ljubljana v ilegali*, published by Regional Board of the Socialist Alliance of the Working People, Slovenia, 1961, p. 259.

13   Edvard Kardelj, *Iz obrambe v napad (From Defence to Attack) 1941*, quoted in *Ljubljana v ilegali*, p 92.

14   Boris Mlakar, *Slovensko domobranstvo 1943–1945*, Slovenska matica, Ljubljana, 2003, p 24.

15   Kardelj, op. cit., pp 91–92.

16   Ilija Jukič, op. cit., p 135.

17   John Keegan, op. cit., p 53.

18   Milovan Djilas, *Wartime*, Harcourt Brace Jovanovich, New York, 1977, p 338.

19   Fitzroy Maclean, *Eastern Approaches*, Jonathan Cape, London, 1949, p 426.

20   Barbara Jelavich, *History of the Balkans*, Cambridge University Press, 1983, pp 298–230.

21   Bert Pribac, *Slovenske spravne motnje (Slovenian Reconciliation Troubles)*, Canberra, 1998.

22   Metod M. Milač, op. cit., pp 73–86.

23   Monsignor Jože Jagodič, *Mojega življenja tek*, Klagenfurt, 1974.

24   Monika Kokalj Kočevar, *Gestapo Volunteers: The Upper Carniola Home Defense Force 1943–1945 (originally: Gorenjski domobranec – Gorenjski kraji in ljudje XVIII)*, Axis Europa Books, New York, 2000, p 36.

25   Matija Žganjar, *Slovenski partizani in zavezniki (Slovene Partisans and the Allies)*, p 139.

26   Mlakar, op. cit., p 136.

27   Monika Kokalj Kočevar, op. cit., p 39.

28   See www.tuskegeeairmen.org 21 January 2004.

**Chapter 3**

1    Nigel Nicolson, in a report written shortly afterwards, quoted by Nikolai Tolstoy in *The Minister and the Massacres*, Century Hutchinson Ltd, London, 1986.

2    Jane Balding, unpublished diary quoted by Nikolai Tolstoy, op. cit.

3    Marijan Tršar, *Dotik Smrti*, Nova Revija, Ljubljana, 2000.

4    Interview 11034/3/1, Imperial War Museum, London, p 1.

5    Marko Bajuk, *Annual Report for the School Years 1944/45 and 1945/46, Peggetz-Lienz*, undated, 23-page text, Studia Slovenica Archive, Šentvid, Ljubljana.

6   Interview with Imperial War Museum historian, 1989.
7   Bert Pribac, *Slovenske spravne motnje (Slovene Reconciliation Troubles)*, Canberra, 1998.
8   *Encounter*, December 1979, pp 10–42.
9   Dušan Biber, *Tito-Churchill, Strictly Confidential*, Zagreb, pp 512, 514, quoted by Boris Mlakar, *Slovensko domobranstvo 1943–1945*, Slovenska matica, Ljubljana, 2003, pp 499–500.
10  Ian Mitchell, *The Cost of a Reputation*, Topical Books, Scotland, 1997, p 32.
11  Anthony Cowgill, Lord Brimelow, Christopher Booker, *The Repatriations from Austria, Report of an Inquiry*, London, 1990, p 248, quoted by Mlakar, op. cit.
12  Nicholas Bethell, *The Last Secret*, Penguin, 1995, pp 58–59.
13  Interview 10968/2/2, Imperial War Museum.
14  WO 170/4184, quoted by Mitchell, op. cit., p 26.
15  WO 170/4241, quoted by Mitchell, op. cit., p 28.
16  Kirk Papers in US National Archives, quoted by Mitchell, op. cit., p 31.
17  Cowgill, op. cit., pp 297–298, quoted by Mlakar, op. cit, p 504.
18  *British Documents on Foreign Affairs, Part III, 1940–1945, Series F, Europe*, University Publications of America, pp 450–453.
19  WO 106/4059, quoted by Tolstoy, op. cit., pp 321–322.
20  Alistair Horne, *Macmillan 1894–1956*, Macmillan, London, 1988, p 276.
21  Interview 10968/2/2, Imperial War Museum.
22  Nigel Nicolson, *Long Life*, Weidenfeld & Nicolson, London, 1997, p 121.
23  Last quote is from Pernišek's diary.
24  The account is based on: *Matica mrtvih (The Registry of the Dead), Specific data on Slovenians who were murdered by the criminal Liberation Front 1941–1945*, Cleveland, US, 1968, iv, pp 7–9; *Vetrinjska tragedija*, Cleveland, US 1960, pp 26–38; Vladimir Kozina, *Slovenia, the Land of My Joy and My Sorrow*, Cleveland, US pp 228–232 Tolstoy, op. cit., pp 156–169.
25  Tone Ciglar, *Dr Janez Janež, Utrinek božje dobrote*, Ljubljana, 1993, pp 15–16.
26  Interview with Uroš and Milči Roessmann.
27  John Keegan, *The Face of Battle*, Penguin, 1978, pp 185, 191 and 303.
28  John Keegan, *A History of Warfare*, Pimlico, London, 1994, pp 193 and 290.
29  Franc Ižanec, *Odprti grobovi (Open Graves)*, Buenos Aires, 1965.
30  *Independent Magazine*, 22 April 1989.
31  Interview 10968/2/2, Imperial War Museum, p 15.
32  Susan Crosland, *Tony Crosland*, Jonathan Cape, London, 1982, pp 38–39: letter to Philip Williams dated 18 May 1945.
33  Ibid., p.41.
34  Barre interview, 11034/3/1, Imperial War Museum, pp 3–4.
35  From a cyclostyled document in John Corsellis' possession, *Events in Vetrinj in May 1945*, by Dr Valentin Meršol, p 13.
36  Report dated 13 June 1945 *Friends Ambulance Unit – Mediterranean Area: Relief Work in Austria: First Reports*, p 5, from FAU Archives.
37  *OCIT 110, Friends Ambulance Unit, C.M.F., 10 July 1945, 'Austria'*, p.9, from FAU archives, Friends House Library, London.

38  J.A. Selby-Bigge, op. cit., pp 217–219.
39  Tolstoy, op. cit., pp 297–298.
40  Copy in the Friends Ambulance Unit (FAU) archive, Friends' House, London. Copies of the order were given at the time to FAU and British Red Cross field workers for their reassurance.
41  WO 106/4059, quoted by Mitchell, op. cit., p 45.
42  Quoted by Pernišek in his diary and by Meršol in his cyclostyled document.

**Chapter 4**
1   Inscription displayed at headquarters of the International Red Cross.
2   In 1995, the Slovene publisher Mohorjeva družba published a book, *Onstran samote*, containing an unpublished novel and short pieces by Ludve Potokar, and a biography on him by Franc Pibernik.
3   Božo Repe interview with Marcus Ferrar, 14 October 2003.
4   *Encounter*, December 1979, pp 10–42.
5   *Slovenski poročevalec newspaper*, 27 May 1945.
6   Quoted by Drago Jančar in *The Dark Side of the Moon*, (English version), CIP – kataložni zapis o publikaciji, Narodna in univerzitetna knijižnica, Ljubljana, 1998.
7   Milan Zajec, *Ušli so smrti (They Escaped Death)*, edited by Ciril Turk, Mohorjeva založba, Celovec-Ljubljana-Dunaj, 1998. First published in Argentina in 1949.
8   Franc Ižanec, *Odprti grobovi (Open Graves)*, Buenos Aires, 1965.
9   Besides his interview with Marcus Ferrar, France Dejak also spoke with Slovene journalists Ivo Žajdela and Milovan Dimitrič. Excerpts of their interviews were made available to the authors and are included in the account.
10  Magazine article published in 1995 by France Dejak, edited by Slovene journalist Ivo Žajdela.

**Chapter 5**
1   Milovan Djilas, *Wartime*, p 447.
2   Account based on an article by Father Blatnik in the weekly journal *Ameriška domovina*, Cleveland, USA., issue no. 201, 20 October 1971.
3   Vladimir Kozina, *Slovenia Land of My Joy and My Sorrow*, published by Historical Commission of TABOR ZDSB, Cleveland, USA. and Toronto, Canada, 1980, p 250.
4   Ibid., p 181.
5   Pernišek's diary is the source of this account.
6   Duplicated seven-page report headed Headquarters Military Government Land Kaernten Ref: MGK/3870/DP, signed Baty (Deputy Controller, Education Br., Allied Comm. For Austria), dated 12 August 1945, Studia Slovenica archive, Ljubljana-Šentvid.
7   Tape-recorded interview with Jože Jančar, September 1991.
8   Quotes from Metod M. Milač, from his own book, *Resistance, Imprisonment and Forced Labor, A Slovene Student in World War II*, Peter Lang Publishing Inc., New York, 2002, pp 216–222, and in France Pibernik's memoir of Ludve Potokar, *Onstran samote*, Ljubljana, 1994, pp 219 and 330.

9   Colin Parkes, *Bereavement: Studies of Grief in Adult Life*, Penguin, London, 1972, p 187 and 206.

**Chapter 6**
1   Richard Lamb, *Churchill as War Leader: Right or Wrong?* Bloomsbury, London, 1991, p 253.
2   Adam LeBor and Roger Boyes, *Surviving Hitler*, Simon & Schuster, London, 2000, p 29.
3   Article entitled *The Slovene Social Committee paved the way for our emigration* signed by D.R.F. in *Koledar svobodne Slovenije*, Buenos Aires, 1949, pp 162–165.

**Chapter 7**
1   *Koledar svobodne Slovenije (Free Slovenia Almanac)*, Buenos Aires, 1949.

**Chapter 10**
1   *Koledar svobodne Slovenije (Almanac of Free Slovenia)*, Buenos Aires, 1949/50.
2   Anthony Cowgill, Lord Brimelow, Christopher Booker, *The Repatriations from Austria, Report of an Inquiry, Vol II*, pp 292, 299, 300, London, 1990, quoted by Ian Mitchell, *The Cost of a Reputation*, Topical Books, Scotland, 1997, p 70.
3   Mitchell, op. cit., pp 69–80.
4   Cowgill, op. cit., *Vol I*, p 171, quoted by Mitchell, op. cit., p 77.
5   Chapter *The official British answer concerning the repatriation of the domobranci* in *The Viktring Tragedy*, Association of Anti-Communist Fighters, Cleveland, Ohio, 1960.
6   General Sir William Jackson, *The Mediterranean and the Middle East, Vol.6, Part 3: Victory in the Mediterranean, November 1944–May 1945*, HMSO, London, 1987.
7   Letter dated 15 December 1947, shown to John Corsellis.
8   Editorial of 20 February 1978, quoted by Nicholas Bethell, *The Last Secret*, Penguin, 1995, p 281.
9   Nigel Nicolson, *Long Life*, Weidenfeld & Nicolson, London, 1997, pp 120–123.
10  Nikolai Tolstoy, *The Minister and the Massacres*, Century Hutchinson Ltd, London, 1986, pp 214, 219, 307. Cf also Nicolson, op. cit.
11  J.A. Selby-Bigge, typescript memoirs, loaned to John Corsellis, pp 217–219.
12  Lyn Smith, *Pacifists in Action*, William Sessions Ltd, York, England, 1998, pp 177, 201, 408, 411.
13  Richard Lamb, *Churchill as War Leader: Right or Wrong?* Bloomsbury, London, 1991, p 273.
14  cf John Keegan, *The Second World War*, Penguin, 1990, pp 483–502.
15  Richard Lamb, op. cit., pp 250–273.
16  Fitzroy Maclean, *Eastern Approaches*, Jonathan Cape, London, 1949, pp 402–403.
17  Winston Churchill, House of Commons, 13 May 1940, *The Speeches of Winston Churchill*, Penguin Books, London, 1990, p 149.

18   See Chapter 3.
19   Nicholas Bethell, op. cit., pp 282–289.
20   Interview, Imperial War Museum, 10968/2/2, p 15.
21   *Zaveza*, no. 45, June 2002.

**Chapter 11**

1   Žarko Lazarevič, catalogue of the exhibition *Over the hill is just like here* in the Museum of Contemporary History, Ljubljana, 2002, p 79.
2   Božo Repe, *Rdeča Slovenija (Red Slovenia)*, Založba Sophia, 2003, p 62.
3   Arrigo Petacco, *L'Esodo: La Tragedia negata degli Italiani d'Istria, Dalmazia e Venezia Giulia*, Mondadori, Milan, 1999, pp 59–66.
4   Vladimir Kozina, *Slovenia, the Land of My Joy and My Sorrow*, Tabor, Cleveland/Toronto, 1980, pp 303–304.
5   Bert Pribac, *Slovenske spravne motnje (Slovene Reconciliation Troubles)*, Canberra (Australia) 1998, Sergasi (Slovenia) 2002, Založba 2000, p 91.
6   Nataša Urbanc, catalogue of the exhibition *Over the hill is just like here* in the Museum of Contemporary History, Ljubljana, 2002, pp 74–75.
7   Božo Repe, op. cit., p 31.
8   cf. Boris Mlakar, *Slovensko domobranstvo 1943–1945*, Slovenska matica, Ljubljana, 2003. Mlakar, a historian at the Slovene Institute of Contemporary History, named a few of the alleged perpetrators in this book.
9   Source: Tine Velikonja, in an interview, 17 August 2002.
10  Quoted by Bert Pribac, ibid, p 52.
11  Interview with Slovene state television, 1 November 2004.
12  Speech by President Milan Kučan at a meeting of Allied veterans at Priložje, Slovenia, 28 June 1998.
13  http:www.orf.at – August 2004.
14  The authors know M.'s name. Marcus Ferrar interviewed her at her home, 29 October 2002.

**Chapter 12**

1   CNN, 7 January 2002.
2   Quoted in *Fifty Years of United Slovenia Association in the Argentine Republic*, Buenos Aires, 1998, p 777.
3   Marko Kremžar, *Med smrtjo in življenjem*, Družina, Ljubljana, 2000, pp 109–113.

**Chapter 13**

1   Nataša Urbanc, catalogue of the exhibition *Over the hill is just like here* in the Museum of Contemporary History, Ljubljana, 2002, p 70.
2   Drago Jančar, *The Dark Side of the Moon: A Short History of Totalitarianism in Slovenia, 1945–1990*, CIP – kataložni zapis o publikaciji, Narodna in univerzitetna knjižnica, Ljubljana, 1998, pp 5–19.
3   Drago Jančar, article *Nikdar več (Never more)* reviewing a book by an ex-*domobranec* Marijan Eiletz *Moje domobranstvo in pregnanstvo (My domobranci service and banishment)*, published in a collection of Jančar essays entitled *Brioni in drugi zapisi (Brioni and other writings)*, Mladinska Knjiga, Ljubljana, 2002.

4   Bert Pribac, *Slovenske spravne motnje (Slovenian Reconciliation Troubles)*, Canberra, 1998, p 49.
5   James Gow and Cathie Carmichael, *Slovenia and the Slovenes*, Hurst & Company, London, 2000, p 127.
6   Interview with Slovene state television, 1 November 2004.
7   Jonathan Fenby, *On the Brink: The Trouble with France*, Warner Books, 1999, pp 209–225. See also Robert Gildea, *Marianne in Chains*, Pan Books, 2003.
8   Richard Wagner, *Der leere Himmel: Reise in das Innere des Balkan*, Aufbau-Verlag, Berlin, 2003, pp 185–186.
9   Interview with Slovene state television, 1 November 2004.
10  Drago Jančar, op. cit. – *Nikdar več*.

**Chapter 14**

1   The Slovene National Anthem is a song, *Zdravljica (A Toast)*, written by the 19th century Slovene poet, France Prešeren. Translation by Janko Lavrin, *A Selection of Poems by France Prešeren*, Basil Blackwell, Oxford 1954.
2   Mark Wyman, *Europe's Displaced Persons, 1945–1951*, Cornell Paperbacks, 1998.
3   Slovenec newspaper, Ljubljana, 21 April 1944, also quoted by Božidar Fink, *Na tujem v domovini*, Mohorjeva založba, 1999, p 49.
4   Janez Kos, *O prisegi slovenskih domobrancev (About the Slovenian domobranci oath)*, Dnevnik Forum, 5 November 2004.
5   *Ljubljana v ilegali*, published by the Regional Board of the Socialist Alliance of the Working People, Slovenia, 1961.
6   Janko Prunk, *A Brief History of Slovenia*, Založba Grad, Ljubljana, 2000, p 149.
7   Quoted by Slovene politician Janez Stanovnik in *Delo* newspaper, Ljubljana, 15 November 2003.
8   Bert Pribac, *Slovenske spravne motnje (Slovene Reconciliation Troubles)*, Canberra, 1998, p 173.
9   Boris Mlakar, *Slovensko domobranstvo 1943–1945*, Slovenska matica, Ljubljana, 2003, pp 288–298.
10  Typewritten statement given to Marcus Ferrar, Buenos Aires, 8 October 2002.
11  Tine Velikonja, *General Leon Rupnik*, www.zaveza.org, 4 September 1996.
12  Milovan Djilas, *Wartime*, Harcourt Brace Jovanovich, New York, 1977, pp 229–245.
13  Milan Kučan, speech in Nova Gorica, 14 September 1997.
14  cf. Antony Beevor, *Berlin: the Downfall 1945*, Penguin, 2003.
15  *The Economist*, 17 August 2002.
16  Ivan Matičič, *On the Fields of Blood*, quoted by Petra Svoljšak in *The Front on Soča*, Cankarjeva založba, Ljubljana, 2002, p 78.

# Acknowledgements and Verbal Sources

This book is based on memory, diaries and dozens of interviews with Slovenes who fled their country in 1945. The memory is John Corsellis'. He was there in Viktring shortly after the Slovenes arrived. As an aid worker, he looked after them for the next two years in refugee camps in Austria. He witnessed some of the events himself and became well acquainted with many of the protagonists. He wrote regular letters to his mother, which she kept. They constitute a journal of his experiences in the camps, and he was able to quote from the originals in this book.

The late France Pernišek, a Catholic social insurance official, kept a diary until he reached his country of emigration, Argentina, in 1949. Before his death, he gave permission to John Corsellis to use it. Corsellis has facsimile copies of the original hand-written diary, as well as its serialisation in an emigrant publication in Argentina in 1979–1980. As the handwriting was not always decipherable, the quotes come from the serialised version, in which Pernišek edited a few passages. Sister Agnes Žužek, a Medical Mission Sister and relative, kindly translated it into English. The Bajuk family provided a translated version of the typescript memoirs of Director Marko Bajuk. Corsellis also has a copy of a cyclostyled memoir by Dr Valentin Meršol.

The core of this book is the testimony given by the emigrants in interviews. Unless otherwise stated, the quotes attributed to specific emigrants were given directly to the authors, who wish to thank them warmly for their willingness to spend time and effort sharing their stories. Corsellis made a series of interviews in the US, Canada, Britain, Argentina and Slovenia in the early 1990s. Marcus Ferrar supplemented these with further interviews in the same countries at the beginning of the 21st century, investigating the continuing conflict between the emigrants and their opponents in Slovenia, and the impact of Argentina's economic collapse.

A large number of the interviews were taped and transcribed, while others were recorded in notes. In the case of those in Argentina, some emigrants made a written response to questions, followed by interviews.

The authors owe much to many institutions and individuals. Among institutions, the Refugee Studies Centre, University of Oxford and its Documentation Centre, the Bodleian Library, Cambridge University Library, Chatham House Library, Friends House Library, Graduate Institute of International Studies (HEI) Geneva, Imperial War Museum Department of Sound Records, London School of Slavonic and East

European Studies Library, Public Record Office, UN Archives New York and Westminster School. Among individuals, Mark Almond, Mary Armstrong, Dr Janez Arnež, Ann Avery, Božidar and Marko Bajuk, Professor Ivo Banac, David Blamires, Richard Burns, James Catford, Father Čeglar, Henry and Naida Christie, Father Stanislav Čikanek, Sarah Collinson, Dennis Conolly, Professor Peter Conradi, Leopold and Marija Čop, Christopher Cviic, Janez and Marija Dernulc, Barry Eliott, Tim Evens, Peter Fabian, Simona Ferrar, Professor Marta Haines Ferrari, Otto Fisher, Carol Gardiner, Philip and Barbara Giles, Dr James Gow, Laurence Harbottle, Dr Melissa Hardie, Dr Barbara Harrell-Bond, Graham Howes, Bo and Mary Eiletz, Margaret Jaboor, Dr Jože and Marija Jančar, Professor Ewald Koren, Janez and Alice Kovic, Marko and Paula Kremžar, Karl and Dora Lavrenčič, The Lazarist Fathers, Ljubljana, Jan and Zdenka Lovro, A.H. MacKinnon, Ciril Markež, Lord Mayhew, Grigor McClelland, Mitja Meršol, Val and Patty Meršol, Keith Miles, Ian Mitchell, Dame Iris Murdoch, Nigel Nicolson, Jože and Božena Opara, Stanislav Pevec, Frances Pinter, Ken and Rosemary Polack, the Earl of Portsmouth, Michael Pountney, Dr Gwyn Prins, Peter and Majda Remec, David Roberts, Dr Elizabeth Roberts, Uroš, Milči and Cathy Roessmann, Anita Sanders, John Saunders, Dr Brendan Simms, Ifigenija Simonović, Dr Catherine Simpson, Lyn Smith, Dr Jonathan Steinberg, Dr Gabriela Stieber, Dr Anton Stres, Geoffrey and Anka Stuttard, H.A. Swan, Donald Swann, Richard Symonds, Gordon Tilsley, Nikolai Tolstoy, Dr Nicholas Van Hear, Tine Velikonja, Antonella Vitale, Professor Sidney Waldron, Dr Mark Wheeler, Robin Whitworth, Anica Wilkinson, Anthony Wilson, Dr Ken Wilson, Maria Zorc (Rus) and Ann, Emily, Gillian, Peter and Tom Corsellis. Evelina Ferrar, who is Slovene, interpreted during interviews, translated texts and helped with research.

Claudio Ceni, c.ceni@iprolink.ch, created the maps. Except where otherwise indicated, photos are reproduced with kind permission of Studia Slovenica, Ljubljana-Šentvid, Slovenia.

For his research and visits to refugees overseas, John Corsellis received grants from the Joseph Rowntree and Barrow and Geraldine S. Cadbury Trusts and from a private family trust in Cambridge.

## Dramatis Personae
### (those quoted in the text are marked with *)

*British Military:*

Alexander, Field Marshal Lord, Supreme Allied Commander Mediterranean *
Ames, Lieutenant, OC Viktring military camp
Barre, Major Paul, Canadian, OC Viktring civilian camp *
Bell, Major, Scottish, OC Viktring civilian camp
Crosland, Captain Antony, Royal Welch Fusiliers *

Dufour, Lieutenant-Colonel, Head, DP Branch, AMG Austria
Floyd, Major-General Sir Henry, Chief-of-Staff, British 8th Army *
Hall, Colonel, Deputy Head, DP Branch, AMG Austria
Johnson, Major William, Head, DP Branch, AMG Carinthia *
Keightley, General Sir Charles, OC 5 Corps, British 8th Army *
McCreery, General Sir Richard, OC British 8th Army in Austria
Nicolson, Captain Nigel, Officer i/c liaison, Viktring camp *
Steele, General Sir James, British Commander-in-Chief in Austria

## (British and UNRRA staff – civilians and former military)

Balding, Sister Jane, BRC nurse *
Barton, Dr, UNRRA Chief Medical Officer, British Zone, Austria
Baty, CW, Deputy Director of Education, Allied Commission Austria *
Boester, Florence, UNRRA welfare officer, Lienz and Spittal camps
Chalmers, Wing Commander, Director of Lienz UNRRA camp
Chapman, Major C.D., Australian, Director UNRRA, British Zone, Austria*
Corsellis, John, FAU/BRC field worker, later UNRRA*
Cottrell, Colonel, UNRRA Director of medical services in Austria
Couper, Joan, supervisor, BRC contingent in Carinthia, Austria
Cullis, Michael, diplomat i/c Yugoslav Section, Foreign Office *
Falmouth, Lady, senior BRC official from London HQ
Gibson, Peter and Rose, John, senior FAU officials from London HQ
Jarvie, Major, Australian, Director of Spittal UNRRA camp
Lieven, Dara, Russian émigré, UNRRA nurse, IRO welfare officer
Maclean, Brigadier Fitzroy, MP, chairman of commission screening refugees *
Meredith, Miss, welfare officer, Spittal UNRRA camp
Michell, Miss, Australian, welfare officer, Spittal UNRRA camp
Pearson, David, Welsh, leader of FAU team in Austria
Selby-Bigge, John, OBE, BRC Asst. Commissioner, Civ. Relief Austria *
Strachan, James, FAU/BRC relief worker, Lienz camp
Thurstan, Miss Violet, i/c Tuberculosis Sanatorium Seebach *
Young, Group Captain Ryder, Director, Lienz UNRRA camp

## Refugee personalities

Ambrožič, Lojze, chairman of Lienz camp welfare committee
Bajuk, Božidar, son of Marko Bajuk, teacher: home, flight *
Bajuk, Marko, Director of camp grammar school *
Basaj, Dr Jože, President of National Committee of Slovenia
Blatnik, Dr Franc, Salesian priest, teacher, editor of camp papers *
Drčar, Colonel Ivan: Viktring
Hladnik, Father Janez, émigré Slovene priest in Argentina
Jagodič, Monsignor Jože, Apostolic Delegate to Refugees in Austria
Jančar, Jože, spokesman for university students *
Janež, Dr Janez, surgeon, reported forcible repatriations *
Kozina, Father Vladimir, refugee priest in parish west of Lienz *

Krek, Dr Miha, former Vice-Premier, leader, Slovenes in exile
Kremžar, Franc, editor of camp newspaper
Krener, General Franc, *domobranec* leader
Mašič, Pavle, former state auditor, active in camps
Mernik, Father Janko, teacher in camp secondary school
Meršol, Dr. Valentin, physician, camp leader and spokesman *
Mihelič, Professor Silvin, music teacher in camp secondary school
Novak, Jože, chief Communist agent in Spittal camp
Pernišek, France, secretary of Slovene camp committee *
Puc, Dr Franc, children's clinic and TB sanatorium
Rjahin, Dr, Russian émigré doctor in Lienz and Spittal camps
Rožman, Dr Gregorij, Bishop of Ljubljana, lived near Lienz camp *
Sever, Professor Janez, teacher in camp secondary school
Škrbec, Monsignor Matija, senior Catholic priest in Lienz camp
Tavčar, engineer: Viktring
Trobec, Mr, Communist agent in Spittal camp
Vračko, Dr Edvard, Judge, i/c legal affairs in Lienz camp

*Interviews with refugees (name, age/occupation in 1945, context, country of emigration, dates of interviews)*

Ambrožič, Aloysius, pupil (son of L. Ambrožič, later Cardinal): home, camps, Canada: March 1991, September 1993, 7 April 2002
Aršič-Bajuk, Vera: wartime, Argentina: 8 October 2002
Bajuk, Božidar, pupil, son of teacher Božidar Bajuk: camps, Argentina: October 1995, 10 October 2002
Bajuk, Marko, pupil, son of teacher Božidar Bajuk: flight, camps, Argentina: 9 October 2002
Bertoncelj, Dinko: wartime, Argentina: 15 October 2002
Bohinc, Julia, pupil: Argentina: February 1994
Bratina, Gloria, 19, student: flight, camps, Graz, Canada: March 1991, September 1993, 8 April 2002
Cenkar, Franc, 21: home, camps, USA: March 1991
Cof, Colonel Emil: wartime, flight, Argentina: 7 October 2002
Čop, Leopold and Marija, students: Bolivia, Canada: April 1991, 7 April 2002
Dejak, Franc, policeman: wartime, flight, USA: 11 April 2002
Dernulc, Janez, 24: home, camps, England, Wales: September 1991
Eiletz, Bo and Mary: wartime, flight, Argentina: 6 October 2002
Fink, Božidar, lawyer: wartime, flight, Argentina: 7 October 2002
Grebenc, Stanko, schoolboy: flight, camps, Argentina, Slovenia: 7 October 2002
Grintal, Luka, farmer: wartime, camps, Argentina: 17 October 2002
Guden, Anica and Marija, 16 and 19 (later A.Jug and M.Dernulc): home, England and Wales: September 1991
Hirschegger, Marija, small girl: flight, camps, Argentina: 18 October 2002
Hribovšek (later Kremžar), Paula, schoolgirl: camps, Argentina: October 1995
Jančar, Jože, spokesman for university students: September 1991, 8 June 1994
Jančar (née Hribar), Marija, medical student: home, flight, camps: September 1991, 20 February 2002
Jeglič, Dr Frank A., schoolboy: wartime, camps, USA: 12 April 2002

Jerebič, Stanko, 13, pupil: Argentina: February 1994

Kolarič, Rudy, schoolboy: flight, camps, USA: September 1993, 10 April 2002

Kozina, France, farmer: wartime, flight, Canada: 9 April 2002

Kremžar, Marko, student (son of Franc Kremžar): Graz, Argentina: February 1991, 5 October 2002

Kuk, Gustl, law student: life outside camps, Toronto: April 1991, September 1993

Kukovica, Ivan, student: flight, repatriations, Canada: September 1993

Lekan, Jože, *domobranec*: wartime, flight, US: May 1991, 10 April 2002

Loboda, Marian, 10, pupil: home, flight, Argentina: May 1994, 6 October 2002

Lovro, Jan, *domobranec*: wartime, flight, camps, Argentina: 18 October 2002

Maček, Pavči, 16: repatriations: October 1995

Markež, Ciril: wartime, Argentina: 19 October 2002

Markež, Francisco: wartime, Argentina: 3 October 2002

Markež, Irenej: flight, Argentina: 18 October 2002

Meršol, Val, 14, pupil (son of Dr V. Meršol): wartime, camps, USA: March 1991, September 1993, 12 April 2002

Mizerit, Tone, schoolboy: wartime, Argentina: 5 October 2002

Oblak, Anton, 22, farmer: USA: March 1991

Odar, Miroslav, 18, pupil: Lienz camp: March 1991

Opara, Jože, engineering student: camps, Canada: April 1991, September 1993

Pavlin, Peter: home, Canada: September 1993

Pavlin, Stefania, 15, pupil (née Stukelj): life outside camps: September 1993

Pernišek-Žužek, Cirila, schoolgirl: flight, camps, Argentina: October 1995, 3 October 2002

Plevnik, Joseph, pupil: wartime, camps, Canada: April 1991, 8 April 2002

Puc, Marija (later Remec: daughter of Dr Puc): USA: September 1993

Rak, Max, *domobranec*: wartime, flight, USA: April 1991, September 1993, 12 April 2002

Roessmann, Matej and Pepca, students: wartime, flight, camps, USA: March 1991, September 1993, 11 April 2002

Roessmann, Uroš and Milči, 20 and 17, medical student and schoolgirl: wartime, flight, camps, USA: March 1991, 10 April 2002

Rosenberg, Vida, 20, law student: flight, camps, Canada: April 1991

Sekolec, Franjo and Bernarda: camps, England: August 1991

Sfiligoj, Marko and Heda, 19, pupils: camps, USA: March 1991, September 1993

Snoj, Stane: Argentina: May 1994, 5 October 2002

Starman (née Šimenc), Magdalena, 8, flight: January 1996

Suhadolc, Tone and Maria (née Plevnik), students: camps, Canada: April 1991, September 1993, 9 April 2002

Tomaževič, Jože, schoolboy: 5 October 2002

Voršič, Jorge, engineering student: Argentina: May 1994

Vračko, Majda, 16 (later Remec), pupil: flight, camps, USA: March 1991

Ziernfeld, Henry (Riko), engineering student: Canada, Argentina: March 1991, September 1993, 8 April 2002

Zorc (Rus), Maria, schoolgirl: wartime, Argentina: 4 October 2002

Žonta (Loboda), Albina, small girl: flight, camps, Argentina: 6 October 2002

## Interviews in Slovenia

Arnež, Dr Janez, archivist, Studia Slovenica, Šentvid, Ljubljana: 29 January 2002
Bajuk, Andrej, Prime Minister of Slovenia, 2000: 17 April 2002
Godeša, Dr Bojan, historian: 7 January 2002
Grobovšek, Bojan, Slovene Ambassador to Argentina (interviewed in Buenos Aires): 7 October 2002
Hribar, Dr Spomenka, journalist: 28 October 2002
Jančar, Drago, writer: 14 October 2003
Kučan, Milan, President of Slovenia, 1990–2002: 19 April 2002
Mikeln, Miloš, writer: 30 October 2002
Repe, Božo, Professor of Contemporary History, Ljubljana University: 14 October 2003
Rode, Dr Franc, Metropolitan Archbishop of Ljubljana (from February 2004: Prefect, Congregation for Religious, Vatican): 17 April 2002
Stanovnik, Justin, teacher: 29 January 2002
Velikonja, Tine, doctor: 21 August and 30 October 2002
Žajdela, Ivo, journalist: 13 October 2003

## Interview in UK

Lavrenčič, Karl (Drago), ex-BBC World Service: 16 February 2002

## Interview in Geneva

Williams, Wendy, Population Movement Officer, International Federation of Red Cross and Red Crescent Societies: 22 May 2002

## Abbreviations

BRC British Red Cross
DP Displaced Person
FAU Friends Ambulance Unit
FSS [British] Field Security Service
HQ Headquarters
IRO International Refugee Organisation
MG Military Government
OC Officer in charge of
OZNA Odeljenje za Zaščitu Naroda [Department for Protection of the People – Slovene state security service]
UNRRA United Nations Relief and Rehabilitation Administration

# Selected Bibliography

**Britain**

Aarons, M./Loftus J., *Ratlines*. Mandarin Paperbacks, London 1991

Alanbrooke, Field Marshal Lord, *War Diaries 1939–1945* (edited by Danchev, Alex and Todman, Daniel.) Weidenfeld & Nicolson 2001

Allcock, John B., *Explaining Yugoslavia*. Hurst & Company, London 2000

Almond, Mark, *Europe's Backyard War: The War in the Balkans*. Heinemann, London 1994

Banac, Ivo (editor), *Eastern Europe in Revolution*. Cornell University Press, Ithaca and London 1992

Beevor, Antony, *Stalingrad*. Viking, London 1998

Bennett, Christopher, *Yugoslavia's Bloody Collapse: Causes, Course and Consequences*. Hurst, London 1995

Bernières, Louis de, *Captain Corelli's Mandolin*. Vintage, London 1994

Bethell, Nicholas, *The Last Secret*. Andre Deutsch, London 1974 – reissued with a new epilogue, Penguin 1995

Bethell, Nicholas, *Spies and Other Secrets*. Viking 1994

Booker, Christopher, *A Looking Glass Tragedy*. Duckworth, London 1997

Colville, Sir John, *Footprints in Time*. Collins, London 1976

Conradi, Peter, *Iris Murdoch*. HarperCollins, London 2001

Cornwell, John, *Hitler's Pope: The Secret History of Pius XII*. Penguin 1999

Corsellis, John, *Yugoslav Refugees in Camps in Egypt and Austria 1944–1947*. Refugee Participant Network 17, Oxford University Refugee Studies Programme 1994

Corsellis, John, *Friendly Persuasion: How 6,000 Refugees were Saved in 1945*. The Friends' Quarterly, London October 1995

Cowgill, Anthony; Booker, Christopher; Brimelow, Lord, *The Repatriation of Surrendered Enemy Personnel from Austria: The Report of an Enquiry (2 vols.)*. Sinclair-Stevenson 1990

Crankshaw, Edward, *The Fall of the House of Habsburg*. Macmillan, London 1963

Crosland, Susan, *Tony Crosland*. Jonathan Cape, London 1982

Cruikshank, Charles, *The German Occupation of the Channel Islands*. Imperial War Museum / Guernsey Press, Channel Islands 1975

Cviic, Christopher, *Remaking the Balkans*. Chatham House Papers, The Royal Institute of International Affairs, London 1991

Davies, A. Tegla, *Friends Ambulance Unit: In the Second World War 1939–1946*. Allen & Unwin London 1947

Deakin, F.W.D., *The Embattled Mountain*, Oxford University Press, 1971

Fenby, Jonathan, *On the Brink: The Trouble with France*. Warner Books 1999

Foot, M.R.D., *S.O.E. The Special Operations Executive 1940–1946*. Mandarin 1993

Glenny, Misha, *The Balkans 1804–1999*. Granta Books, London 1999

Glover, Jonathan, *Humanity: A Moral History of the Twentieth Century*. Pimlico, London 2001

Gow, James/Carmichael, Cathie, *Slovenia and the Slovenes*. Hurst & Company, London 2000

Goodwin-Gill, Guy S., *The Refugee in International Law*. Clarendon Press, Oxford 1996

Greenwood, John Ormerod, *Quaker Encounters: Volume 1, Friends and Relief*. William Sessions, York 1975

Harrell-Bond, Barbara E., *Imposing Aid: Emergency Assistance to Refugees*. Oxford University Press, Oxford 1986.

Horne, Alistair, *Macmillan*. Macmillan, London 1989.

Jelavich, Barbara, *History of the Balkans: Twentieth Century*. Cambridge University Press 1983

Johnson, Paul, *A History of the Modern World, from 1917 to the 1980s*. Weidenfeld & Nicolson, London 1983

Keegan, John, *The Face of Battle*. Pimlico 1978

Keegan, John, *The Second World War*. Penguin 1990

Keegan, John, *A History of Warfare*. Pimlico, London 1993

Knight, Robert, *Harold Macmillan and the Cossacks: Was there a Klagenfurt Conspiracy?* Intelligence and National Security, May 1946

Kujundzic, Zeljko, *Torn Canvas*. Paterson, London 1957

Lacaze, André, *The Tunnel*. Hamish Hamilton, London 1980

Lamb, Richard, *Churchill as a War Leader: Right or Wrong?* Bloomsbury, London 1991

LeBor, Adam/Boyes, Roger, *Surviving Hitler*. Simon & Schuster, London 2000

Maclean, Fitzroy, *Disputed Barricades*. Jonathan Cape, London 1957

Maclean, Fitzroy, *Eastern Approaches*. Jonathan Cape, London 1949

Macmillan, Harold, *The Blast of War*. Macmillan 1967

Macmillan, Harold, *Tides of Fortune*. Macmillan 1969

Macmillan, Harold, *War Diaries: The Mediterranean 1943–1945*. Macmillan 1984

McNeill, Margaret, *By the Rivers of Babylon: A Story of relief work among the Displaced Persons of Europe*, Bannisdale Press, London 1950

Marrus, Michael R., *Unwanted: European Refugees in the Twentieth Century*. Oxford University Press, 1985

Mendl, Wolf, *Prophets and Reconcilers: Reflections on the Quaker Peace Testimony*. Friends Home Service Committee, London 1974

Mitchell, Ian, *The Cost of a Reputation*. Topical Books, Scotland 1997

Nicolson, Nigel, *Alex: The Life of Field Marshal Earl Alexander of Tunis*. Weidenfeld & Nicolson, London 1973

Nicolson, Nigel, *Long Life: Memoirs*. Weidenfeld & Nicolson, London 1997

Parkes, Colin Murray, *Bereavement: Studies of Grief in Adult Life*. Penguin, London 1975

Pears, Iain, *The Dream of Scipio*. Jonathan Cape, London 2002

Rogers, Lindsay, *Guerilla Surgeon*. Collins, London 1957

Rootham, Jasper, *Miss Fire: The Chronicle of a British Mission to Mihailovich 1943–1944*, Chatto & Windus, London 1946

Rosenberg, Tina, *The Haunted Land, Facing Europe's Ghosts After Communism*. Vintage, London 1995

Rothschild, J./ Wingfield, N.M., *Return to Diversity: A Political History of East Central Europe since World War II*. Oxford University Press, Oxford 2000
Seton-Watson, Hugh, *The East European Revolution*. London, 1956
Silber, Laura/Little Allan, *The Death of Yugoslavia*. Penguin/BBC 1995, 1996
Simms, Brendan, *Unfinest Hour: Britain and the Destruction of Bosnia*. Allen Lane the Penguin Press, London 2001
Smith, Lyn, *Pacifists in Action*. William Sessions Ltd, York, England 1998
Somerfield, M./Bellingham, A., *Violetta Thurstan: A Celebration*. Jamieson Library, Cornwall 1993
Steinberg, Jonathan, *All or Nothing: The Axis and the Holocaust 1941–1943*. Routledge, London 1990
Thompson, Mark, *A Paper House: The Ending of Yugoslavia*. Hutchinson/ Radius, London 1992
Tolstoy, Nikolai, *Victims of Yalta*. Hodder & Stoughton, London 1977
Tolstoy, Nikolai, *Stalin's Secret War*. Jonathan Cape, London 1981
Tolstoy, Nikolai, *The Minister and the Massacres*. Century Hutchinson, London 1986
UNRRA, *Helping the People to Help Themselves: The Story of UNRRA*. UN Information Organisation/HM Stationery Office, London 1944
Ward, Barbara, *Healing Grief: A Guide to Loss and Recovery*. Vermilion, London 1993
Wilson, M. Francesca, *Aftermath*. Penguin Books London 1947
Wilson, M. Francesca, *They came as Strangers: The Story of Refugees to Great Britain*. Hamish Hamilton, London 1959
Wilson, Roger C., *Quaker Relief: An Account of the Relief Work of the Society of Friends 1940–1948*. Allen & Unwin, London 1952

**Slovenia**
Arnež, Janez, *Slovenski tisk v begunskih taboriščih v Avstriji 1945–1949*. Studia Slovenica, Ljubljana–Washington 1999
Arnež, Janez, *Življenje in delo Slovencev v Argentini*. Ljubljana–Washington 1994
Ciglar, Tone, *Dr Janez Janež, Utrinek bozje dobrote*. Ljubljana 1993
Corsellis, John, *The Slovene Political Emigration 1945–1950*, Dve Domovini Migration Studies, Centre of Scientific Research of the Slovene Academy of Sciences and Arts, The Institute for Slovene Emigration Research, Ljubljana 1997
Čebulj-Sajko, Breda, *Med srečo in svobodo: Australian Slovenes about Themselves*. The Institute for Slovene Emigration Research, Ljubljana 1992
Dolničar, Ivan/Klanjšček, Zdravko/Kocijan, Lado, *Kako se je končala druga svetovna vojna na Slovenskem*. PKK, Ljubljana 2001
Dornik Šubelj, Ljuba, *OZNA za Slovenijo*. Ljubljana 1999
Eiletz, Marijan, *Moje domobranstvo in pregnanstvo*. Mohorjeva družba, Celje 2001
*Farne spominske plošče, druga knjiga*. Družina, Ljubljana 2000
Ferenc, Tone, *Rab-Arbe-Arbissima*. Ljubljana 2000
Godeša, Bojan, *Kdor ni z nami, je proti nam*. Cankarjeva založba, Ljubljana 1995
Grgič, Silvo, *Domobranstvo – zamikanje kolaboracije*. Ljubljana 2000

Grgič, Silvo, *Zločini okupatorjevih sodelavcev*. PKK, Ljubljana 1997

Jančar, Drago, *The Dark Side of the Moon: A Short History of Totalitarianism in Slovenia 1945–1990*. National Museum of Contemporary History, Ljubljana 1998

Jančar, Drago, *Brioni*. Mladinska Knjiga, Ljubljana 2002

Janša, Janez, *The Making of the Slovenian State 1988–1992*. Mladinska knjiga, Ljubljana 1994

Kokalj Kočevar, Monika, *Gorenjski domobranec*. Gorenjski kraji in ljudje XVIII. 2000

Kraigher, Živa, *Ljudje in kraji na Pivškem med NOB 1941–1945*. PKK, Ljubljana 2002

Kremžar, Marko, *Leto brez sonca*. Družina, Ljubljana 2002

Kremžar, Marko, *Med smrtjo in življenjem*. Družina, Ljubljana 2000

Kremžar, Marko, *Prevrat in spreobrnjenje*. Mohorjeva družba, Celje 1992

Kremžar, Marko, *Sivi dnevi*. Mohorjeva družba, Celje 1995

Mikeln, Miloš, *Veliki Voz (Great Bear)*. Knjižna Zadruga, Ljubljana 1995

Mlakar, Boris, *Slovensko domobrantstvo 1943–1945*. Slovenska matica, Ljubljana, 2003

Mlakar, Boris, *Tragedija v Cerknem. Pozimi 1944*. Goriška Mohorjeva družba, Gorice 2001

*Over the Hill Is Just Like Here*. National Museum of Contemporary History, Ljubljana 2002

Peršič, Marijan, *Na usodnem razpotju, per aspera ad A(u)stra(lia)*. Združenje Slovenska izseljenska matica, Ljubljana 2001.

Pribac, Bert, *Slovenske spravne motnje (Slovene Reconciliation Troubles)*. Založba 2000, Canberra (Australia) 1998, Sergasi (Slovenia) 2002

Prunk, Janko, *A Brief History of Slovenia*. Založba Grad, Ljubljana 2000

Repe, Božo, *Rdeča Slovenija (Red Slovenia)*, Založba Sophia, 2003

Svoljšak, Petra, *The Front on Soča*. Cankarjeva založba 2002

Tišler, Janko/Rovšek, Jože, *Mauthausen na Ljubelju*

Toš, mag. Marjan/Cerjak, Vladimir/Lorbor, Franc, *Slovenci v tuji vojski*. Celje 2002

Tršar, Marijan, *Dotik Smrti*. Nova Revija, Ljubljana 2000

*Tudi mi smo umrli za domovino: zamolčani grobovi in njihove žrtve*. Društvo za ureditev zamolčanih grobov. Ljubljana/Grosuplje 2000

Žganjar, Matija, *Slovenski partizani in zavezniki*

Židar, Alojz, *Il popolo sloveno ricorda e accusa*. Založba Lipa, Koper 2001

Žigon, Zvone, *Iz spomina v prihodnost, slovenska politična emigracja v Argentini*. Založba ZRC, Ljubljana 2001

**Published by Yugoslavs abroad**

Ambrožič, Archbishop Aloysius/Corsellis, John/Tolstoy, Nikolaj/Zdešar, Janez, *Testimony, Proceedings of the Historical Symposium at Tinje / Teinach. 30 June 1995*

Bajuk, Marko, *Še bomo peli…* Buenos Aires 1988

Bela knjiga: *The White Book on Slovene Anti-Communist Resistance* (two volumes). ZDSPB Tabor, USA 1970

Beljo, Ante, *Yu-Genocide*. Northern Tribune Publishing, Toronto-Zagreb 1995

Blatnik, Rev Dr Franc, *Kako sem pripravljal atentat na Tita*. Paterson, New Jersey 1972

Blatnik, Rev Dr Franc, *Tudi slovenski mučenci morajo biti vpisani v seznam svetnikov*, Buenos Aires 1985

Djilas, Milovan, *Wartime*. Harcourt Brace Jovanovich, New York 1977

Djilas, Milovan, *Tito: the Story from Inside*. Harcourt Brace Jovanovich, New York and London 1980

*Fifty Years of United Slovenia Association in the Argentine Republic*. Buenos Aires 1998

Fink, Božidar, *Na tujem v domovini*. Mohorjeva založba, Celovec-Ljubljana-Dunaj 1999

Grum, France/Pleško,Stane, *Svoboda v razvalinah: Grčarice – Turjak – Kočevje*. Cleveland US 1961

Jagodič, Monsignor Jože, *Mojega življenja tek*. Klagenfurt 1974

Jukič, Ilija, *The Fall of Yugoslavia*. Harcourt Brace Jovanovich, New York and London 1974

Ižanec, Franc, *Odprti grobovi (Open Graves)*. Buenos Aires 1965

Kolarič, Jakob, *Škof Rožman*. Klagenfurt 1977

*Koledar svobodne Slovenije (Almanac of Free Slovenia)*. Buenos Aires, from 1949

Kozina, Vladimir, *Slovenia, the Land of My Joy and My Sorrow*. Tabor ZDSB, Cleveland, Ohio, Toronto, Canada 1980

Kozina, Vladimir, *Communism as I know it*. Brentwood, California 1978

*Matica mrtvih (The Registry of the Dead), Specific data on Slovenians who were murdered by the criminal Liberation Front 1941–1945*, Cleveland, US, 1968. Vetrinjska tragedija. Cleveland, US 1960

Milač, Metod M., *Resistance, Imprisonment and Forced Labor*. Peter Lang, New York 2002

Pernišek, France, *Pred štiridesetimi leti: odlomki iz dnevnika slovenskega begunca (40 Years Ago: Excerpts from the Diary of a Slovene Refugee)*. Published serially in Duhovno življenje, Buenos Aires, May 1985– February 1990

Potokar, Ludve, *Onstran samote*. Mohorjeva družba, Klagenfurt, Austria 1995

Sluga, Dore, *The Orchard*. Historical Commission of Tabor ZDSPB Toronto, Canada 1978

Svetek, Lev, *Pri svojih na svojem: spomini s poti po Reziji in Beneški Sloveniji v vojnem letu 1944*. Založništvo tržaškega tiska, Trieste 1987

Tolstoy, Nikolai/Klepec, Matjaž/Kovač, Tomaž, *Trilogija: Vetrinj-Teharje-Rog*. Reprint 1991

Vrninc, France (editor), *Pričevanja: Graški zbornik:* Kapellari, Egon/Kvas, Jože/Velikonja, Tine/Millonig, Stana/Vrbinc, France/Zerzer, Janko/Kopeinig Jože/Corsellis, John/Tolstoy, Nikolaj/Ambrožič, Alojzij/Zdešar, Janez/Srienc, Kristo. Mohorjeva založba, Klagenfurt 1996

Zajec, Milan/Kozina France/Dejak, France, *Ušli so smrti (They Escaped Death)*. Mohorjeva založba, Celovec-Ljubljana-Dunaj 1998

Zveza slovenskih protikomunističnih borcev, *Vetrinjska tragedija*, Cleveland Ohio 1960

Žebot, Ciril, *Neminljiva Slovenija*. Klagenfurt, Austria 1988

## Other

Bartov, Omar/Grossmann, Atina/Nolan, Mary, *Crimes of War, Guilt and Denial in the Twentieth Century*. The New Press, New York 2002

Beloff, Nora, *Tito's Flawed Legacy: Yugoslavia and the West since 1939*. Westview Press, Boulder, Colorado 1985

Carr, Caleb, *The Lessons of Terror*. Random House, New York 2002

Casaroli, Agostino, *Il martirio della pazienza: La Santa Sede e i paesi comunisti (1963–1989)*. Einaudi 2000

Cohen, Lenard J., *Serpent in the Bosom: the Rise and Fall of Slobodan Milošević*. Westview Press, Boulder, Colorado 2001

Corsellis, John, *Refugiados Eslovenos en Argentina*. Todo es Historia, Buenos Aires February 1996

Corsellis, John, *Yugoslav Refugees in Camps in Egypt and Austria 1944–1947*. North Dakota Quarterly, USA 1993

Courtois, Stéphane et al., *The Black Book of Communism*. Harvard University Press (English version), Cambridge, Massachusetts 1999

Deuer, Wilhelm, *Viktring/Stein, Kaernten: Ehemalige Zisterzienserabtei Viktring*. Verlag St Peter, Salzburg 1992

Feldman, L/Prica, I/Senjkovic, R (editors), *Fear, Death and Resistance: An Ethnography of War; Croatia 1991–1992*. Matrix Croatica, Zagreb 1993

Griesser-Pečar, Tamara, *Das zerrissene Volk Slowenien 1941–1946: Okkupation, Kollaboration, Bürgerkrieg, Revolution*, Boehlau Verlag, Cologne, Graz 2003

Hemingway, Ernest, *A Farewell to Arms*. 1929

Kaplan, Robert D., *Balkan Ghosts*. Vintage Books, New York 1993, 1995

Krulic, Josip, *Storia della Jugoslavia: Dal 1945 ai nostri giorni*. Bompiani, Milan 1999

Kundera, Milan, *Ignorance*. Faber & Faber, South America, Germany and UK 2000

Lees, Michael, *The Rape of Serbia*. Harcourt Brace Jovanovich, New York 1990

Levi, Primo, *Se Questo è un Uomo (If This is a Man)*. 1947.

Munoz, Antonio J., *Yugoslav Axis Forces in Pictures 1941–1945*. Axis Europa Inc., Bayside, New York.

Muravchik, Joshua, *Heaven on Earth; the Rise and Fall of Socialism*. Encounter Books, San Francisco, 2002

Petacco, Arrigo, *L'Esodo: La tragedia negata degli Italiani d'Istria, Dalmazia e Venezia Giulia*. Mondadori, Milan 1999

Reed, John, *Ten Days that Shook the World*. 1926

Rossi Kobau, Lionello, *Prigioniero di Tito 1945–1946: Un Bersagliere nei campi di concentramento Jugoslavi*. Mursia, Milan 2001

Sebald, W.G. (translated by Bell, Anthea), *On the Natural History of Destruction*. Alfred A. Knopf, Canada 2003

Steiber, Dr Gabriela, *Nachkriegsflüchtlinge in Kärnten und der Steiermark*. Leykam, Graz 1997

Wagner, Richard, *Der leere Himmel: Reise in das Innere des Balkan*. Aufbau-Verlag GmbH, Berlin 2003

West, Rebecca, *Black Lamb and Grey Falcon*. Viking Press, US 1941

Winchester, Simon, *The Fracture Zone*. Perennial, New York 2000

Wyman, Mark, *Europe's Displaced Persons, 1945–1951*. Cornell Paperbacks 1998

# Index

## People

Alexander, Field Marshal Lord 34, 48, 49, 65, 66, 183, 186, 249
Alexander, King 23, 24, 208
Ambrožič, Aloysius (later Cardinal) 11, 24, 33, 92, 169, 170, 176, 192, 241
Ambrožič, Lojze 105, 144, 169
Ames, Lieutenant 60, 61, 66
Anders, General Władysław 45
Arbuthnott, Major-General Robert 189
Armstrong, Arthur 171
Arnež, Dr Janez 76
Aršič-Bajuk, Vera 197, 229, 237
Avšič, Jaka 248

Bajuk, Director Marko (father) 17, 44, 45, 58, 61, 91, 92, 104–106, 108, 110, 116, 124, 130, 132, 140–142, 158, 159, 161, 163, 173, 178, 199, 215
Bajuk, Prof. Božidar (son) 17, 19, 20, 45, 91, 110, 141, 159, 160, 163, 164
Bajuk, Andrej (grandson) 17, 215–217
Bajuk, Božidar (grandson) 140, 159, 160, 163, 164, 229
Bajuk, Marko (grandson) 90, 140, 142, 163, 223, 230
Balding, Jane 41, 43, 44, 66, 190
Barre, Major Paul 41, 43, 44, 45, 58, 60, 61, 62, 64, 65, 93
Baty, C.W. 104, 106
Beamish, Major Tufton MP (later Lord Chelwood) 188
Bedo, Dr 119
Bell, Major 95
Beneš, Edvard 250
Benson, Air Commodore Constantine 63
Bentley, Captain 74
Bertoncelj, Dinko 31, 197, 199, 200, 226, 227
Bertoncelj, Romana 227
Bethell, Nicholas 188, 192

Blair, Tony 238
Blake, Major 122
Blatnik, Dr Franc 99, 135, 187
Bohinc, Juliana 165
Brandt, Willy 236
Brash, Captain Maurice A. 38
Bratina, Gloria 11, 18, 20, 44, 55, 168
Breznik, Mr 146

Cankar, Ivan 236
Cenkar, Franc 116, 179
Chamberlain, Neville 116
Chapman, Major C.D. 115, 130
Chirac, President Jacques 237
Churchill, (Sir) Winston 7, 48, 98, 117, 122, 137, 190–192, 210, 249
Cof, Lt.-Colonel Emil 55, 56, 192, 223, 224, 251
Čop, Leopold 22, 23, 26, 108, 144, 155, 169, 197
Čop, Marija 37, 155
Corsellis, John 4, 43, 45, 58, 63, 88, 91, 92, 95–97, 99, 103, 104, 106, 107, 110, 112–117, 121–125, 130, 132, 134, 135, 141, 142, 144, 146, 147, 187, 190, 192, 234
Cottrell, Colonel 131
Crosland, Captain Antony (later MP) 59
Cullis, (Sir) Michael 121, 122

Daley family 170, 171
Dejak, France 29, 74–83, 174, 200
Dernulc, Janez 69, 181
Dežman, Jože 206, 236, 240
Djilas, Milovan 34, 47, 48, 70, 87, 249
Dodds-Parker, Colonel Douglas MP (later Sir) 147, 190
Drčar, Colonel Ivan 50, 54
Drnovšek, Janez 195, 196, 216
Dufour, Lt.-Colonel 62, 63

Eiletz, Bo 37, 227
Eiletz, Mary 227
Elizabeth, Queen 208

## Subjects and places